Armed Struggle in Palestine:
A Political-Military Analysis

Armed Struggle in Palestine:
A Political-Military Analysis
Bard E. O'Neill

Bard O'Neill investigates the Palestinian guerrilla movement and assesses the probability that the fedayeen will achieve their aim of liberating Palestine—including Israel—by means of protracted revolutionary insurgency. His analytic framework incorporates several factors that have a critical bearing on the outcomes of protracted insurgencies; these include government response, environment, popular support, organization, cohesion, and external support. A discussion of these factors is followed by a general summation and an examination of the implications of the longer, more enduring trends that have emerged since the October War. Major O'Neill concludes that a Palestine state under PLO control may not be a real threat to Israel's security and existence.

Bard E. O'Neill is director of Middle East Studies at the National War College and senior research fellow in the National Defense University Research Directorate. Major O'Neill holds a Ph.D. in International Relations from the University of Denver. His publications include *Revolutionary Warfare in the Middle East, The Energy Crisis and U.S. Foreign Policy,* which he coedited, and a number of articles dealing with Middle Eastern affairs.

Armed Struggle in Palestine:
A Political-Military Analysis
Bard E. O'Neill

Published in cooperation with
the National Defense University

Westview Press ● Boulder, Colorado

Dawson ● Folkestone, England

This volume is included in Westview's Special Studies on the Middle East.

Published in 1978 in the United States of America by
  Westview Press, Inc.
  5500 Central Avenue
  Boulder, Colorado 80301
  Frederick A. Praeger, Publisher

Published in 1978 in Great Britain by
  Wm. Dawson and Sons, Ltd.
  Cannon House
  Folkestone
  Kent CT19 5EE

Library of Congress Catalog Card Number: 78-2285
ISBN (U.S.): 0-89158-333-5
ISBN (U.K.): 0-7129-0883-8

Printed and bound in the United States of America

To my parents

Andrew Thomas O'Neill
Edith May O'Neill

Contents

Preface

In November 1977 Egyptian President Anwar as-Sadat shocked the world with his momentous decision to cross the psychological barrier dividing Arabs and Jews by visiting the state of Israel. Within a few weeks, the representatives of Israel and the Arab Republic of Egypt sat down at Mena House in Cairo to begin a new stage of direct negotiations that hopefully would culminate in the long sought after "just and durable peace."

Though the full implications of the fast-moving events in the Middle East had yet to be digested, scholars and observers quickly agreed that in spite of the hopes engendered by the Sadat initiative, peace would not come easily because two major issues continued to divide the two sides—the eventual disposition of the occupied territories and a settlement of the Palestinian question. This book deals with the latter of the two issues, which all parties have acknowledged is a core consideration. Specifically, it analyzes the strategic accomplishments and role of the Palestinian Liberation Movement and assesses its future in light of past and present capabilities.

Addressing the Palestinian issue is, of course, fraught with peril for the scholar. The emotions that have built up on both sides of the conflict over thirty years compel many advocates to demand total adherence to their version of events. Words, phrases, and sentences that appear perfectly innocuous to the writer may become suspect in the eyes of the zealot. For example, from the Israeli perspective, the matter of using Tel Aviv rather than Jerusalem to refer to Israel is assumed to be an indication of latent hostility. On the Arab side, meanwhile, an acknowledgement of the centuries of suffering and persecution of the Jews is often viewed as a sign of pro-Israeli tendencies. In view of these and other examples, it is important, I believe, that my personal view be stated forthrightly.

Simply put, I have no axes to grind on this issue. I believe that there is more than enough tragedy and blame on both sides of the conflict and that if there is to be peace, *all* parties will have to make substantial, though not necessarily parallel, compromises.

My own thoughts about some of the possibilities with respect to a solution of the Palestinian issue are put forth in the final chapter. The conclusions are the product of several years of research and analysis during which I have been blessed with generous assistance and advice.

A number of colleagues gave of their time in order to read and critique all or portions of the manuscript—Professors Peter Van Ness, Paul D. Whelan, and Joseph S. Szyliowicz; Captain Jerome O'Brien, U.S. Navy; Colonel Thomas Pianka, U.S. Army; Ms. Sheila Buckley, International Security Agency, Department of Defense; and Mr. George Maerz and Mr. Greg Diercks, editors, National Defense University Research Directorate. Others, including Professors Joseph J. Malone and Adrea Rosenberg, thoughtfully provided documents and information that proved to be most useful.

Commander Frederick T. Daly, assistant director for administration and publications, National Defense University Research Directorate, patiently took care of administrative arrangements and clerical assistance. Several individuals—Mrs. Ginny Lanz, Miss Deborah Zambreny, Mrs. Evelyn Lakes, Miss Susan O'Keefe, and Mrs. Corinne Dodge—helped with the typing of initial drafts. Special recognition along these lines must go to Mrs. Gloria Eakin for her splendid cooperation in both typing the final manuscript and offering many constructive suggestions.

Finally, I would like to acknowledge Colonel Andrew J. Dougherty, Colonel Ralph Hoffman, Captain Jerome O'Brien, Major General Harrison Lobdell, Jr., and Lieutenant General Robert Gard for supporting and encouraging me during this effort.

Responsibility for the final result of this lengthy effort is, of course, solely my own. The views expressed herein do not necessarily represent those of either the Department of Defense or the U.S. government.

Bard E. O'Neill
Washington, D.C.

Abbreviations

ALF	Arab Liberation Front
ANM	Arab Nationalist Movement
AOLP	Action Organization for the Liberation of Palestine
APO	Arab Palestine Organization
BSO	Black September Organization
CCPR	Central Committee of the Palestinian Resistance (now defunct)
HPCPA	Higher Political Committee for Palestinian Affairs (Lebanon)
IDF	Israel Defense Forces
MLC	Military Leadership Committee
PASC	Palestine Armed Struggle Command
PDF	Popular Democratic Front for the Liberation of Palestine
PFLP	Popular Front for the Liberation of Palestine
PFLP-GC	Popular Front for the Liberation of Palestine-General Command
PLA	Palestine Liberation Army
PLF	Palestine Liberation Front
PLO	Palestine Liberation Organization
PLO-CC	Palestine Liberation Organization Central Committee (or Council)
PLO-EC	Palestine Liberation Organization Executive Committee
PNC	Palestine National Council
PPNLF	Palestine People's National Liberation Front
PRC	Palestinian Revolutionary Council
PRFLP	Popular Revolutionary Front for the Liberation of Palestine
PSF	Popular Struggle Front
UCPR	Unified Command of the Palestinian Resistance (now defunct)

1
Introduction

Armed struggle is hardly a new phenomenon in Palestine. Indeed, for millennia men have turned to violence in order to satisfy their claims and ambitions in the area. The types and forms of wars they have waged have varied considerably over the centuries, ranging from conflicts between major political groups (empires, colonial systems, and nation-states) to those involving small units such as tribal or insurgent groupings.

Historical Sketch

The Battleground of Empires

During the many centuries which spanned the pre-Christian era, Palestine was the scene of continual clashes between decaying and newly emergent empires. Some, like the Egyptian, Hebrew, Babylonian, and Hittite, were indigenous to the area surrounding Palestine; others, such as the Greek and Roman, constituted more distant intrusions. The period of Roman rule, which began in approximately 63 B.C., was marked by recurrent conflict with both outside invaders and dissidents within. The extension of Islamic rule to the area by 640 A.D. did not bring an end to the conflict and violence as the great Ummayyad, Abbasid, and Fatimid dynasties struggled against various enemies to assert their dominance.

The year 1099 A.D. saw a new force, the Christian Crusaders, enter the region in their quest to liberate the Holy Land. While successful in establishing a Crusader kingdom, they eventually met defeat at the hands of the Kurdish warrior Salah ad-Din al-Ayyubi in 1187. Though the Crusaders returned again in the thirteenth century, their stay was short lived and their presence was finally expunged once and for all.

As the Crusader episode drew to a close, Mongols from the East seized control in 1250. The next great invasion came in 1512 when the Ottoman

Turks implanted an empire that would last for four centuries, although not without eventual challenge from European powers which, at the end of the eighteenth century, began to move into the area because of global balance of power considerations.

By the time of World War I, a disintegrating Ottoman Empire found itself opposed by one of those powers, Great Britain, which managed to align with the local Arab leaders seeking to expel the Turks. When the war ended, it was the European powers, rather than the Arabs, who asserted control in the Levant, with the French ensconced in Syria and Lebanon and the British in Iraq, Transjordan, and Palestine.[1] European dominance proved to be relatively brief, however, since the global process of decolonization, expedited by World War II, engendered the transformation of mandates and protectorates into independent political units. Unhappily, the extension of the modern nation-state system to the area did not bring a new era of peace and tranquility, for the new nations soon crossed swords because of historical animosities, ideological differences, and territorial disputes.

The Conflict of Jewish and Arab Nationalism

Armed confrontation involving large collectivities was not the only sort of organized violence between social groupings in Palestine and its environs. The region also had a long legacy of conflicts among tribal and religious groups as well as localized rebellions against imperial, colonial, and indigenous authorities. In the contemporary era, such uprisings, for the most part, reflected the global trend towards national self-actualization—that is, the desire by people who share a common sense of identity to establish autonomous political units within which they can shape and control their own destiny. It is the intersection of two such nationalist movements, the Jewish and Palestinian Arab, that has generated the problem which is the focus of this study. Essentially, the current dilemma centers around the fundamental fact that, since the creation of the British mandate in 1922, both Jewish and Palestinian nationalists have laid claim to the same geographic area—the area that today is comprised of Israel, the Gaza Strip, the West Bank, and a small portion of the Golan Heights. (The precise boundaries of "Palestine" have varied throughout its history. Today, for instance, the Israelis would argue that from an historical point of view the East Bank of the Jordan also should be considered part of Palestine.)

Zionism and Palestine

The Jewish nationalist movement received its initial impetus from members of the diaspora in Europe at the end of the nineteenth century. In 1896, its founder, Theodore Herzl, published a book entitled *Der Judenstaat,* which called for the formation of a Jewish state, hopefully in Palestine. After the idea was endorsed at the first World Zionist Congress in Basel a year later, the Zionists organized an extensive effort to persuade the major powers, especially Turkey, to adopt policies favorable to their aims.

Support from the Turks was crucial in view of the fact that permission for the emigration of a large number of Jews to Palestine was considered a sine qua non for success, given the Arab majority in the area. Though the Turks refused to allow European Jews to purchase a large tract of land, limited immigration nonetheless commenced, thereby giving rise to protestations by local Arabs whose own sense of nationalism was beginning to crystallize.

When the British consolidated control in the area during the war, they, too, were subjected to Zionist pressures. On November 17, 1917, the British foreign secretary, Arthur J. Balfour, indicated in a written declaration that Britain viewed with favor the establishment of a national home for the Jews so long as it did not prejudice the civil and religious rights of the existing non-Jewish communities in Palestine. The vigorous efforts of the Zionists and continued immigration following the Balfour declaration increased tensions in the area; over the course of the next two decades the Zionists and Arabs clashed violently, not only with the Mandatory Power but also with each other. Of the two nationalist movements, the Zionist was by far the more successful. It proved able, although not without considerable effort and cost, to create and sustain a Jewish state (Israel). The Palestinian Arabs (hereafter referred to as Palestinians), by contrast, were denied concrete expression of their nationalism in the form of an independent state, because, unlike their Zionist adversary, they were plagued by inept political leadership, poor organization, strategic miscalculations, and a lack of resources.[2] Political and material deficiencies such as these played a major part in the genesis and outcome of the first Arab-Israeli war in 1948.

The Creation of Israel and the 1948 War

Throughout the history of the Mandate, commissions of various sorts had investigated the Palestinian problem, but the British government, preoccupied with the Second World War, had postponed a major decision, confining itself instead to the immediate issue of regulating Jewish immigration. In the aftermath of the war, a weakened Britain, beset with economic difficulties, decided to turn what seemed to be an unsolvable problem over to the United Nations. After several months of intensive and skillful lobbying by the Zionists, the UN approved a partition plan on November 29, 1947, which made provision for both Jewish and Palestinian states.

When the Palestinians rejected the plan, fighting ensued between the two sides. Taking advantage of the absence of a UN plan to implement the partition, the Zionists seized the initiative by acquiring weapons and training the forces necessary not only to defend their communities, but also to sustain the state that would be established after the British withdrew in May 1948. On the other side, the Palestinians proved unable to mobilize and organize the capability necessary to undercut the partition plan. A poorly coordinated intervention of regular Arab military forces did not spare the Palestinians from a major defeat, the consequences of which they would suffer for the next twenty-eight years.[3]

The Legacy of the 1948 War

Three specific outcomes of the 1948 fighting were especially significant for the Palestinians: the flight of the refugees; the expansion of Israel; and the extension of Egyptian and Jordanian control to the Gaza Strip and the West Bank, respectively. The large exodus of refugees from Israeli-controlled zones was due to the convergence of several factors. Many Palestinians fled because of systematic and deliberate coercion by the Zionists while others merely followed the example of their own leaders who had departed. There were also cases of notables encouraging the people to flee in the belief that the exodus would only be temporary. Finally, of course, there were the untold numbers who always seek refuge from the ravages of war. More important than the specific causes of the exodus, as far as this study is concerned, is the fact that hundreds of thousands were displaced and dispossessed.[4] For the next three decades most would languish in refugee camps in the Arab states contiguous to Israel, while the remainder would disperse throughout the Middle East and other parts of the world.

Though the members of the Palestinian diaspora were separated from their homeland, they did not forget it.[5] Yet, while the attachment to Palestine was kept alive, strengthened, and, at times, idealized in the art, literature, and poetry of the Palestinians, reconquest was left to the Arab states. Thus, for the better part of twenty years, the Palestinians waited in vain for the Arab armies to transform their longing for return into a reality. Because the June 1967 war seemed to shatter that possibility permanently, a new generation of Palestinian leaders surfaced. Determined to deal with these matters themselves, they turned to the restive masses in the camps for support—especially the younger elements that had been brought up to hate Zionism and Israel.[6]

The failure of the Arab states to regain the losses of 1948 was related partially to the second outcome of the 1948 war, namely, the expansion of Israel to a size far more viable and defensible than it had been under the original partition plan. Taking advantage of breakdowns in cease-fire arrangements that punctuated the 1948 fighting, Israel seized the Negev and Upper Galilee, both of which were considered vital to its future security.

The death knell for the Palestinian state that was called for in the partition plan was sounded shortly after the final armistice, by the extension of Egyptian administration to the Gaza Strip and the annexation of the West Bank by Jordan. This third consequence of the war meant that the Palestinians were not only denied any form of statehood, but that they also became the political pawns of the Arab states. Moreover, it made subsequent Israeli arguments that there is no such thing as Palestinian nationalism appear credible to some listeners.

Palestinian Nationalism: 1949-1967

Despite the desperate circumstances of the Palestinians after the 1948 war, the fires of Palestinian nationalism still flickered. Though a younger generation of leaders had appeared in the 1950s, their dispersion had led them to identify with various ideological currents in the area (e.g., Nasserism, Ba'thism, Marxism). These conditions, as William B. Quandt has noted, " . . . did little to foster a sense of purpose and unity among the Palestinian elite."[7]

In the 1960s two major organizations emerged that sought to rectify this desultory situation—the Palestinian Liberation Organization (PLO) and *Al-Fatah*. (Fatah means "conquest" and is an acronym that reverses the order of the letters of the Arabic name of the Palestinian National Liberation Movement: *Harakat at-Tahir al-Watani, al-Filistini.)* The PLO was established at an Arab summit conference in 1964 as the official voice of the Palestinian people, and shortly thereafter it proceeded to organize a military component, the Palestine Liberation Army (PLA). In spite of its claim to autonomy, the PLO was, in fact, heavily influenced by Egypt. Since the PLO's main base of operations was the Gaza Strip, Cairo kept the organization on a short leash lest it cause problems with Israel at inopportune moments. Moreover, the PLA, equipped with tanks and artillery, had a conventional force structure, which was somewhat anomalous for a contemporary liberation organization. Since both the linkage to Cairo and the conventional force structure resulted in a low level of insurgent activity, the PLO was criticized by a number of Palestinian organizations as being insufficiently revolutionary.[8] When war did come in 1967, Israel crushed the PLA with relative ease.[9]

Shortly after the formation of the PLO, a rival organization, *Al-Fatah*, made its presence felt. *Fatah* was a strong proponent of irregular, rather than conventional, warfare, as the means to liberate Palestine, regardless of the strategy and views of the Arab states. Accordingly, it spent several years following its formation in the late 1950s, planning guerrilla raids against Israel.[10] In 1965 it carried out its first attacks under the name *Al-Assifa* ("the storm"). According to Leila S. Kadi, this name was chosen so that in the event of a failure *Fatah* might continue its secret preparations for armed struggle.[11] Following several operations, *Fatah* decided to continue using the appellation *Al-Assifa,* and the latter became synonymous with its military wing.

With the exception of Syria, the Arab governments were either opposed or indifferent to *Fatah,* and many of its recruits ended up in Arab jails. Furthermore, there were a number of armed clashes with Jordanian and Lebanese forces seeking to prevent guerrilla raids from originating in their territories for fear of Israeli reprisals. This interference, plus the fact that *Fatah* was operating with a total strength of no more than two to three hundred men, rendered it incapable of inflicting serious military damage on Israel. Despite such problems, *Fatah's* operations were nevertheless a factor which helped precipitate the June war.[12]

The June War and the Palestinian Resistance Movement

The war, of course, was a great disaster for the Arab states, whose armies emerged from the conflict in defeat and disarray. While the outcome was a far cry from the war of liberation envisaged by the fedayeen,* it had the paradoxical effect of strengthening the latter. Two factors accounted for this: the new military situation and Israeli occupation of several Arab territories.

The magnitude of the defeat suffered by the Arab armies led Palestinian leaders to once again question the feasibility of conventional combat against Israeli forces. The thought of a regular armed confrontation with an enemy, whose relative military strength had increased substantially as a result of the war, seemed ludicrous. Minimally, such a course of action would require many years of preparation, years that the new, more militant fedayeen leaders, believed they could ill afford to lose. Moreover, the Palestinians, along with many Arabs outside the resistance movements, felt a strong psychological need to redeem their wounded honor and dignity. In a military-psychological setting such as this, the renewed call for an active and immediate armed struggle using unconventional techniques became an increasingly attractive alternative strategy for many Arabs.

The receptivity to the notion of a people's war was further increased by

---

*The term *fedayeen*, derived from the Arabic word *feda* or sacrifice, means "Men of Sacrifice." It is used to refer to all Palestinian insurgents, regardless of their organizational affiliation.

the spatial and demographic changes affecting the area which Israel controlled. Prior to the war, the idea of conducting a people's war in Israel, relying on some 300,000 Arabs living amidst 2.5 million Jews seemed absurd. When the war ended, however, some one million Arabs found themselves under Israeli control and the potential area of operations had expanded to include the occupied territories as well as Israel. Consequently, some Arabs concluded that armed struggle, in the form of guerrilla warfare and terrorism, had become a more plausible course of action.

The Strategic Aim of the Palestinian Resistance Movement

Taking advantage of the new developments, the fedayeen moved with alacrity to begin guerrilla and terrorist attacks and to organize for a protracted struggle against Israel. As part of this effort, the Palestine National Council (PNC) adopted a Palestinian National Charter in July 1968 which, in a series of articles, formally codified the ultimate aim of the movement as the total liberation of Palestine from Zionist control.[13] It was beyond debate that the Palestinian aim was tantamount to the destruction of the existing political-social-economic system of the Jewish state. As a *Fatah* pamphlet put it:

> The liberation action is not only the removal of an armed imperialist base, but, more important—it is the destruction of a society. [Our] armed violence will be expressed in many ways. In addition to the destruction of the military force of the Zionist occupying State, it will also be turned towards the destruction of the means of life of Zionist society in all their forms— industrial, agricultural and financial. The armed violence must seek to destroy the military, political, economic, financial and ideological institutions of the Zionist occupying State, so as to prevent all possibility of the growth of a new Zionist society. The aim of the Palestine liberation war is not only to inflict a military defeat but also to destroy the Zionist character of the occupied land, whether it is human or social.[14]

Since the fedayeen considered the attitude of the international community to be important in the liberation struggle against Israel, they made a concentrated attempt to transform their pre-1967 public image as a group that merely wished to "throw the Jews into the sea" by stressing two points. First, non-Zionist Jews would be allowed to remain in the new Palestine, and second, the new nation would be a "secular, democratic, nonsectarian state." Unfortunately for the fedayeen, there was sharp disagreement within their own ranks on both points, especially the meaning and implications of a "secular, democratic, nonsectarian state."[15] More specifically, there was (and still is) no agreement on the role of a Jewish population in such a state, the nature of that state's relationship to the Arab world, and the state's political-economic order (e.g., Marxism or some variant of Arab socialism).

Since the majority of Israelis considered Zionism the raison d'etre of their state, to speak of destroying it was to speak of eradicating Israel and its people. Thus, it was not surprising that the new fedayeen propaganda line had little impact within Israel and that the Jewish population remained distrustful, unresponsive, and unimpressed.

The Strategy of Protracted Armed Struggle

Since the Palestinians fully expected Israel and its international supporters to oppose strongly the political transformation called for in the National Charter, they reconfirmed their commitment to a strategy of people's war. Inspired by the Chinese Communist, Algerian, Cuban, and Vietnamese examples, the fedayeen argued that revolutionary warfare was a historically proven means that would bring success against Israel. That is, by conducting a protracted popular war of national liberation, by emphasizing armed struggle, and by employing guerrilla, terrorist, and political-psychological tactics, the Palestinians contended they could succeed where the Arab armies previously had failed. While there was no agreement on precisely which of the revolutionary warfare experiences should be emulated or emphasized, there was an abiding faith that revolutionary warfare could and would succeed in the Palestinian situation.[16]

Of the specific forms of warfare associated with the strategy of protracted armed struggle, guerrilla warfare was singled out as being particularly important. Article 10 of the National Charter referred to commando action as the nucleus of the liberation war that had to be sustained and escalated by mobilizing, organizing, and unifying the Palestinians and the Arab masses.[17] Though the resources and forces of the Arab world were also considered important, the fedayeen recognized that it would take a considerable effort to bring them to bear.[18] In the meantime, self-reliance was critical; after 1970, as we shall see later, it became imperative.

The Purpose of the Study

The Palestinian commitment to a strategy of protracted insurgency necessarily placed many complicated demands on the leadership, demands it may not have appreciated fully. Indeed, when one goes beyond the romanticism and folklore surrounding contemporary insurrections, it becomes readily apparent that the successful conduct of an insurgency involves the interplay of many complex factors. The primary purpose of this study is to analyze the strategic accomplishments of the fedayeen carefully and systematically in light of these factors. Since protracted insurgency is as much a political phenomenon as a military one, both dimensions will be accorded proper attention.

Methodology

The political-military assessment undertaken herein will rely on a framework for analysis which is based upon an extensive review of the literature on insurgency. This literature includes works by practitioners and academicians, as well as by historians and political scientists. Moreover, both the perspective of insurgency and counterinsurgency have been incorporated. The resulting synthesis, which is presented in the following chapter, in no way purports to be a probabilistic theory of insurgency, for the simple fact is that we are still a long way from any such theory in the scientific sense. Instead, the conceptual framework employed in this study is closer to what Lawrence Mayer has referred to as concatenated theory—that is, it explicitly identifies a number of factors having a major bearing on some outcome or dependent variable (in our case, the success or failure of a strategy of protracted revolutionary insurgency).[19] Though it is beyond the state of current knowledge to assign precise weights to the major causal factors, largely because they interact in a highly dynamic way, there is nonetheless an effort to suggest conditions under which specific factors are more critical than they might otherwise be. Since one of those conditions is the particular strategy employed by the insurgents, four separate strategies are discussed, and the importance of particular factors in each case is briefly noted.

Several advantages derive from the use of an explicit framework for analysis. First of all, a careful examination of past cases enables the analyst to ascertain key strategic questions that must be addressed. This, in turn, facilitates the ordering and interpretation of a large amount of data. Secondly, a framework for analysis directs attention to the interrelationships among the factors that are vital for a comprehensive understanding of strategy. Closely related to this is the fact that the framework suggests a number of general hypotheses relating two or more factors which can then be tested in future cases. A number of these are set forth at the end of Chapter 6. Finally, of course, the use of an explicit framework for analysis is an important device for explaining the particular case under investigation. Moreover, it is flexible enough to integrate the unique aspects of the Palestinian case.

One should not infer from this that a strategic assessment is the only way to approach the Palestinian issue. Indeed, there is already an insightful body of historical and analytical commentary on the topic by such experts as William B. Quandt, Michael Hudson, Fuad Jabber, Ann Mosley Lesch, John K. Cooley, and Edgar O'Ballance that has done much to enhance our understanding. This study seeks to complement (and update) these writings by looking at the problem from a different point of view.

A strategic assessment of the Palestinians is important because it helps us to understand why things did not unfold in the manner the fedayeen hoped they would. Equally important, it directs our attention to many of the underlying and more enduring realities that have affected and continue to affect the nature and destiny of the resistance since the October 1973 war.

Framework for Analysis

The Nature of Insurgency

Insurgency may be defined as a struggle between a nonruling group and the ruling authorities, in which the former consciously employs political resources (organizational skills, propaganda, and/or demonstrations) and instruments of violence to establish a legitimacy for some aspect of the present political system which it considers illegitimate. Legitimacy and illegitimacy refer to whether or not existing aspects of politics are considered moral or immoral, or, to simplify, right or wrong by the population or selected elements therein. For our purposes politics is defined as the process of making and executing binding decisions for a society and, accordingly, all behavior associated with this enterprise comprises the "political system." On a general level, the major components of the system may be identified as: the political community, the regime, the authorities, and policies. Any or all of these may be considered immoral by insurgents, and it makes a great deal of difference precisely which one is at stake.[1]

The political community consists of those who accept interacting together in a situation where binding decisions will be made for all. In the contemporary international system this is, for the most part, equivalent to the nation-state. On this very basic point, violent conflict may result from considerations of legitimacy. In Burma, for example, there are a number of groups such as the Shan, the Karen, and the Kachin which do not accept the notion that they should be a part of the nation-state, and thus have sought through violent means to separate themselves from existing arrangements and establish separate political communities. In the United States, Great Britain, France, and Japan, by contrast, there is a general acceptance of the morality of the political community rooted in common history, tradition, and language.

Where there is a consensus on the morality of the political community, there can nevertheless be other grounds for violent conflict. For instance, there may be considerable discord over the salient values and structures which provide the basic framework within which binding decisions and policies are made. Thus, while the Tudeh party in Iran has accepted the political community, it has used violence in an attempt to expunge monarchical principles and values, and to destroy the patrimonial structures of the Iranian government, hoping to replace them with a system in which binding decisions would presumably be made within the framework of a one-party regime, in which the value of equality would replace elitist values that reflect private and aristocratic interests.

On another level some groups may grant legitimacy to the regime but reject the specific individuals in power. This is exemplified by coups in which insurgents seize the key decision-making offices without changing the regime of their predecessors. Besides the well-known Latin American cases of the 1950s, one could point in this regard to the 1970 overthrow of the sultan of Oman, Said bin Taimur, by his son Qabus.[2]

Finally, violence may be used by nonruling groups in an effort to change existing policies detrimental to their interests. One illustration is the terminal phase of the recent insurgency in the Sudan, where the blacks in the South demanded a change in policies to enable them to obtain a greater share of the political and economic benefits of the society.

The important thing to remember in this discussion is that insurgency is essentially a political legitimacy crisis of some sort. The first task of the analyst, therefore, is to ascertain exactly what the issue is. In seeking an answer to this question, it is useful to examine carefully the articulated aims of the insurgents.

By focusing on the ultimate goal of the insurgents and relating it to the aspects of politics discussed above, one can identify six types of insurgent movements: secessionist, revolutionary, restorational, reactionary, conservative, and reformist. *Secessionist* insurgents, such as the aforementioned Karen in Burma, reject the existing political community of which they are formally a part; they wish to separate from it and constitute a new autonomous political community. *Revolutionary* insurgents seek to impose a completely new set of values and structures (regime) within an existing political community (e.g., Marxist insurgents). While *restorational* insurgent movements also desire to displace the regime, the values and structures they champion are identified with a political order of the recent past. The followers of the Imam in the Arab Republic of the Yemen and Sultan Ali Mirrah's Afar Liberation Front in the Haoussa region of Ethiopia are contemporary manifestations of this type. Although *reactionary* insurgents likewise seek to change the regime by reconstituting a past political order, their vision is one that relates to an idealized, golden age of the distant past. The Moslem Brotherhood in Egypt and other Arab countries, which seeks to recreate the flowering Islamic society of centuries ago, is a case in point. *Conservative* insurgents, on the other hand, seek to maintain the existing regime in the face of pressures on the authorities to change it. This type of insurgent movement is illustrated by the Protestant defense organizations in Ulster who wish to retain the regime in Northern Ireland which they see as threatened by the Irish Republican Army, the Irish Republic, and "British capitulationists." Finally, *reformist* insurgents, such as the Kurds in Iraq and the Anayanya movement in the southern Sudan, have attempted to obtain more political, social, and economic benefits without necessarily rejecting the political community, regime, or authorities. They are primarily concerned with policies which are considered discriminatory.[3]

To accomplish their objectives, insurgent movements use political resources and instruments of violence against the ruling authorities. As far as political resources are concerned, organization is the critical dimension. This can be one of two types: conspiratorial, where small elite groups carry out and threaten violent acts; or internal warfare, where insurgent elites attempt to mobilize large segments of the population on behalf of their cause.[4] While the latter phenomenon is the most familiar to students of insurgency because of the well-known Vietnamese, Cambodian, Chinese, Algerian, and Portuguese colonial conflicts, there are also ample cases of conspiratorial insurgencies such as those led by the Bolsheviks in Czarist Russia, the Red Army in Japan, and the Moslem Brotherhood in Egypt.

In movements such as the last named, the organizational effort necessary for coordinating both violent and nonviolent activity is not as demanding as in an internal war setting, since there is far less concern with linking the insurgency to the mass population. This neglect of the population, however, often renders such groups impotent and, hence, has provided one of the key issues dividing insurgent strategies.

Turning to the violent aspect of insurgency, one can identify different *forms* of warfare. A form of warfare may be defined as one variety of organized violence emphasizing particular armed forces, weapons, tactics, and targets. Naval blockades, ground combat, air campaigns, and guerrilla operations are forms of warfare. Three forms of warfare are normally important in insurgent conflicts: terrorism, guerrilla war, and conventional warfare.

Terrorism, a form of warfare conducted either by individuals or very small groups, involves the threat or use of covert and sporadic violence— for example, murder, torture, mutilation, bombing, arson, kidnapping, and hijacking—in order to achieve both long- and short-term political aims; unlike conventional soldiers and guerrillas, terrorists direct their operations primarily against unarmed civilians, rather than enemy military or economic targets. Moreover, the longer-term aim is not so much the desire to deplete the government's material resources as it is to erode its psychological support by instilling fear among officials and segments of the population at large. Though the general purpose of terrorism is to alter the behavior and attitudes of specific groups, this does not exclude the simultaneous pursuit of more proximate objectives, such as extracting particular concessions (e.g., payment of ransom or the release of prisoners), gaining publicity, demoralizing the population through the creation of widespread disorder, provoking repression by the government, enforcing obedience and cooperation from those inside and outside the movement, fulfilling the need to avenge losses inflicted upon the movement, enhancing the political stature of specific factions within the insurgent movement, and undermining policies of rival insurgent groups.[5] Since the particular aims being pursued will vary from incident to incident (even in the cases of those which are similar), it is difficult and sometimes dangerous to generalize about terrorist acts.

Julian Paget has characterized guerrilla warfare as a form of warfare based on mobile tactics used by small, lightly armed groups who aim to harass their opponent rather than to defeat him in battle.[6] Guerrilla warfare differs from terrorism in that its primary targets are not unarmed civilians but usually the government's armed forces, police, or their support units and, in some cases, key economic targets. As a consequence, guerrilla units are larger than terrorist cells and tend to require a more elaborate logistical structure as well as base camps. Like terrorism, however, guerrilla warfare is a weapon of the weak; it is decisive only when the government puts a low value on defeating the guerrillas, and fails to commit adequate resources to the conflict. In most cases it has been necessary to accompany guerrilla warfare with other forms of violence or to develop into mobile conventional warfare (the direct confrontation of large units in the field) in order to achieve success.[7]

Whether or not an insurgent organization will have to move to conventional warfare is, in part, related to whether or not the insurgency is auxiliary or independent in nature. In the former case, suggests Otto Heilbrunn, the insurgents pursue only tactical aims, for they do not have to defeat the enemy; a regular army will be charged with that mission (e.g., Yugoslavia in World War II). Independent insurgent movements, on the other hand, have strategic aims, because they often must regularize their forces in order to be successful on their own. Even if regularization of forces is unnecessary, the independent insurgent movement must still rely largely on its own capability if it is to succeed.[8]

Major Analytical Variables

In their quest for victory, insurgents have devised various strategies intended to maximize the effectiveness of political techniques and violence. These strategies can be differentiated by examining six general variables—popular support, organization of the insurgent movement, cohesion of the insurgency, external support, the environment, and the effectiveness of the government. Since these variables have a major impact on the outcome of insurgencies, they will constitute the criteria for assessing the political and military achievements, as well as the strategy, of the PLO in later chapters. After discussing each of these, we shall consider their relative importance in the context of various insurgent strategies.[9]

Popular Support

For many insurgent leaders, popular support is an overriding strategic consideration. In the words of Mao Tse-tung, "the richest source of power to wage war lies in the masses of the people."[10] The significance ascribed to civilian support can be understood by viewing it as a means to offset advantages which the government possesses by virtue of its control of the administrative apparatus of the state and, most especially, the army and police. Since insurgents know that they would risk destruction by confronting government forces in direct conventional engagements, they opt instead to erode the strength and will of their adversary through the use of terrorism and/or guerrilla warfare, which are designed not only to increase the human and material cost to the government but, also, to demonstrate its failure to maintain effective control and provide protection within the country. Eventually, according to insurgent logic, the government will grow weary of the struggle and seek to prevent further losses by either capitulating or negotiating a settlement favorable to the insurgents.

For the purposes of this study, popular support is divided into two categories: active support and passive support.[11] The latter includes individuals who merely sympathize with the aims and activities of the insurgents, while the former includes those who are willing to take risks and accept personal sacrifices on behalf of the insurgents. In the active support category are individuals who provide insurgents with supplies, intelligence information, shelter, concealment, liaison agents, and who, in some cases, carry out acts of disobedience or protest, all of which risk severe punishment by the government. Although most discussions of popular support tend to emphasize active support, passive supporters are important in the sense that, at a minimum, they are not apt to betray or otherwise to impede the guerrillas.

In focusing on the need for active and verbal support from the masses, insurgents do not neglect the role of the intelligentsia, since it is the principal source for recruitment into both high- and middle-level leadership positions (e.g., commanders of guerrilla units and terrorist networks and political cadres).[12] The importance of the intellectuals has been noted by Ted Robert Gurr, who points out that their desertion from the government has repeatedly been a harbinger of revolution.[13]

It has been argued that community support and security are "safeguarded best when the native population identifies itself spontaneously with the fortunes of the guerrilla movement."[14] However, since spontaneity is often lacking, the insurgent movement must actively proselytize the people. Generally, insurgents will employ one or several of the following methods to gain desired support and recruits: (1) esoteric appeals (2) exoteric appeals, (3) terrorism, (4) provocation of government counter-terrorism, and (5) demonstrations of potency. All of these, in one way or another, aim at convincing the people to render support because the insurgents' goal is both just and achievable.

Esoteric appeals, directed at the intellectuals, seek to clarify the situation by placing it in an ideological or theoretical context that orders and interprets political complexities. In the words of Gabriel Almond:

> An ideology imputes a particular structure to political action. It defines who or what the main initiators of action are, whether they be individuals, status groups, classes, nations, magical forces, or deities. It attributes specific roles to these actors, describes their relationships with one another, and defines the arena in which actions occur.[15]

Marxist revolutionaries, for example, have found that Lenin's exegesis on imperialism has powerful intellectual attraction in Third World countries because it provides a coherent, logical, and all-encompassing explanation of the poverty, illiteracy, and oppression which characterize the political and social milieu. Furthermore, by pointing a finger at indigenous feudal or capitalist classes and their links with external imperialist elements, it provides an identifiable target for the frustrations of the intellectuals, many of whom are either unemployed or underemployed.[16] Although Almond has suggested that ideology is rarely perceived by persons on the point of admission to political movements, one must still account for those few who do respond to ideological incantations.[17] This analysis is especially important in circumstances where intellectuals join one insurgent group, as opposed to its rivals, because it is more ideologically oriented and provides intellectual satisfaction.

Even though the esoteric appeal is primarily directed at the intellectuals, it is also relevant to the masses, who often need to focus their discontent on a real villain if they are to be galvanized into action. One of the functions of ideology, the identification of friend and foe, meets this need. Indeed, identifying the source of frustration and grievances is important because "discontented people act aggressively only when they become aware of the supposed source of frustration, or something or someone with whom they associate frustration." Moreover, doctrinal justifications for violence can themselves intensify discontent by raising expectations and defending violence as a means to their attainment. This, of course, presupposes that there are existent grievances—the exoteric dimension—"because men's susceptibility to these beliefs is a function of the intensity of their discontent."[18]

Exoteric appeals focus on concrete grievances of both the intelligentsia and the masses. In the case of the former, the issues of unemployment and underemployment are often exploited, whereas for the latter, emphasis is directed to the more varied matters, such as corruption and repression by local officials as well as the need for food, land reform, jobs, medical assistance, and other social services.[19] If they are successful in achieving their goal, the insurgents promise, such problems will be effectively dealt with.

In those situations where foreign nations either impose their authority directly (imperialism), exert tremendous influence through international economic networks (neoimperialism), or intervene in support of the local authorities, the insurgents will frequently merge nationalist themes with esoteric and exoteric appeals. Relying on a formulation such as Lenin's theory of imperialism, they will identify the external enemy as the source of national deprivations. For many intellectuals this, again, provides both a cogent explanation and target, while for the masses it is manipulated in such a way as to provide a simplified explanation and tangible enemy.

Where esoteric and exoteric appeals are unsuccessful or difficult to implement because of effective government action and/or environmental disadvantages, the insurgents may turn to terrorism or the provocation of counterterror. In this context, the purpose of terrorist acts is to obtain popular support by demonstrating the government's weaknesses and the insurgents' strength.[20] Whether or not the insurgents will be successful in this undertaking, however, depends on two factors: the target of terror and the duration of the terrorist campaigns.

As far as the target is concerned, if terror is aimed at individuals or groups disliked by the people, it can facilitate the identification of the insurgents with repressed and exploited elements. By manipulating resentment (based on grievances), and using selective terror against hated individuals and groups, the insurgents may well be able to increase popular support. Such was the case in the Cypriot insurrection against the British, according to Paget. On the other hand, if, at the outset, potential support is low, terror can create hostilities toward the insurgents.[21] Whatever the case, it can end up alienating potential domestic and international supporters if it becomes indiscriminate and unduly prolonged.[22]

A fourth means which the insurgent utilizes in winning popular support is "catalyzing and intensifying counterterror which further alienates the enemy from the local population."[23] In other words, the guerrillas seek to provoke government reprisals against the population which, in turn, will increase resentment and win the insurrectionary forces more adherents and support. Whether such an insurgent ploy will succeed, however, will be determined largely by the nature of the government response and by ethnic considerations. If the government's actions are violent—wanton killing, as in the case of the Pakistani army in Bangladesh in 1971—and widespread, they would appear to effect more resentment and hatred than, say, such nonviolent actions as curfews, resettlement, etc. While ruthless methods by the government might restore law and order in the short run, the long-term effect may be, as Richard Clutterbuck suggests, to provide the seeds for further insurgency.[24]

The effect of the ethnic variable is less clear. Jerry Silverman and Peter Jackson have argued that ethnic solidarity between the people and guerrillas may be important in terror-counterterror situations, since it can cause the population to forgive insurgent excesses but not the government's.[25] In light of the fact that this analyst found situations in Vietnam where the people reacted to American air and artillery strikes by blaming the revolutionary provocateurs, the ethnic factor cannot be considered foolproof. Nevertheless, on balance, it seems sound and suggestive.

The final means the insurgents employ to establish popular support, demonstration of potency, has two dimensions: retaining the military initiative and meeting the needs of the people through social services and a governing apparatus. The latter aspect demonstrates not only the reality of the guerrilla presence, but the corresponding government failure to deal with shadow government political cadres. Besides governing, guerrilla political operators will seek to meet some of the people's basic needs and cooperate with them in essential tasks.[26] Quite often extension of such aid to the people will be the first step in involving them with the insurgent movement, either actively or passively. This would seem to be especially true in those contexts where the regime has been delinquent in responding to popular demands.

The second feature of demonstration of potency is gaining the military initiative in order to create the impression that the insurgency has momentum and will succeed. A number of writers have stressed the importance of initiative to the guerrillas because, in addition to winning adherents for the movement, it boosts and sustains morale within insurgent organizations. "Units that are active and successful in the accomplishment of assigned missions build up a high espirit de corps and attract followers; success is contagious." Putting it another way, "no guerrilla movement in the field can afford to remain inactive for long; by so doing, it loses its morale and sense of purpose."[27]

In his quest to gain the initiative, the insurgent has at his disposal a flexible arsenal—ambushes, sabotage, kidnapping, assassination, mass attacks, etc. In order to employ such diverse methods effectively, however, the insurgent must have a coordinated strategy, a requisite that involves another major criterion, cohesion. Although the question of cohesion will be discussed in a separate section, a few comments about its relationship to popular support are necessary at this point. Of special significance is the fact that an insurgent movement with competing focuses of loyalty will not only raise command and control problems that undercut military operations and initiative, but will lead some potential supporters to believe the resistance is in a state of confusion. As a result, the corresponding image of weakness may dissuade many from joining. Moreover, any violent conflict between rival factions will undoubtedly sap the movement's strength, divert it from the main enemy, and deny it a positive image in the people's eyes. The spectacle of various guerrilla organizations criticizing each other in order to enhance their stature is bound to be bewildering to potential supporters.

Military initiative will require continuous local victories. Since the guerrilla is usually weak at the outset of hostilities, these may be only small successes, but such tactical modesty at the beginning may be necessary for eventual victory.[28] Local victories in guerrilla war, however, are heavily dependent on popular support; hence initiative and popular support are interdependent.

Initiative will require freedom of action. In Mao's words, "Freedom of action is the very life of an army and once this freedom is lost an army faces defeat or annihilation."[29] Although freedom of action is normally associated with operations in the target country, there are circumstances in which it is related to sanctuaries outside the territory being contested. These sanctuaries, which involve external support, are of great importance if, during the incipient stages of the conflict, the resistance movement has difficulty operating within the target country's borders. In such situations the attitude of contiguous states will assume a major role in the conflict for, in a sense, they are the insurgent's last fallback position. One should not conclude from this, however, that guerrillas can indefinitely operate from outside the target state. In most cases, they must, at some point, organize the population and establish a popular base within the target country. Douglas Hyde, for instance, has called attention to the fact that guerrillas from Sarawak found that operating from bases across the border in Indonesia had a deleterious effect on the revolutionary movement, because it prevented direct and continuous contacts between leaders and the guerrillas in Sarawak. As a result the insurgents had to make an effort to set up bases in Sarawak itself.[30]

A final aspect of initiative which deserves mention is what Hyde calls the dramatic gesture. This tactic, which involves terrorism such as kidnapping and hijacking, is employed by the insurgents in order to convince world and domestic opinion that they are to be taken seriously, as a movement actively fighting for a worthwhile goal.[31]

To summarize, popular support is often crucial for the success of an insurgency. In light of this fact, the insurgent movement will use esoteric and exoteric appeals, terrorism, provocation of counterterrorism, and demonstration of potency to win adherents to its cause. Such a campaign is quite complex, and its outcome can be heavily influenced by other major variables considered in this chapter, most especially by the government's response and the insurgents' organizational dexterity.

Organization

Organization is a major factor enabling insurgents to compensate for the material superiority of opponents. Indeed, when scholars emphasize the point that insurgency is more a political phenomenon than a military one, they often have in mind the great amount of effort insurgents devote to organization, either on the elite level, if it is a conspiracy, or the mass level, if it is an internal war. When examining an insurgent organization, three structural dimensions—scope, complexity, and cohesion—and two functions—provision of instrumental services and provision of channels for expressive protest—are of primary interest.[32] Given the particular salience of cohesion in the Palestinian case, it will be treated as a major factor and discussed in a separate section below.

Scope refers to the number of people who either play key roles in the movement (terrorists, guerrillas, or political cadres) or provide active support. How many people will be controlled by the insurgent movement is partially a function of complexity and cohesion. If an insurgent organization perceives a need to augment its membership, it will normally increase its level of differentiation or complexity, and, through the efforts of its political cadres, penetrate the hamlets, villages, and cities of the nation, especially in contested areas (i.e., areas in which neither the government nor the insurgents have firm control). Insurgents often establish what Bernard Fall has called parallel hierarchies, which rival government institutions. The parallel hierarchy can take two forms: use of existing administrative structures through the infiltration of subversive individuals, or creation of new clandestine structures designed to take over full administrative responsibility when military-political conditions are appropriate. The importance of this type of organization is well-known to students of World War II partisan movements and the two Vietnam conflicts. Moreover, in some cases the insurgency organization may go beyond the government structures it seeks to imitate, and create new branches or structures in order to entice more people into the movement. Examples of such additions would be youth groups, peasant organizations, workers' groups, and women's organizations.[33] The purpose is to widen the base and increase the number of people in the insurgency movement by integrating these auxiliaries with the main guerrilla organizational structure (the new entity is often referred to as a front). The effectiveness of winning adherents by increasing the differentiation of the organization is exemplified by the case of the Philippines, where many joined the Huks through front organizations, often without even knowing the party's aims.[34]

In the early stages of an insurgency, the viability of parallel hierarchies in government-controlled areas is dubious. Organizational structures usually exist in the guerrilla-controlled base area; the aim of the insurgents is to spread them to partially controlled government regions. The first step in this undertaking is the formation of small, secretive cells to assess the revolutionary potential of the people and to recruit followers and supporters. Should the insurgents fail to establish cells, more sophisticated organizational development is doomed.

In addition to differentiation of political structures, insurgents— especially those engaged in a protracted revolutionary war—may diversify their military organization by creating logistics units, terrorist networks, and guerrilla forces, with the last-mentioned being divided into full-time and part-time fighters. Full-time guerrilla units, operating from secure bases, attack government military units and installations on a continuous basis, and will form the nucleus of a regularized force if the movement progresses to mobile-conventional warfare. The part-time or local guerrillas, on the other hand, stay in their communities and provide a number of invaluable services, such as collecting intelligence, storing supplies, and providing a coercive arm to protect the political organizers. In addition, the local guerrillas can attach themselves to main force units for local attacks either as combatants or as scouts and guides.[35]

The continual functioning of both parallel hierarchies and military units may itself convert people by simply demonstrating the insurgents' ability to control an area in defiance of the government (a linkage of demonstration of potency and organization). Such differentiation is particularly important in situations where the regime is reasonably strong.

By increasing the complexity of their organization, the insurgents will be better able to perform the instrumental and expressive functions that attract adherents. Participation can yield both material benefits, if the organization has the resources, and interpersonal satisfactions such as companionship, self-definition, and reinforcement of shared beliefs.

Although external support and control of base areas by dissidents help meet material needs, most dissident organizations lack the capability to meet economic demands. To compensate, great stress is placed on psychosocial requirements for status, communal solidarity, ideational coherence, and expression of hostility.[36]

Cohesion

The third major variable associated with the outcome of an insurgency is cohesion. Indeed, many experts and practitioners of insurgency have stressed the importance of unity within insurgent ranks. John J. McCuen, for example, contends that unifying the effort is the basic principle behind all effective revolutionary strategy, planning, tactics, and organization. "This has been so ever since 1902 when Lenin's *What Is To Be Done?* made revolution into a science."[37] Although the conduct of operations and responsibility may be delegated to local leaders, there should be a general headquarters in charge of policy, discipline, ethics, and ideology.

An insurgent movement which lacks unity will face a host of problems, not the least of which is an inadequate sense of direction. Moreover, as Mao pointed out in *The Strategy of Partisan Warfare*, "without centralized strategic command the partisans can inflict little damage on their adversaries, as without this, they can break down into roaming, armed bands, and then find no more support by the population."[38]

Although unity is usually important for insurgent movements, its absence is not always a barrier to success. Despite ideological divisions and internecine violence between the groups in Algeria and between the Tito and Mihailovitch factions in Yugoslavia, both the FLN and Tito achieved their political goals. However, in each case, other major developments offset the lack of cohesion. In Algeria it was a breakdown of French resolve to stay on, despite the fact that the military insurrection was brought under control, that enabled the insurgents to succeed; in Yugoslavia it was the thrust of the allied armies (an external support) that defeated the Germans and created a power vacuum in the country. It seems, therefore, that if the regime loses its will or if outside forces intervene in a substantial way, insurgent disunity need not be a critical failing. On the other hand, where the regime is strong, insurgents court disaster by fighting among themselves and failing to coordinate their efforts.

In order to achieve unity, insurgent movements stress proper attitudes, sanctions, and organizational schema. While ideology can be a basis for cohesion, because it provides members of an insurgent movement with shared values and orientations toward the political world, it can be a double-edged sword in situations where the insurgent movement contains rival factions, each of which has a different ideology. In the latter case ideology militates against cohesion and may even lead factions to split from the movement and reconstitute themselves as separate groups.

Organizational formats are also important in establishment of cohesion, and there are three general outlines: control by politicians, independent political and military commands, and control by the military. Even though each organizational scheme is partially aimed at unifying the revolutionary forces, rival movements may continue to exist and operate. Where this happens, the insurgents may attempt to coordinate activity by creating a unified command for a particular operation, by arriving at a division of labor among the various groups, or by establishing a unified command for all operations. Of the three possibilities, a unified command for all operations appears most promising, since it is most conducive to giving insurgents a sense of strategic direction and to dealing with the ideological, tactical, and personal differences which divide the movement in the first place. For a unified command to be successful, however, rival organizations must agree to subordinate parochial interests to the overall interests of the movement, as defined by the unified command. And, if the unified command's decisions are to be considered authoritative and legitimate, competing groups must reach a consensus on the mechanics of the decision-making process and on methods for invoking sanctions against deviationists.

External Support

Perhaps the most publicized aspect of insurgent strategy is its frequent stress on external support as an important means to offset the government's advantages. Indeed, all one has to do is pick up a newspaper or watch television news broadcasts to become acquainted with such notable examples as Chinese and Soviet aid to insurgent groups, the People's Democratic Republic of the Yemen's support for the Popular Front for the Liberation of Oman, the Sudan's assistance to the Eritrean secessionists, and so forth. The question of just how important such support is and precisely what it consists of, however, merits closer examination.

There are four categories of external support: moral, political, material, and sanctuary. *Moral* support is least costly and risky for a donor, for all it involves is public acknowledgement that the insurgent movement is just and admirable. *Political* support advances a step further since the donor nation actively champions and supports the strategic goal of the insurgent movement in international fora. Both of these types of intangible support can be effective against a wavering government which must, as the French found out in Algeria, bear the additional burden of international pressure and censure. Of the two, political support clearly is more desirable because of its potential in adding to the insurgent movement's allies and increasing support in some or all categories. One final point here: foreign states are not the only sources of political and moral support. In colonial settings, insurgents will seek to obtain backing from dissident groups in the mother country (e.g., the Algerian and Vietnamese relations with the French left and peace groups).

In contrast with moral and political support, *material* assistance is more concrete and risky for an outside power. Consisting of such things as weapons, ammunition, medical supplies, food, training, and perhaps even the provision of military advisors, fire support, or combat units, it becomes particularly important as the insurgents increase the scale and intensity of violence, since such a development necessitates greater logistical inputs (e.g., the Viet Cong after 1965).[39] Before this period, the insurgents may rely on the populace or materials seized from the government for their sustenance.

When insurgents conclude that external logistical inputs are essential, the role of sympathetic major powers can be very important. Accordingly, insurgent leaders will expend great efforts to persuade them to provide material assistance. Success in this endeavor is not the end of the story, however, for in some cases the provision of aid may be dependent on third parties who control overland transportation routes. In light of this problem, the attitude of states contiguous to the area being contested may be vital. A positive response on their part will facilitate the flow of materials; a negative reaction may neutralize the entire effort.

Besides facilitating the supply flow or actually making materials available to the insurgents, foreign states may be important as *sanctuaries* in which the guerrillas can be trained, arms stockpiled, operations planned, leadership secured, and perhaps a provisional government established. While both sanctuaries and material aid are usually more important in the final stages of an insurgency, there are circumstances which can make them indispensable early in the struggle. Such may be the case in situations where the insurgents are unable to establish a secure base in the target country and lack popular support. With such an inauspicious start, the insurgents are literally forced to rely on adjacent countries, for, at a minimum, security and freedom of movement must be guaranteed if the insurgents are ever to establish bases, organize the people, and obtain popular support and commitment. The Sarawak insurgency, which has relied on bases in Indonesia, is an example here.[40]

When seeking to obtain support in the international system, the insurgents must first attract the attention of outside states or groups. One method is to use dramatic gestures such as kidnapping or skyjacking. Usually, however, such acts must be followed by actions which can demonstrate that the insurgency is substantial. In this connection, military successes against the regime, backed by good organization and demonstrable popular support, are crucial. In contradistinction, a poorly organized, disunited guerrilla movement with little popular backing is unlikely to attract significant external support.

While the types of external support discussed thus far are very often important to the fortunes of insurgent movements, there have been cases where only low-level outside help has been sufficient. In these instances one usually finds that the insurgents have benefited from other favorable factors (e.g., a weak regime or substantial popular support). A case in point would be the Castro revolution in Cuba, during which the insurgents did not have a contiguous friendly country to function as a sanctuary or logistics area, although they did receive some arms via flights from Mexico, Venezuela, and the United States. Given an inept, corrupt, and insecure government and a demoralized army, however, this level of aid was sufficient to help topple the Batista regime and to obviate the need for a protracted guerrilla war based on the Chinese and Vietnamese models.

Environment

The fifth major variable used to assess an insurgency is the environment. Among other things, this includes terrain, climate, the road and communications network, ethnicity, religion and culture, size of the country, and the size and distribution of the population.

Rugged terrain—vast mountains, jungles, swamps, forests, and the like—usually helps guerrilla operations, because it hinders movement by government troops and provides inaccessible hideouts for the guerrillas' main bases. The triple-canopied jungles of Indochina, which were a tremendous asset to the forces of Ho Chi Minh in two wars, are an example of excellent terrain for guerrilla operations and the establishment of base areas. Although deserts have sometimes proven to be advantageous for guerrilla operations—one such case being the Arab Revolt led by the legendary T. E. Lawrence from 1916-1918—the advent and development of air surveillance and attack have made guerrillas more susceptible to detection and destruction.

Along with the makeup of the terrain, one must consider the size of the base of operations. If the base of operations is small, it can easily be isolated and penetrated; if the terrain, on the other hand, is vast, and guerrillas take advantage of this by expanding their area of operations, government administration will be complicated, firepower concentration reduced, and supervision of the populace made more difficult. Considerations such as these led Mao to view a vast countryside as a sine qua non of successful protracted war.[41]

Although a lack of favorable terrain can be a drawback to insurgencies, there are instances (the 1945-1948 Jewish insurrection in Palestine, for instance) where it was overcome. The key here appears to be a weak or wavering government that is prone to capitulate early when faced with sustained terrorism. Where the regime is resolved to pursue the conflict, favorable terrain is crucial to the insurgent side.

The importance of terrain is accentuated further by Heilbrunn's suggestion that geography is the main consideration in the establishment of the guerrilla bases which he believes are necessary for the success of a revolutionary movement. It is in the base area that the guerrillas first establish the parallel hierarchy which rules the population; from there the guerrillas will seek to expand into areas partially controlled by the government. As important as such base areas usually are, however, there are cases where they may be dispensable. Thus, Heilbrunn argues that where popular support is high and the army is demoralized or in sympathy with the revolutionaries, bases may not be important because the government will collapse without a long struggle. If these conditions are reversed, a prolonged war will be necessary, and in that situation bases will be required in order to wear down the enemy.[42]

The relationship of climate to guerrilla success has not received the attention that terrain has in the writings on insurgency. Perhaps this is because climate can favor either the regime or the insurgents. Severe weather, for example, can hinder both guerrilla and government movement and increase the logistical needs of both. In the Vietnam conflict, the North Vietnamese campaigns frequently coincided with favorable weather, facilitating supply movement, while bad weather often brought lulls in fighting. Yet, in military actions, the Viet Cong used poor weather to advantage because it hampered government air support. Severe weather may also benefit the guerrillas by preventing government attacks and allowing the revolutionary side to regroup and reorganize. All told, however, climate is difficult to isolate and define as crucial in any way to insurgent success.

An aspect of environment that seems to have more bearing on the fortunes of an insurgency than weather is the state of the transportation-communications network. Suffice it to say that if the road and communications systems are highly developed and extensive, regular government forces are favored because they can move about expeditiously and make better use of their technological superiority. On the other hand, poor roads and communications favor the guerrilla side. Gurr comments on this point as follows:

> Guerrilla war is common in underdeveloped countries because of poor transportation and communications networks and the isolation of rural

areas, which facilitate guerrilla incursions. Free access to rural people enables guerrillas to propagandize, control, and secure support from them. . . .
Given the technological capabilities of the best-equipped modern military
forces, the terrain that offers the most physical protection for the guerrillas
must be mountainous, without roads or tracks, and almost continuously
cloud-covered.[43]

The size and distribution of the population will also have an impact on
an insurgency. Where the number of people is small and concentrated, it
will facilitate government efforts to control the population and sever its
links with the guerrillas. The concentration of people in cities does not
appear as favorable to insurgent movements as their dispersal in rural
areas, although, as we shall see later, some contemporary insurgent
strategists believe otherwise. If a society is mostly urban, it is easier for a
government to control the people and to prevent the establishment of
guerrilla bases. However, if the government is weak and the insurgents
have a significant degree of international support, it is possible that some
of the aims of the insurgents may be achieved in an urban setting. Again, an
example is Palestine, where Jewish terrorism combined with pro-Zionist
currents in the international arena to force a British retreat. When the
authorities demonstrate both the resolution and the competence to combat
the insurgent threat, and thus force the insurgents to plan for protracted
warfare, an urban environment, although conducive to terrorist activities,
hardly suffices; a rural, underdeveloped society, is more promising.

Conflict caused by ethnicity, religion, and language may be helpful to
guerrilla elements. This would seem to be especially true where the
majority of the population is from the same ethnic, religious, and/or
language group as the insurgents, while the authorities are not.[44] Although
the colonial systems are classic examples, the same dynamics apply in
independent states ruled by minority factions. The tendency of an
individual to sympathize with his kinsman rather than with an outsider is
important to the insurgent. Nevertheless, as the first Indochina war shows,
it will require an assiduous political effort to actualize the potential of such
a population and turn it against the regime.

As the preceding discussion indicates, in situations where the regime
displays the ability and willingness to resist and the army is not
demoralized, the insurgent movement must prepare itself to wage a
prolonged conflict. In that case, it will be necessary for the insurgents to
organize the population effectively, unify the movement, obtain external
support, and exploit what advantages the environment has to offer, if they
are to have any hope of succeeding.

One conclusion that seems inescapable after considering the first five variables is that government response is the crucial variable in insurgent conflicts. Where that response is poor or uneven, the insurgents can tolerate shortcomings in popular and external support, organization, cohesion, and the environment. Conversely, where the government manifests strength, such failings can spell defeat. Since it is important, the government response must be examined in some detail.

The Government Role

Professor Walter Sonderland has pointed out that the government's response to an insurgent challenge is critical. As he puts it:

> as soon as the challenge is in the open the success of the operation depends not primarily on the development of insurgent strength, but more importantly on the degree of vigor, determination and skill with which the incumbent regime acts to defend itself, both politically and militarily.[45]

Carrying this argument a step further, one might suggest that whether a given insurgency can succeed by confining itself to low-level activity or will have to take on the dimensions of a protracted internal war, is largely determined by the nature of the government and its response to the incipient actions of the insurgents. Therefore, the counterinsurgency aspect merits closer and extended examination.

Governments facing an insurrection may confront one or more of the political challenges or forms of violence discussed earlier, namely: (1) propaganda-organizational activity, (2) terrorism, (3) guerrilla warfare, and (4) mobile-conventional warfare.[46] Since each type of threat involves different techniques and poses a unique problem for the government, effective and appropriate countermeasures are heavily dependent upon the willingness and ability to differentiate among them. Each type of insurgent threat compels the government to emphasize a particular facet of counterinsurgency. Hence, McCuen has argued, to cope successfully with the organizational challenge the government will have to stress civic action, administration, and low-level police activity. A terrorist threat will necessitate intensified police work. Guerrilla warfare calls for a low-level military response. Mobile-conventional warfare will require conventional military operations by the government.[47]

The creation and implementation of a counterinsurgency program along these lines is complicated by the fact that, in practice, the insurgent threats not only overlap and are cumulative, but also may emerge in different regions of the country. Thus an effective government response is associated not with a single strategy applied indiscriminately in all sectors, but rather with the adoption of a flexible policy that coordinates a variety of countermeasures in different areas, depending on the nature of the threats. For example, a government facing a substantial mobile-conventional threat in one sector and low-level guerrilla activity in another would seem to find little utility in extending its search and destroy operations against conventional formations to the guerrilla area, since such a move would constitute a costly, and perhaps counterproductive, overreaction. Guerrillas can easily blend back into the population, and thus raise the possibility of frustrated government units striking out against the people, many of whom may be quite innocent. What appears more appropriate in such circumstances is search and destroy operations in one area and patrols in the other.

The execution of a multifaceted counterinsurgency program obviously requires coordination of political, administrative, military, police, and intelligence efforts; this is essential if the various counterinsurgency agencies are to avoid working at cross-purposes. The problem here, however, is that the optimal organizational conditions of an effective administration—a tradition of civilian primacy and an adequate number of good leaders—are often missing; in fact, their very absence may be one of the reasons for the insurgency.[48] While the question of civilian leadership is perhaps the most difficult to resolve in the short term, the other aspects can be improved.

As with the insurgent side, the government will find organizational efforts are facilitated when its officials have a common purpose and direction. This, in turn, places a premium on the articulation and communication of an overall program for the future.[49]

Since the national program is also instrumental in gaining the support of the population, ascertaining the people's aspirations, which vary from one insurrection to another and from one region to another within the same country, becomes important. Land reform, for instance, may be a basic grievance in some circumstances but not in others. History provides a number of cases sustaining the thesis that benevolent treatment of the population and reforms designed to meet the basic needs of the people can go a long way toward undermining the support of the insurgents.

The behavior of the German administration in the Ukraine during World War II was a striking example of the government being its own worst enemy, especially since the Ukranians had no love for Stalin and seemed ready to help the Germans. As it happened, German exactions and repression against the Ukranians eventually turned the population against the Third Reich. Benevolent administration and effective reforms such as those carried out by Colonel General Schmidt might have proved effective in harnessing popular support; however, they were few and far between and were undercut by general Nazi policies.[50]

A classic case of a government winning popular support is the Philippine campaign against the Huks. In that instance, Ramon Magsaysay's election to the presidency led to a number of social and military reforms which mobilized popular support. Combined with the use of ruthless force against the insurgents, this turn of events brought victory.[51]

Devising a program to satisfy the grievances of the population is, of course, no easy undertaking, especially for a developing nation, with poor resources and capabilities. It is frequently necessary for the governments of such states to seek economic assistance from external sources. Demands for redistribution of existing economic or political power, on the other hand, are largely internal matters that can be accommodated by the government from within.[52]

The most difficult demand for a government to meet is that it abdicate in favor of insurgent rule at the highest level. However, since popular support for an insurgent organization with such a formidable objective is usually based on lesser socioeconomic needs, the government can seek to undercut the basis of insurgent support by attenuating the concrete grievances of the masses. In other words, the lesser demands of the people are distinguished from the ambitions of the insurgent leadership. While the government cannot accommodate the latter, it may well be able to deal with the former, and by so doing deprive the insurgent movement of its main source of strength and resources, the people.

Clearly, it will be more difficult to design an effective counterinsurgency program in colonial situations where not only the insurgent leadership but also the people are motivated by the nationalist aim of independence. Faced with such circumstances some regimes have sought to contain the situation by improving the well-being of the population in the hope that the latter would support the existing political order in return for short-term benefits. Where the population is divided into rival ethnic groups, the government may also seek to sustain or exacerbate societal cleavages in order to keep the insurgent movement divided (the well-known strategy of divide and rule).

The execution of a general program to deal with the needs of the people depends upon an effective administration staffed by local personnel if possible.[53] History is replete with cases in which a government vacuum has been exploited by insurgent forces establishing their own organizational apparatus, however rudimentary. The initial British inattention to the Chinese squatters in areas bordering the jungles during the Malayan Emergency is a case in point.

An essential component of any organizational effort by a government is forging a sense of loyalty between itself and the people. To facilitate this task, potential groups and leaders to serve the government and provide personnel for the auxiliary police and militia forces are identified and organized. The role of the police and militia is to isolate the people from infiltrators, prevent exactions from being made on the people by the insurgents, and provide security against terrorism and low-level guerrilla operations. Since most people place the highest value on personal security, the government which expects to gain and benefit from the cooperation of the people must ensure their personal protection at the earliest possible moment.

Along with the political and administrative action outlined above, effective counterinsurgency invariably involves a number of security measures—detention without trial, resettlement of sections of the population, control of the distribution of food, curfews, restrictions on movement, the issuance and checking of identification cards, and the imposition of severe penalties for carrying unauthorized weapons—in order to separate the population from the insurgents. While such sanctions may be undesirable from an ideal or moral standpoint, they can be and have been effective, when applied consistently, fairly, and judiciously.[54]

Resettlement, for example, may be necessary if the government is to sever the links between the insurgents and the populace, particularly when terror and/or guerrilla attacks persist and are attributed, at least partially, to support rendered the insurgents by portions of the population. Civic action and political organization are extremely important during resettlement; indeed, they are often viewed as concomitants of that technique. The Briggs plan for moving the Chinese squatters in Malaya, the Kitchener resettlement scheme during the Boer War, and the relocation program during the Mau Mau uprising are examples where transporting segments of the population was instrumental in denying insurgents support of the population. Conversely, the resettlement carried out by the regime of Ngo Dinh Diem in South Vietnam failed, largely because it was overextended, too rapid, procedurally deficient, and inadequately supported by the police establishment.[55]

Whenever the government invokes security measures directed at individuals or the collectivity, it can expect the insurgents to make use of the legal structure in an attempt to portray the regime as a violator of civil and human rights, and to protect their personnel. Essentially, the insurgents will seek to have those under detention treated as peacetime offenders. This ploy, which will make it even more difficult for the government to avoid alienating the population, is another reason for imposition of such measures in a judicious and limited manner.

The fairness of security measures is contingent upon accurate information about the insurgent organization, including the identification and location of its members and the detailing of its intended activities.

The easiest way for the government to obtain the necessary information is to establish effective rapport with the people by means of good administration and prudent and diligent police work. The latter requires well-trained interrogation experts, who can minimize violence by knowing the right questions to ask, and agents who can penetrate the insurgent apparatus.[56]

Since insurgents themselves are a potentially valuable source of intelligence, their treatment by government forces is important. While it is unlikely that members of the hard core will defect, it is possible that less dedicated insurgents may be induced to surrender, especially if insurgent prospects are not bright. Psychological warfare designed to increase the number of defectors by promising them amnesty, security, and material benefits has often been used to exploit such situations.

As far as military measures designed to deal with insurgent threats are concerned, four responses have been suggested, based on previous cases.

McCuen, for instance, argues that to cope with an insurgent *organizational* threat and the low-level terrorism and sporadic guerrilla attacks which often accompany it, the military must be oriented toward population contact. Thus, military units should be positioned in a large number of small posts allowing for protection of and mixing with the local people. If there is a small-scale guerrilla threat, the territorial defense force must make extensive use of ambushes and patrols in an effort to intercept insurgent bands. Moreover, the government should provide back-up mobile air, naval, and ground forces to assist ambush patrols that engage the enemy, and to conduct harassment operations against insurgent units in underpopulated hinterlands. But, in no case can the mobile forces be considered a substitute for territorial defense forces.[57]

Where the insurgent movement has been able to mount a substantial *terrorist* campaign, the government must consolidate its own areas and then, operating from these secure bases, seek to destroy the political-military structures of the insurgent organizations by locating and detaining its members. Police forces, which have received quasi-military training for operations in the contested areas and the hinterlands, can concentrate on this action while lesser duties are performed by the auxiliary police.[58]

When insurgents have begun to conduct large-scale *guerrilla* actions, the government faces a serious threat. In response, it must first consolidate the areas it does hold, and then gradually expand from there with the objectives of gaining control of the population, food, and other resources, while inflicting losses on guerrilla-units and defending vital lines of communication. In McCuen's view, an essential component of the antiguerrilla campaign is a nomadic territorial offensive that emphasizes patrols, attacks, and ambushes by small dispersed units during both day and night hours. Once an area has been cleared of guerrilla bands, it is important that the government establish an administrative presence, if only initially by civic action teams.[59]

To further deprive the guerrillas of the initiative, the government can employ mobile forces, commandos, airpower, and artillery to harass insurgents in remote and thinly populated hinterlands where they are likely to have established bases. Eventually these areas should also be organized by the government. If forbidden zones (i.e., areas that can be fired into at will) are to be created, experience suggests that great care should be taken to assure that innocent civilians are not endangered, otherwise such military actions may prove to be counterproductive in risking creation of more insurgents than are eliminated.

If the government finds itself confronted by *mobile-conventional* warfare, then it is near defeat, a situation which may require a call for outside assistance. McCuen argues that the first countermove by the government should be to consolidate base areas, even if this means sacrificing large areas of the country. After securing base areas and expanding from them, mobile strike forces are used against insurgent bases in the manner of the assaults on the Greek guerrilla strongholds during the Greek civil war. If the government is lucky, the guerrillas may choose to defend their bases, thus violating the cardinal guerrilla principle which warns against engaging a superior force. In the event that insurgents decide to revert to guerrilla warfare, the government should respond likewise, taking appropriate steps as summarized above.[60]

If the government concludes that sanctuaries across the border are playing an important role in sustaining the insurgent activities at any time, it can attempt to create a cordon sanitaire. Should jungle and mountain terrain make this task impossible or difficult, the government may opt to establish forbidden zones, conduct a nomadic territorial offensive, build barriers, infiltrate counterguerrillas across the border, or directly strike the sanctuary country. Since the last-mentioned tactic can be a casus belli that might widen the conflict, the government must weigh its aims, possible costs, and risks carefully.[61]

Although the insurgent threat is largely a political-administrative one, this does not mean that military success is unimportant. Besides inflicting material and personnel losses on the insurgent movement, and in some cases forcing the insurgents from familiar operating terrain, military victories can enhance government morale, undermine the insurgent image, and impress the population. It must be remembered that the insurgents are trying to establish an image of strength in order to convince the people that they will succeed; when most of the victories go to the government side, the insurgents' credibility suffers.

One caveat here, however. If military victories are achieved at the expense of the local population—in terms of casualties and property losses—they may prove to be counterproductive in that the alienation engendered may increase the ranks of the disaffected. The inescapable conclusion is that all military operations must be planned and executed in such a way as to minimize civilian losses, for as Richard Clutterbuck has pointed out, one misplaced bomb or artillery shell can undo countless hours of political effort.[62]

In summary, the government faced with an insurgency must combat four different types of threat with four different types of responses. Insurgent organizational and propaganda efforts must be countered by government counterorganization and psychological warfare as well as by police operations designed to uncover insurgent political cadres; terrorism must be countered by security measures and intensified police and intelligence operations; guerrilla warfare must be dealt with by low-level military action (the nomadic territorial offensive) which puts a premium on small unit patrolling, mobile operations against hinterland guerrilla bases, and the defense of vital lines of communication; and, mobile-conventional warfare must be countered by conventional military operations on the part of the government's mobile units. Furthermore, the government must be prepared to deal with each of these threats simultaneously.

Regardless of how one looks at it, the effort required by a counterinsurgency program is substantial. The demands in terms of morale, patience, and determination become greater as the insurgent movement progresses. To be successful, the counterinsurgency forces need the firm backing of their government and people. Whether or not such support is forthcoming will be partially determined by the strategy the regime uses and by the way in which this strategy is implemented. Signs that things are not going well include serious dissent in favor of the guerrilla objective (explicit or implicit), desertions from government forces, general lack of combativeness, poor local law enforcement, guerrilla operations carried out by increasingly larger units, lack of informants among the people, and a low surrender rate. Conversely, the opposite of each of these indicators would suggest that the government is succeeding.

If the government has been able to devise and apply the types of programs suggested above, insurgents will have little chance of success. Moreover, even if the government does a mediocre job, it may still succeed, depending upon how well the insurgents perform in relation to other major criteria for success. Which of those factors is important and how the insurgents will perform is, in large part, a function of the particular strategy they adopt, the final consideration in this chapter.

Insurgent Strategies

There are a myriad of insurgent strategies in the real political world. Although in specific situations it is necessary to consider unique historical and cultural factors, on a more general level several patterns of strategic thought are discernible. We shall focus on three—the Maoist, Cuban, and urban strategies.

The Maoist Strategy

No doubt the most elaborate insurgent strategy is articulated by Maoist theoreticians. They ascribe great significance to popular support, extensive organizational efforts, and the environment as resources necessary for a prolonged conflict with an enemy perceived as being in a superior position prior to hostilities. What is more, the Maoist approach is par excellence a sequential strategy—i.e., it unfolds in distinct steps, each of which is partially designed to achieve the goal and is dependent on the outcome of the step before it. Both scholars and practitioners have identified these steps or "stages" as political organization-terrorism, guerrilla warfare, and mobile-conventional warfare.

In the organizational stage, cellular networks are created, around which the guerrilla builds political-propaganda groups to win popular support and trains teams of terrorists to engage in selective intimidation of recalcitrant individuals. At this point, fronts may be organized along with pressure groups and parties in order to aid in gaining popular support. Simultaneously, insurgents usually try to infiltrate enemy institutions, foment strikes, demonstrations, and riots, and perhaps carry out sabotage missions.[63]

During the first stage, the insurgents stress esoteric and exoteric appeals and social services and mutual help aspects associated with demonstrations of potency. One key objective at this time is the recruitment of local leaders among political dissidents,who, once in the organization, will then go forth and attempt to win the people away from the government.

In order to institutionalize support, insurgents begin to construct parallel hierarchies. If the regime fails to react, it will lose by default; if it responds successfully, the insurgents may suffer a fate similar to that suffered by the Tudeh insurgents in Iran.[64]

Terrorism during this period serves many functions, including the acquisition of both popular and external support. It may be very significant where the insurgent organization and/or terrain are inadequate for guerrilla warfare. In situations where the regime's strength has been the key reason for the use of terror, the insurgent movement is worse off than where organizational deficiencies are the problem. Organizational failings can conceivably be rectified and the insurgency may then evolve toward guerrilla warfare.

Guerrilla warfare is the second stage in the Maoist scheme. The earliest part of this stage will be characterized by armed resistance carried out by small bands operating in rural areas where terrain is rugged and government control weak. If the guerrillas face significant government opposition, they have the option of reverting to an earlier phase. Factors most likely to be involved in the decision-making process are: vitality of the incumbent regime, its projected capability against guerrilla warfare, and external political-military factors.

The insurgents' aim in the earliest part of stage two is to isolate the people from the government. The organizational apparatus established in phase one begins to supply small guerrilla units and full and part-time personnel play a more prominent role. Yet, during the early part of stage two, there is still a lack of organization above village level, and groups operate from shifting and remote bases. Militarily, actions in early stage two are small hit-and-run attacks against convoys, military and economic installations, and isolated outposts. These scattered attacks are intended to goad the enemy into adopting a static defensive posture which stresses the dispersal of forces in order to protect many potential targets.[65]

If there is satisfactory progress during the early phase of stage two, insurgents normally move into the second half of that stage and expand their organization in the regions they control. In addition, regional forces emerge, which, along with the full-time forces, enable the insurgents to join villages together into a political network which constitutes a major base area. At this point the guerrillas step up the mobilization of the population by exploiting and satisfying (as best they can) popular aspirations. Meanwhile, there is usually a stress on ideology which is designed to supplant the traditional ideas of legitimacy which sustain the existing regime.[66]

During stage two the parallel hierarchy is more visible than during stage one. Besides resembling the state apparatus, it also includes auxiliary organizations controlled by revolutionary cells linked to the central political structure. Moreover, a government-in-exile may be created.[67]

The organizational evolution in late stage two includes the establishment of arsenals, arms production facilities, and hospitals. The logistics operation encompasses activities that range from procurement of basic foodstuffs and war supplies to acquisition of material aid from external sources. Once base areas are set up, the delivery of supplies from nearby friendly states becomes less risky and more likely.

In the military realm, recruitment of full-time guerrillas, establishment of an extensive reserve system, and creation and training of regular army units are emphasized. If voluntary recruits are insufficient, there may be forced abductions. Since those forced into service often make poor fighters, however, voluntary enlistments are stressed.

Three operational levels often comprise the military organization in late stage two: regional, district, and local. The regional troops, the best armed and trained, form the strike forces, which are the backbone of the movement. At the next level, the district battalion is led by full-time cadres, though the subordinate companies are composed of part-time soldiers. Local forces are made up of both full and part-time guerrillas, with the latter predominant. All three levels are coordinated by a central headquarters in pursuit of common military and political objectives.

Even though the parallel hierarchy and military organizations may be relatively secure in late stage two, the guerrillas usually do not elect to fight positional battles or even to defend their base areas. Instead, the insurgents avoid large government sweeps and patrols in order to demonstrate the government's inability to destroy them and to contrast the regime's ephemeral authority with the insurgents' permanency.[68]

While base areas are being constructed, the insurgents will continue to establish bands and to send agents into contested or government controlled areas with the purpose of implanting new cells, networks, and bands in these sectors. A major effort is made to deceive the government in the hope that its response will be tardy, insufficient, and tactically misdirected. Military actions in stage two are basically large-scale guerrilla attacks carried out from secure base areas. In addition to operations designed to acquire additional supplies and reduce areas of government control, armed propaganda teams are dispatched to further undermine the enemy. Considerable attention is devoted in the terminal part of this stage to seizing and securing large areas and preparing the physical battlefield for mobile-conventional warfare. Thus, military considerations receive as much attention as political calculations when it comes to target selection.[69]

The third and final stage of a Maoist-type insurgency is civil war, characterized by regularization of guerrilla forces and mobile-conventional warfare. In the past, the objective at this point has been the displacement of the regime and authorities. Regular units conduct conventional operations, with small bands supporting the main effort in an ancillary role. Ordinarily, external support is important at this time, unless the regime has totally collapsed from within.[70]

It should be readily apparent from the preceding discussion that the Maoist insurgent strategy is a multifaceted one which emphasizes several interrelated elements: popular support, organization, and the environment. Whereas the first two factors can be directly affected by the conscious decisions and skills of the insurgents, the environment is a given to which they must adapt. Through a combination of propaganda efforts and organizational dexterity, the insurgents prepare the people for prolonged conflict with the government and, once conflict has commenced, sustain and gradually expand popular support to the point where the insurgents control the countryside, thereby isolating the urban centers. Since such an enterprise requires flexibility and coordinated efforts on the part of many activists, it is vulnerable to government psychological, organizational, and military-police countermeasures at many points. In a very real sense, the outcome will be determined by the side manifesting superior political and military skills, as well as emotional commitments. Despite external influences on both parties, in the final analysis it was these ingredients which prevailed in China, Cambodia, and Vietnam.

Environmental characteristics are also important in the Maoist strategy. In the three cases just mentioned, the insurgents were able to build and expand their organization and base of popular support in relative security because of favorable topographical and demographic patterns. By contrast, if the contested country is small and relatively open, if the population is concentrated in areas that can be isolated, and if the road and communications systems are developed, the insurgents find it very difficult to organize and gain support.

External support has a rather ambiguous place in the framework of Maoist strategy. Although self-reliance is said to be the overriding consideration, in practice, moral, political, material, and sanctuary support have played a key role, especially in offsetting similar assistance to the government.

The Cuban Strategy

An alternative to the Maoist protracted warfare strategy is provided by the Cuban model. Che Guevara, a much publicized figure in insurgent folklore, opened his book *Guerrilla Warfare* with the following comments:

> We consider that the Cuban Revolution contributed three fundamental lessons to the conduct of revolutionary movements in America. They are:
> 1. Popular forces can win a war against the army.
> 2. It is not necessary to wait until all the conditions for making revolution exist; the insurrection can create them.
> 3. In underdeveloped America the countryside is the basic area for armed fighting.[71]

While one may debate the originality of points one and three, the second claim merits attention because Guevara seems to give more scrutiny to the initial phase of insurgency than does Mao. John Pustay has suggested that one reason for this may be that Castro and Che had to start by recruiting at the grass-roots level, whereas Mao did not have to start from scratch. In his words:

> Castro, Guevara, and their eleven cadre men, on the other hand, were forced to form guerrilla insurgency units by drawing upon recruitment sources at the grass-roots level. They had to start essentially from nothing and build a revolutionary force to achieve victory. It is reasonable, therefore, for Guevara to discuss in detail the initiatory steps in creating a viable guerrilla force. Of priority is the assembly of revolutionary leaders and cadre guerrilla fighters in exile or in some isolated spot within an object country "around some respected leader fighting for the salvation of his people." Guevara then calls for elaborate advanced planning, for the advanced establishment of intelligence networks and arsenals, and above all for the continued maintenance of absolute secrecy about the potential insurgency until overt resistance is actually initiated. Thus Guevara fills in the details, overlooked by Mao and only slightly covered by Giap, of the initiatory phases of the first general stage of Maoist insurgency warfare.[72]

While one may interpret this as little more than an effort by Che to refine and elaborate the Chinese leader's scheme, a closer look at the Cuban case reveals substantive divergences from the Maoist strategy.

It was Guevara's contention that insurgent leaders did not have to wait for the preconditions of insurgency to appear, since they could act to catalyze existing grievances required for positive action. Thirty to fifty men, he believed, were adequate to start an armed rebellion in Latin American countries given "their conditions of favorable terrain for operations, hunger for land, repeated attacks upon justice, etc."[73] In other words, Guevara was arguing that the mere fact of taking up arms in situations where grievances existed would create suitable conditions for revolution.[74] One of the major characteristics of the Cuban revolution, according to Regis Debray, was rejection of the idea of subordinating the guerrilla force to the party, in favor of placing primary emphasis on the army as the nucleus of the party. Putting it another way, he suggests that the guerrilla force was a political embryo from which the party could arise. Whereas Mao stressed the leading role of the party and the need for political preparation before military struggle, Debray argues that the Cuban case made it clear that military priorities must take precedence over politics. "Psychological warfare," he asserts, "is effective only if it is introduced into war itself."[75]

Debray contended that it was an old obsession to believe that revolutionary awareness and organization must and can, in every case, precede revolutionary action. Rather than wait for the emergence of an organization, it is necessary to proceed from what he calls the guerrilla foco, nucleus of the popular army. This foco is referred to as "the small motor" which sets "the big motor of the masses" in action and precipitates formation of a front, as victories of the small motor increase.[76]

Underlying all this is the idea that all Latin American conditions would preclude parties from leading national liberation movements.

As Debray puts it:

> The guerrilla movement begins by creating unity within itself around the most urgent military tasks, which have already become political tasks, a unity of non-party elements and of all the parties represented among the guerrillas. The most decisive political choice is membership in the guerrilla forces, in the Armed Forces of Liberation. Thus, gradually this small army creates rank-and-file unity among all parties, as it grows and wins its first victories. Eventually, the future People's Army will beget the party of which it is to be theoretically, the instrument: essentially the party is the army.[77]

Then, returning to the same point, he continues:

> The Latin American revolution and its vanguard, the Cuban revolution, have thus made a decisive contribution to international revolutionary experience and to Marxism-Leninism.
> *Under certain conditions, the political and the military are not separate, but form one organic whole, consisting of the people's army, whose nucleus is the guerrilla army. The vanguard party can exist in the form of the guerrilla foco itself. The guerrilla force is the party in embryo.*
> This is the staggering novelty introduced by the Cuban Revolution.[78]

For insurgents who see the Cuban experience as analogous to their own situation and believe that the Vietnamese and Chinese models are inapplicable because of unfavorable circumstances—poor chances of substantial external support and a small country—there is another way, the way of Fidel, wherein the key ingredients are violence in the form of small to moderately sized guerrilla attacks, limited organization, popular support, and perhaps most important, a weak government. Indeed, it is questionable whether Castro could have achieved his aims if the Batista government had not been in a state of profound decay.[79] As a matter of fact, in any of the types of insurgency that threaten either the political community or the regime, a reasonably strong government could be expected to take resolute steps to eradicate the insurgents. On the other hand, where conservative or reformist insurgents are operating, the Cuban approach might prove effective even in the face of a strong government for the latter might decide to reduce its losses by initiating policy changes that do not threaten the integrity of either the political community or the regime.

Urban Strategy

A third strategy, which many insurgents in the 1960s and 1970s have found attractive, is the urban terrorist model (sometimes referred to as the urban guerrilla model). As in the case of the Maoist and Cuban schemes, emphasis is placed on popular support and erosion of the enemy's will to resist, rather than on defeating the enemy in classical military engagements. Unlike the Maoist and Cuban examples, however, the locus of conflict during initial phases is the cities rather than in the countryside, a development related to the fact that the increased size and socioeconomic differentiation of urban centers make them especially vulnerable to terrorism and sabotage.

The essential strategy of the urban terrorist, according to Carlos Marighella, its foremost proponent, is to "turn political crisis into armed conflict by performing violent actions that will force those in power to transform the political situation of the country into a military situation. That will alienate the masses who, from then on, will revolt against the army and the police and thus blame them for this state of things."[80] To effectuate this transformation, urban terrorists stress organization, propaganda, and terrorism as techniques. Organizationally, urban terrorists rely on small cells of three to five men, with a link man in each. Although this has the advantage of limiting exposure and police penetration, it severely undercuts the insurgents' ability to mobilize significant sectors of the population.[81] The aim of terrorism is to create havoc and insecurity, which will eventually produce a loss of confidence in the government.

For such a strategy to be successful, however, it would seem that the regime would already have to be on the brink of collapse. It is not surprising, therefore, that Marighella himself acknowledges that the function of urban terrorists is to permit the emergence and survival of rural guerrilla warfare, "which is destined to play the decisive role in the revolutionary war."[82] Accordingly, the major question is how effective urban terrorism is in undermining the government and in gaining popular support, not whether urban terrorism alone can be successful. And this, in turn, brings us back not only to the Maoist and Cuban examples, but to the criteria for successful insurgency discussed earlier.

The perceived need to transfer the conflict to the rural areas stems from the belief that widespread popular support will be required to defeat an adversary which controls the state apparatus and which is unlikely to remain passive in the face of a challenge to the political community or the regime. Although such reasoning certainly makes a good deal of sense, it overlooks the possibility that urban terrorism might serve the aims of reformist and conservative insurgents quite well. Again, the point to be made is that it is easier for the authorities to make concessions when demands assume the maintenance of the regime or its policies rather than the overthrow of the regime.

Concluding Note

As the foregoing discussion indicates, insurgency is a complex and multifaceted phenomenon, having wide variations with respect to specific goals and strategies. In order to cope with the analytical difficulties inherent in such a situation, several factors which can have a major bearing on the outcome of insurgent conflicts were identified: popular support, organization, unity, external support, environment, and the government role. Each of these was then discussed in some detail. Finally, it was suggested that the salience of individual factors could be ascertained by reference to their relative importance in different strategic contexts.

Commencing with chapter 4, the Palestinian guerrilla movement will be analyzed in terms of its goal, and the factors that its strategy suggests are vitally important. In this undertaking, the most relevant portions of the framework for analysis will naturally receive greater and more explicit emphasis than other sections.

3
The Political Context

An appreciation of the general political context of the Arab-Israeli conflict during the period 1967-1976 is necessary for a meaningful examination of the Palestinian resistance movement. This examination is especially important if one is to comprehend the increased power and influence of the Palestinians in the Middle East after the June 1967 war, as well as their strategic adjustments in the wake of the 1973 war. Accordingly, the following chapter will summarize salient aspects of Arab-Israeli interactions and Israeli domestic politics between 1967 and 1973, leaving the analytical dimension to the subsequent chapters.

The Formative Period—1967-1969

In the aftermath of the Six-Day War, Israel found itself in control of several Arab territories, having occupied the Gaza Strip, the Sinai, the West Bank of the Jordan River (including East Jerusalem), and the Golan Heights. Almost immediately, differences of opinion began to surface within the Israeli political system over the question of the future disposition of the territories. Not surprisingly, the security establishment argued forcefully that the strategic gains accruing to Israel were of profound significance. All major population centers and most of Israel's farms were out of artillery range and the new borders were more defensible. The Jordanian border, which always troubled Israeli generals because of their fear that an armored thrust from there might cut Israel in half, had been pushed back to the Jordan River and shrunk from 180 miles of undemarcated hill country to 60 miles of more easily defensible river line. In the south, the Egyptian border had been reduced from 160 miles of unmarked desert to 107 miles of canal. Moreover, whereas it had taken

Egyptian aircraft only seven minutes to reach the Israeli heartland before the war, under the new conditions it would take them sixteen, thus allowing Israel more time to scramble its interceptors. Finally, in the north, Israel's control of the Golan Heights not only brought an end to the threat of bombardment of Israeli settlements, it also provided for defense against an invasion of the Hula Valley below.[1] While the validity of some of these assumptions would be hotly debated after the October War some six years later, the point to remember is that from 1967 onward they comprised the mental framework of nearly all major defense officials in Israel.

Even if one granted the Israeli generals their case, there were, nevertheless, contervailing arguments. First of all, since approximately one million Arabs had been added to the Israeli domain,[2] a question concerning their political status arose, which had unfavorable longer-term security implications. It was not clear, for example, how Israel could retain its democratic character and anticolonial image if such a large group was deprived of equal political rights. The difficulty was that to grant such rights would mean that in the short term the Arabs would constitute some forty percent of the Israeli body politic, while in the longer term, the higher birth rate among Arabs could make them a majority. Should the latter occur, Israel could lose its Jewish character and hence its security could be undermined by demographic factors. Despite the dilemma created by such questions, security considerations were given priority, a priority accentuated by fedayeen hostilities, which began along the Jordanian border shortly after the war.

Jerusalem, the principal religious center of Judaism, presented a special problem for Israel. Since the Jordanians denied the Israelis access to the Jewish holy places prior to the war, Israel adamantly opposed their return to the Hussein regime, and thus moved to proclaim the administrative unity of the city. Foreign Minister Abba Eban, no doubt concerned about international reaction, avoided the term "annexation" and sought to convince interested parties that the measures taken were intended to create "municipal unity." Other officials argued that such steps in no way represented a political solution.[3] Yet, in July 1967, Prime Minister Levi Eshkol was reported to have told a German publication that Israel intended to keep Jerusalem as well as Gaza.[4]

During July, it was also reported that the Israeli cabinet had decided to tighten up the administration of Gaza and the West Bank because of growing opposition and civil disobedience. In conjunction with this move, a decision was taken to have Israeli officials report to the military and to bar Israeli political leaders from activity in the occupied areas. A few days later an economic survey of the West Bank proposed that large-scale public works be undertaken in order to prevent a crisis.[5]

By August, the Israelis had made the pound the official legal tender in Gaza, the Sinai, and the Golan Heights; in the last-named area, which was virtually deserted, Israelis began to settle in the Baniyas River region. Meanwhile, on the West Bank the military government responded to subversive activities by exiling the ex-mayor of Jerusalem and initiating a series of punitive measures.

During the same month, Israeli leaders tried to alleviate international apprehensions about their intentions concerning the occupied areas by pointing out that their economic plan for the next decade included no occupied areas except Jerusalem. But, in an unofficial speech, Defense Minister Moshe Dayan said that Israel would not return to its prewar borders, and asserted that Israel's security was dependent on East Jerusalem and the West Bank. Another influential minister, Yigal Allon, also addressed the security situation in a speech in which he proposed the establishment of paramilitary settlements in Golan, the Jordan Valley, and southern Gaza, and the creation of a border with Jordan based on the Jordan River and the middle of the Dead Sea.[6]

Near the end of the summer, the Arab leaders met at a summit in Khartoum and decided to seek a nonmilitary solution to the conflict with Israel, while avoiding negotiations with or recognition of Israel. This decision brought an angry response from Premier Eshkol, who indicated that his country was more determined than ever to keep positions which were vital to its security. Israel was not the only party chagrined with developments at Khartoum. Ahmad ash-Shuqayri, who was still at the helm of the PLO, had boycotted the meetings because of their emphasis on a political settlement.[7]

On the operational level, Israel responded to rising terrorism with a security crackdown and, no doubt in reaction to both the terrorist activity and the general defense needs against the Arab states, began to set up paramilitary settlements called *Nahals* in the West Bank and Baniyas area near Golan. To head off any criticism of the move, Israeli sources stressed that the *Nahal* settlements implied no decision on the future of the area, a theme echoed by Eban, who said that the establishment of military positions on the West Bank and the Syrian Heights would not preclude a territorial settlement. Still, the situation clearly remained rather confused when fifteen members of a *Nahal* indicated at Kfar Etzion that they considered themselves the vanguard of Israelis who would settle the West Bank while, at the same time, the Israeli ambassador was telling the United States that Israel was setting up military strong points, not settlements, on the West Bank, and that this represented no political change.[8]

In October, Eshkol officially outlined Israeli policy to the cabinet. He indicated that Israel no longer recognized Egyptian claims to the Gaza

Strip and Jordan's claims to Arab Palestine (the West Bank), since both areas were taken in 1949 as the result of military aggression and occupation. The prime minister then went on to say that the Golan Heights would not be returned to Syria, "whose guns had threatened havoc and destruction for our villages in the valley." Eshkol insisted on an Israeli voice in the Sinai question, in order to assure free passage of Israeli ships through the Suez Canal and the Straits of Tiran and proposed a demilitarized Sinai, partly policed by Israel. Jerusalem, he said, would remain under Israeli control at all costs, because, as a divided city, it was "a security danger and an economic absurdity."[9]

On the Arab side, meanwhile, Jordan employed a carrot-and-stick approach. On the political front, King Hussein continued his efforts to achieve a political settlement to include a total Israeli withdrawal from the occupied areas. In a New York television interview, the Jordanian monarch said that he was prepared to recognize Israel's right to exist in peace and security as part of an overall settlement. However, during his visit to the United States, he also indicated that recognition of Israel as a "fact of life" did not mean diplomatic recognition. His views, he asserted, were similar to those of Nasser, a claim confirmed by an Egyptian spokesman during a Cairo press conference. This diplomatic activity was accompanied by pressure in the form of Jordanian cover fire for guerrilla operations.[10]

The passage of United Nations Security Council Resolution 242 (SC-242), on November 22, 1967, did little to change the situation, inasmuch as Egypt and Jordan interpreted it one way and Israel another. (See Appendix A for full text of SC-242.) For the Arab states, SC-242's principal stipulation was an immediate and total Israeli withdrawal from the occupied territories; for Israel the key provision of SC-242 was the objective of establishing a durable peace as a necessary precondition to any withdrawal steps. Another difference between the Arab states and Israel revolved around the clause calling for a withdrawal from territories occupied in June 1967. To the Arabs this meant complete withdrawal, while to the Israelis it meant and continues to mean partial withdrawal to secure and defensible positions. As far as the fedayeen were concerned, SC-242 was anathema because it implied a political solution that would fall short of the liberation of all Palestine, including Israel. This attitude was underscored by increased guerrilla activity, especially from Jordan. Israeli concern over the increased fedayeen activity was evident in a February 1968 speech by Eshkol, who warned that Israel would retaliate against the guerrillas. The fact that Amman was criticized for letting its territory be used by saboteurs and for directing artillery fire against the Israel Defense Forces (IDF) left no mystery as to who would bear the brunt of Israeli reprisals.[11] The ongoing guerrilla actions certainly did little to dissuade Eshkol from announcing at the end of February that seventeen *Nahals* would be established north of the Dead Sea on the West Bank.[12]

When its warnings went unheeded, Israel decided that military action was necessary. Hence, in mid-March, following an attack on a school bus (the bus incident provided a pretext since Israel was planning the raid before it occurred), Israeli air, armor, and infantry units struck several targets in Jordan, the principal one being the fedayeen base at Karamah. At Karamah, the Israeli force encountered stiff resistance from both the Palestinian commandos and the Jordanian army. Although Hussein's forces did most of the fighting, the incident was publicized in the Arab world as a victory for the guerrillas, with the result that it greatly boosted the guerrillas' prestige and numbers.[13]

Later in the spring, political discussions and maneuvering over the question of the occupied areas picked up. Perceiving a need to clarify his government's policy, Prime Minister Eshkol delivered a major policy statement on Israeli radio. Israel, he said, would insist on the Jordan River as its security border, the implication being that while the political border might be elsewhere, Jordan's troops would be barred from the West Bank. When determining the political border, he suggested, the government would have to weigh Israel's historic rights and the location of Arab population concentrations. A few days later he told the Central Committee of Mapai (the Labor party) that Israel would never surrender absolute rule of Jerusalem as her capital and called for stepped-up settlement of the former Arab sector and establishment of religious institutions and government ministries there.[14] The congruence between official policy and public opinion could be seen in a poll on attitudes toward the occupied territories conducted by Israel's Dachaf Agency. The results showed that while 87 percent of the population approved the government's policy of not returning any territory until the Arabs agreed to direct talks, 78 percent were willing to give back one or more pieces of occupied territory once negotiations began. In terms of specific areas, 21 percent wanted to retain Sinai, 47 percent the West Bank, 61 percent Sharm el-Sheik, 88 percent the Golan Heights and 95 percent Jerusalem.[15]

Consideration of the security and Arab population problems gave rise to three approaches: the Dayan plan, the Sapir plan, and the Allon plan. The Dayan plan called for the economic integration with Israel of a large part of the West Bank, the Arab half of Jerusalem, Bethlehem, and Hebron. The Sapir plan (named after Finance Minister Pinhas Sapir) proposed returning most of the West Bank to Jordan, thereby freeing Israel from the burden of ruling a large Arab population.[16] The antithetical nature of these two schemes became even more evident when Dayan offered his personal view that the area from Jordan to the

Mediterranean was the land of Israel, and that the Jordan River and the mountain tops to the west of the Jordan River should be the basis for defending Israel's borders.[17]

Within the government, albeit unofficially, the Allon plan seemed to enjoy the most support. In its final form, the plan called for a ten- to fifteen-mile-wide security belt along the sparsely populated edge of the Jordan River, which would be considered Israel's new security frontier. Guarded by a string of paramilitary settlements, the strip would contain fewer than 20,000 Arabs. New towns were to be constructed to overlook the Arab population centers of Jericho and Hebron, and a 4.3-mile-wide corridor linking Jordan with the West Bank was to be created. With the exception of Jerusalem and areas near Latrun and Hebron, the rest of the area outside the paramilitary strip, which contained most of the Arab population, would either be permanently demilitarized and given an autonomous status or be linked to Jordan, depending on negotiations with the Jordanians. Moreover, Hussein's government would be asked to accept 200,000 refugees from Gaza. Besides providing for defense against conventional attacks—the Jordan River was a natural tank ditch—the Allon plan, with its paramilitary settlements, was also directed at the problem of guerrilla infiltration. Clearly, training of the *Nahal* personnel would allow them to carry out the patrolling and other tasks associated with territorial defense (as discussed in Chapter 2).[18] Finally, to the south, Allon's scheme called for a demilitarized Sinai and a new Israeli town near Sharm el-Sheik, to protect a north-south line to El-Arish that represented the Israeli withdrawal area.

The Allon plan was perceived by some as a tentative and personal idea spawned by public relations needs and political maneuvering. From this standpoint, the plan was viewed as giving the world a general outline of the Israeli peace plan, while at the same time boosting the prestige of Allon, a contender for the premiership.[19] Although such observations were certainly plausible and probably contained some truth, they overlooked the profound problems of security and of ruling a million Arabs which the Allon plan sought to reconcile.

As far as the security aspect was concerned, the most dramatic development in 1968 occurred in Athens near the end of December: an attack by terrorists from the Popular Front for the Liberation of Palestine on an El Al airliner. The incident brought immediate Israeli warnings that Arab airliners were as vulnerable as Israel's and that Israel considered Lebanon partially responsible for the episode because it allowed the PFLP to train openly in its territory. In order to reinforce its admonitions to other Arab states that allowed fedayeen to operate from their territories, Israel carried out a spectacular helicopter raid against the Beirut airport that destroyed or damaged some thirteen airliners. At the United Nations, the Israeli ambassador argued that the strike was in retaliation for the Athens incident and other Lebanese aggressions. In support of his case, the Israeli delegate called attention to statements by the Lebanese premier and press acknowledging Lebanon's active support of the guerrillas and argued that the PFLP operated openly in Beirut with the blessing of the government. Nevertheless, the United States representative, in remarks characteristic of the initial wave of international reaction, termed the raid an "act of arrogance and disproportionate."[20]

Responding to the international protestations, Eshkol declared that the countries supporting the fedayeen must take responsibility for the terrorists' acts. In a warning that seems prophetic in light of the events of September 1970, the prime minister pointed out that the terrorists were capable of significantly interrupting international civil aviation.[21] The criticism in world fora was not totally devoid of effect, however, for over the course of the next several months, the Israelis refrained from dramatic reprisal attacks and focused instead on a policy of "active self-defense" which entailed direct strikes against fedayeen bases.[22]

The gulf separating the diplomatic positions of Israel and the Arab states remained through the summer of 1969, with Israel moving to consolidate its hold on East Jerusalem by announcing that the Arab inhabitants could become Israeli citizens without meeting a three-year residency requirement.[23] The death of Prime Minister Eshkol in late February and the succession of Golda Meir had no effect on the direction of Israeli policy. At her swearing-in ceremony, Mrs. Meir stressed that her government's policy would be the same as the old one's, stating, "We are as resolutely determined as the previous government that there shall never again be a return to the borders and conditions which existed on June 4, 1967." She also indicated that her government would continue to hold the Arab states responsible for terrorist raids and would pursue the policy of "active self-defense."[24] Although the prime minister let it be known that she had serious reservations about Dayan's economic integration scheme, the defense minister continued to press his views, as did Allon.[25]

As events in Israel were taking their course, Jordan was active in the diplomatic arena. During an April visit to Washington, King Hussein, contending that both he and Nasser wanted a peace settlement, put forth a six-point peace plan. For the first time, Israel was to be guaranteed free passage through the Suez Canal and the Gulf of Aqaba, pending a complete Israeli withdrawal from the occupied territories. Although a clear statement recognizing Israel was avoided, Hussein acknowledged that Israel was "there to stay." Regarding the Palestinian refugees, the king said Israel should accept their right to compensation or repatriation.[26] While all this was transpiring, Egypt was busy on the military front, shelling Israeli positions across the canal and conducting commando raids. Not surprisingly, these actions led to Israeli reprisal strikes rather than political concessions.

If both ongoing clashes with the Arab states and the fedayeen and the Israeli political debate over the occupied areas seemed to preclude a softer Israeli diplomatic stance, the outcome of Israel's October 1969 election was, if anything, less encouraging. Although there was no drastic alteration in the composition of the Knesset, the acquisition of four additional seats by the Gahal party (from twenty-two to twenty-six) signified a slight shift to the right. As usual, the Mapai party, despite a loss of seven seats (from sixty-three to fifty-six), was the dominant party in a new, enlarged coalition government approved by the Knesset on December 15. The new cabinet, with seven new members (four from Gahal), was expected to be no less militant on the question of the occupied areas than its predecessor. While the Israeli right was welcoming the appointment of one of Israel's most outspoken hawks, General Ezer Weizmann (Gahal), as minister of transportation, the Israeli left and center took some consolation from the fact that the new Greater Israel party, which advocated an expansionist policy and more repressive measures in the occupied areas, had not won a single seat. Nevertheless, the electoral outcome did suggest that while a new government would be free to continue ignoring the most extreme of the expansionists, it would be restricted as far as any conciliatory adjustments to existing policy were concerned, since, if nothing else, hard-liners in the Labor party, such as Dayan, could count on Gahal's support.[27]

Between the elections and the formation of the Israeli cabinet, a political crisis arose within the Israeli government over Dayan's policy of neighborhood punishment. Designed to curb fedayeen activity and deny the insurgents the support of the people, neighborhood punishment entailed destruction of houses belonging to Arabs who the Israelis believed were reasonably likely to have known about terrorist attacks.[28] When several ministers, including Eban, challenged the measures, both Dayan and General Shlomo Gazit, head of the military government, responded by arguing that the policy was directed only at those who the authorities were convinced harbored terrorists, an apparent narrowing of the criteria for punishment.[29] Though a report in *The New York Times* the following month indicated that those who withheld information on terrorist acts were still liable for punishment, a cabinet consensus on the policy of punishing proven guerrilla supporters eventually led to the issue's fading in importance.[30]

In Israel's last major political event of 1969, Prime Minister Meir presented her coalition government to the Knesset and delivered a major policy speech, which, among other things, emphasized the need for more immigration and the intention to intensify "the establishment of security outposts and permanent settlements on the soil of the homeland." The last phrase was variously interpreted in Israel. To Gahal it meant all areas occupied since 1967; to Mapam (a left-wing party) it stood for little more than prewar Israel.[31]

Diplomatic Immobilism and the War of Attrition—1970

By 1970 the major aspects of both Israeli and Arab policy toward the occupied territories had solidified and, consequently, it was not surprising that military activity picked up in all sectors early in the year. Even though the *London Financial Times* reported on January 28 that incidents associated with the so-called "war of attrition" along the Suez Canal had dropped and daily artillery exchanges had largely been replaced by small arms fire, the Israelis during the same period made their deepest air assaults inside Egypt. Ironically, on the very day of the *Financial Times* article, Israeli fighter-bombers struck closer to Cairo than at any previous time, hitting army camps six miles from the center of the city. A February 12 mission hit a metal processing plant in the Cairo suburb of El-Khanka and killed a reported seventy civilian workers. Although Israeli officials said the attack was a mistake and Dayan telephoned the chief of the United Nations observers, General Odd Bull, to warn him that the bombs contained delayed fuses, the action, mistake or not, increased both tension and Arab bitterness and was instrumental in a Soviet decision to bolster the Egyptian air defense system.

While there were also significant military actions along the Jordanian and Syrian borders, the most dramatic acts of violence involved two mid-air explosions outside the Middle East, one on an Austrian Airlines plane carrying Israeli mail bound from Frankfurt to Vienna, which managed to land safely, the other on a Swissair Coronado going from Zurich to Tel Aviv, which killed forty-seven people, including a number of Israelis. Quite naturally, Israel reacted with indignation when credit for the act was claimed by a small fedayeen splinter group, the Popular Front for the Liberation of Palestine-General Command (PFLP-GC). Mrs. Meir warned on February 23 that either all airlines in the Middle East would fly safely or none would. Moreover, the Israeli press expressed unhappiness with the feeble nature of past actions by governments and the airline pilots' associations in dealing with assaults on civil aviation. Although the PFLP-GC later denied carrying out the operation, the Israelis remained convinced—rightly so—that it was done by the fedayeen.[32]

The costs of hostilities to Israel were reflected in the February budget proposal, which called for higher taxes, a slowdown on developmental projects, and heavier outlays for defense. Of a total of $2.831 billion budgeted for the fiscal year beginning April 1, 1970, $1,089 billion was allotted for direct expenditures on defense, and Finance Minister Sapir indicated that when indirect military spending was considered, close to $100 million could be added to the defense spending figure. Conceding that the gap in the balance of payments would be enormous, the finance minister said the deficit, as in the past, would have to be made up from grants and loans from governments, individuals, and Jewish agencies abroad, and from West German indemnities.[33]

As spring was settling in, a new political crisis was brewing, this time over a March 25 announcement by Allon in the Knesset that the Israeli government was going to assist in settlement of some fifty Jewish families in the Arab West Bank town of Hebron.[34] Although the deputy premier contended that the move had no political significance for the future of the West Bank, there were those in the Mapai and Mapam parties and among students and intellectuals who thought otherwise. Their essential criticism was that Jewish settlement would, by signifying an intent to stay, make it much more difficult to make a compromise in the interest of peace. The move, opponents added, was influenced by right-wing extremist elements in Israel.[35] Yet, despite continuing Israeli dissent, including a student demonstration in Jerusalem, the Israeli government proceeded on its intended course in Hebron.

When he had announced Israel's intentions in Hebron, Allon indicated that the Jewish settlement had security implications, since it would be the largest of thirty-one civilian and paramilitary outposts established in the occupied areas or planned for 1971. Fourteen settlements were to be in the Golan area, seven in the Jordan Valley, five in northern Sinai and Gaza, three in Etzion, and one to be moved across the old Jerusalem border. In April, a defense ministry spokesman announced that Israel was taking over the Hebron region for military purposes, and Israeli forces launched a major operation against guerrillas in the area because, it was contended, Hebron was the main staging area for guerrilla operations on the West Bank.[36] Having invoked security considerations—with some justification, since Hebron was a trouble spot—the Israelis requisitioned the land and Allon announced in mid-May that construction would begin on 250 houses.[37]

Arab reaction to the Hebron decisions was hardly enthusiastic. At a meeting of the city's leading citizens, a decision was taken to form a delegation led by the mayor, Sheik Mohammad Ali Ja'abari, to appeal to the Israeli government to drop its plans, a plea the mayor had already registered on Israeli radio. The best he could achieve was a promise from

Dayan that measures would be taken to prevent difficulties with the population arising out of military actions in the area.[38]

Military and terrorist activity along the border continued through the summer of 1970, at which time American efforts to halt the fighting finally brought an end to the war of attrition on the Egyptian front. Prime Minister Meir's decision to accept the cease-fire exacerbated the already strained relations with Gahal, and led the latter to withdraw from the government, thus breaking up the National Unity Cabinet.[39]

While details of the cease-fire, effective on August 7, were to be kept secret, several provisions were divulged to the press by informed sources. Of particular importance was the Israeli contention that Jordan would remain legally obligated to prevent cease-fire violations by both fedayeen and regular forces from its territory. Although Hussein disclaimed responsibility for the guerrillas, the parties reportedly reached agreement that the guerrillas would probably continue to stage incidents and that Israeli retaliation against the fedayeen would not give anyone the right to void the cease-fire.[40] The fact that Israeli reprisals against guerrilla bases in Jordan and Lebanon during August were not used by either of the two Arab states to openly disavow the cease-fire appeared to confirm the reports.[41] Despite sporadic exchanges of fire across the Jordan River, some reportedly involving Jordanian forces, Israeli officials noted a marked decline in Jordanian cooperation with the commandos near the end of August.[42]

The Egyptian-Israeli truce greatly angered the fedayeen, especially the militant PFLP. Consequently, in September, PFLP terrorists hijacked several airliners and flew them to Jordan, where they held the passengers hostage while demanding that Israel release fedayeen prisoners. Since the fate of a number of Jewish hostages was involved, Israel focused its attention on events in the Hashemite kingdom.

One Israeli countermove was to arrest and eventually release some 450 Arabs in the occupied areas. Although the minister of police said that security precautions necessitated the action, Arab residents perceived the move as an Israeli attempt to exert pressure on guerrilla leaders, by reminding them that Israel could retaliate if the airline hostages were harmed.[43]

When the hijacking incident triggered a full-scale civil war in Jordan, Israel became additionally concerned about the nature of any agreement between the king and the fedayeen that might result from the fighting. Thus, near the end of September, when an accord between Jordan and the guerrillas was being worked out, Israeli officials went to great lengths to warn that guerrilla operations against Israel from Jordan would be completely unacceptable. Chief of Staff Haim Bar Lev said Israel's reaction to border attacks "would differ in scope and nature" from past reprisals, while Allon, in a more explicit statement, indicated that the IDF would no longer differentiate between the fedayeen and the Jordanian army during retaliation raids.[44]

When Hussein and the guerrillas reached an agreement in Cairo on September 27, it seemed that the fedayeen were to be given some freedom of action against Israel. The possibility of a guerrilla free zone would, Israeli strategists thought, put a legal framework around Hussein's refusal of responsibility for fedayeen activity at the time of the cease-fire. This consideration, along with the final article of the Cairo agreement, which endorsed the liberation of Palestine (including Israel), convinced Israel that the chances for serious negotiations had been undermined. On the other hand, Israeli analysts doubted that the Jordanian-fedayeen compromise would last, implying that the situation might change for the better in the future.[45] The unexpected death of Nasser on September 28 merely added to the uncertainty.

During the crisis in Jordan, Israel faced two considerable challenges. First of all, the PFLP insisted that fedayeen prisoners in Israel be released in return for the safety of some 300 hostages, among whom were a number of Israeli citizens. The Israelis, as might have been expected, flatly rejected this demand. Fortunately, the fighting in Jordan, worldwide criticism of the PFLP actions, and pressure from the Arab states and from within the Palestinian movement combined to effect the release of the hostages, thus saving the Israelis from an agonizing decision.

The other major concern of Israel during the September War was the intervention by Syria on behalf of the fedayeen. It was quite likely that had the Syrian move brought the Jordanian army to the brink of defeat, Israel would have intervened to preclude Jordan being turned into a guerrilla state. Once again, however, Israel was spared a difficult decision when Hussein's forces more than held their own and international pressure forced Damascus to desist from further intervention. An important factor was clearly the Syrian decision not to use its superior air force against Jordanian planes attacking armored units coming from Syria. Since Damascus had contended that the armored units were components of the PLA, it could not throw its air force into the battle without emasculating its claim that it was not directly involved in the invasion.

With the end of the civil war in Jordan, Israel turned its attention to the Suez front. Although it had suspended participation in United Nations negotiations in protest over the Egyptian movement of surface-to-air missiles on the east bank of the Canal, Israel decided to return to the talks near the end of September, when the United States committed itself to providing political and military support to offset the Egyptian advantage. Nevertheless, Mrs. Meir made it clear that the decision in no way lessened

Israel's demand that it was entitled to defensible borders. International guarantees, she asserted, could not substitute for secure borders and the maintenance of Israel's capability to defend itself.[46] Given the November 19 policy statement by President Anwar as-Sadat of Egypt that "there must be a complete liberation of all the Arab territories occupied by Israel in 1967" if there were to be peace, both sides could look forward to a difficult new year. Pessimistic projections were supported by the fact that, as international events were unfolding, Israel had proceeded on its course of either planning or building new settlements in the occupied areas and integrating Gaza with the Israeli economy.[47]

The Political Freeze and the Drift toward War—1971-1973

While the military situation along Israel's borders was relatively quiet during the first half of 1971—the main problem area being the Lebanese frontier—the same could not be said for events in the political arena. On the international level, the Israelis returned to the United Nations talks and, although there was a good deal of discussion on several issues, there was little movement toward a settlement. As for the occupied areas, Prime Minister Meir, in a series of interviews, indicated once more that secure and defensible borders were a sine qua non of any settlement. In an interview with *The Times* of London, the prime minister conceded that the Gahal party and religious groups wanted to keep the West Bank, but added that she did not want to rule 600,000 Arabs. What Israel did want was an arrangement along the lines of the Allon plan which would allow an Israeli presence in the Jordan Valley. On the question of Golan, it was suggested that while Israel might give up part of the area, it would insist on retaining the Mount Hermon section overlooking the Lebanese border, a demand no doubt influenced by fedayeen activity in this region. As for Gaza, Israel's position was that, although it did not wish to retain the strip, it would not allow Egypt to return. Instead, it was proposed that Israel take care of the refugees and that Gaza be a port for Jordan.[48]

Besides the territorial demands, Israel pressed to have guerrilla activity curbed. On this point, the Israelis received some satisfaction when, on February 15, Cairo agreed to a proposal by UN negotiator Gunnar Jarring which included a section calling on both Egypt and Israel to assume responsibility for preventing guerrilla operations from their territories.[49]

On the domestic level, Mrs. Meir's remarks about withdrawal from most of the West Bank (and the Sinai) generated a round of political debate with right wing parties. When Gahal introduced a no-confidence motion, Mrs. Meir forced a strict party-line vote in order to defeat the move 62-0 in the 120-seat Knesset. (The entire hard-line bloc walked out in protest over the government's political tactics.) The Knesset meeting was described as stormy; both hawks and doves demonstrated in downtown Jerusalem. The precarious political situation facing Mrs. Meir was due to the fact that the National Religious party, with twelve seats in the Knesset, held the balance in a working majority for the government. Its defection, after the Gahal departure the previous August, would have left the premier with only sixty votes, including four members of the minority Druze and Israeli Arab parties.

Within the occupied areas, meanwhile, the Israelis continued to build settlements, an activity the Arabs interpreted as confirmation of their fears that Israel did not intend to withdraw. One issue generating a special outburst of Arab protest was a controversial Israeli plan to build a number of housing developments on the hills around the Arab sector of Jerusalem. The basic Arab concern was that the new houses would attract a large number of Jewish residents to the area, thus altering the demography in favor of the Jews. Besides the chorus of Arab protests from Jordan, Egypt, and the Supreme Moslem Council of Jerusalem, there was considerable foreign opposition and a domestic debate between liberals who opposed the move and conservatives who favored it.[50]

When Israel, nevertheless, moved ahead with its plan, the international community registered its impatience and disapproval with Israeli policy, passing a resolution in the United Nations calling on Israel to take no further steps to change the character of Jerusalem and to rescind all steps taken to date to that effect. The Israeli delegate to the United Nations responded by declaring that Israel would ignore the Security Council order and the Israeli government rejected the resolution.

The importance of security considerations in Israel's overall settlement policy had become even more obvious by the end of January 1971. An article in *The Daily Star* (Beirut) by Walter Schwarz pointed out that the construction of hotels, petroleum stations, and other tourist facilities on a permanent basis underscored Israel's decision to retain Sharm el-Sheik.[51] In another area the Israelis were keen on retaining, the Golan Heights, eleven settlements had been built. Most significant was the fact that nine of the settlements were civilian; civilians meant to stay whereas military settlers could quickly pack up and move on.

The settlement pattern on the West Bank also reflected the strategic intention of Israel, which was to return a large part of the region to Jordan. Seven settlements were in existence on the West Bank, five paramilitary and two civilian. Two more were located near Hebron, and in that city was the previously mentioned fledgling Jewish community. Schwarz concluded that most of the Jordan River posts were set up as part of a provisional enactment of the Allon plan, strategic concerns being the major consideration. In the Gaza area, a new Israeli civilian settlement a few miles from the strip was viewed as the beginning of a defensive chain of settlements. The implication was that if Israel was committed to return the Sinai to the Arabs, it would probably ask for some marginal frontier modifications in the north. All told, it seemed that Israel was committed to return most of the occupied areas, with the exception of points along the Jordan River, Sharm el-Sheik, the Golan Heights, the Gaza Strip, and East Jerusalem.[52]

It became evident that not all Israeli political leaders shared this view during a Mapai convention in April 1972, when Dayan indicated that he supported a National Religious party proposal that all of the West Bank be retained. In reference to David Ben Gurion's stated willingness to return the West Bank, the defense minister argued that the Jordan of Ben Gurion's time was not the Jordan of Arafat and Habash, a point which ignored the fact that Hussein had crushed the fedayeen and banned the PFLP from his country.[53] In an address made in the capacity of defense minister, Dayan evinced a skepticism about the readiness of Egypt and Jordan to sign peace treaties, stressing that it might be a ploy aimed at obtaining withdrawal from the occupied areas as a first step to destroying Israel. Arguing that readiness for peace could not be judged by speeches, Dayan went on to state that "the real touchstone is the basic attitude in the Arab nations regarding the existence of Israel, and I feel I have not detected any change."[54]

On the other side of the debate on the occupied areas, Eban told *The Jerusalem Post* in April that the territorial demands Israeli leaders had made—control over the Straits of Tiran, the Golan Heights, the Gaza Strip, a united Jerusalem, and demilitarization of the West Bank—constituted a negotiating position broad enough for flexibility and not so rigid as to be an ultimatum.[55] Obviously, there was still no consensus within the ruling establishment about the final disposition of the occupied areas.

Unperturbed, Dayan returned to the political offensive during August, calling on Israel to establish a permanent government in the occupied areas. Sensitivity to hints of annexation was reflected in the subsequent omission of the word "permanent" from the official English translation of the defense minister's speech.[56] Despite Dayan's remarks and the adverse reaction they generated both abroad and in Israel, Israel's policy remained essentially the same for the remainder of the year. Given the delicate diplomatic activity between Israel and the United States over a plan to open the Suez Canal, the decision makers in Israel probably had no inclination to consider any policy demarche on the occupied areas which might further complicate matters by causing more acrimonious debate within Israel and possible dissent from abroad. Indeed, as far as the occupied areas issue was concerned, it was likely that Israel welcomed the prolonged consideration of the Suez Canal proposals, since it deflected attention from the question of withdrawing from strategically more important areas.

The Israeli diplomatic position remained essentially the same from 1972 through October 1973. One reason for this was the government's preoccupation with a wave of terrorist incidents, both within Israel and abroad, which were perpetrated by several fedayeen organizations, including the Black September Organization, the PFLP, and several small groups sponsored by Libya. Palestinian terrorism became part of a cycle of violent action and reaction. Terrorist acts included hijackings, massacres (e.g., Lod Airport, May 1972; Munich, September 1972; Athens airline terminal, August 1973), assassinations (e.g., American diplomats in Khartoum, March 1973; an Israeli military attaché in Washington, July 1973), letter bombs, kidnappings, and plans to shoot down civilian airliners with surface-to-air missiles. Also involved were Israeli reprisals against fedayeen bases in Lebanon and Syria, the mailing of explosive packages and letters to PLO representatives abroad, downing of a Libyan 727 civilian aircraft by Israeli fighters (February 1973), killing of key PLO leaders in Beirut (April 1973), abduction of an Iraqi airliner (April 1973), and arrest and eventual conviction of Israeli assassins in Oslo, Norway. The situation, as if not bad enough, was further complicated by violence and intrigue among various Palestinian groups and Arab states.

The emotionally charged atmosphere produced by such activity was hardly conducive to a more conciliatory policy on Israel's part; to the contrary, a survey conducted by the Israel Institute for Applied Research shortly after the Munich incident confirmed a continuing trend toward a harder line than had been evident in previous polls. These results were published a few months before Mapai, on Dayan's insistence, adopted the so-called Galili Document which called for increased settlements in the occupied areas, a new town near the Gaza Strip to be populated by immigrants, and purchase of Arab land by the Jewish Development Agency.[57]

The Mapai decision no doubt reinforced a conviction President Sadat had increasingly come to hold since 1971, i.e., that only force could transform immobility in the international arena into an active diplomatic process involving major powers, especially the United States. Such a process, Sadat reasoned, was indispensable if the occupied territories were ever to be returned. As is well known, Presidents Sadat and Hafez al-Assad of Syria had begun planning for war in the spring of 1973, and the Egyptians had already completed much diplomatic and military preparation by the time of the Mapai conclave.[58]

Thus it was that on October 6, 1973, Arab armies began a two-front war against Israel. To nearly everyone's surprise, the Arabs achieved notable success in the early fighting as they took advantage of Israel's lack of preparedness and their own improved military capabilities. Unfortunately for the Arabs, the time taken to consolidate the bridgeheads on the east bank of the Suez Canal eventually cost them the initiative. After locating a weak point at the juncture of the Egyptian Second and Third Armies, Israeli tank columns surprised the Egyptians by crossing the canal and proceeding to cut off the rear of the Third Corps of the Egyptian Third Army, the southern bridgehead. Had it not been for superpower intervention and the cease-fire of October 23, it is likely that the Israeli forces would have cut off the rear of the Second Army as well, and thus completed the defeat of the Egyptian forces. (The Syrian forces, after costly and bitter fighting, had already been pushed to a point halfway between the Golan Heights and Damascus.)

While the Israelis eventually prevailed militarily, the Arabs achieved considerable political success. They accomplished a number of limited aims which they had set for themselves, namely, inflicting substantial human and material losses on the IDF, seizing and holding the canal bridgeheads, enhancing the legitimacy of the authorities in Cairo and Damascus, redeeming Arab honor and dignity, and, above all, compelling the United States to play a more active and balanced role in the peacemaking process. Yet, as the euphoria of victory subsided, strategists in the Arab states reawakened to the cold fact that Israel still held the territories and was more determined than ever to assure its security through defensible borders. Indeed, although Arabs argued that their early victories had demonstrated that occupying territory as a means to security was anachronistic in an age of missiles and sophisticated weapons, the Israelis drew exactly the opposite conclusions when they asked themselves what their fate would have been in the early fighting without the defense-in-depth afforded by the Sinai and Golan Heights.

Summary and Conclusions

As the preceding narrative indicates, the Israeli wish to retain selected parts of the occupied areas was intended to serve the objective of creating "secure and recognized borders." A number of factors accounted for this policy.

First and foremost was the concern for national security, a concern rooted in both distant and contemporary history. The persecution of the Jews over several centuries, culminating in the terror of the Nazi holocaust, left an indelible mark on the Zionist leadership and increased its conviction that security of Jews could only be assured in Israel. That is to say, it was in Israel that the Jews at last were to find a security from persecution.

Unhappily for the Zionists, the creation of a Jewish state did not bring the long-sought-after security. Instead, Israel, threatened with extinction from its very inception, engaged in four wars with neighboring Arab states. Moreover, even in the relatively stable interludes after 1948, Israel was subjected to small-scale guerrilla attacks and periodic shellings from Arab states, especially Syria, some of which were provoked, some not. Accordingly, Israel was adamant about its demand for secure borders after the June 1967 war. Furthermore, since Israel, rightly or wrongly, believed that the international community was incapable of providing such security, it decided it had to rely on its own resources, a position that made Sharm el-Sheik, the Golan Heights, Gaza Strip, and areas along the Jordan River strategically important.

While security per se was a sufficient reason for demanding secure borders and certain territorial adjustments, other factors appeared to influence the making of Israeli policy. In the first place, the Arab states adopted what in Israeli eyes was a hard line at the Khartoum Conference in the summer of 1967, when they pledged neither to recognize nor to negotiate with Israel. Although Egypt and Jordan eventually moderated their stance by suggesting that they would accept the existence of Israel, Israel remained skeptical about the ultimate aims of the Arab states. Such skepticism, moreover, was reinforced by Egyptian, Syrian, and Jordanian military actions and by the support, however uneven, these states gave to the fedayeen.

The guerrilla and terrorist activities of the fedayeen were also a factor that reinforced Israel's policy on the occupied areas. Not only did such behavior demonstrate the continuing hostility of the Arabs, it also underscored the importance of military defense. Thus it in turn reinforced the perceived need to hold strategic points seized in June 1967.

The de facto implementation of the Allon plan, partly a response to border incursions, also influenced Israel's policy. Indeed, the very fact that the new border settlements played an important role in controlling the fedayeen probably increased Israel's reluctance to dismantle them as part of a peace settlement.

The domestic political situation in Israel, too, affected Israeli policy. In the first place, public opinion was in general agreement with the minimalist policy of returning most of the occupied areas while retaining East Jerusalem, Sharm el-Sheik, the Golan Heights, points on the West Bank, and Gaza. The Israeli public, like the political leadership, opposed the return of East Jerusalem to Jordan. Unlike the other areas, the main consideration in the Jerusalem case was religious, with the Israelis unwilling to risk the denial of access to Jewish religious shrines which had prevailed under Jordanian rule prior to June 1967.

Another factor influencing Israeli policy was party politics. Although right-wing parties like Gahal wished to retain most of the occupied areas, including all of the West Bank, Mapai and other left-wing groups rejected the idea of an expansionist Israel. Despite the right wing's gains in the 1969 elections, its strength remained insufficient to change the main directions of Israeli policy. What the gains probably did, however, was to reinforce the minimal policy of secure borders. Indeed, the latter seemed to be the lowest common denominator holding the National Unity Cabinet together until the summer of 1970. Furthermore, even after Gahal left the cabinet in protest over acceptance of the Rogers plan, the Israeli leadership was concerned lest a compromise on its minimalist program give the opposition a chance to increase its influence. As things turned out, a new right-wing alignment, the Likud, did come to power in 1977, albeit for domestic political and economic reasons rather than out of general dissatisfaction with Mapai's national security policies.

To sum up, the Israeli political objective of achieving secure borders and the related policy of retaining several important strategic areas were primarily the result of security considerations. Furthermore, both the objective and the policy were reinforced by perceived Arab hostility and intransigence, continuing violence involving both the Arab states and the fedayeen, military advantages of the Allon plan, public support, and party politics. Paradoxically, however, while Israel's policy was intended to provide security, it also contributed to insecurity, since it was a major factor accounting for the rise of the fedayeen. Retention of the occupied areas helped to galvanize what support the guerrillas enjoyed, and to revitalize the Palestinian aspect of the Arab-Israeli conflict. Besides giving the fedayeen a cause celebre, the Israeli occupation provided a potential rallying point for the popular support necessary to a revolutionary "people's war." As noted in Chapter 1, prior to June 1967 the fedayeen organizations were in the rather ludicrous situation of relying on some 300,000 Arabs in Israel as a popular base for a revolutionary war. With the occupation of 1967, however, the million Arabs who came under Israeli rule and the increase in territory under dispute made the fedayeen strategy of protracted armed struggle more plausible.

The fedayeen did not miss the significance of the new situation created by the June War. As one insurgent put it:

> I knew we were going to lose the war . . . but that didn't bother me as much as the possibility that the Israelis would withdraw immediately. If they had, our cause would have been set back for years: the Palestinians would have been further demoralized, Israel would have won a tremendous moral victory, and the Arab governments would have agreed to suppress the resistance as part of

the price for withdrawal. Fortunately, the Israelis gave us a break.[59]

Hussein, too, cited the nexus between the occupation and Palestinian resistance by indicating that a peace settlement, by removing injustice, would remove the need for the existence of the fedayeen.[60] Putting it in Maoist terms, the occupation of the Arab territories created the water (support) within which the fish (guerrillas) might swim.[61]

The fedayeen effort to exploit this situation within the context of a strategy of protracted revolutionary insurgency is the subject of the analysis which follows.

4
Israeli Counterinsurgency
and the Environment

The analysis of the Palestinian armed struggle from June 1967 to October 1973 begins with an assessment of the Israeli response. This is in keeping with the assumption advanced earlier that government response is the central consideration in insurrections. Moreover, the environment will be discussed concisely in this chapter. Modifying the sequence of Chapter 2 in this manner makes it possible to concentrate initially on two factors which critically affect insurgent performance and options in the areas of popular support, organization, unity, and external support. Since this particular arrangement tends to accentuate the role of the government and the environment as independent variables, it is important to reiterate that in reality all of the factors are interdependent.

Government Response

The substantive analysis of the government response is organized into six major sections. In the first, the nature of the threat is examined in terms both of the type of insurgency represented by the Palestinian resistance and of the techniques the insurgency employs to achieve its aims. There follows a discussion of the security sanctions, economic programs, and administrative policies adopted by Israel to control the population of the occupied areas. The third section, the military dimension of the Israeli counterinsurgency effort, contains a detailed investigation of the measures taken in response to internal terrorism, guerrilla raids along the borders, and transnational terrorism. In the next two sections, the analysis focuses on the outcome of the Israeli actions in the two most important occupied areas, the West Bank and Gaza Strip, and the legal and moral implications of Israeli security sanctions. The sixth section summarizes the analysis of the Israeli government response.

The Nature of the Threat

As pointed out in previous chapters, the Palestinian resistance believes that the demographic, geographic, and psychological effects of the 1967 War created a situation more favorable than ever for protracted armed struggle as a means to liberate Palestine from control by a Zionist regime which it considers completely illegitimate. Palestinian rhetoric notwithstanding, the notion of destroying Zionism says little about the actual nature of the resistance. To ascertain the type of insurgency that the Palestinian resistance represents requires some brief comments on the values and political structures envisaged for the regime of a Palestinian state.

Though there has been a great deal of diversity among Palestinian groups with respect to values, there is an overriding consensus that a new Palestinian regime must reflect Arab dominance. Moreover, most organizations demonstrate a commitment to socialism, albeit of different kinds (e.g., Marxist, Ba'thist, or Nasserist) and in varying degrees. Although democracy is identified as another important value in the new political order, its meaning remains vague and its normative and structural requisites receive little attention. While it is difficult to say what the new institutions of a Palestinian state would be like and how they would function, one may speculate that the orientations which characterize Arab political culture generally would foster a tendency towards some form of authoritarianism.[1]

Whatever the ambiguity surrounding future structural arrangements, the fact remains that the particular admixture of Arab and socialist values articulated by the fedayeen is antithetical to the current Zionist regime in Israel. Accordingly, the Palestinian insurgency is basically revolutionary, at least in the political sense of that term as set forth in Chapter 2. Whether or not the current leaders could or would engineer a social revolution, should they come to power, may be more doubtful, given the traditional orientations of many in the movement. In any case, this book is primarily concerned with political revolution, not the longer-term, more complex, and more conjectural question of social revolution.

In order to achieve their revolutionary goal, the fedayeen have emphasized means that are familiar to students of insurgency, namely political organization and propaganda, as well as instruments of violence in the form of terrorism and guerrilla warfare. Although there have been both disagreement and imprecision within Palestinian ranks concerning the proper strategy for conducting the conflict, on a more general level there has been commitment to protracted warfare. As we shall see later, a number of problems emerged between 1967 and 1973 relative to the specific application of such a strategy to the realities of the contested area.

Although they disdained the Palestinian notion of carrying out a protracted revolutionary insurgency in Israel and the occupied areas, the Israelis confronted an adversary who thought and behaved otherwise. This challenge compelled the Israelis to adopt a counterinsurgency policy, regardless of their doubts about the relevance and utility of revolutionary warfare to the situation. We now turn to an examination of the nature and effectiveness of that policy.

Population Control

Of the four territories taken by Israel in June 1967, only the West Bank and the Gaza Strip contained populations large enough to sustain insurgent activity of any consequence. Recognizing this, fedayeen leaders began almost immediately to organize the people for a campaign of violence and dissidence against the military government. In order to cope with this situation and prevent the insurgents from forging strong links with the population, Israel adopted a population control policy that combined forceful security sanctions with economic development and liberal administration.

Security sanctions and problems. The sanctions Israel imposed on those associated with terrorism and civil disobedience were based on both existing laws in the occupied areas and administrative orders (proclamations) issued by the Israeli Defense Forces. A *Compilation of Proclamations and Orders* was published in both Hebrew and Arabic and distributed to all local officials such as mayors, judges, and village leaders; and a detailed code containing ninety-five sections (the *Order Concerning Security Instructions*) established military court procedure and defined administrative powers and offenses against security.[2]

The IDF indicated that it would prosecute all prisoners charged with possession of illegal weapons, incitement to riot, membership in illegal organizations, infiltration, espionage, and terrorism. No favoritism was shown toward particular groups or individuals; all violators who committed acts of terror were arrested, tried by military court, and, if proven guilty, given long prison terms. Others were detained without trial, in accordance with the *Order Concerning Security Instructions*.[3]

Once in prison, most fedayeen served their full sentences with little or no chance of pardon.[4] In fact, it took an unusual situation, such as the hijacking of an El Al airliner to Algeria, to secure the release of prisoners. The sixteen released in the hijacking were freed as a gesture of gratitude to the Italian government for obtaining the release of the plane. Moreover, those released were limited to prisoners incarcerated before the June War who had not been charged with violent crimes. By March 1971, the number of security prisoners in Israeli jails was 3,400 according to the minister of police.[5]

Although the penalties given to the fedayeen and other security offenders were substantial and the chances for pardon nil, the Israelis, in 1971, promised lenient treatment to Gaza-based guerrillas who surrendered. This pledge was underlined by a decision to release some one hundred fedayeen who had fled from Jordan and surrendered to Israel in the summer.[6] While such moves were aimed at encouraging other guerrillas to defect, there was no significant response.

Besides detaining fedayeen, Israel used several other techniques to dissuade the people from supporting terrorists. In January 1968, for example, a wave of sabotage in Gaza brought a general curfew, a house-to-house search, a number of arrests, and the destruction of homes belonging to supporters of the terrorists. In the midst of these operations, there were charges that the Israelis had not made proper provisions for the distribution of food and water during the curfew, that arrests were arbitrary, and that the destruction of homes was on a random basis and not connected to fedayeen activity.[7]

Another troublesome problem that Israel faced after the June War was an outbreak of civil disobedience. When the Arab leaders on the West Bank were warned by the Jordanians and the fedayeen not to collaborate with Israel in administering or developing the area, muncipal council members and judges responded by refusing to perform official duties. The displeasure of the Israelis was soon evidenced by the arrest of five Arabs caught distributing a blacklist of all those who were collaborating.[8]

The military government also acted to counter other forms of civil disobedience. In early 1967, four East Jerusalem stores were padlocked, arrest warrants issued, and a company closed in response to a strike carried out in protest against the high taxes associated with the occupation; a few days later Israel sentenced a former Jerusalem judge and a prominent Arab businessman to three months as strike instigators, contending that they were organizers of the hostile Committee for the Defense of Arab Jerusalem. In addition to arrests and sanctions against businesses participating in the strikes, the Israelis also invoked curfews to deal with civil disobedience. One such case was the Sinai town of El Arish, where in August 1967 a full curfew was put into effect and twenty strike instigators were detained after a strike by merchants and the blockage of traffic.[9]

Despite the Israeli countermeasures, there were periodic strikes on the West Bank and in Gaza during most of 1968, often involving school girls. In response, Israeli security forces moved firmly against the strikers, detaining participants, imposing curfews at the first sign of trouble, restricting trade and visits, and, on occasion, deporting Arab leaders who were guilty of agitating the population.

Several times Dayan, who habitually kept in personal touch with events, talked with Arab leaders in major urban centers, and warned them that the Israeli military would have to take over law enforcement if they did not control the strikes and demonstrations. In a number of cases the Arab notables did respond by promising to control the demonstrators.[10] Nevertheless, since there were recurring incidents of civil disobedience, the military government was forced to apply sanctions on many occasions.[11]

Deportation, as noted above, was another measure used by the Israelis in dealing with civil disobedience. As early as July 1967, Israel moved to underscore its warnings to Arab leaders about noncooperation and civil disobedience by banishing to northern Israel the ex-governor of East Jerusalem, Ruhi al-Khatib, and three other political personalities because of alleged subversive activities. For his part, the banished governor asserted that he was cooperative and had tried to suppress opposition.[12] That religious leaders were not exempt from punishment for subversion or civil disobedience was demonstrated near the end of September 1969, when Israel deported the chief justice of the Moslem High Court in Jerusalem, because he allegedly played a role in a strike ordered by Amman. The tactic of deportation would continue to be used by Israel against those who either instigated civil disobedience or consorted with the fedayeen. By late 1970 the total of those exiled was placed somewhere between 90 and 130, depending on whether one accepts Israeli or Arab figures.[13] After the Jordanian civil war, however, Israel apparently felt the security situation in the occupied areas was stable enough to allow some deportees to return.

Yet another technique used by Israel to deal with the civilian unrest, particularly terrorism, was restrictions on movement. The military government made it explicit to Arab leaders that the continuance of terrorist activity could adversely affect the economic well-being of the people because it would force Israel to restrict their mobility. Mayor Kollek, for example, warned East Jerusalem Arabs, near the end of November 1968, that persistent terrorism could isolate the city and result in an exodus.[14] The previous month an admonition by Dayan to Hebron's leaders about terrorism elicited a message from the latter, expressing disapproval of a grenade attack and promising to send a delegation to Amman to request an end to such incidents.[15] In short, Israel had decided in 1968 that one way to lessen support for fedayeen activity was to inconvenience the people with roadblocks and restrictions on movement.[16] While obviously displeasing to those in the occupied areas, such steps were nowhere near as costly and controversial as the tactic of neighborhood punishment.

During a campaign against the terrorists in August 1967, Israeli security forces had destroyed a home in Jenin that contained footprints of a sniper. Likewise, in September, Israel responded to fedayeen sabotage and terrorist activities in Jabaliya and Tulkarem by destroying the homes of suspected terrorists and their supporters.[17] As time passed, this sanction, known as neighborhood punishment, was increasingly used by the Israelis to deal with the fedayeen and their supporters; it would, as indicated in the previous chapter, generate a serious political crisis in Israel in the late fall of 1969.

Since not all Israeli leaders approved of destroying homes of fedayeen and suspected supporters, there had been several disputes within the Israeli establishment before 1969. In March 1968, for instance, when several homes in Jerusalem were razed without the government informing Mayor Kollek, the mayor said Dayan had not explained the practice and that the city would repair the homes and apologize.[18] Such inconsistency and lack of coordination within the Israeli government was not indicative of sound counterinsurgency policy. In fact, it was not until the political crisis the following year that a consensus was achieved on this controversial measure, a consensus that resulted in neighborhood punishment being used less frequently and with a good deal more circumspection.

Another problem that could have caused serious trouble was the tendency of irate Jewish citizens to attack Arab residents indiscriminately in reaction to terrorist bombings within Israel and the occupied areas. Following four explosions in Jerusalem on June 18, 1968, for instance, Israeli youths began to attack Arabs and to smash and stone the Arab sector, a response that the fedayeen could only welcome, since it would further alienate the Arab population and perhaps swing it toward the guerrillas. In a prudent move, Israeli security forces cordoned the area and arrested a number of the Jewish rioters; Defense Minister Dayan then visited the Arab sector of Jerusalem in order to restore calm and to severely reprimand the guilty youths.[19]

Unfortunately for the Israelis, Dayan's strong words did not deter a similar response by Israeli citizens after an explosion in a Tel Aviv bus station on September 4, 1968, which killed one and wounded fifty-one. In retaliation, a Jewish mob attacked Arabs in the terminal, beating eight severely, and then turned on Arabs arriving in buses, none of whom were among the suspects in the incident. When the mob drifted toward the Arab quarter of Jaffa, quick action by police and soldiers, who sustained a number of injuries, averted more serious disorders. The following day one of Israel's most respected newspapers, *Ha'arez*, said the hooligans "must be considered active, unwilling allies of the Arab terrorists."[20]

Obviously aware that the warnings of Dayan were insufficient to prevent further counterterror episodes, the Israeli government began an intensive education drive to prevent any recurrences. The campaign stressed that terrorism was not succeeding, urged citizens to remain alert for terror incidents and to be calm when they did occur, and pressed the point that violent mob reactions were precisely what the insurgents desired. To help heal the wounds, meanwhile, government representatives visited Arab leaders in an attempt to convince them that the mobs did not reflect the attitudes of the Israeli people or government.

The Israeli attempt to curb mob responses to fedayeen terror incidents was tested by a mid-November bomb explosion in a Jerusalem market area, which killed eleven and wounded fifty. This time, to the satisfaction of Israeli officials, the Israeli civilians generally refrained from attacking Arabs in the area.[21] In the same month, the Israeli policy of preventing counterterror was underscored by the sentencing of two Israeli frontier police to life imprisonment for murdering two local Arabs the previous year. Three months later it was announced that an Israeli captain would be tried for the killing of an Arab woman and the wounding of several others in Rafah during January.[22]

Although the Israelis were successful in preventing a pattern of counterterror from emerging, isolated incidents, such as an attempt by Jewish youths to attack the Arab quarter of Acre following a bombing in Haifa in November 1969, continued to cause problems. The incident forced Israel to deploy hundreds of soldiers and police in order to block a major riot and to arrest several Israelis for assaults on Arabs.[23] In general, however, such episodes became the exception rather than the rule.

Economic policy and civic action. Even though Israel implemented a firm security policy, backed by harsh measures against those guilty of civil disobedience, sabotage, and terrorism, it did not neglect the people's standard of living and general welfare. As a first step, the Israeli Ministry of Finance allotted over $800,000 to stabilize the economies of the occupied areas until the end of July 1967, at which time an economic survey of the West Bank was completed, calling for large-scale public works to forestall an economic crisis.

The Agriculture Department of the administration sponsored a number of innovative projects—demonstration plots, mechanization, agricultural stations, the teaching of new farming techniques, and the increased use of fertilizers and pesticides—which contributed to the gradual increase in the total value of West Bank agricultural production from 114 million Israeli pounds in 1968 to 350 million Israeli pounds in 1972. Further improvement along these lines was provided by a marketing policy which not only retained traditional markets in the East Bank and neighboring Arab states through the open bridges, but also opened up new ones in Israel (after 1971), the Gaza Strip, and Europe.[24] On the debit side, thirty-one Arab

banks were closed because of Arab refusals to operate separately from
Jordan and there were Arab complaints about the imposition of taxes, and
the disruption of the traditional labor force and marketing channels, and
the checks by security forces.[25] Nevertheless, there seemed to be little doubt
that the improved standard of living, the rise in consumption, and the
increased trade were partially responsible for tranquilization of the West
Bank and undermining of fedayeen attempts to set up clandestine bases
there.[26]

Another program designed to raise the standard of living and to cope
simultaneously with a manpower shortage in Israel was the employment of
Arabs in Israel. In October 1969 the minister of labor indicated that since
Israel was already employing more than 16,000 Arabs from the West Bank
and Gaza in Israel, he might ask for permission to give more Arabs jobs in
Israel. Nevertheless, a plan to stop relief and public works in the occupied
areas in order to increase the number working in Israel appeared to give
substance to fedayeen charges of Israeli exploitation.[27] Offsetting this
objection was the statement issued in the spring of 1970 by the Ministerial
Committee for the Administered Territories, directed at expanding
employment opportunities through economic development of the
occupied areas. Among other provisions was a program to provide loans
and capital for modernization programs.[28]

By 1973, the number of Arabs working in Israel had risen to more than
80,000, or roughly one-third of the Arab labor force of the occupied
territories. Although Arab employment in Israel fostered a better standard
of living for workers over the short term, it undermined the emergence of an
autonomous economic base for development in the occupied areas, and
raised the possibility that a recession in Israel could create a sudden mass
unemployment and lead to a recrudescence of grievances and perhaps
violence, inasmuch as the Arabs would no doubt be the first to be laid off.[29]
Moreover, as time went by, the proclivity of settlers to rely on local Arabs,
including children, for cheap labor threatened to undermine the
pioneering ethos of Zionism and gave credence to Arab propaganda
concerning Israeli "colonialism." Furthermore, this practice was criticized
by Dayan because it brought Bedouins back into areas from which they had
previously been moved in the name of security.[30]

· In spite of these problems Israel was, on balance, quite successful in
improving the economic well-being of the population, a situation that
stood in marked contrast to the prewar Jordanian regime's discrimination
against Palestinians in favor of Bedouins. Under the occupation, the new
economic opportunities provided the Palestinians gave them something to
lose if they supported the fedayeen, a fact not lost on the guerrillas.[31] As far
as the longer term was concerned, Israel hoped that economic cooperation

and development, as well as civic action programs (education, vocational training, medical services, and social welfare programs), would have the effect of convincing the Arabs that Israelis and Arabs could interact in a peaceful and mutually beneficial way.[32]

Administration: liberalism, localism, and flexibility. The administration of the occupied areas was the responsibility of the military government. An official government publication outlined the structure of the administrative apparatus as follows:

> The Minister of Defense is responsible for the Military: a Cabinet committee under the Prime Minister advises him. Another Minister plans and coordinates economic development and refugee rehabilitation; for administration there is an advisory committee of Directors-General of Ministries concerned, and for political and security problems an interministerial committee.
>
> An IDF (Israel Defence Forces) officer commands each of the four "regions," namely, the Golan Heights, Judea and Samaria, the Gaza Strip and North Sinai, and South Sinai; to every headquarters representatives of the Ministries are attached.[33]

This organizational scheme, which provided coordination between the civilian and military sectors, was in consonance with the need for a unified government effort as discussed in Chapter 2. Furthermore, this coordination was strengthened by the appointment of civilian advisers to local commanders. The civil-military links on both central and local levels, in addition to fostering coordination, functioned as a check on possible arbitrary measures against the people by overzealous military personnel.

In terms of policy, the military government sought to minimize the presence of Israelis and to rely on Arab administrators for maintenance of essential services. The Israelis encouraged an approach as liberal as possible to relations with the Arabs, given security demands. Indicative of Israel's flexible policy toward the Arabs was a 1968 decision to permit 500 residents of Gaza to visit the West Bank daily.[34] On the other hand, the Israelis, citing security reasons, were reluctant to allow a large number of Arabs, who had fled to Jordan during the war, to return to the West Bank. Thus, only 14,000 of the 170,000 refugees listed by the International Red Cross as applying for return had crossed into the West Bank before the Israelis closed the Jordan River bridges.[35]

Despite Israel's refusal to accept a large number of returnees, it adopted an open bridges policy with Jordan, in order to facilitate trade and increase the standard of living of the West Bank population; even when fedayeen terrorism and guerrilla raids threatened this policy, it was not discarded. Indeed, by July 1971, the favorable security situation in the occupied areas prompted Israel to further liberalize travel between Israel and the West Bank by allowing visitors to cross into Israel without permits between 5 a.m. and 1 a.m., and in May 1973 permission for visits from the neighboring Arab states was extended from the summer to a year-round program.[36]

The underlying philosophy of the military government was guided by three principles: minimal presence, minimal interference, and open bridges. As General Gazit, a former head of the military government, summarized them:

> The aims of the Military Government were, in principle, that an Arab resident of the area could be born in the hospital, receive his birth-certificate, grow up and get his education, be married, raise his children and his grandchildren and live to a ripe old age, all without the help of an Israeli government employee or clerk, and without even setting eyes on him . . . . The Military Government is guided by the following principle in these matters: the population must take care of itself, with its own people and in the way it deems best. This policy is reflected by the small number of Israelis who deal with civil and economic matters in the areas.[37]

In keeping with this general policy, the occupation forces attempted to minimize their presence and to avoid shows of force, except when violence and demonstrations required it. Unlike some armies of occupation in the past, IDF personnel were instructed to pay for goods and services rendered by the local population and to eschew antagonizing the latter. Ironically, it was Israeli citizens visiting the occupied territories who demonstrated less sensitivity to Arab feelings.[38]

In order to put into operation the policy of minimal interference and minimal presence in the occupied areas, and also to avoid the unnecessary deployment of scarce manpower, Israel decided shortly after the war to leave local administration largely in the hands of the Arabs. Departments were managed by previous directors from the Egyptian and Jordanian civil services and, in cases where directors left, their deputies took over. The few Israelis who were involved functioned as behind-the-scenes overseers and final arbiters. Thus, in the spring of 1968 it was reported that health services were administered by seven Israelis and 2,900 Arabs, education by nine Israelis and 4,600 Arabs, agriculture by five Israelis and 1,300 Arabs. Overall, by March 31, 1970, the civil administration of the West Bank was carried on by 8,395 local employees and 389 Israelis, while the Gaza-northern Sinai figures were 4,087 and 145, respectively.[39]

In a complementary move, Dayan reinstated the Arab police force in each city and made it responsible for law and order, much to the consternation of some security experts.[40] Like the administrative policy, this policy was reflective of sound counterinsurgency tactics, because it lessened the manpower demands on Israel and removed the potential for friction which might arise if Jews were responsible for day-to-day law enforcement.

In line with its stress on using local manpower where feasible, the Israelis hoped to tap the resources of some 5,000 Druze in the Golan Heights. The latter were allowed to stay in place with the hope that they might be of assistance against the fedayeen since they had no particular love for the Arabs.[41] As it developed, the decision to establish good relations with the Druze had mixed results. On the one hand, some Druze elders complained because the Golan was not formally annexed by Israel and a number of Druze joined the Histadrut (the Israeli Labor Federation); however, others, such as the youth in the village of Majdal Shams, remained sympathetic to the Syrian Ba'th and few responded to Israel's invitation to join the army.[42]

In a similar action aimed at obtaining ethnic group support, Israel extracted a promise, in October 1968, from Bedouin sheikhs in the Sinai and Negev that they would help combat terrorists and saboteurs. Eight days later, however, Reuters reported that tribal leaders were refusing to cooperate. Just how successful Israel was in this endeavor was not entirely clear, although a fedayeen charge in the spring of 1970 that Israel exploited the Negev Bedouins with token assistance and concessions seemed to imply that some progress had been made.[43]

Even though the administration in the occupied areas functioned in a relatively smooth fashion, there were problems from time to time. During the incipient stage of the occupation, the Israeli military government was confronted by a crisis involving the reopening of schools. When the Ministry of Education attempted to replace virulent anti-Israel textbooks with pro-Zionist books, the result was a parent-teacher strike which closed the schools. Despite Arab objections and refusals to teach, Israeli officials proceeded to reopen the schools and to arrest a former Jordanian education aide and his assistant for trying to impede their opening. At the same time, however, the military government registered its opposition to the actions of the Ministry of Education, contending that the replacement of the former texts deprived the Arabs of the last thing they had to cling to, their dignity. In the face of the objections of the military government, the Ministry of Education compromised and left the Arab texts, removing parts considered anti-Israel. In the end, however, all except 10 of 120 purged passages were reinstated and schools opened in November. It was clear that crisis had passed the following year, when attendance at school was reported to be back to prewar levels.[44]

A less important point of friction, the administration of Moslem shrines by the Israeli Ministry of Religious Affairs, quickly abated when autonomy was restored to the Arabs.[45] On both the educational and religious issues the

Israelis displayed a flexible posture, which helped preclude unnecessary frictions from undercutting the generally liberal occupation policy. From a counterinsurgency point of view, this policy was sound.

The political program. While the administration of the occupied areas—especially the West Bank—proved to be effective, the political uncertainty surrounding both the eventual disposition of the areas and the possibility of serious negotiations with the Arab states (see the previous chapter) caused problems. The Israeli preference for negotiations with Hussein, rather than the West Bank Palestinians, led Israel to oppose any significant political activity until 1972, save in Jerusalem. The sensitivity about politics was such that even a meeting to plan a West Bank university was vetoed due to the fear it might turn into a political forum and that the university might increase the division between the West Bank and Amman by enhancing the West Bank's independence. During periods when negotiations seemed possible, some members of the Arab population tended to take symbolic steps, like protesting annexation or resigning from municipal tax committees, in order to disassociate themselves from Israeli rule. Such Arab political reactions illustrate a shortcoming of Israeli counterinsurgency policy, the inability to devise a complete program for dealing with the occupied areas. Since negotiations with the Arab states were at an impasse, Israel could not promise an early end to the occupation. Nor, in light of the stated desires to return most of the West Bank population to Arab rule, could Israel promise a permanent government. Hence, despite an effective stop-gap, liberal administration, uncertainty remained in the West Bank.[46]

Counterinsurgency: The Military Dimension

On the military level, Israel was faced with a three-fold threat from the fedayeen: terrorism within the occupied areas, hit-and-run guerrilla attacks in the border regions, and transnational terrorism. In dealing with these, the military government used a number of measures, some of which have already been mentioned in the discussion of security sanctions.

Internal terrorism. The Israeli security forces began to move quickly and efficiently against the insurgents operating within the occupied areas shortly after trouble began, arresting some twenty-four men from a *Fatah* terrorist ring in October 1967. As the weeks passed into months, the Israelis repeatedly uncovered sabotage rings and cells, with the result that the fedayeen could not establish a widespread and efficacious underground resistance in the occupied areas, and thus eventually had to withdraw most of their personnel across the borders.

As noted previously, one measure employed frequently by the Israeli security forces was cordon and search operations after major terrorist incidents. Although it inconvenienced the local population, this tactic often led to the detention of the perpetrators of attacks.[47] Even the fedayeen, albeit unconsciously, admitted the efficiency of the security forces. The "speedy arrest" of the arsonist responsible for a fire at al-Aqsa Mosque, for example, was referred to as "still another proof of the efficiency of that state's security forces."[48]

The fact that in a number of instances the Israelis were tipped off in advance to the movement of infiltrators was partially responsible for the effectiveness of the security forces. Not only did Arab informers provide tips on the establishment of new cells (thus enabling Israeli forces to destroy them before they were able to act), but captured guerrillas showed a penchant for divulging information about their compatriots, a tendency which often led to the latter's arrest. Within hours after the detention of participants in a September 1968 bombing in Tel Aviv, for instance, the captives had given the names and addresses of their comrades to Israeli intelligence officers.[49] If the success of the interrogation is judged by the ability to get needed and vital information, the Israelis proved their competence in this undertaking.

In the Gaza Strip, where terrorism remained a problem through 1971, the Southern Command adopted a strategy of surprise and movement of its security forces to keep the fedayeen off balance. Abandoning routine movements, Israeli patrols operated at different times and along different routes. This flexible approach, combined with solid intelligence, played a major role in apprehension of terrorists and the consequent reduction of incidents in the area.

Although the Israelis proceeded to uncover sabotage networks within the occupied areas, it would be a mistake to say they enjoyed total success. Indeed, throughout the period 1967-1977, there were continued efforts by the fedayeen, particularly the Popular Front for the Liberation of Palestine, to organize sabotage units and a number of costly terrorist incidents did occur. In February 1969 there was an explosion in a Jerusalem market, followed by a blast in a Hebrew University cafeteria the next month. Although the first led to the rounding up of several PFLP members and the discovery of political and sabotage cells, observers took the Hebrew University blast as confirmation that the PFLP had been able to establish a new apparatus.[50] While it would be an exaggeration to imply that any kind of cohesive and continuously active sabotage network had been restored, the continued existence of terrorist cells was verified by periodic incidents over the next few years, such as three blasts at the Wailing Wall in Jerusalem and the destruction of a oil pipeline at Haifa in June 1969, a rocket attack on Jerusalem in August 1969, bombings in Haifa in October 1969, a Tel Aviv bombing on November 6, 1970, the Petah Tikvah rocket attack in July 1971, and bombings in Jerusalem and Tel Aviv in July 1973. In spite of these sensational attacks, by 1970 a combination of economic measures and effective police work had led to the breakup of many terrorist groups, thus reducing the problem to manageable proportions.

Perhaps the most dramatic indication of the difficulties and frustrations the fedayeen experienced in regard to their terrorist campaigns inside Israel and the occupied areas was the Lod Airport Massacre of May 1972. This attack took the lives of twenty-six people, including a number of Puerto Rican religious pilgrims, and wounded over seventy others. Although the PFLP took credit for the incident, the fact that it was carried out by three Japanese members of the United Red Army, who had entered Lod on an Air France flight, said much about PFLP weakness.

In response to the Lod incident, the Israelis tightened security at their air terminals considerably, criticized France for its poor airport security procedures, and blamed Beirut for allowing the terrorists to train and plan the operation on Lebanese soil. As the months went by, this incident, combined with periodic raids against Israel from across the border and terrorist operations abroad, led to a number of Israeli military operations against the terrorists in Lebanon.

One detrimental effect of the Lod attack was that it so sensitized the Israelis to internal terrorist incidents originating abroad, that they overreacted to an inadvertent overflight of the Sinai by a Libyan civilian airliner in February 1973 and forced it to crash. While accepting blame for the error, the Israelis nonetheless said that, based on intelligence reports, they feared the terrorists might load an aircraft with munitions and crash-land it in a settled area.[51] The explanation did little, however, to stem the tide of international criticism.

Border security: territorial and mobile defense. In order to deal with fedayeen infiltration and hit-and-run raids along the borders, Israel combined a nomadic, territorial offensive in its own area of control with attacks against sanctuary countries. The internal measures along the border included the removal of selected Arab villages, small-unit patrolling, the construction of security fences, and mobile pursuit of infiltrators seeking to flee across the border.

The destruction of Arab villages in sensitive border areas had debatable effects. While it may have facilitated security operations, the destruction of the villages also provided fedayeen publicists with good propaganda material inasmuch as thousands of Arabs were left homeless.[52]

More clearly effective was the establishment of outposts and settlements in frontier areas to provide local bases for patrols by both military units and local personnel, including the soldier-farmers of the *Nahal* movement. The substantial number of casualties inflicted on infiltrators bore testimony to the success of the active territorial defense strategy. By emphasizing aggressive patrols as the centerpiece of their counterguerrilla effort, the Israelis avoided the mistake of yielding the initiative to the guerrillas, a mistake which often occurs when a conventional force posture is stressed.[53]

The nomadic territorial offensive was facilitated by the construction of a security fence along the Jordan River. Although a similar scheme had been entertained in 1966 and rejected, the Israelis felt that the shorter border resulting from the 1967 War had changed the situation. Thus, the Israelis erected a barrier composed of mines, trip wires, and other devices along a fifty-mile strip from the Dead Sea to the Beisan Valley; at the time of the September 1968 Tel Aviv bombing, its effectiveness was credited as a factor in the curbing of infiltration and the increase in guerrilla losses.[54] In 1971 a similar barrier was completed along the Lebanese border.

Besides the internal operations, which were based on *Nahals,* border security forces, the security border, the Israelis also used mobile strike forces for the pursuit of guerrillas who were within the occupied areas and trying to escape to sanctuary countries. Mobile forces—moved by ground vehicles or helicopters—were also employed upon occasion against guerrilla locations in Jordan and Lebanon. Since the cross-border operations of the IDF turned out to be a crucial component in Israel's counterinsurgency programs, they merit closer examination at this point.

In November 1967 an Israeli communiqué reported that Jordanian cover fire had aided a dramatic guerrilla escape across the Jordan River following a raid on an Israeli settlement. Within days Israel responded by shelling Jordanian army positions and sending its jets across the border. By January 1968, top officials in Israel were reported as saying in private that Israel might have to launch retaliatory raids against Jordan and Syria in response to fedayeen activity. Presumably, the previous reprisal raids were related to supporting actions of the Jordanian army and not exclusively to guerrilla attacks.[55]

Whatever the case, after stepped-up activity by the Jordanians and the fedayeen along the border in February 1968, Israel launched another air and artillery barrage across the river. This resulted in Jordan's King Hussein saying that he would no longer allow the guerrillas to provide Israel with pretexts for attacks against his country. Whether or not this incident was important in sowing the seeds of future Jordan-fedayeen strife can only be answered by the king and his confidants. If, as seems likely, the Israeli operation did make concern about Israeli reprisals a key factor in Jordanian decisions affecting the guerrillas, then it had hidden long-term payoffs.[56]

If the February action by Israel had unseen benefits, the March assault on the fedayeen base at Karamah, discussed in the preceding chapter, was perhaps Israel's greatest failure in the cross-border campaign. Even though, in a military sense, the operation may have been a marginal Israeli victory, it was also a Pyrrhic one that unsettled many Israeli citizens.[57] Politically, the fact that the Jordanian army and the fedayeen held their ground and inflicted substantial losses on the Israeli force did wonders for the guerrillas.[58] Overnight they became the heroes of the Arab world and applications for membership in fedayeen organizations—especially *Fatah*—soared, a development that few observers, impartial or not, disputed.[59] When the condemnation of the raid by the world community was added to the political-psychological gains of the fedayeen, the inescapable conclusion was that the raid was, on balance, counter-productive.

Nevertheless, Karamah was not a total loss for the Israelis. Psychologically, at least that segment of the population demanding retaliation for fedayeen incidents was undoubtedly assuaged by the attack. In security terms, Israel claimed that the operation had forced the fedayeen to postpone a planned offensive, a contention based on "highly authoritative information" obtained before the attack and upon interrogation of a number of captured guerrillas after the attack.[60] Furthermore, the fact that the Karamah episode, the first instance of Israeli forces crossing the border in strength, did not result in a military response by the Arab states, seemed to establish the premise that future strikes across the border would not entail the risk of generalized war. Thus, one of the options for dealing with a sanctuary country, striking it directly with mobile troops, became feasible for Israel, and fears that direct ground attacks could be a casus belli were quelled as far as future operations against fedayeen sanctuaries were concerned. For the time being, however, Israeli leaders, stung by worldwide criticism and Israeli citizens' chagrin about the losses at Karamah, indicated that different methods for dealing with the fedayeen would be used.[61]

One sidelight to the operation which deserves mention is the fact that the Israeli forces did try to minimize civilian losses by dropping leaflets warning Jordanian villagers to put any arms they might have outside and to stay in their homes. Whether this was instrumental in villagers leading the Israeli forces to fedayeen weapons caches during the operation could not be established.

One thing the Karamah battle did not do was curb guerrilla activity along the border in the short run, a fact attested to by Dayan, who warned in a speech at Beisan in late April that the Jordan Valley would be a battlefield if the guerrillas were not restricted and Jordanian artillery barrages were not terminated. In the same month, the chief of staff, Bar Lev, conceded that although *Fatah* was damaged, he expected terrorism to increase.[62]

As guerrilla activity intensified, Israeli forces once again crossed the Jordanian border, this time claiming that the operation was only a helicopter pursuit of saboteurs.[63] The aim was, no doubt, to draw a distinction between the large-scale Karamah operation and this smaller-scale mobile pursuit operation in the hope of avoiding adverse world reaction.[64] In an associated development, meanwhile, Israeli officers let it be known that on April 17 Israel had begun to attack the fedayeen by sending its own guerrillas across the border. Besides inflicting losses on the fedayeen and keeping them off balance, the commando raids appeared to be aimed at attenuating international protest and at avoiding casualties similar to those suffered at Karamah.

Another tactic designed to inflict losses on the fedayeen was the stepped-up use of air strikes against guerrilla positions, the large July 1968 air strike against the fedayeen training base at Salt being a case in point. A secondary purpose, according to Bar Lev, was to keep the Jordanians aware of the possibility of reprisals if fedayeen operations were allowed to continue. Even though Prime Minister Eshkol claimed that his pilots avoided the civilian population of Salt, the guerrillas asserted that Israeli aircraft had inflicted substantial civilian casualties.[65]

In spite of Arab protests, the Israelis continued to cross the Jordanian border, in response both to fedayeen incidents and to the shelling of Israeli settlements by Jordanian artillery. Such forays included air strikes, not only against the fedayeen but also against the Jordanian and Iraqi units. By December 1968, Israeli officials admitted that their policy was to use jets, sometimes one at a time, in response to border actions by guerrillas.[66]

At the end of December 1968, within a context of continued terrorism, hostilities along the borders, and a domestic Israeli debate over the best means for dealing with the fedayeen problem, two PFLP members opened fire on an El Al airliner in Athens. Following warnings by Israel that Arab planes were vulnerable to interference and that the PFLP operations in Lebanon were unacceptable, the Israelis carried out the dramatic helicopter operation against Beirut airport, which had the twin aims of deterring further attacks against airliners and of motivating Lebanon to curb guerrilla activity within and along its borders. The raid destroyed or damaged further some thirteen airliners. While critical international reaction led Israel to refrain from any further such operations in the next three years, the possibility that the raid helped engender a climate leading to later clashes between the Lebanese and the fedayeen could not be discounted.[67]

Some aspects of Israeli policy did not change, however. For one thing, Israel continued to insist that Arab states would be held responsible for guerrilla acts, a point underscored by new warnings to Lebanon after the

Beirut attack.[68] Bar Lev agreed that reprisals were beginning to have good results, and suggested that the Israelis were not about to end them. Not only had the number of cross-border incidents declined, according to security sources, but since the air strikes had begun in December, the firing against Israeli settlements took place from points farther from the cease-fire lines.[69]

Since the number of Israeli casualties and of incidents along the Syrian, Lebanese, and Jordanian borders rose during 1969, Israeli optimism seemed a bit premature. Yet, the fact that the casualties per incident dropped sharply seemed to suggest that operations against the fedayeen were becoming effective.[70]

In early February 1969, there was increased concern over a buildup of some 300 to 500 guerrillas in southern Lebanon, and over the possibility that the fedayeen might be trying to establish a new front. When guerrilla activity from Syria began to increase and the PFLP carried out an attack in Zurich against an El Al airliner in the same month, the stage was set for another reprisal. This time, however, Israel avoided a dramatic response like the Beirut raid in favor of a new policy called "active self-defense." Essentially, this meant that Israel, instead of merely responding to fedayeen incidents at home and along the borders, would take the initiative in an active campaign against guerrilla bases in border states. Thus, Israeli jets took to the air and struck guerrilla bases in Syria in the first such strike against that country since June 1967, while at the same time, a mechanized force pursued guerrillas across the Jordanian border and clashed with Jordanian troops. The Syrian attacks, according to Israel, caught hundreds of fedayeen by surprise in tents and buildings.[71]

The following month a series of strikes against guerrilla bases in Jordan and Syria left no doubt about the existence of a new Israeli policy. On the Lebanese front, the extension of air strikes to the southern slopes of Mount Hermon did not begin until July, although Israeli patrols did cross the border.[72] The air strikes against Jordan continued intermittently until the civil war in 1970.

At the time the spring 1969 air strikes were taking place, an Israeli assessment concluded that increased domestic terrorism and increased airline incidents abroad were indicators that border incursions were being effectively stymied (see Table 1). Yet, since internal terrorist activity, largely by the PFLP, caused right-wing politicians to challenge the wisdom of the liberal occupation policy, the government could not be completely happy with events.[73] On the other hand, one long-term plus, unseen at the time, was the movement of many fedayeen into the towns in Jordan as a result of Israeli military actions. In time, the behavior of the fedayeen in the urban centers, particularly Amman, would be a major contributor to the friction between the guerrillas and Jordan, a clash which eventually led to the crackdown on the fedayeen.

Table I

FEDAYEEN INCIDENTS AND ISRAELI CASUALTIES ALONG
THE JORDANIAN BORDER: JUNE 1967-JULY 1971

Year	Incidents	Israeli casualties	Casualties per month	Casualties per incident
1967	97	38	5.4	.39
1968	916	273	22.7	.29
1969	2,432	243	20.2	.099
1970	1,887[a]	111	13.8[b]	.063
1971	45	——	0.0	——

[a] January-August (pre-civil war): 1,845 incidents
[b] January-August only. No casualties after civil war.

In order to increase the cost to Jordan of acquiescing in fedayeen activity, Israel commandos sabotaged the East Ghor Canal on June 5, 1969, following two warnings to Hussein about incidents along the border. Since many of the farmers benefitting from the canal had moved as a result of military activity in the area, the effectiveness of the operation as a deterrent was questioned by some observers.[74] A second strike against the repaired canal in August, following an increase in guerrilla actions, gave credence to the Israeli view. The effects of the attack left fruits and vegetables dying on 500 square miles of Jordan's principal agricultural land. The facts that the Jordanian government negotiated a tacit accord with Israel in the fall of 1969, agreeing to curb guerrilla activity in return for being allowed to repair the canal, and that Israel again hit the canal in January 1970, also pointed to the importance of the waterway.[75]

To reinforce its military operations, Israel, on the political-psychological level, let it be known that it would not tolerate a guerrilla state in Jordan. Statements to this effect were especially prominent during the Jordanian-fedayeen clashes of June and September 1970, and seemed to have the twofold objective of admonishing the guerrillas not to overthrow Hussein, and of preventing Jordan from reaching an agreement allowing the fedayeen unrestricted freedom of movement.[76] In fact, when it appeared that the agreement which ended the June 1970 Jordanian-fedayeen clashes was going to result in fedayeen freedom of movement in Jordan, Israeli forces struck not only commando positions, but also the Jordanian army. The raid against the latter on July 13, 1970, was explained in Tel Aviv as a warning that Jordan would be regarded as an accomplice of the fedayeen if the July agreement had adverse effects on Israel.

Similar concern was shown by Israel over the Cairo agreement that ended the Jordanian civil war in September. Since the extent of the damage inflicted on the guerrillas by the civil war was not evident at the time, both

Allon and Bar Lev felt it necessary to warn that continued activity along the border would bring action differing in nature and scope from previous actions.[77] What Israel had in mind remained unknown, given the sharp decrease in guerrilla activity after September 1970.

Though the situation on the Jordanian border became rather placid, the same could not be said of the Lebanese frontier. By the summer of 1969 the border fighting had spread along the southern sector of Lebanon and the Israelis were responding to guerrilla raids with air strikes, artillery barrages, occasional search and destroy operations (some as long as two days), smaller mobile operations, and police actions by small patrols. In many cases homes lodging guerrillas were destroyed, and occasionally prisoners were taken. Like those along the Jordanian border frontier, the periodic thrusts into southern Lebanon were designed to not only inflict losses on the fedayeen, but also to remind the sanctuary state that Israel would not tolerate fedayeen attacks from across the border. Although not totally successful on this score, Israeli pressure did contribute to several clashes between the fedayeen and the Lebanese army, and to the eventual restriction of fedayeen activity by the government of Lebanon.

During the army-fedayeen clashes in Lebanon, Israeli spokesmen indicated that Israel would not stand by if the government fell or if a foreign army entered Lebanon. And, although a November 1969 guerrilla-Lebanese accord restricted guerrilla activity, Israeli spokesmen made it clear that Israel would not allow guerrillas a free run at northern Israel. Eban reiterated that Israel would hold Lebanon responsible for a quiet border. These admonitions were sharply underlined by the Israeli commander of the northern district, who said that if the raids continued, a six-mile stretch of southern Lebanon would be turned into a scorched-earth desert. On the diplomatic level, meanwhile, Israel made efforts to get other governments—the United States, Britain, and France—to persuade Lebanon to curb the fedayeen.[78]

Along their side of the Lebanese border, the Israelis proceeded to construct fortifications, surrounding settlements with barbed wire, erecting watchtowers, clearing infiltration routes, and installing lights. Though such measures enhanced internal security, the cross-border operations had greater impact against southern Lebanon, since they were partially responsible for efforts by Beirut to curb the guerrillas. A series of Israeli operations and air strikes in early 1970 causing the flight of 17,000 refugees from southern Lebanon, for example, was a major factor in a government decision to ban firing rockets from Lebanese territory and planting explosives near the border.[79] Nevertheless, since fedayeen activity, as anticipated by Bar Lev, was not completely ended, Israel felt compelled to continue periodic counterguerrilla operations.

South Lebanon & Vicinity

International boundary
Israel-Jordan/Lebanon/Syria Armistice
  Line (20 July 1949)
Demilitarized Zone Limit
  (20 July 1949)
All-weather road
Unsurfaced road or vehicle track
Railroad
✛ Airfield
Built-up area
Israeli settlement

Transverse Mercator Projection
Spot elevations in meters

0 — 15 Miles
0 — 15 Kilometers

503160 3-77

From the fall of 1970 onward, however, the military situation was favorable to Israel. Besides the internal defense measures and border operations, Israel had created a "dead zone" six miles deep along the border, and reports indicated that the guerrillas had been forced to withdraw deeper into Lebanon.[80] The improved security was soon reflected in the drop from 14.5 casualties per month along the Lebanese border in 1970 to 3.2 in the first seven months of 1971.[81] Inside Lebanon, meanwhile, the continuing Israeli military actions led to the rare spectacle of Arab peasants in southern Lebanon protesting guerrilla activities—especially rocket firing against Israel—because such acts led to Israeli operations against their villages.[82]

In 1971 Israel was still sending periodic patrols into Lebanon in order to dislodge fedayeen reportedly in the area. Reports received by the Lebanese Higher Defense Council in April 1971 indicated that Israel seemed to be well informed on guerrilla movements; no sooner had a number of fedayeen arrived at a village than they would be subjected to an Israeli operation.[83] When such actions did not prevent an upsurge of rocket and mortar attacks against Israeli settlements in the final months of 1971, Israel responded with several search and destroy operations against guerrilla areas, which were accompanied by air strikes, occasionally extending to bases in Syria following infiltration from the Golan Heights. (A February raid was the largest in an Arab country since 1967.) During these operations, roads were bulldozed into Lebanon for possible future use and observation posts were set up. As a consequence of Israeli actions, the Lebanese army moved into the area for the first time since 1969 and the fedayeen were ordered not to enter populated areas and to shift to flexible bases.[84]

Further limitations on guerrilla activity were imposed in 1972. As Yasir Arafat was meeting with the Lebanese prime minister in June in an effort to reach a new accord on regulating the insurgent presence, the Israelis struck the guerrillas with air and artillery attacks. Besides being a reprisal for the bombing of an Israeli village from Lebanon, the attack was also intended to influence the Arafat talks, and it probably had some effect, for the guerrillas reportedly agreed to withdraw from several frontier villages and to freeze operations against Israel.[85]

While a relative lull in activity obtained along the border for the next few months, the death of seventeen Israeli Olympic athletes at the hands of the terrorists in Munich during September led to renewed Israeli air strikes and a large search and destroy operation, during which villages were destroyed and property looted. In addition to inflicting losses on fedayeen units in southern Lebanon and keeping them off balance, a central purpose of the attacks was to force Lebanon to crack down on the planning, training, recruiting, and financing of transnational terrorism from within its borders.[86] Once more the Lebanese responded by moving troops into southern regions to control the fedayeen, a move that fell short of Israel's new demands.

Recognizing that guerrilla and terrorist threats from Lebanon and Syria were far from ended, Israel sought to gain the initiative through preemptive strikes against insurgent areas in Lebanon and Syria in mid-October. Although it was acknowledged that the new stress on preemption would not eliminate the fedayeen capability, IDF spokesmen indicated that it was intended to reduce the problem to manageable proportions.[87] While a concentrated attack against guerrilla bases in Syria two weeks later was depicted by the Israeli chief of staff as part of the new policy, there were suspicions that it was also a reprisal for the hijacking of a flight originating in Damascus which resulted in West Germany's release of three Munich terrorists.

Whatever the case, problems on the Golan Heights continued in the fall of 1972 and gave rise to the heaviest fighting in the area since the 1970 cease-fire. At one point in the midst of the air and artillery battles, an Israeli commander freely admitted that six civilian villages in Syria had been shelled to make examples of them.[88]

Though Foreign Minister Eban acknowledged that military operations could only interfere with rather than end insurgent terrorism, the clashes did usher in a period of relative calm along the borders between January and the October (1973) War, and led both the Lebanese and Syrian governments to prevent fedayeen attacks against Israel. In Lebanon, furthermore, the army clashed with the Palestinians during December when the latter refused to withdraw from a prohibited zone (the area of the September Israeli incursion). The two groups clashed again in the spring when the government moved to restrict the insurgents in Beirut, fearing that the PLO might use Lebanon as a base for attacks to avenge an Israeli raid that had resulted in the death of three PLO leaders in Beirut. In the latter instance, the Lebanese president was quoted as saying that his government would not allow guerrillas to kidnap and terrorize, and that Lebanon was sick and tired of being the victim of Israeli raids because of the fedayeen.[89] Concerned lest the Syrians move substantial forces across into Lebanon to aid the beleaguered Palestinians, Prime Minister Meir warned that Israel would act in such a case, and the IDF underscored the warning with large-scale maneuvers in the Golan Heights.[90]

As far as Syria was concerned, a January report indicated that the Syrian army had not only ordered the fedayeen out of all villages bombed by Israel earlier in the month but had also served written notice to the Palestinians to avoid operations unless approved by the army.[91] There was no explicit proscription against possible future operations as there had been in Lebanon. In a discussion with the author in February 1973, a high-ranking Israeli officer indicated that Syria was, in fact, controlling the guerrillas. The arrest of sixteen members of *Fatah* in September and closure of guerrilla trails and bases in the wake of fedayeen public criticism of the Syrian rapprochement with Jordan simply reinforced existing conditions. These acts also, and perhaps purposely, added to the deceptive calm before the October War.

Transnational terrorism. The Israeli military operations along the borders achieved their proximate aims of decreasing and mitigating border attacks, as well as pressuring the Arab governments to crack down on the fedayeen. Meanwhile Lebanon, as noted above, was still subjected to Israeli military operations due to Palestinian terrorist operations outside the Middle East that were planned, prepared, and frequently directed from Beirut. In dealing with this phenomenon, Israel's first impulse was to hit the Arab country from which the terrorists had departed (e.g., the Beirut raid of December 1968). Given strong and adverse international criticism, Israel suspended similar counteractions for a period of time, turning instead to a combination of vigorous diplomacy and veiled threats against Arab states in the hopes of preventing such terror in the future. In light of a number of incidents in the following years, the Israelis were not completely successful in their efforts.

Subsequent to one of the more costly incidents, the mid-air explosion of a Swissair plane in February 1970, Israeli officials met with representatives of foreign governments and called upon governments, civilian airlines, and pilots' organizations to take a strong stand against transnational terrorism. In addition, the Israeli propaganda apparatus stressed the abnormality of such behavior and Premier Meir warned that other Arab states in the area could not expect to enjoy uninterrupted air traffic if Israel did not have the same privilege. On a practical level, Israel tightened security precautions and placed armed guards on its aircraft. It was also reported that Israeli counterterrorist specialists were assigned to cities outside the Middle East.[92]

In the face of the fedayeen's most complex act of external terror, the multiple skyjacking of September 1970, Israel stood firm in refusing to meet demands by the PFLP that guerrillas held in Israeli prisons be released, and initially encouraged other governments to do likewise. On September 14, however, Israel backed away from the latter position by indicating that it would not oppose release of fedayeen held in Britain in return for release of all hostages held by the PFLP. On the other hand, Israel for the first time warned that if the hostages were harmed, the death penalty might be invoked against PFLP prisoners in Israeli jails.[93]

In a move associated with the skyjacking crisis, Israeli security forces arrested more than 450 Arab residents in the West Bank and Gaza, some of whom were understood to be relatives of guerrillas in Jordan. Although Israel said that the detention was for the purpose of interrogating suspected PFLP members, the action was generally interpreted as a ploy to bring pressure to bear on the PFLP to release hostages in Jordan. In fact, *The New York Times* reported that there was widespread skepticism in urban centers that the detainees were involved with the fedayeen, and pointed to the fact that Israeli officials had themselves said subversive activities and connections were negligible in occupied areas. Knowledgeable sources in Jerusalem, meanwhile, indicated that the roundup was instigated by the Defense Ministry without approval by the cabinet or foreign minister. By September 18 all detainees were released.[94]

Even though Israeli officials contended that the detentions were for the purpose of finding out how the PFLP worked, it was doubtful that this was the primary aim, since Israel already had a number of PFLP members under arrest who presumably had been interrogated. The thesis that the action was intended as counterpressure against the fedayeen to secure the release of hostages, or, short of that, to prevent them from being harmed, seemed more plausible. Whatever the truth, the action achieved little and tarnished Israel's liberal occupation policy.

The heavy losses sustained by the Palestinians in Jordan during the civil war intensified the bitterness and frustration among the more radical elements of the PLO and gave rise to a new, clandestine arm of *Fatah* known as the Black September Organization. The BSO in the months to come would, along with other groups, extract revenge, release psychological frustrations, publicize the Palestinian cause, and try to compensate for political and military weakness along the borders and within Israel and the occupied areas. This would be accomplished by carrying out terrorist actions that victimized scores of civilians and innocent third parties. In response, the Israelis mounted a multifaceted and systematic campaign involving diplomacy, military operations, enhanced security for Israelis abroad, and attacks against terrorists abroad.

As noted in the previous section, in September 1972 the death of seventeen Israeli athletes, taken hostage by Black September terrorists during the Munich Olympic games, led to major air strikes against fedayeen bases and naval installations in Lebanon and Syria.[95] Judging that retaliatory strikes would be insufficient, Israeli officials promised a continuous war against the terrorists, indicating that preventive measures would be taken wherever warranted in the world, including Europe.[96] An intelligence officer also informed an American news magazine that Israel was considering a counterterrorist campaign, using tactics as vicious as those of the Arabs.[97] Support for the latter came from *Ha'arez*, which urged the government to form a special network of terrorists which would not be restricted by the limitations of various authorities and bodies.[98] In response to this and pressures from Gahal, Prime Minister Meir said that Israel would track down terrorists wherever it could reach them.[99] To strengthen Israeli defense against terrorists, three senior officials in the security service were dismissed for negligence and security of embassies was upgraded to the point where they became veritable fortresses.

On the diplomatic level, Israel actively sought to exploit the carnage of Munich by persuading European governments to curtail Palestinian activities, and threatening to abandon peace talks until the terrorist problem was dealt with.[100]

These steps failed to deter the fedayeen, and for the next thirteen months the Israelis and the terrorists became locked in a deadly cycle of violence. Letter bombs mailed to Jews were countered by letter bombs mailed to Arabs, and assassinations of Jews in Europe were answered by the murder of Palestinians, in what came to be known as the "war of the spooks." On the Israeli side, such efforts came under the direction of a special advisor to the prime minister (first Major General Aharon Yariv, and then his successor Brigadier General Lior) and were reportedly carried out by *Ha Mossad L'Tafkidim Meyuhadim* (The Institute for Special Tasks).[101] Although Israel refused to acknowledge such activity, the arrest of two Israelis in Norway in July 1973, their admitted role in Israeli counterterror operations, and the expulsion of an Israeli security official for harboring them merely confirmed what informed observers had known all along.[102] In addition to the violence, Israeli agents also penetrated Palestinian organizations and engaged in a war of nerves with their Palestinian counterparts by placing obituaries of men still alive in newspapers and sending Arabs letters about their private lives.

While the war of the spooks was running its course, the IDF was also busy. In February 1973 Israeli commandos raided *Fatah* and PFLP bases in the Nahr al-Baddawi refugee camp in northern Lebanon, reportedly using maps and diagrams supplied by agents in Europe.[103] Two months later, in a raid which shook the PLO leadership, Israeli commandos struck in the heart of Beirut, killing three Palestinian leaders—Abu Yussef, chairman of the PLO Political Department; Kamal Adwan, who the Israelis claimed was responsible for terrorism within Israel; and Kamel Nasser, the official spokesman of the PLO. Although Arafat and the other leaders remained safe, Israel's capability to strike at the leadership was hardly lost on them. One positive by-product of the raid was the acquisition of plans for further attacks in Israel and of radio codes used by fedayeen to communicate with their agents. (The guerrillas knew that their codes had been broken and warned their agents.)[104] On the negative side, the raid moved the Saudis to renew contributions to the PLO which had been suspended since the BSO seizure of the Saudi embassy in Khartoum and the murder of two American diplomats the previous month. Sudanese President Ja'far al-Numayri also used the raid as a pretext to postpone the trial of the BSO members arrested in Khartoum.

In the wake of the Beirut raid, Arafat promised revenge, including attacks on American interests. This led, in turn, to the security crackdown by the Lebanese government which precipitated a new, serious round of fighting between the fedayeen and the army.

If the raids in Lebanon were successful, the same could not be said of an Israeli attempt to capture George Habash, leader of the PFLP, by forcing a Middle East jet airliner to land in Israel. Among the many critics of this episode were the Israeli pilots' association, the UN Security Council, and *Ha'arez*, which said Israel's image as a country that supported free international aviation was damaged.

The vulnerability of the aviation industry to both sides was again manifested in September when Italian police seized two SA-7 Strela missiles intended for use against El Al aircraft departing from Rome. The extremely grave nature of this development generated an intensive diplomatic effort, including requests that the United States and the USSR intervene jointly.[105]

The final major terrorist incident prior to the October War was the seizure of hostages in Vienna by Palestinians demanding the closure of transit facilities for Jewish immigrants coming from Russia. When the Austrian government capitulated, Israel denounced the move and Golda Meir made a personal, albeit unsuccessful, visit to Prime Minister Bruno Kreisky. The fact that the action was carried out by *As-Sa'iqa (Sa'iqa)*, a Syrian-sponsored fedayeen organization generally eschewing external terrorism, suggested that it may have been a deliberate ploy to divert Israeli attention prior to the war Damascus knew would commence within a week.[106]

Although transnational terrorism did not end after the October War, the mainstream of the PLO, led by *Fatah*, took a stand against it. While it is tempting to attribute this stance to pressures from the Arab states seeking to exploit the war politically, it is not unreasonable to suggest that the costs inflicted by the Israelis also had something to do with the decision.

Commentary on Israeli Counterinsurgency in the Territories

As the preceding chapters make clear, the Israelis had to cope with three threats normally associated with insurgent warfare. Inside the occupied territories, there was both terrorism and an effort by the fedayeen to organize the population for a people's war; along the Jordanian, Lebanese, and Syrian borders there were fedayeen raids, some of which were terrorist actions aimed at civilians, others guerrilla attacks against military units, outposts, and economic targets. Finally, of course, there was the upsurge in transnational terrorism outside the Middle East. The peak of the violence was 1969.

Although Israel employed a number of military and nonmilitary measures soon after the June War in order to thwart a serious threat from the fedayeen, the fact remained that the Palestinian guerrillas did gain momentum in 1968-1969. The rise in Israeli casualties and the number of fedayeen incidents during this period, particularly in 1969, testified to the increased threat posed by the insurgents, as did the tightening of security measures. *The International Herald Tribune* reported on November 3, 1969, that experienced observers in Israel generally agreed that the problem was worrying Israeli authorities more than they wished to admit, and that its scope was greater than the public had been led to believe.[107]

Both the upsurge in violence and fedayeen political activity were designed to achieve the central operational goal of creating and intensifying a people's war in the occupied areas. Accordingly, this section will focus on the Israeli efforts to thwart that aim in the critical West Bank and Gaza Strip regions in 1969 and thereafter.

The West Bank. During 1969, fedayeen activity on the West Bank was countered by an Israeli security crackdown, which included neighborhood punishment, curfews, confiscation of shops (in Hebron), restrictions on movements from the East Bank into the occupied areas, deportations, and arrests. The increased use of Israeli security measures was attributed by General Gazit to an upswing in support for the guerrillas, a phenomenon ascribed to fedayeen threats against collaborators.[108] The rising Israeli frustration could be seen in remarks by an Israeli spokesman on November 4, who said that Arabs in Hebron had three choices: fight the terrorists themselves; assist Israelis by supplying information; or accept neither alternative and pay the consequences. Dayan chimed in with a general warning that Arab residents could not have both normal functioning services and the fedayeen operating.[109]

Since Hebron was a particular problem area, the military governor of the West Bank, General Raphael Vardi, announced in mid-September that residents would be denied movement to any other part of the occupied territories, and for four days imports and exports between Hebron and Jordan were suspended. When student protests followed, Israel closed Arab schools and deported five teachers for instigating the student uprising.[110] Furthermore, in an effort to curb the smuggling of arms into the occupied areas, Israel imposed new restrictions on trucks entering from Jordan. No longer would trucks be allowed to carry hollow objects such as water or gas containers.

Paradoxically, the period during which insurgents seemed to be most effective was also the time when they experienced great difficulties within the West Bank. During November 1969, Israeli security forces captured Captain A. L. Rsheid in the most important arrest since the June War. Rsheid, according to Israel, was the key figure in the largest network of terrorist cells operating since the June War and the organizer of the Acre ring. After his capture, Rsheid readily admitted his role and led the Israelis to an arms cache. He himself had been identified by a member of a cell he once set up. In reaction to the Rsheid arrest and Israel's uncovering of other cells, "The Voice of *Fatah*" broadcast coded messages for two days instructing members in all cells in the West Bank and Israel to disband.[111]

The situation along the Jordanian borders added to Israel's problems during 1969 on the West Bank, as both border incidents and Israeli casualties increased. The border security and cross-border operations undertaken by the IDF eventually had their desired effects, however. Not only did casualties and incidents drop in 1970, but the casualties per month and casualties per incident in the first eight months before the Jordanian civil war also tailed off.[112]

The improved security situation on the West Bank brought with it an Israeli decision to allow political participation during 1972 in the form of elections to municipal councils, a move strenuously opposed by both the fedayeen and Jordan. Though the latter eventually withdrew its objections, and actively championed royalist candidates after threats by Dayan to halt the free movement of people and goods across the bridges, the Palestinians threatened the candidates with assassination. In spite of this, over 80 percent of the electorate voted (compared to 75 percent in the last Jordanian election in 1963). Five traditionalists were returned to office and five candidates favoring an independent Palestinian state were elected; none were known to be sympathetic to the PLO. A month later, there was an even heavier vote turnout in twelve other towns (87.8 percent) in defiance of the fedayeen.[113] These developments led Arafat to concede, in a speech to the **Palestine National Council in January 1973, that Israeli policies had** slowed the radicalization of the West Bank and that the elections had accomplished something.[114] In spite of occasional protests, such as a strike by Arab merchants in East Jerusalem on the anniversary of the Six-Day War, the West Bank remained quiet. The trouble during the October War was limited to the tossing of a few Molotov cocktails.

Although one could see these developments as clear testimony to the effectiveness of Israel's counterinsurgency policies, they in no way suggested Arab contentment with the occupation, for following the October conflict, there was a recrudescence of nationalism which included support of the PLO. The reasons for this renewed nationalism, however, had less to do with strategy of protracted armed struggle than with the decision of key Arab states to support the idea of a small Palestinian state, a point to which we shall return in the concluding chapter.

Gaza: the neutralization of terrorism. While Israel was able to establish relative tranquility on the West Bank during 1970, the situation in Gaza had remained unsatisfactory from a counterinsurgency point of view. During the 1967-1969 period, Gaza had been the scene of substantial civil unrest, marked by strikes, demonstrations, and terrorism, particularly grenade tossing incidents. In response, Israel restricted movement in and out of the strip (all travel except that into Israel was barred), imposed frequent curfews, and made use of deportation, detention without trial, identification checks, cordon and search operations and neighborhood punishment.

In spite of Israeli admonitions, the situation seemed to go from bad to worse in the spring of 1970. The estimated 10,000 Gaza residents working in Israel and labor exchanges in the strip became the targets of terrorist grenade attacks, the fedayeen argument being that every Arab working in Israel released an Israeli for the front. Another group that increasingly became the object of guerrilla terror was collaborators. In addition, a number of murders were caused by rivalry among fedayeen groups. It was not surprising that the Arab casualty toll was greater than that of the Israelis, due to these developments.[115]

A multiplicity of factors converged to make Gaza a hotbed of turmoil and conspiracy. A report by *The Times* of London on March 15, 1970, that sixty percent of the people in Gaza were hardship cases, illustrated the well-known fact that the area was poverty-stricken. The demographic density—350,000 Arabs living in a strip of land twenty-five miles long and eight miles wide—seemed to exacerbate the economic dilemmas of an area already poor in resources. Also contributing to the turmoil was the fact that most of the refugees, who had never left Gaza, had a low educational level and had been subjected to intensive anti-Israel propaganda for two decades. Moreover, since much of the PLA, which had been recruited in the strip, evaporated into the population after the June War, the population was well provided with individuals who hated Israel.[116]

As the civilian resistance and terrorism continued unabated into 1970, Israel, perhaps due to the drop in fedayeen effectiveness on the West Bank and along the border, began to give more attention to the integration of Gaza with the Israeli economy. A port at Gaza was to be restored, a new industrial center was being built at Beit Hanun near the Israeli border, and more jobs in Israel were opened to Arabs. The philosophy behind the last measure was aptly summed up by one Israeli official who commented on the Arabs working in Israel by saying: "If they're picking strawberries in Israel, they're not throwing grenades in Gaza."[117] On the other hand, the

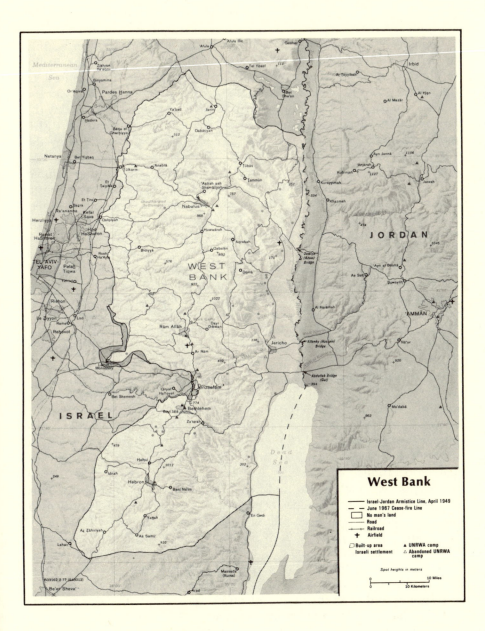

West Bank

— Israel-Jordan Armistice Line, April 1949
-- June 1967 Cease-fire Line
☐ No man's land
— Road
+++ Railroad
✛ Airfield

◻ Built-up area ▲ UNRWA camp
● Israeli settlement △ Abandoned UNRWA camp

Spot heights in meters

0 ___ 10 Miles
0 ___ 10 Kilometers

increasing use of Arab labor resurrected Zionist fears that the Arabs would become "the hewers of wood and drawers of water" in a mixed society.

Unhappily for Israel, the Gaza situation had not improved perceptibly by early 1971.[118] In Tel Aviv, the Defense Ministry announced that the mayor of Gaza City had been removed because of a failure to cooperate with the military government and refusal to use the city's surplus funds for the benefit of the people. Early in January, a curfew was imposed following the killing of two Israeli children. The subsequent killing of three PFLP guerrillas by Israeli patrols on January 9 led to a strike called by the fedayeen which shut down Gaza City. Cooperation in the strike was attributed to intimidation resulting from grenade attacks that injured twelve Arabs. In a radio interview, Major General Yeshayahu Gavish, former commander of the southern front, pointed to a serious counter-insurgency failing when he said that it had been a mistake for Israel to have closed their eyes while the guerrillas assassinated dozens, and perhaps hundreds, of local Arabs. The local population, he contended, was entitled to the full protection of the Israeli government. In another insightful remark, Gavish indicated that it had been an error to apply identical policies in the West Bank and Gaza, since the West Bank insurgents were infiltrators whereas those in Gaza were part of the local populace. This difference, he suggested, made the policy of unobtrusive military rule, which was a success on the West Bank, unsuitable for Gaza. He then said that the Israelis in Gaza should demonstrate their power.[119]

Whether influenced by Gavish or acting on its own initiative, the military government did move firmly in the wake of the January difficulties. Eighty shopkeepers were put on trial for closing their establishments during strikes on December 31 and January 9 and 11, 209 residents who formerly held Egyptian citizenship were transferred to Egypt through the International Red Cross, a curfew was imposed, and vigorous search operations were carried out. Most significant was a decision to move border police, mostly Druze and Bedouin volunteers, into the strip. This proved to be a counterproductive endeavor because the border police used harsh measures and were, according to *The Times* of London, January 19, 1971, guilty of a number of "ugly incidents." Some military officials were chagrined since they believed their efforts over three and one-half years had been undermined. In the midst of protests from the Arabs, the Israeli press (e.g., *Ha'arez*, January 27, 1971), military officials, and the military governor agreed to an investigation, and Dayan said that he was opposed to heavy-handed action taken out of anger.[120]

The following month an Israeli spokesman announced that eleven soldiers, including an officer, would be tried on charges of "unwarranted violence, including use of batons and truncheons against a number of

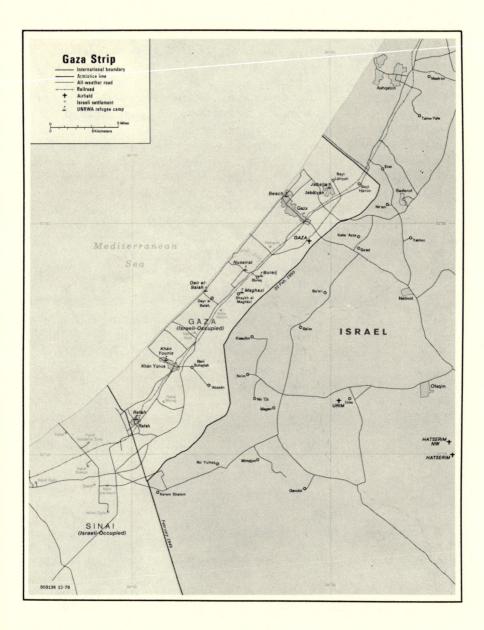

Gaza Strip

International boundary
Armistice line
All-weather road
Railroad
Airfield
Israeli settlement
UNRWA refugee camp

5 Miles
5 Kilometers

Mediterranean
Sea

Ashqelon
Mash'en
Talme Yafe
Erez
Bayt Lāhiyah
Jabalia
Bayt Hānūn
Beach
Jabālyan
Sederot
Gaza
Nir'am
GAZA
Kefar 'Azza
Yakhini
Sa'ad
Nuseirat
Bureij
Bureij
22 Feb. 1950
Be'eri
Deir el-Balah
Maghazi
Netivot
Dayr al Balah
Shaykh al Maghāzī
Kefar Darom
GAZA
(Israeli-Occupied)
Re'im
Nahal Oz
Kissufim
ISRAEL
Khān Yūnis
Bani Suhaylah
Nirim
Khān Yūnus
'Abasān
Nir 'Oz
Ofaqim
Magen
URIM
Uria
Rafah
HATSERIM
NW
Rafah
HATSERIM
Yamit
Rafah Approach Zone
Yamit
Nir Yizhaq
Mivtahim
Nahal Bukkati
Sadot
Gevulot
Nahal Hu Atsva
Keram Shalom
February 1949
Nahal Ogda

SINAI
(Israeli-Occupied)

residents, causing damage to buildings." Three other officers, two of high rank, were, according to the same announcement, given administrative reprimands for authorizing violence or failing to control their men. Coincident with the legal action, Israeli psychologists, sociologists, and educators were asked to work out methods to mentally prepare young soldiers for enforcement operations and searches in occupied areas. On February 17, Dayan admitted the excessive violence and put the number of injured at thirty. In the meantime, security measures were enforced and a number of PFLP guerrillas were apprehended.[121]

In March, Israel separated responsibility for government and civil affairs from responsibility for security, a move designed to expand civilian authority in Gaza and the northern Sinai. On the security level, ongoing grenade attacks and murders resulted in the Israelis detaining families of twenty-nine suspected terrorists in Sinai camps. The measure, according to Dayan, had been instituted nine weeks earlier in order to deny guerrillas the aid, shelter, and comfort afforded by their families.[122]

The next month saw a shift in Israeli policy in Gaza. A report on the Gaza situation appearing in *The Daily Star* of Beirut said that in April Israelis had initiated a number of tactics designed to limit repressive actions against guerrillas and their families. The objective was to get the population to concentrate on economic development and to eliminate the status of refugees by transferring some to the West Bank and building permanent houses and securing jobs for others. The new Israeli plan, it was suggested, aimed at raising the standard of living, in order to isolate the fedayeen from the rest of the citizenry.[123]

While the approach just described seemed sensible, the Israelis did not act prudently in all situations. One such instance was the reported demand that Arab notables in Gaza sign a pledge to report every case of assassination, beating, and threatened terror, or be removed from office. Since it was clear at the time that Israelis could not protect those who signed from the fate of other collaborators, the demand was ill-advised.

By July 1971, Israeli dissatisfaction with the security situation in Gaza resulted in one of the most significant chapters in the Gaza story. This was an Israeli plan to resettle a large number of refugees outside the large incident-prone camps such as Jabaliya. Other aspects of the scheme included the construction of new roads inside the camps to facilitate policing and the installation of electric lighting to improve security conditions. Following a second stage that involved building new housing and furnishing electricity, water, and recreational facilities, Israel hoped that a series of small, manageable camps, with security reasonably assured, would exist.

It was the resettlement aspect, however, which caused the greatest furor.

Resettlement actually began in late July with movement of some 100 families from Jabiliya to al-Arish. While the purpose given by Israel was the need to decrease the camp's population and make way for new patrol roads, the local Arabs remained unconvinced and a wave of protests ensued. Israeli promises that choice of new housing or compensation would be tendered along with employment opportunities proved similarly unpersuasive. After a month of protests and a successful general strike, informed sources in Tel Aviv reported that the resettlement scheme had been halted, pending further decisions by the government.

As far as counterinsurgency practice was concerned, the technique of resettlement, as noted in Chapter 2, was potentially helpful, as long as it was explained and new conditions were better than old ones. Given the chronic insecurity, poverty, and overcrowding in Gaza, all of which were interrelated, the resettlement program was a bold and wise step that, despite short-range political problems, could have the long-term effect of significantly pacifying the area. Even though short-term political factors intervened to block the rapid completion of the program, Israeli security actions dramatically reduced the level of fedayeen activity in Gaza during the last half of 1971.[124] Though there was a brief upsurge of fedayeen activity in the Gaza Strip during August and September, 1972 was a generally quiet year. Thirty-three terrorist networks had been uncovered (six were extensive); arms and sabotage equipment were said to be in short supply; 726 persons were arrested, including 200 terrorists; and 1,000 detainees were in custody.[125] The new stability was both reflected and reinforced by the nearly full employment of the Gaza Strip's labor force (some 25,000 went daily to Israel). The curfew that dated back to the time of the Egyptian administration was lifted; border police were withdrawn; and visits to the area by relatives were allowed.

While terrorist incidents did occur from time to time and the Israelis periodically uncovered cells, the major problem in the area in 1972 and 1973 was political. In October 1973, Israel dismissed the Gaza town council and mayor, using some minor terrorist incidents as a pretext. The real issue, however, was refusal of the Arab leaders to supply the Shati refugee camp with water, for fear that such a step not only would alter the inhabitants' status as refugees and hence cost them their UN benefits, but would also set the stage for an Israeli annexation of the Gaza Strip. The extension of Israeli electrical and telephone grids to the area of construction of new roads and housing, and Israeli settlement plans for Jews near Rafah, were interpreted in a similar way.[126]

In short, by the time of the October War, two results had become clear. First, the Israeli counterinsurgency measures had effectively tranquilized the Gaza Strip. (No incidents were reported during the year.) Secondly, despite the absence of violence, the Arabs still detested the occupation and feared annexation by Israel.

Security Sanctions: The Moral and Legal Critique

The actions taken by Israel in Gaza, like punitive measures elsewhere, generated charges that Israel was guilty of atrocities and violations of several international agreements on the treatment of both prisoners and civilians during an occupation. Although the Institute for Palestine Studies and the Arab Information Center produced a plethora of documents purporting to demonstrate the widespread torture of prisoners by the Israelis, specific claims were almost impossible to verify, since, in the final analysis, they were based on statements by individuals who may or may not have been telling the truth. Yet, such allegations could not be dismissed as mere propaganda in view of similar reports issued by independent observers such as Amnesty International and a London *Sunday Times* Insight Team. After gathering and analyzing data as well as interviewing former prisoners, the Insight Team concluded that torture of prisoners was so widespread that it appeared to be sanctioned as official policy.[127]

While the Insight Team report was generally persuasive when arguing the point that torture frequently occurred, its attribution of this pattern to deliberate policy was misleading, in that it implied that torture was officially sanctioned by Israel. A closer look at the report suggested that if allegations of widespread torture were accurate, it was due either to negligence or approval by a military government which was violating the laws, norms, and regulations of the state and government of Israel.

Not surprisingly, the Israelis denied the allegations noted above. Such denials were given at least some credence by the decision of approximately 100 fedayeen to surrender to Israel rather than to the Jordanian army during the July 1971 fighting in Jordan. Though this choice was understandable in light of the treatment meted out by the Jordanians, it nonetheless raised the question of whether the fedayeen really accepted the notion that Israel maltreated prisoners on a systematic basis. As it happened, Israel decided to treat the surrendering insurgents as civilians rather than as prisoners of war, no doubt hoping that leniency might bring information, cooperation, and more surrenders. In September 1971, the fedayeen who had surrendered in July were released because Israel claimed it could not establish the fact that they carried out any hostile acts against Israel.[128]

In the absence of definitive data, objective observers can only speculate as to the true scope of torture and responsibility for it. To the extent that widespread torture did exist, Israeli officials had a serious problem that involved morality, counterproductive effects, and discipline.

As far as misuse of force against the general populace was concerned, the major question was whether or not an obvious pattern of brutality against the Arabs existed. A close reading of the public accounts over several years of occupation led to the conclusion that Israel 'did not systematically terrorize or exploit the population. There were, as indicated earlier in this chapter, several incidents in which Jewish citizens or security forces did inflict undue harm on Arab citizens, many of whom were innocent. What appeared most significant, however, was the trenchant evidence that such acts were in violation of official policy—to wit, punishment of guilty individuals only, with efforts to avoid unjustified harm to Arab citizens. Indeed, Israeli concern about brutality stood in marked contrast to other insurgencies (e.g., Bangladesh), and suggested that Israel did not wish to repeat mistakes made elsewhere.

This conclusion does not ignore obvious punitive measures—detention without trial, cordon and search operations, identification checks, resettlement, destruction of homes of guerrillas and supporters and so on— used by Israeli security forces to thwart the fedayeen and deny them links with the population. Although the Arabs and some outside observers argued that such actions were harsh and immoral, it is necessary to remember that they were not unusual counterinsurgency practices. In fact, as noted in Chapter 2, several experts on counterinsurgency indicated that there are situations in which punitive measures like those just noted are necessary in order to establish security.

Another charge made against Israeli occupation policies and punitive measures is that they were violations of international law. International legal prohibitions against such things as resettlement and destruction of property are invariably qualified by clauses allowing for the actions in case of military necessity. The invocation of military exigencies could be and was used by the Israelis to justify their measures.

Government Response: Summary and Conclusions

An analysis of Israel's antifedayeen program from a counterinsurgency point of view leads to the conclusion that it was generally successful. Operating from a secure base in Israel, the military government moved into the occupied areas and took a number of steps aimed at neutralizing an enemy that had posed a terrorist threat, despite serious organizational shortcomings. Following sound counterinsurgency principles, the Israelis moved to eliminate the nascent insurgent organization through effective security and intelligence operations, and to counterorganize the population. The counterorganization efforts sought not to encourage the people to identify with the state of Israel, but to restore normal life patterns and increase the people's stake in tranquility by improving their material well-being.

Although the military government was in charge of administration of the occupied territories, provision was made at both central and local levels for civil-military coordination. In order to restore essential services and, at the same time, to avoid both unnecessary friction with the local population and imposition of a manpower burden on Israel, administration was left largely to the Arab population, a decision which proved to be very successful, particularly on the West Bank.

On the security level, the treatment of the Arab populace was a blend of liberalism toward those who wished to pursue life as normal, and firmness toward those who joined or supported the fedayeen. As has already been indicated, within the occupied areas the Israelis used a number of punitive measures to establish order and security, and to isolate the fedayeen from the people. Those found guilty were given stiff sentences, and there was no tendency to release prisoners on pardons, even in the face of fedayeen blackmail (e.g., September 1970). The fact that the Israeli Minister of Police could report in March 1971 that the number of people detained on security grounds was only 3,400, and that the number held for interrogation for long or short periods since June 1967 was 10,000, seemed to suggest that Israeli detentions were not indiscriminate or on a mass scale. In any event, there were few experienced observers in the Middle East who denied that, with the partial exception of Gaza, Israel had been able to thwart fedayeen attempts to galvanize active popular support for resistance within Palestine. Few, also, denied that the effectiveness of the Israeli intelligence and security apparatus, economic policy, and liberal administration policy were major factors in Israel's success.

Since the sanctions used by Israel were high-level sanctions, the possibility remained that over the long run, they might lead to renewal of political violence. Several factors seemed to militate against this tendency. For one thing, the relative stability in 1971 meant that such measures were employed infrequently. Moreover, it seemed clear that the increased standard of living had taken the edge off some discontent that existed in the early phases of the occupation. Finally, the belief among sectors of the Palestinian elite on the West Bank that an end to the occupation could come peacefully suggested that political violence was not the only option being entertained. Whether hopes for a peaceful transition would remain viable or eventually be replaced by frustration and despair was a question only the future could answer.

While the Israelis were taking action against terrorism within Israel and occupied areas, they were also faced with guerrilla-type raids from across the borders. Although the infiltrators were at a disadvantage because they had no popular bases in the occupied areas, the casualties they inflicted and their eventual objective of getting a foothold on the West Bank could not be ignored. Thus, Israel, in line with counterinsurgency principles, acted to establish control of border areas through nomadic territorial offensive operations and strikes by mobile forces against commando sanctuaries. A blend of constant patrolling, security barriers, good intelligence, air strikes, and search and destroy operations was employed to increase guerrilla losses and to successfully reduce the infiltration problem to a negligible threat by December 1971.

Aside from the direct material and human losses inflicted on the fedayeen, the cross-border attacks appeared to have the long-term effect of contributing to Lebanese and Jordanian moves against the Palestinian guerrillas.

While the September 1970 civil war in Jordan proved to be a major factor behind the decreasing fedayeen raids, it must be remembered that Israeli countermeasures had already begun to achieve results. Using Israeli casualties along the Jordanian frontier as an index of the effectiveness of the border attacks, one finds that casualties per month were decreasing prior to September 1970. In 1969, a total of forty-seven Israelis were killed, an average of 3.9 per month, while in the first eight months of 1970, twenty-two Israelis were killed, an average of 2.7 per month.

In addition to the fact that Israeli forces enjoyed military and technological superiority, there were more general reasons for Israel's success. Perhaps most important was the fact that, in addition to proven excellence in leadership and combat ability, the military, police, and border forces had strong backing from the government and from the Jewish population. Time and again the citizens of Israel had demonstrated their willingness to make substantial human and material sacrifices on behalf of security needs. Even though by October 1970 Israel had suffered 788 soldiers and civilians killed and 2,738 wounded in the post-June 1967 fighting with the fedayeen and the Arab states, and the Israelis had become the world's most highly taxed citizens, there was no indication of weakening resolve.[129] Unlike the mixture of apathy and alienation in the population that had undermined past regimes engaged in insurgency—Batista in Cuba, for example—the Israeli people supported their government in its operations against the fedayeen.

Obvious reasons for the Israeli unity of effort were, of course, the antipathy between Jews and Arabs and the more than twenty years of hostilities and threats of destruction associated with it. A more revealing but related explanation is the fact that unlike some regimes, such as the French in Algeria and Indochina or the British in Cyprus, the Israelis could not afford to tire of the struggle and withdraw to the metropole, since the primary fedayeen target for liberation, Israel, was the metropole. One knowledgeable commentator on Palestinian activities, who was also sympathetic with the Palestinian cause, Gerard Chaliand, stressed this point when asked to compare the situation of the Vietnamese with that of the Palestinians. As he cogently noted:

> In one case you have a foreign invader with a metropole. I don't say that the Israelis were not foreign. They were foreign; they were part of the European expansion, the colonial expansion. Even if you can't call them classical colonialists because they have not used Arab manpower. But, they have no metropole. The Americans, they will get tired, they can't win militarily, so they have a cease-fire, etc. The same with the French in Algeria or in Indochina. In the case of Israel, these people, whether they are right or wrong, they believe that they are home. They won't go.[130]

Such an attitude on the part of the Israelis reflected not only the immediate situation in the Middle East, but also a consciousness of centuries of persecution of the Jewish people and the desire to end it, once and for all.

Since 1948, the people of Israel have demonstrated their commitment to the survival of the nation of Israel by a willingness to engage in periodic wars and to stand fast in the face of intermittent fedayeen activity. In fact, having become accustomed to low-level terrorism, the Israelis did not let the shock value of fedayeen actions after the June War undercut their determination. Furthermore, it should also be pointed out that prior to 1948, the Israelis themselves were guerrillas and terrorists, and thus had some appreciation of the workings of and motivation behind insurgent organizations.

The fact that Israel was such a formidable foe had important implications for the fedayeen strategy of a people's war. Since the Palestinian guerrillas were unable to count on a collapse of the Israeli military government or of popular will that would smooth their path to success, they would have to rely on their capabilities. Essentially, this meant that the fedayeen would have to exert great efforts to build a cohesive and differentiated organization, win popular support, and obtain external support (moral, political, material, and sanctuary), if the Israeli strengths were ever to be offset. This conclusion is reinforced by a review of the environmental situation facing the fedayeen.

Environment

As Chapter 2 pointed out, the environmental variable becomes very important to an insurgent movement in situations where strength and resolve of the regime necessitates a prolonged armed struggle. Since precisely this situation exists in Palestine, it is important to examine the terrain, size and distribution of the population, linkage between topography and demography, transportation and communications network, primordial cleavages in the area, and climate.

Terrain

Succinctly stated, the terrain in Palestine is unfavorable to guerrilla operations (especially when compared to places like Algeria and Vietnam), in light of its limited size and the absence of jungles, extensive swamps, or forested mountain chains.[131] In fact, much to the detriment of the fedayeen cause, the largely flat and barren landscape has facilitated Israeli counterinsurgency operations, the detection of guerrilla units, and the use of air power. Moreover, the topography of the area, when combined with the effectiveness of the Israeli air force, has made it extremely hazardous for commandos to operate in large units and creates serious doubts as to whether the fedayeen can ever risk the regularization of their forces.

Firsthand observation makes it evident that the few areas where guerrillas can find some cover—the Mount Hermon region of south Lebanon, part of the Golan Heights, the bushes along the banks of the Jordan River, and some of the hills in Galilee—are either across borders or easily isolated by the Israeli forces. The poor topography of the West Bank (small size and open terrain), in particular, has made it impossible for guerrillas to create and secure anything resembling decent base areas for guerrilla operations.

Faced with such unhappy facts of nature, the fedayeen have reacted in a number of ways. Usually they and their supporters have simply belittled the importance of the terrain factor, or ignored it altogether.[132] At other times, the fedayeen have acknowledged limits imposed by the environment, but suggested that the support of the masses would overcome this deficiency. One organization, for example, has assured its followers that "dense human forests" would enable the resistance to succeed.[133]

Size and Distribution of the Population

The population statistics also have been unfavorable to guerrilla operations. As the editor of *Al-Ahram* once pointed out, the Jewish population within the target area exceeds that of the Arabs, thus reversing the situation which prevailed in both Algeria and Vietnam.[134] Given this situation, it is difficult to envisage the establishment of a popular base and the swallowing up of the Israelis by "dense human forests."

The population has been a problem for the guerrillas in another way. Although the majority of the population was engaged in agriculture—a seeming advantage—the small overall size of the area has enabled Israeli military forces to react quickly to problems anywhere. Furthermore, geographic separation of the West Bank from Gaza has facilitated Israel's efforts to isolate the people of the two areas and compounded the coordination problems of the fedayeen.

Topographical-Demographic Linkage

In most cases of protracted internal war, the two variables of popular support and favorable terrain have had to merge. That is to say, inaccessible areas could be turned into popular bases only if there was a local population willing to assist guerrilla forces. Since, in the case of Palestine, the few areas which do provide some natural concealment for guerrillas are both small and sparsely populated, there was never much chance that a thriving popular base would emerge. Thus, the demographic-topographic mix was another factor which forced the fedayeen to rely on refugee camps in the states surrounding Israel.

Although there was a large population within the West Bank which the fedayeen hoped to exploit, the small area and flat nature of the terrain conspired against the guerrillas and made establishment of a guerrilla base area a practical impossibility, despite fedayeen claims that they had set up bases. And, without such bases, intensified and successful guerrilla warfare became extremely unlikely. Instead, hit-and-run raids often degenerated into terrorist attacks. While this may have yielded some successes in the short run, it became counterproductive in the long term, because it demonstrated a lack of revolutionary progress and alienated the affected population. Since an attempt to overcome the handicap by conducting guerrilla operations in a small and open area would have been suicidal, the fedayeen were caught in a dilemma from which there was no obvious escape.

Road and Transportation Network

Another debit on the fedayeen environmental balance sheet was the existence of an effective transportation and communications system in the area. In fact, as far back as 1964, a distinguished Egyptian scholar had warned that fedayeen operations would be severely hampered by the extensive road network in Palestine, which facilitated regular army movements.[135] Thus, it is not surprising that the IDF has stressed the element of mobility against the guerrillas, and in areas where there were some problems, proceeded to bulldoze new roads. In general, then, the good state of the transportation system in the target area was a distinct advantage to the counterrevolutionary side in their antiguerrilla operations.

Primordial Cleavages

In contrast to the rather dismal environmental conditions just noted, one facet of the milieu favored the fedayeen, namely, the linguistic, cultural, religious, and economic cleavages separating the Arabs from the Jews. While the volatile mix of conflicting cultural, religious, linguistic, and economic elements and the serious concrete conflict over control of Palestine have created a situation ideally suited for insurgent exploitation, the fedayeen, for a number of reasons discussed in previous and subsequent chapters, have been unable to exploit the situation to their full advantage.

Climate

The climate has not emerged as a decisive factor in the Palestine case. In the few situations where it has played a role, it appeared to cause the guerrillas more difficulties than it did the Israelis. In early 1969, for example, bad weather in the area was cited as a factor which curtailed guerrilla operations; in the fall of 1969, the need to overcome the interruption of fedayeen supplies caused by the snow on Mount Hermon was thought to have been a consideration motivating the guerrillas to extend their operational areas.[136] This move, as noted earlier, was a key reason for the guerrilla-Lebanese fighting. All things considered, however, the climate does not appear to be a crucial variable in the fedayeen situation.

The Environment: Summary and Conclusions

Like the government factor, the environment was not favorable to the fedayeen. The nature of the terrain, location of the population, small size of the target area, and good transportation and communications systems all favored the Israelis and hence facilitated their counterinsurgency effort. Whether the fedayeen could offset these serious disadvantages by mobilizing the people, creating an effective organization, and gaining substantial external support is the subject of chapters which follow.

Popular Support

The Palestinians recognized that popular support is a crucial ingredient of successful protracted revolutionary warfare; indeed, they even went so far as to call this a "revolutionary law."[1] Consequently, they made a considerable effort to gain active support, using esoteric and exoteric appeals, terror, provocation of counterterror, and demonstrations of potency as techniques for convincing the people to provide food, shelter, information, and concealment for their forces. The purpose of this chapter is to analyze how the fedayeen utilized these means and how successful they were in gaining popular support in Israel, the occupied areas, and the refugee camps located in Jordan, Lebanon, and Syria.

As the preceding chapter pointed out, the situation in the occupied areas in the summer of 1967 was characterized by a significant degree of more or less spontaneous civil unrest. What did not exist was a systematic allegiance to the fledgling fedayeen organizations that could be properly characterized as active popular support. The previous chapter also noted that the military government undertook a number of measures immediately following the June War designed to contain civil disobedience and to preclude the guerrillas from obtaining mass support. In light of the fact that the Israelis started from a position of strength in that they possessed a highly efficient security system, fully backed by the government and people of Israel, it was obvious that the task of gaining popular support would require substantial efforts on the part of the fedayeen. As time went by and it also became evident that Israel's counterinsurgency policy was increasingly effective, it was even more urgent that the fedayeen attempts to gain popular support achieve a high degree of sophistication. How the Palestinian guerrilla organizations responded to this challenge is the subject of the discussion which follows.

Techniques for Gaining Popular Support

Esoteric Appeals

Following the June War, it was clear that the fedayeen were going to use esoteric appeals in order to gain support from the intellectuals and buttress the exoteric appeals directed at the masses. In the case of the latter, the objective was to identify the villain responsible for nearly twenty years of deprivation and frustration. On the ideological level there were two important trends: Fanonism, a rather loose ideology based on the thought of Frantz Fanon, which influenced the *Fatah*-PLO wing of the fedayeen movement; and the Marxist-Lenist approach of smaller left-wing groups such as the PFLP and the Popular Democratic Front for the Liberation of Palestine (PDF).

Fatah's theoretical approach was generally eclectic. It sought to establish the point that classical imperialism, represented by Zionism, was the underlying cause of the loss of Palestine.[2] Borrowing from Fanon, *Fatah* depicted the Palestinians as "the wretched of the earth" who could only achieve national and personal liberation through violence.[3] The strategy for employing violence was a curious blend of Maoism and Castroism. It incorporated the Chinese concept of protracted armed struggle but rejected party control and extensive political preparation. Instead, it favored immediate military action along the lines of the Cuban experience. Intertwined with all of these philosophies was an obvious nationalist dimension aimed at the ultimate liberation of Palestine and the establishment of a new state which would give concrete expression to the emergent Palestinian national awareness.[4]

Although *Fatah* had a loosely articulated ideological explanation for the Palestinian situation, it displayed far less attention to ideology than did the PFLP and PDF. The latter organizations, in typical Marxist-Leninist fashion, argued that only a scientific appreciation of class conflict could lead to an effective revolutionary movement. An analysis of the social structure would, they contended, demonstrate clearly that before Palestine could be liberated, there had to be a wider revolution in the Middle East to purge reactionary elements which, because of their own interests and integral ties with world imperialism, opposed change. The implication was that non-Marxist regimes, especially right-wing ones in Jordan, Lebanon, and Saudi Arabia, would have to be toppled prior to any serious attempt to liberate Palestine from the Zionists. This view led to profound and continuing differences with the PLO and *Fatah*, since the latter organizations were trying to obtain support from the very regimes the left wing wished to destroy.[5]

Inasmuch as nascent Palestinian nationalism merged inextricably with frustrations born of a deep sense of deprivation, particularly in the refugee camps, it is impossible to establish with certitude that esoteric appeals were the major reason individuals joined the movement. Nevertheless, esoteric appeals do appear to have had some impact. If it is assumed that ideological appeals have something to do with the recruitment of intellectuals, then the rather large number who flocked to the resistance, especially to left-wing groups, seems to suggest that the esoteric appeal was of some significance.[6] Indeed, there were many reports that doctors, businessmen, scholars, etc., were taking up the cause of the fedayeen. *Le Monde*, in a survey published in 1969 of 1,000 fedayeen, revealed that only six percent were illiterate, whereas fifty-four percent had primary education, thirty-two percent secondary education, and eight percent had been to a university.[7] Even Dayan, in March 1969, called attention to the fact that many infiltrators were highly educated and more ideologically motivated than in the past. Another observer claimed that approximately half of the members of *Assifa* were college graduates or students.[8]

Although it was undoubtedly true that ideological appeals attracted some recruits to the fedayeen movement, it was probably also true that ideology, particularly that propagated by left-wing groups, repelled a number of would-be commandos. As an experienced Middle Eastern correspondent of *The Guardian* observed, the ideological positions of the PDF and PFLP alienated "much of the middle- and upper-class support... which could otherwise be theirs."[9]

Exoteric Appeals

No doubt the strongest appeal made by the fedayeen was their emphasis on concrete grievances, aimed at both the masses and the intelligentsia. The dispossession of Palestinians from their land and the exile from their homes and communities provided ready-made issues which propagandists exploited by poster, pamphlet, newspaper and radio.[10] Added to the stress on deprivation was the argument that only the Palestinians themselves could redress the wrong, a point reinforced by the repeated failures of the Arab states.

Closely related to the exoteric appeal was the notoriety of Yasir Arafat, who, especially in 1969, was being heralded as a contemporary Salah ad-Din by the Arab press. In an Arab culture which had always extolled hero figures, Arafat was probably the best-known leader after Nasser, at least among the masses.[11] Yet, as will be indicated later in this chapter, by 1971 the star of Arafat had faded and a number of rivals had surfaced to challenge his authority.

Terrorism

Although the fedayeen did carry out a considerable number of terrorist operations in the years after the June War, it did not appear that terrorism was directed as much at gaining popular support as it was at disrupting Israel's economy and undermining the morale of its citizens. Terrorist attacks against Jewish civilians, both within the conflict area and outside the Middle East, were an explicit policy of the PFLP, BSO, and several other organizations. Although the *Fatah*-PLO grouping claimed that its policy was to avoid attacks on civilians, there were enough incidents directed against civilians to cast doubt on these claims; and once *Fatah* spawned the BSO, the policy became clear. However, there did not seem to be a systematic terrorist effort which was aimed at Arab citizens in the occupied areas and Israel, and which sought to coerce the target populations to render active support to the guerrillas. At best, terror appeared to be used indirectly to win support. This is to say, by successful and dramatic terrorist attacks on Israelis, the fedayeen intended to demonstrate their own potency and the corresponding inability of the Israeli authorities to provide security. However, since the fedayeen proved incapable of the transition from terrorism to systematic guerrilla warfare within the target areas, it appeared to many observers that terrorism, rather than demonstrating strength, reflected weakness and lack of progress. Worse yet was the fact that a combination of effective intelligence and security actions by Israel, facilitated on a number of occasions by information supplied by the Arabs, led to the destruction of a large number of terrorist networks. This setback resulted in an increased effort on the part of the fedayeen, particularly the PFLP, to assassinate collaborators, a development that the military governor conceded was largely responsible for increased cooperation with the guerrillas in 1969.[12] By 1970 the state of affairs had deteriorated to such an extent, however, that instead of using terror to gain popular support, the fedayeen were forced to use it negatively—that is, to deny Israel the support and information being rendered by certain Arab residents of the occupied areas.

The use of terror complicated the quest for popular support, since incidents directed at disrupting the occupation often resulted in Israeli restrictions against the local population which, in turn, led the latter to criticize the fedayeen. In October 1968, for example, a grenade attack in Hebron led the Arab mayor to send a message of regret to Dayan and to charge that those who encouraged such actions did not want a single Arab left on the West Bank. The next month the Arab paper *Al-Quds* registered a similar condemnation of an explosion in Jerusalem.[13] Even more counterproductive was the fact that terrorist attacks frequently resulted in more Arab than Israeli casualties.[14]

In addition to casualties inflicted by indiscriminate terrorism, there were a few cases where Arab areas were deliberately targeted. In May 1969, for instance, the Arab town of Jericho was attacked with rockets two nights in a row. *Fatah* charges that Israel carried out the attacks in order to force the population to flee were unconvincing in light of the fact that later the fedayeen carried out their first attack on an Arab village.[15] Suffice it to say, such attacks against the Arab population were costly to the insurgency in terms of popular support.

Provocation of Counterterror

Through terror operations against the Jewish population, the fedayeen, besides demonstrating their potency and Israeli weakness, hoped to provoke Israeli security forces and citizens to attack innocent Arabs, causing the latter to be alienated and thus support the fedayeen.[16] Although there was some success in this endeavor, the military government made conscious efforts to control the situation. Rather than adopt a complacent attitude, Israel acted vigorously to curb excessive reactions by its citizens and security forces. The fact that on a number of occasions Dayan and other ministers became personally involved indicated that the prevention of counterterror had received attention at the highest levels of government. This effort, plus the punishment of those responsible for attacks on innocent Arabs, prevented the emergence of a pattern of counterterror which would have undoubtedly played into fedayeen hands.[17]

Demonstration of Potency

The fifth means of gaining popular support, demonstrations of potency, was also used by the fedayeen. Through terrorism within the target area, dramatic gestures abroad (e.g. hijacking of airliners), and an organizational presence, the fedayeen sought to convince their Palestinian brethren and the world that they were a force to be reckoned with. In conjunction with terrorism, guerrilla attacks—especially in 1969-1970—were designed to demonstrate fedayeen potency by gaining the military initiative.[18] Unfortunately for the insurgents, it was necessary, as suggested in Chapter 2, to gain freedom of action in order to sustain the momentum required for keeping the military initiative. Yet, because of Israeli countermeasures and their own inability to systematically organize within the occupied areas and Israel, the Palestinians were forced to operate from contiguous countries. In such a disadvantageous position, it was imperative that freedom of action be retained in Jordan, Syria, and Lebanon, if the intensity and number of attacks were to increase to the point where Arabs in the target area would be convinced the guerrillas were succeeding. As it turned out, several considerations led the regimes of the adjacent states, particularly Jordan, to restrict fedayeen activity. By 1971, freedom to operate from Jordan, the front the guerrillas considered the most important, was totally proscribed and activities in Lebanon were sporadic.

The last element of demonstration of potency, an organizational presence, had an important bearing on the acquisition of popular support. Though material assistance made available by the insurgent organizations no doubt had a positive effect on recruitment, a more important factor seems to have been the opportunity for political action as a means to redress grievances that was provided by the Palestinian groups. In an empirical study of the political socialization of young fedayeen, Yasumasa Kuroda found a strong positive relationship between political activism and joining a guerrilla organization. Since membership in a Palestinian insurgent group fulfilled a pre-existing need for political activity, the presence of organizational structures emerged as an important variable in recruitment.[19]

Where the fedayeen were able to create a viable organizational apparatus, as in the refugee camps in the Arab states surrounding Israel, they enjoyed impressive support. Their failure to establish a functioning shadow government anywhere in the occupied areas, by contrast, meant that they were unable to fashion and maintain systematic linkages with the population. Since the Israeli institutions proved more capable of meeting at least the material needs of the people, whereas the Palestinian guerrillas could provide little in terms of material and psychological inducements, it was not surprising that the fedayeen were confronted with a good deal of indifference and, at times, hostility.

The fedayeen failure to establish an effective organization in the crucial West Bank and the Israeli success in apprehending terrorists and political cadres were not unknown to the Palestinians on the West Bank. Nor were they unaware of the willingness of captured fedayeen to inform on their comrades. All of this seemed to demonstrate impotency rather than potency.[20]

The Palestinian propaganda apparatus was another factor which, in the long term, contributed to fedayeen problems in winning support. While the insurgents were successful in portraying Karamah as a great victory, although the Jordanians did a good deal of the fighting, the credibility of fedayeen was being questioned by Israelis and Arabs alike by 1970. Indeed, any review of fedayeen claims, in publications or the press, led to the inescapable conclusion they were inflated. E. Naawas, an Arab writer, noted the wide disparity between fedayeen and Israeli reports caused bewilderment among Arabs, while the editor of PFLP's *Al-Hadaf* ("The Aim") criticized the tendency to report fedayeen actions without any effort to establish the accuracy of the information. In short, Arabs themselves were doubtful about the veracity of insurgent claims.[21]

The fact that Palestinian ranks contained a number of "opportunists" and individuals who exhibited "conceit and exhibitionism" was also a problem that, in the long run, detracted from their image as self-sacrificing revolutionaries. Moreover, Farouk Qaddumi of *Fatah* cited the domineering attitude of some fedayeen as a factor which contributed to the September 1970 clash with the Jordanian army.[22]

In 1970-1971, the fedayeen movement had reached a low point. The inability to gain systematic active support was partially responsible for this development. Nevertheless, since it would be a mistake to argue that the fedayeen enjoyed no support from the people during the 1967-1973 period, it is necessary to review briefly popular support as it relates to Israel, the occupied areas, and refugees in the contiguous states.

Popular Support Constituencies

Israel

In 1967, there were over 300,000 Arabs in Israel, located, for the most part, in exclusive villages or urban areas. Although granted full citizenship—including the right to serve in the Knesset—and enjoying higher educational and economic standards than their brethren outside Israel, the Arabs suffered economic, political, and psychological deprivation. While the military administration and travel restrictions under which they had lived since 1948 were eliminated in 1966, the Arabs remained the object of distrust, a point clearly evidenced by their exemption from military duty and prohibition from participating in classified defense projects and holding posts in the Ministry of Defense. Though such security restraints may have contributed to Arab alienation, a more profound and enduring cause was the inevitable tension that resulted from being an Arab in a Jewish state. As Professor Leonard Fein has put it:

> Nearly all the symbols which unify Israel's Jews are meaningless to its Arabs. Ingathering of the exiles, reviving the Hebrew language, the Bible's centrality, the army, Israel's independence day, elicit either no response or antagonism. That the Government has sought, for various reasons, to encourage local responsibility and to promote economic development is paltry compensation for the Arab's certain knowledge that he is an outsider. Moreover, economic development is a mixed blessing, for its obvious advantages are limited by the threats it poses to the traditional order. Similarly, local responsibility, where it means deviation from clan politics, is a troublesome innovation.[23]

Then, commenting on Israel's efforts to bridge the gap between Arab and Jew, Fein further remarks:

> Yet all this is insufficient, for in the final analysis both Jew and Arab are aware that the Arabs are not truly welcome. Few Jewish tears would be shed were all of Israel's Arabs voluntarily to leave the country. Israel's ideology,

however, is still a Jewish ideology, in which the Arabs have no role to play. Efforts made prior to the State's establishment to move towards some kind of binational policy, based on communal autonomy, have long since become irrelevant. It is quite clear that, at least as long as we can see, no Arab could occupy a major cabinet position. But at the heart of the matter it is not at all clear that, according to Israel's public ethic, an Arab should be able to hold such a position. In the United States, where until recently no Negro could have been appointed to the cabinet, the public ethic suffers no such confusion: any American has the right to such an appointment. The Israeli dilemma is that the very powerful ethic of equal opportunity and full political equality must compete against the equally powerful ethic of a Jewish state. It is not a question of simple bigotry, in the sense in which the American South, for example, has known bigotry, nor a sham defense of "separate but equal" facilities. Rather the notion of an Arab President of Israel is rejected by the Jewish population because of its historical impropriety, because it would introduce fundamental doubts about the reasoning behind Zionism and about the most basic understandings of what Israel and Israelness mean.[24]

As if the situation were not bad enough, the Arabs' identity crisis was exacerbated by the fact that they were regarded with some suspicion in the Arab world. Indeed, there was even fear of Jordan among Israeli Arabs because the latter country regarded them as traitors, a situation that partially explained what one Arab member of the Knesset described as the Israeli Arabs' ambivalence concerning which side they wished to see win the June War.[25]

Given the land grievances, economic inequalities, and psychological identity crisis, Israeli Arabs appeared to be a potential source of support for a strong Palestinian national liberation movement. That the fedayeen did enjoy some success in recruiting Israeli Arabs was demonstrated as early as June 1968, when twenty-four Israeli Arabs were arrested for subversive activity. The following year one commentator reported more Israeli Arabs arrested for "acts against the state" than in the whole previous decade.[26] Yet, since the fedayeen were unable to extend their organization into Israel in any substantial way whatsoever, the Israelis found it relatively easy to maintain the balance of coercive and institutional control in their favor; thus, Israeli Arabs could only join or actively support the fedayeen at very high risk of capture, reprisal, and punishment. As it happened, despite some increased concern that Israeli Arabs were becoming more responsive to the fedayeen and were joining their ranks in 1969, the majority avoided giving active support to insurgents. Not only was the number of Arabs directly associated with fedayeen organizations insignificant, but the population largely ignored fedayeen appeals for small sacrifices, such as boycotting the 1969 elections.[27]

The Palestinians from time to time displayed an interest in winning converts within the Jewish population. However, since even Jewish radicals did not accept the Palestinian notion of a "secular, democratic, and nonsectarian state" as a viable one, the chances of gaining, at minimum, a foothold within the Israeli left was very remote.[28] Consequently, the Palestinian guerrillas had to concede that the effort of converting Jews by changing their attitudes would be a long-term affair.

The Occupied Areas: The Crucial Constituency

Of all the Palestinian communities, the ones in the occupied areas, especially the West Bank, were most important, because the success or failure of the strategy of protracted people's war was contingent on their mobilization. If the clandestine bases *Fatah* claimed in early 1968 to have established in the occupied areas were to expand and function effectively, support of the population was absolutely necessary; this was especially true if the efficiency of the Israeli security forces was to be offset.[29]

In the months following the June War, the civil disobedience and restiveness in the occupied areas seemed to suggest the people might support actively a protracted war of liberation.[30] The positive response of segments of the population to the fedayeen cause was indicated both by functioning terrorist cells and other dissident activity as well as by countermeasures the Israelis were compelled to take against the local population.[31]

While there was no question about the existence of popular support for the fedayeen, there was a question about its extent and significance. Besides being unable to establish a widespread network of guerrilla bases, the fedayeen increasingly found the rudimentary underground units they did have being uncovered by the Israelis, often with the help of local Arabs. Instead of finding shelter and concealment within the local milieu, the insurgents often found betrayal.[32] Thus, by February 1969, they were under orders not to contact the local population, since it could not be trusted. When, as noted in the previous chapter, the "Voice of *Fatah*," on November 26, 1969, called on its remaining cells to disband, it seemed quite clear that the fedayeen had not received the support in terms of concealment and shelter which was necessary if they were to move about and operate undetected.[33]

Although some terrorist cells continued to exist in the occupied areas, especially in Gaza, through 1973, they bore little resemblance to the parallel hierarchies that had appeared in successful protracted wars of the past. In fact, as early as 1970, the attitude of the West Bank population toward the resistance had become generally apathetic.

The failure to organize a clandestine network to sustain continuous terrorist and guerrilla operations and the apathy of the people were not the only indications of Palestinian problems. Electoral participation, application for Israeli citizenship, a decline in popularity of fedayeen leaders, and the emergence of proindependence forces in the West Bank also suggested that the insurgents' influence with the people, which was tenuous to begin with, had weakened considerably.

Despite fedayeen assassination threats and pleas for a total boycott, 10,000 of 34,000 eligible voters turned out for the 1969 general election in Jerusalem.[34] Even though the Palestinians subsequently argued that the Israelis threatened the people by implying that those who did not vote would lose municipal services, the fact remained that a significant section of the population displayed little inclination to make any real sacrifice for the revolution.[35] An even more serious deterioration took place in the spring of 1972, when over eighty percent of the eligible voters again defied the fedayeen by voting in twelve municipal elections on the West Bank (see Chapter 4). While the Israeli success was mitigated by the fact that only 10,537 male taxpayers out of a population base of 300,000 were eligible to cast ballots, because of a Jordanian law which barred refugees and women from voting, Arafat, nonetheless, conceded the Israeli gain.[36]

Another index of the Palestinian inability to attract popular support was the February 1970 decision of fifty East Jerusalem Arabs, including the noted personality Hussa el-Alami, to sever their ties with the Arab world and take up Israeli citizenship. Since this group was composed of elite middle and upper-class personages to whom many in the traditional Palestinian community looked for leadership, it was a blow to fedayeen attempts to alienate the people from the military government.[37] While the vast majority of citizens did not take steps similar to this one, neither did they provide meaningful support for the fedayeen.

Also indicative of the decline in popularity of the insurgents was the fading attraction of Arafat, Habash, and other fedayeen chieftains. A poll published by *Al-Quds* on January 15, 1971, revealed that 36.5 percent chose Nasser as the man of the year in the Arab world and 36.5 percent chose Mu'ammar Al-Qadhdhafi of Libya.[38]

The existence of a group within the Palestinian population of the West Bank that sought to play a role independent of the fedayeen in creating a new future provided even stronger evidence that support for the insurgents was lacking. As early as September 1967, a number of professional and business leaders had quietly discussed taking the initiative in reaching a settlement with Israel that might lead to an Arab state separate from Jordan.[39] That such a stance was dangerous, in light of both fedayeen and Jordanian objections, was demonstrated by a December 1967 bazooka attack against the home of Dr. H. T. Faroubi, a leading advocate of the Palestinian state idea.[40] Such events, combined with fedayeen threats, forced those who supported an alternative to the insurgents into silence until 1970. Then, on February 17, 1970, the mayor of Hebron called for creation of a "Palestinian entity" on the West Bank, saying the Arab refugees were being used as pawns by the Arab governments and guerrilla actions were preventing peace in the Middle East.[41] Within a few months, reports, including one in *Al-Haya* in Beirut, claimed that serious consideration was being given by West Bank Palestinians to their role in negotiations and the possibility of creating a Palestinian state. This brought an admonition from the "Voice of *Fatah*" that those supporting the Palestinian state would "pay for their activities."[42] Shortly thereafter, the acceptance of the Rogers peace plan by several Arab states led *Fatah* to warn "Palestinian quarters" against accepting the American plan since the Central Committee of the Palestinian Resistance intended to set up a revolutionary court to try anyone who moved in the name of the Palestinian people outside the framework of the revolution. Moreover, *Fatah* was also perturbed by petitions emanating from the Palestinian community claiming that the people were tired of violence.[43]

In spite of fedayeen threats, the majority of the population on the West Bank was reported to be in favor of Nasser's acceptance of the American plan. One observer commented in September 1970 as follows:

> Indeed, never have the fedayeen organizations been so unpopular in the occupied territories as in the past few weeks; never has the cleavage been so great between the Palestinians living under Israeli control and those outside of Palestine, who claim to represent all Palestinians.[44]

More startling was an indication that Hikmat al-Masri, a West Bank Palestinian, had risked fedayeen fury by traveling immediately to Amman after acceptance of the American plan, with a declaration of support from leading figures on the West Bank.[45]

After the losses sustained by the fedayeen in the Jordanian civil war, the West Bank Palestinians were emboldened to take further steps in defiance of the guerrillas.[46] Several active groups emerged which sought varying degrees of independence, some rejecting the traditional leadership. One organization, the Palestine Nationalist Alignment, composed of middle-class and labor elements, demanded a United Nations referendum to determine the future of the Palestinians in the occupied areas and reportedly rejected both Hussein and the fedayeen. A more traditional group met in Hebron on October 17 and decided to set up a body to represent the Palestinians and ask for Israeli permission to hold a general assembly of mayors, former Jordanian ministers, and other notables from West Bank towns.[47] That the fedayeen considered such independent voices as anathema was clear from their charges that Israel was plotting with "defeatist elements" to set up a "puppet state."[48]

It made little difference to the insurgent leadership that traditional elites and newer leaders opposed Jordan's military operations against the fedayeen. What was significant was their desire to seek a solution, divorced from the PLO, acknowledging Israel's right to exist as an independent state.[49] Fortunately for the insurgents, the Israeli eschewal of political negotiations with the Palestinians on the West Bank, in favor of dealing with Hussein, as well as the hesitation of prominent Arab leaders, emasculated any hopes that schemes independent of the PLO would come to fruition in the near future.[50] This fact notwithstanding, independent political stirrings on the West Bank, which continued through 1973, made it clear that support for the fedayeen had diminished.[51]

By 1970, many of the links the fedayeen had with the West Bank population had been broken. This turn of events, however, did not mean the Arabs had embraced the Israelis; on the contrary, a number of observers were quick to note that most people wanted Israel to withdraw but were not prepared to force the issue.[52]

Where the PLO did retain a significant degree of support was in the turmoil-ridden Gaza Strip. While the continuing detection and incarceration of terrorists through 1971 indicated that the guerrilla underground had not been totally destroyed, it also suggested that the security of the terrorists was precarious, a conclusion buttressed by the guerrilla assassination campaign against collaborators. Nevertheless, since terrorist incidents continued and were attributed to the fedayeen by Israel, the inescapable conclusion was that a modicum of active popular support was forthcoming in Gaza.[53] The geographic separation of Gaza from the West Bank, however, prevented events in the strip from having a contagious effect.

One reason suggested for the disparity of support for the fedayeen between Gaza and the West Bank was that residents of Gaza were "old refugees" (1948) who had little to gain from a settlement, which, at best, might return only some of them to the Israeli portion of Palestine; in contrast, many inhabitants of the West Bank were permanent residents who stood to jeopardize their homes and livelihood by aiding the insurgents.[54] In addition, the West Bank population had experienced the effectiveness of the Israeli security apparatus for over three years and therefore harbored few illusions about toppling the military government.[55] Moreover, the improved standard of living and well-being of people in the West Bank meant that they had more to lose by supporting the guerrillas. This much was admitted by Nabil Shaath, a *Fatah* spokesman, during an interview with *Free Palestine*. Although he attributed the situation to economic exploitation, the point was still clear when Shaath, asked about the failure of passive resistance on the West Bank, commented:

> Yes. It has been a little disappointing—I think compared to Gaza, the West Bank is a disaster. I really think one should talk very frankly about these things and there is no sense in making the picture look any rosier. The West Bank is a situation of classic economic exploitation, there is no better example of a Marxian application of labour exploitation than there is on the West Bank. But you see it takes people time before they start realising that they are being exploited. You get a guy who has been unemployed for years and he has been in Jordanian jails, he has been beaten by Jordanian security officers and has been rotting in the camp for want of employment and if he got employment he got a very low wage and so on. And now he is offered jobs, although he is paid less than half of what an Israeli-Jew gets, he does not yet compare himself with that Israeli-Jew, he still compares himself with the "bad old days," in which he was unemployed. But people don't realise it yet—it takes some time—and that's why I think it was less of a good show than Gaza.[56]

In short, since the old refugees had less to lose than the settled Palestinians on the West Bank, they were more inclined than the latter to support the fedayeen.[57]

The Palestinian Diaspora

The inability to obtain substantial support in the occupied areas, which was due, in large measure, to the effectiveness of the Israelis and the guerrillas' own organizational shortcomings (*Fatah* showed some hesitancy about organizing), forced the fedayeen to turn to the 540,000 Palestinians located in refugee camps in Jordan, Lebanon, and Syria.[58] In this endeavor there was far more success, given the bitterness and frustrations inherent in the consignment of such a large number of people to poverty-stricken camps, the identity crisis stemming from the lack of integration into the host states, and the failure of the refugees to recover their lost lands. One report aptly summarized the grievances that could be exploited by fedayeen exoteric appeals as follows:

> What does distinguish these people is the loss of those things which constitute a heritage—the home which provides privacy for one's family . . . the land and property which belonged to one's ancestors and with which one associates his own childhood . . . a trade or job with which one can relate to his community . . . and a nationality and pride in that nationality. These are the elements of life, the natural rights which do not exist for the refugee. He has

lost, in short, those parts of his identity upon which every individual depends for his self-respect.[59]

When the miserable conditions of the camps were added to the losses just described, the refugee population truly appeared ripe for revolutionary activity.[60]

Within the context of these conditions, the fedayeen argued after the 1967 War that since the Arab governments had not redressed the grievances because of their failure to eliminate the cause, Zionism, the Palestinians had to rely on themselves. The only way to be successful in this undertaking, it was contended, was to wage a people's war of liberation against Israel. When the fedayeen fought successfully at Karamah, the receptivity to this appeal increased dramatically as scores of frustrated individuals were given new hope and joined the insurgents, merging with a number of intellectuals from other sections of the diaspora. As things turned out, Karamah was to be the most significant demonstration of potency during the period covered by this study, a fact which led the Palestinians themselves to claim it as a major turning point in their struggle.[61] Though the fedayeen lost momentum in 1970, the fact remained that Karamah was a key event inspiring active support in the diaspora and moral support in the Arab world in general.

Besides the demonstration of potency at Karamah and the esoteric and exoteric appeals directed at the inhabitants of the refugee camps, the organizational structures of the fedayeen were used to mobilize the people. Through organizations like the Palestinian Red Crescent, the fedayeen sought to provide a number of services—education, medical care, welfare assistance, payments to families of dead and wounded guerrillas, etc.—for the Palestinians in Lebanon and Jordan.[62] In many camps in these countries the fedayeen were reported to be in de facto control, and hence maintained the balance of institutional support in their favor. Although the Jordanian civil war returned the camps to government control, by that time scores of dispossessed refugees had renewed their identification with Palestine as a result of the political socialization they underwent during the years the fedayeen held sway in the camps.[63] It was the author's impression in 1977 that the impact of socialization had not worn off and that the refugees could probably be reactivated, were it not for very tight surveillance and restrictions imposed by the government.

Summary and Conclusions

Like other insurgent organizations, the fedayeen had explicitly recognized the importance of popular support for successful revolutionary warfare. Thus, they tried to win active support by a variety of means.

Esoteric appeals were directed at the Palestinian intelligentsia and, to a lesser extent, at the masses. In the first case, the Fanonism of *Fatah* and the Marxism-Leninism of the PFLP and PDF were used to convince listeners that there was a cogent explanation for the plight of the Palestinian people and a solution to their problems. One could infer from the large number of intellectuals in the left-wing groups that ideology did play a role in recruitment, either per se or as a reinforcement of already existing convictions rooted in concrete grievances. As for the masses, the esoteric approach provided a target for their hatred by emphasizing the centrality of Zionism as the source of all deprivations; it also provided hope for the future by promising that armed struggle would rectify the situation.

The esoteric appeal, particularly the Marxist-Leninist rhetoric, was found to have its disadvantages, since it was repugnant to many members of the middle class, who might otherwise have thrown themselves and their resources behind the revolution. Moreover, the esoteric appeal was a source of friction with the Arab regimes. Since the latter could hardly have been indifferent to organizations calling for their demise, there was bound to be either hostility or limits on support for the guerrillas. In fact, the vitriolic rhetoric and ideologically motivated violence of the left-wing fedayeen were major contributions to the debacle of 1970. The reduction of the guerrillas to relative impotency resulted in a rapid loss of popularity, so much so that one observer reported that they operated in a largely indifferent and often hostile Arab environment.[64] Thus, esoteric appeals indirectly affected popular support in an adverse way.

Nevertheless, to focus solely on the problems caused by the Marxists would be a serious mistake, for it would ignore the powerful attraction of the nationalist appeal which was inherent in the theoretical constructs of all fedayeen groups. While it may not have been sufficient to generate widespread active support, the appeal of Palestinian nationalism did lead to a new sense of identification and communal solidarity, especially among the young. This situation, as we shall see in the final chapter, would shatter Israeli complacency in 1976.

The second and most persuasive appeal made by the fedayeen was exoteric. Given the deprivation and misery in the refugee camps and in Gaza, the insurgents found a tinderbox of revolutionary potential. In contrast, West Bank Palestinians, who had retained their homes and livelihood and had come to experience an improved standard of living under the occupation, were less and less attracted by the fedayeen exoteric appeals. Overall, however, the exoteric appeal seemed to be most powerful, since the foundation of fedayeen strength was in the refugee camps in the adjacent states, precisely the places where insurgents were stressing concrete grievances and were being well received.

Terror was employed by the fedayeen, at least in part, to demonstrate their own strength and Israel's weakness in order to win popular support. Yet its indiscriminate use, often resulting in Arab casualties and/or restrictions on the Arab communities, rendered it counterproductive. Worse yet for the fedayeen image were the well-known and gradually increasing Israeli successes in destroying many terrorist cells and networks. The decline of the fedayeen associated with this development seemed to be confirmed by the penchant of insurgents in 1970 and 1971 to employ terror increasingly against fellow Arabs (collaborators or rivals) and less against Israelis.

The counterterror ploy was also used by the fedayeen, but not with great effect. Though there were cases of overreaction by the Jewish population, the military government's vigorous response precluded a pattern of indiscriminate violence from emerging.

By demonstrating their potency through operations inside the target area and along the border, the fedayeen tried to gain recognition of their cause and to win support of the Palestinian populace, Arab masses, and world opinion. The basic aim was to create the impression that they had the military initiative, and, by so doing, to inspire people to support them. One problem, however, was that freedom to operate and organize from contiguous states was necessary, at least in the early stages, because of the high caliber of the Israeli security forces and the effectiveness of their operations within the target area. Unfortunately for the fedayeen, this freedom was eventually undercut by host governments, with the result that guerrilla and terrorist operations were crippled.

A comparative assessment of various constituencies from which the fedayeen hoped to extract support makes it clear that their greatest success was in the diaspora, particularly in the refugee camps where grievances were many and the fedayeen organization operational. Within the occupied areas, where the establishment of popular bases was considered a sine qua non for a successful people's war, there was an overall failure to obtain active popular support. While some Palestinians did respond to fedayeen appeals, the early network of terrorist cells was neither expanded nor transformed into parallel hierarchies. Nor did the civilian unrest of 1968-1969 increase to the point where a general uprising could be said to have existed. On the contrary, on both these scores the fedayeen retrogressed, with terrorist cells being gradually eliminated and civilian unrest being reduced to sporadic gestures. To make matters worse, a number of Arabs betrayed fedayeen operations, while others eased the administrative task of Israel by staying at their posts. Indeed, there was little the insurgents could do about the latter situation since the West Bank population had come to expect the maintenance of certain essential services. Reestablishment of the standard of living after the June War and gradual improvement thereafter gave the West Bank population an interest in stability, although not in identification with Israel. To accommodate this desire for stability, and at the same time avoid political identification with Israel, independent Palestinians began to probe the possibilities of peace negotiations and a Palestinian state, both of which were considered to be unequivocal evils by the fedayeen. Given the objectives of the fedayeen, the inevitable conclusion was that a large gap separated them from the West Bank population. While the situation in Gaza was somewhat better from the fedayeen point of view, the Israelis were able to isolate the strip and contain the continuing terrorism.

As for Israel proper, the fedayeen were unable to exploit significantly the potential support of an Arab community which could not identify with a Jewish state. The key factor here was, no doubt, that Israeli authority was pervasive. As for the Jewish population, it was quixotic to believe the fedayeen could obtain their support, with the exception of a few youths on the "New Left" fringe.

In the wake of defeat and humiliation in 1967, it was not surprising that successes such as Karamah attracted attention and won the "hearts and minds" of Arabs who were seeking ways to redeem their honor and dignity. With the Arab armies defeated and demoralized, it did not take long for the fedayeen could obtain its support, with the exception of a few youths on fortunes of the fedayeen began to take a negative turn in 1970, their support dropped off sharply. On the eve of the October War it was hard to reach any conclusion other than one which suggested that the insurgents had failed to mobilize the masses for the armed struggle. In short, the fedayeen did not gain the substantial or meaningful active popular support required to conduct a protracted people's war against a strong and determined adversary.

Organization and Cohesion

Organization and cohesion are two factors which have a critical bearing on the overall fortunes and progress of insurgent movements. Accordingly, the Palestinian resistance will be carefully examined in terms of the structural dimensions of scope, cohesion, and complexity, as well as performance of instrumental and expressive functions. At the end of the chapter, some theoretical propositions involving the relationships among organizational variables and other major factors in the study will be developed.

Scope

The scope of the fedayeen movement encompasses the Palestinians in Israel, the occupied areas, the refugee camps in states surrounding Israel, and the Arab world at large. By 1970 there was a general consensus that the combined strength of the major fedayeen organizations was somewhere in the neighborhood of 25,000. In addition, it was estimated that the strength of the regular PLA was about 15,000.[1] The major popular support for these forces came from the diaspora, particularly the refugees in Jordan, Lebanon, and Syria who, according to figures published in June 1971, totalled 766,615, 171,673, and 155,607 respectively.[2] Support from different population segments varied with the complexity and extension of fedayeen organizational structures and their functional performance, a point discussed later. Prior to considering complexity, extension, and functional aspects, however, it is important to assess the overriding problem of unity.

Cohesion

Analyzing cohesion presents a challenge because of the inherent and sometimes bewildering complexity of the Palestinian case. One way to approach this problem is to describe and differentiate among the various organizations. However,while this method has the advantage of accenting the nature of the groups, it tends to place less emphasis on intergroup conflicts and their impact. Since the latter are especially important as far as the study is concerned, the question of cohesion will be examined within a chronological context, which, though complicated, focuses attention on patterns and sources of factionalism, efforts made to overcome it, and the effects it had on external support and relations with the Arab states. Our account begins in 1967.

Patterns and Sources of Disunity—1967-1969

Following the debacle of June 1967, there was a gradual proliferation of commando organizations with a heterogeneity of political and ideological views and various links with the Arab states. Since internal cohesion was viewed as a "practical and theoretical prerequisite to liberation,"[3] there were continued attempts to overcome differences and unify the groups in a common effort against Israel.

Despite the fact that the PLO/PLA role in the June defeat discredited the leadership, its chairman, Ahmad ash-Shuqayri, attempted to establish the PLO as the leading organization in the emerging postwar resistance, an intention underscored by his attendance at the Khartoum Conference in August 1967. Unfortunately for Shuqayri, the PLO's chief rival, *Fatah*, was fast becoming the most popular organization. No doubt encouraged by its progress, *Fatah*, in November 1967, called on the PLO to disband and turn over its funds to *Fatah*, and urged members of the PLA to join *Fatah*'s ranks. Trying to maintain his position within the movement, Shuqayri countered, a few weeks later, with the announcement that the Revolutionary Command Council for the Liberation of Palestine had been set up in order to unify the guerrilla organizations, coordinate military operations, and increase the tempo of activity against Israel. When this move to buttress his position within the resistance movement failed, and most PLO members demanded his resignation, Shuqayri finally stepped aside and was replaced by Yahya Hammouda.[4]

Despite Shuqayri's removal, differences between the PLO and other organizations persisted, and the PLO did not attend three days of meetings in January 1968 involving thirteen guerrilla groups, which set up a joint command, divided into three corps, to direct operations against Israel.[5] The fact that the PLO's principal competitor, *Fatah*, had called the meetings and thus appeared to be assuming direction of the fedayeen movement probably explained the boycott. It no doubt also accounted for a PLO countermove, which called upon the Palestine National Council (PNC), the larger parliamentary-type body of the PLO, to unify guerrilla activity, and for PLO insistence that it was the mother organization of the resistance, not merely one of several parties.[6] In addition to the struggle for power, an important factor in friction between the PLO and *Fatah* at the time was the former's wish to coordinate strategy with the Arab states and the latter's desire to operately independently.[7] As things developed, the fortunes of *Fatah* continued to improve, particularly after its participation in the Karamah battle in March 1968.

In spite of their differences, *Fatah* and the PLO finally agreed that the latter should become the coordinating mechanism for resistance activity.[8] At the fourth session of the PNC in Cairo (July 1968) the PLO and its regular military wing, the PLA, were allocated fifty seats; *Fatah* and the minor groups received thirty-eight.[9] The PFLP, which had surfaced in December 1967 as the result of a merger of the Arab Nationalist Movement (ANM) and two smaller organizations, was given ten seats, a situation which led to eventual difficulties with its larger rivals.[10]

The Cairo meeting confirmed the order of ascendancy of the guerrilla organizations and the gradual reconciliation of the PLO and *Fatah*. The PLO had been reported amenable to a political settlement with Israel if certain rights (unspecified) were protected, whereas *Fatah* opposed a settlement; a PNC resolution rejecting SC-242 and endorsing armed struggle as the only way to liberate Palestine appeared to close the gap. While the formation of a military council made up of representatives from each organization was viewed as a further step toward unity, the failure to agree on the composition of an executive committee suggested that significant differences remained. In fact, *Fatah* voiced the opinion that the resolutions, while outwardly seeking unity, might bring about the liquidation of the resistance.[11]

Shortly after the PNC meeting, *Fatah*'s apprehensions about continued disunity and factionalism were given substance when a major dispute arose between the PLO Executive Committee (PLO-EC) and the PLA. Responding to a PLO-EC announcement on July 31 that General Abd al-Razah al-Yahya was to replace General Subhi al-Jabiri as commander of the PLA, a group of dissident PLA officers, who were said to have been purged in July, placed al-Yahya under house arrest and issued a communiqué demanding that the politicians in the PLO-EC refrain from interfering in command matters. Although the PLO threatened to act against the "mutineers," the latter held out, and on September 1, al-Yahya signed a letter of resignation. When the PLO-EC stood its ground and refused to reverse its decision to relieve Jabiri, he, too, resigned. Even though Misbah al-Badayri was then appointed commander, the PLO-EC was able to reappoint Yahya a year later without a repetition of the incident.[12]

Despite the compromise, most fedayeen leaders continued to view the PLA with suspicion because of its close ties with the Arab governments, especially Syria. For its part, the PLA resented the fact that the fedayeen organizations received all the accolades in the struggle against Israel, as well as the lion's share of the financial support from the Arab states.[13] Both grievances would remain and later merge with personal and ideological factors to produce a PLA challenge to Yasir Arafat in February 1971.

While the PLO-PLA dispute was taking place in September 1968, there seemed to be some minor movement toward fusion when *Fatah* announced that the Palestine People's National Liberation Front (PPNLF) and the Free Palestinians Movement (FPM) had both joined its ranks. A subsequent denial by the former, however, cast doubt on the efforts to achieve unity, as did the breakaway from *Fatah* of a new leftist group called the Popular Struggle Front (PSF).[14]

More important than the fission and fusion involving *Fatah* and the smaller groups was the intensifying rivalry between *Fatah* and the PFLP, a rivalry which time would reveal as the most serious split in the fedayeen movement. In the fall of 1968 the signs of mutual antagonism between the two groups were already evident. As far as the PFLP was concerned, *Fatah* was a reckless, romantic, and ill-disciplined organization that ignored the scientific imperatives of revolutionary warfare and made itself and the people conspicuous targets for Israeli shellings.[15] It also did not help when both groups began to claim credit for the same operations, as was the case, for instance, in the November 1968 market bombing in Jerusalem.[16]

During the remainder of the fall, the uncertainty within the fedayeen ranks continued. In a decision aimed at providing better coordination, a guerrilla organization called Commando Vanguard merged with *Fatah*, and another known as Vanguards of Martyrdom for the Liberation of Palestine announced that it would soon do likewise. Shortly thereafter, the PLO announced that it, *Fatah*, and the Syrian-sponsored *Sa'iqa* were forming a military coordination council, and the PFLP said it would consider participation once it settled a crisis within its own organization.[17] Essentially, the problem within the PFLP involved an attempt by leftist elements to wrest control of the organization from George Habash at a time when he was imprisoned in Syria. The attempted coup, which was led by Nayef Hawatmeh, a thirty-seven-year-old Marxist, came to naught when Habash resumed active leadership of the PFLP after a November 3 jailbreak. The episode, however, proved to be the precursor of more serious events in early 1969.

The lack of unity among guerrilla organizations was a factor contributing to a November clash with the Jordanian army. The fighting, apparently instigated by a unit led by Tahir Dablan which called itself *Kataeb al-Nasir*, eventually involved the main commando organizations. Once the dispute with Amman was resolved, the PFLP, as it would do in similar situations in the future, complicated matters by initially rejecting the agreement. Underlying the rejection was the ideological position of the PFLP, which held that the overthrow of the Jordanian regime was essential for a successful war of liberation against Israel. This view clashed with the PLO-*Fatah* desire to reach a modus vivendi with Amman. Further accentuating the Jordanian distrust of the fedayeen, which had been generated by the ideology of the PFLP, was the fact that other guerrilla groups, such as *Sa'iqa*, were under the influence of Arab states hostile to Jordan. This led King Hussein to comment during the November crisis that *Sa'iqa* was more interested in Jordan than in liberating the occupied areas.[18]

A final aspect of the November crisis that merits attention in this context was the formation of the Palestinian Emergency Council for the purpose of protecting the revolution. As with analogous moves in future crises, this action, which had the appearance of creating unity, proved to be evanescent and ineffective.

If unity proved to be elusive in 1968, events in early 1969 hardly foreshadowed a brighter future. During February, the fifth session of the PNC convened in Cairo and elected a new executive committee with Arafat as its chairman, thus marking the rise of *Fatah* to the position of primacy in the fedayeen movement. In addition, *Sa'iqa* joined the PNC. Offsetting these trends toward unity, however, were the decisions of both the PLA and the PFLP to boycott the PNC conclave because of dissatisfaction with the allocation of seats. In fact, the PLA commander publicly charged that the PLO-EC had ignored his organization's "fair demands and proposals." To compound the problems, the PFLP itself splintered, giving rise to two new organizations, the Popular Front for the Liberation of Palestine-General Command (PFLP-GC) and the Popular Democratic Front for the Liberation of Palestine (referred to variously as PDF and PDFLP). The PDF was composed of the same radical Marxist faction which had been involved in the coup attempt during the fall of 1968. Of the two breakaways from the PFLP, the PDF split was the more serious since attempts by Habash to repress the *Hawatmeh* faction led to a gun battle in Amman. While mediation by *Fatah* eventually brought an end to the violence, the episode created an enduring reservoir of bitterness between the PFLP and PDF.[19]

Habash condemned the clash as "infantile leftism" and asserted it would soon be forgotten. He suggested that the root cause of the conflict was a disagreement over the primary aspect of the struggle: whether to concentrate on efforts against Israel, or, as the *Hawatmeh* faction was urging, to break all relations of subservience with the Arab regimes and devote resources to overthrowing reactionary Arab governments. While Habash could agree with *Hawatmeh* on the question of deposing reactionary regimes, he felt that relations with progressive Arab regimes were important in terms of external support. Such differences, according to PFLP members, reflected a general cleavage between members of the old Arab Nationalist Movement, who emphasized nationalism ahead of socialism, and young idealists, who were more interested in fomenting a socialist revolution throughout the Arab world. In the final analysis, the dispute was not a simple question of nationalism versus socialism, but rather, a question of which was to be emphasized.[20]

In addition to the differences in ideological emphasis, there was a tactical divergence between the PFLP and PDF, since the latter repudiated the PFLP's terrorist operations outside the Middle East, such as plane hijackings, as damaging to the revolution.[21] Although on this point the PDF was in agreement with the non-Marxist wing of the resistance, the link was by no means sufficient to bridge the larger dispute between the PLO-*Fatah* wing and the Marxists, which was rooted in disagreements over external support, tactics, and ideology.

In the view of Habash, the financial support *Fatah* accepted from the "reactionary" states was tantamount to a loss of honor.[22] On the question of tactics, the *Fatah* wing claimed that its operations were designed to avoid civilian casualties, and that operations outside the Middle East cost the movement political, moral, and material support both in the Arab world and outside it.[23] In contrast, the PFLP (but not the PDF) made it known that it would hit Jewish property everywhere. That this was no empty threat was made trenchantly evident by a series of bombing incidents in public places in Israel and the occupied areas, as well as by several operations abroad (hijackings, attacks on aircraft, and attacks on airline and shipping offices).

The differences between Fanonism and Marxism were also a profoundly divisive force within the fedayeen movement. In contradistinction to the PLO-*Fatah* wing's Fanonist orientation, which easily accommodated cooperation with Arab states, regardless of their regimes, the PFLP and PDF visualized the conflict with Zionism as one that involved inevitable class warfare. According to their exegesis, the Zionists and the reactionary Arab classes were inextricably linked to the major capitalist powers (world imperialism) in the pursuit of economic aggrandizement, at the expense of the working classes and peasants of the Middle East. Because of the economic gains accruing from the linkage between the Arab regimes and the world imperialist stystem, the Arab regimes, it was argued, would be compelled to eschew a total commitment to the destruction of Zionism lest they undermine their own interests and source of power and influence. Thus, if the armed struggle against Israel was to be successfully consummated, the Arab regimes would have to be overthrown by revolutionary forces. The fact that the PFLP and PDF might temporize along the way provided little comfort in the Arab capitals.

In practical terms, the left-wing aim of engineering the eventual overthrow of "reactionary" Arab regimes portended the loss of concrete assets that the PLO-*Fatah* wing had accumulated and desperately needed. J. Gaspard identified the crux of the problem when he wrote that:

> The small groups have nothing to lose and much to gain from revolutionary chaos in the host countries. *Fatah* has much to lose: the subsidies from the "moderate" Arab states; its pool of heavy arms and more or less trained military formations that might get broken up in a revolutionary free-for-all; an established diplomatic and political position in the Arab world and in certain international circles; offices in many Arab countries, which are small centers of local government; and a fairly well-oiled propaganda machine.[24]

In short, the ideological and tactical divisions within the fedayeen movement were serious indeed, since they involved a potential loss of much needed tangible and intangible support.

With such problems stemming from disunity becoming ever more evident, there was yet another attempt to increase the cohesion of the resistance movement. Several fedayeen organizations—including *Fatah*, the PLO, *Sa'iqa*, the Arab Palestine Organization (APO), the Iraqi sponsored Arab Liberation Front (ALF),the PLA and the PDF—joined in forming the Palestine Armed Struggle Command (PASC) in the spring of 1969 in order to improve military cooperation. While the participation of the last two organizations was welcomed, the absence of the PFLP was troublesome. Indeed, it did not take long for the independence of the PFLP to complicate matters and cause the fedayeen movement substantial problems.

A case in point was the May 1969 destruction by the PFLP of a section of the Aramco pipeline near the Lebanese border. Since the pipeline brought Saudi Arabia some $150 milion per year in revenues, and Saudi Arabia was providing financial support to *Fatah*, the latter was compelled to publicly apologize to the Saudis; and the Saudi Arabian foreign minister and press demanded that the PASC, if necessary force all guerrilla groups to rally to it. The gravity of the incident was further underscored when all the Arab states except Algeria condemned the action as contrary to Arab interests.[25]

Another aspect of PFLP behavior which caused considerable irritation to

Fatah at the time was the former's claiming credit for operations that the latter contended it had carried out. *Fatah*, for example, argued that the destruction of a pipeline in Haifa and an explosion near the Wailing Wall in East Jerusalem were not PFLP actions, but were carried out by its forces, a claim which could be substantiated, according to *Fatah*, since the operation's plans had been submitted to the PASC prior to the attacks.[26]

The sad state of affairs in the resistance was not lost on Arab observers. Writing in *Al-Ahram* on June 6, 1969, Heikal reprimanded the guerrillas for their divisiveness, untimely ideological debates, and tendency to spend more time making claims than fighting. Referring to *Fatah* as the leading organization, Heikal called on it to coordinate fedayeen activities.[27] *Fatah*, however, did not need much prodding since it was reportedly chagrined by the emergence of four new guerrilla groups. On June 13, 1969, *Fatah* criticized the formation of the organizations, charging that Zionism, the United States, and counterrevolutionary forces were responsible, because they wished to strain the fedayeen movement, stretch its manpower, and create dissension.[28]

During July 1969, the representatives of fedayeen organizations held a three-day meeting in Jordan and tried to reconcile their differences. Although *Al-Jumhuriyah* (Cairo) said that the PASC would oppose the formation of new groups and would seek to dissolve and absorb existing organizations, it was also reported that the representatives at the meeting agreed that the existence of numerous groups was a sign of vitality as long as they all aimed their guns at Israel. Perhaps the most significant accomplishment of the July conclave was the establishment of a unified command in Jordan and a committee to eliminate fedayeen misunder-standings, a development which most observers interpreted as an attempt to close ranks in response to political and military changes in Jordan, which portended possible trouble for the fedayeen. The ranks were, in fact, closed somewhat when it was announced on July 12 that the ALF and the PSF had decided to join the PASC. Still absent, however, were the PFLP, the PFLP-GC, and the Action Organization for the Liberation of Palestine (AOLP).[29] The fact that the PASC had yet to play the leading role in the resistance was conceded the following month.[30]

In the meantime, the independently operating PFLP was busy carrying out acts of terror outside the Middle East, including two fire-bombing attacks on London stores with links to Israel's ZIM shipping line. The incident no doubt increased *Fatah's* impatience with the PFLP, since the latter, although eventually assuming responsibility, had left plaques saying "this is the work of *Fatah*." At the end of August, Habash warned there would be more attacks on Jewish establishments in London and all over the world.

Habash's warnings were soon borne out by grenade attacks against the El Al office in Brussels and the Israeli embassies in Bonn and The Hague. Besides the aforementioned fact that the PLO-*Fatah* group questioned the prudence of external terror because of the alienation it caused, the moderate organizations appeared to be disconcerted with the publicity the PFLP was getting and reports that the latter was the fastest growing guerrilla organization.

In spite of its increased popularity, the PFLP was unable to obtain equal representation at the sixth PNC meeting in September 1969 and hence it boycotted the session. As a consequence, Arafat's reelection as chairman of the PLO-EC and the placement of the PASC under his direct command were facilitated, as was passage of a communiqué pledging noninterference in the affairs of Arab countries, provided they did not obstruct the revolution.[31]

In the next two months there were more organizational moves intended to foster cohesion. On October 14 the PFLP-GC joined the PASC, and on November 26 the formation of the secret Palestinian Revolutionary Council (PRC),which was to include members of the central committees of *Fatah*, the PSF, and *al-Ard* (a nationalist group banned by Israel in 1964), was announced. Since the PRC was designed to enhance the effectiveness of insurgent operations inside the occupied areas, the announcement of its formation, on the same day that *Fatah* was calling on its terrorist cells to disband in the wake of Israeli security operations, was hardly coincidental. Indeed, it seemed to suggest that existing organizational structures were failing and that any attempt to regain lost ground would have to be preceded by cooperation among the fedayeen organizations.

In November a clash with the Lebanese army affected the cohesion of the resistance movement. When Arafat finally reached an agreement with the Lebanese in Cairo, he was faced with protests from the PFLP and the AOLP, which said it was not bound by the accord because it was not represented.[32] Two weeks later, however, Cairo Radio said the PFLP had decided to recognize the agreement and *Al-Sayyad* (Beirut) claimed that contacts had been made between the PFLP and the PASC, with the former promising to help implement the Cairo agreement. At the time of a visit to Iraq by Habash on November 12, 1969, it was suggested by the Baghdad weekly *Alef-Baa* that the PFLP was interested in unity.[33]

The inconsistencies characteristic of fedayeen efforts to unify their movement were again demonstrated in December. Although *Fatah* and the PFLP held talks in Libya to try to reconcile their differences, the PDF announced it would suspend participation in the PASC because of attempts by one organization (*Fatah*) to dominate the movement. A PASC spokesman retorted that the real reason was a disagreement over the size and effectiveness of a raid the PDF claimed to have carried out.[34] In any case, the PDF withdrawal suggested that what coordination had been achieved rested on a very fragile foundation.

Indeed by the end of 1969 the basic patterns and sources of disunity had solidified. Though the integration of the more moderate, pragmatic elements in the PLO with *Fatah* provided a concentration of power that was necessary for a cohesive movement, it was by no means sufficient, for a number of other organizations had emerged which acquired enough capability to operate independently. In some cases, that capability was generated through their own organizational dexterity (e.g., the PFLP), while in others it was provided by parent Arab states (e.g., *Sa'iqa* and the ALF). Whatever the reason, these independent capabilities meant that any effort on the part of *Fatah* to discipline dissident groups would result in a sanguinary internal battle, the outcome of which was most uncertain, especially in view of the possibility of intervention by the Arab states on behalf of their clients. In short, while the PLO-*Fatah* constellation found itself in the position of *primus inter pares* in the resistance movement, its margin of power and influence was not decisive, and accordingly it was reluctant to force a showdown with the left. Instead, *Fatah* and its supporters within the PLO tended to rely on structural remedies such as the PASC and the PLO-EC in the hope of overcoming ideological, tactical, and personal divisions. In the final analysis, however, these nascent institutions merely masked the absence of strong authority and legitimacy at the central level.

The effects of this disunity were becoming evident from 1967 and 1969, namely internecine fighting, strife with the regimes in Jordan and Lebanon, and poor crisis management during conflicts with the Arab states. In 1970, the patterns of disunity would continue and the effects would prove to be dramatic and catastrophic.

Fission, Fusion, and Fratricide: 1970

In January 1970 Arafat indicated that the number of commando groups had decreased from thirty-three to twenty-three, with the ten organizations disappearing of their own accord. After promising there would be no violent attempts to liquidate other lesser groups, Arafat went on to compare *Fatah*'s role in the Palestinian movement with that of the Viet Cong in Vietnam, and attributed its strength to having turned neither left nor right.[35] The fact that the Viet Cong organization was a cohesive structure, led by a small Marxist-Leninist party at the apex, and devoid of serious splits over tactical and ideological questions, was conveniently ignored by the PLO chairman. When it came to practical manners, as opposed to rhetoric, Arafat was compelled to pursue the quest for unity. In early 1970 this effort resulted in the formation of another supraorganizational structure, the Unified Command of the Palestinian Resistance (UCPR). This achievement was considered to be a significant step forward, since the UCPR brought the hitherto independent PFLP into an organizational structure with the other major groups. Moreover, the PDF, which had suspended its participation in the PASC, came back into the fold.[36]

The major factor expediting formation of the UCPR was a crisis in Jordan over the issuance of a decree banning the carrying and firing of weapons in the cities. Fearing that the Jordanian army might enforce the regulations, the fedayeen decided to close ranks within the UCPR "to face any action undertaken against the guerrillas."[37] Besides serving a defensive function against perceived threats from Amman, the UCPR was to be responsible for dealing with and ending any serious errors or disturbances caused by its members. A tacit admission that the indiscipline of the fedayeen groups had been a cause of the clash with Jordan was contained in a twelve-point order of the day, issued by the UCPR, which dealt with general behavior, behavior at road checks, shooting, relations with the army and public security forces, maneuvers inside towns, burial ceremonies, smuggling in the name of the resistance, collection of contributions, inspection of houses, discipline in bases, dealing with government officials, and rumors.[38] Similar steps aimed at disciplining the guerrillas were also being taken in Lebanon by the Higher Political Committee for Palestinian Affairs (HPCPA), a structure made up of representatives of fedayeen organizations in that country. While the UCPR was to complement the PASC, it remained to be seen if, unlike the latter organization, it would overcome ideological, tactical, and personal differences, and obtain full compliance with the political, military, and disciplinary instructions that it was issuing.

In April, the Palestinian organizations met in Amman to prepare for another session of the PNC and to consider the institutionalization of the UCPR. Of primary interest were unanswered questions about the internal statutes of the UCPR, its political and military programs, and its relationship to the PNC, the PLO, and the PASC. In view of the persistence of ideological differences, which had been highlighted once more the previous month during two seminars on the Palestinian question, no one was under the illusion that definitive and authoritative solutions would easily be found.

At the first seminar, *Fatah* had proposed the formation of a movement united with the other organizations, only to have the PFLP and PDF reply that there was no chance of unity as long as *Fatah* rejected Marxism. During the second meeting *Fatah* said that it would welcome the Marxist organizations into its group as long as they did not attempt to indoctrinate members from within; Habash, meanwhile, excoriated Arab socialists, governments, and commando groups, saying that the PFLP refused to be associated with them or to recognize them. After noting the hopes raised by the fedayeen after June 1967, Professor Walid Khalidi, a distinguished Palestinian scholar, addressed the seminar and summed up the situation prevailing at the time as follows:

> These hopes have now faded, . . . we have found that the *fedayeen* were no less shortsighted than were the Arab Governments. The *fedayeen* have split into nationalists, Marxist-Leninists, left-wingers and even Baathists. Each faction claims to be the one true spokesman for the Palestinians and some go even further and fight the others . . . and it seems to me that the *fedayeen* leaders are determined to maintain these divisions. . . .
>
> Thus the roads that lead to Arab progress, strength and freedom have been closed by men who appear to be incapable of understanding the meaning of unity of purpose let alone realize it. However, difficult as it may be, it is not impossible to overcome these obstacles and open the road to a better Arab future.[39]

In addition to the left-right differences that emerged at the two seminars, there were reported fissions within *Fatah* which centered around a struggle between Arafat and one of his leading deputies, Salah Khalef (alias Abu Iyad). Khalef was said to have charged Arafat with being soft with Jordan and Lebanon, and with having gone too far toward association with China and not far enough toward the Soviet Union. Moreover, Khalef urged the *Fatah* executive committee to follow the PFLP example of extending the war against Israel to Israeli property, aircraft, and interests, wherever they might be found.[40]

With this atmosphere of discord as a backdrop, attempts to make the UCPR an authoritative structure were abandoned and the fedayeen leaders returned to the organizational drawing boards. After extensive deliberations, eleven groups, including the PFLP, issued a communiqué during May announcing that the PLO would become the main resistance body and that a new central committee made up of the PLO-EC, the president of the PNC, the commander of the PLA, representatives of the guerrilla organizations, and a number of independents would replace the UCPR. Plans for a unified military command to develop the armed struggle and carry it through to a new stage of guerrilla action were also revealed. On the other hand, the statement also indicated that issues on which no agreement had been reached would be pursued by each organization at its own discretion.[41] This last point made it apparent that while some organizational accommodations had been arranged, essential differences among the fedayeen groups remained outstanding.

As the seventh PNC was about to convene at the end of May, fedayeen divisions were again manifest. On May 22 an ambush of an Israeli school bus by the PFLP-GC near the Lebanese border killed eleven and wounded twenty-one. *Fatah* immediately rebuked the PFLP-GC, saying that the attack was contrary to its policy of avoiding civilian targets. Then, when Israel retaliated with heavy shellings of Lebanese areas and began patrolling both sides of the border, the Lebanese cabinet announced that it would henceforth ban the firing of rockets from Lebanon and the planting of explosives near the border. Shortly thereafter, the PFLP rejected Lebanon's demands as an attempt "to impose tutelage on commando activity in the name of coordination."[42] The fact was clear that terrorist operations, which diverged from the stated norms of the PLO, had once more complicated relations with a sanctuary state.

The reaction to the divisiveness was not long in coming. In his opening address to the PNC at the end of May, the president urged the fedayeen organizations to unify and criticized wasteful side battles which reduced efforts against Israel. Saying the number of guerrilla groups was unjustified, he went on to call for the elimination of personal and ideological differences and for the creation of a single command to guide fedayeen action in all fields.[43] The futility of these remarks was already painfully obvious, inasmuch as the PFLP had decided to limit its participation at the conclave to one "nominal representative."

A number of factors were believed to be behind the PFLP decision, not the least of which was Habash's concern over the relative power and influence of his organization. For one thing, there was reported disenchantment with the reduction of PFLP seats from the fifteen agreed on in early May to five. Sources close to the PFLP said that the organization also disagreed with the way a number of issues were to be handled. Furthermore, the PFLP wanted the PLA to shed its conventional stance, break its ties with the Arab states, and become involved in the fighting. On the military level there was dissatisfaction with the absence of a unified command, while on the financial level the PFLP wanted to see all funds consolidated into one pool. There was also renewed anxiety expressed about the ways some organizations acquired their funds and about their affiliations with particular Arab governments. Finally, the PFLP was reported to be alarmed about an informational credibility gap between the fedayeen and the masses.[44]

Fatah, in the meantime, had suggested three conditions were necessary for the success of the PNC session. First, the independence of the Palestinian revolution was stressed. A call to end "Arab camps within Palestinian unity" was interpreted as a demand that the fedayeen organizations, such as *Sa'iqa* and the ALF, avoid entanglement in inter-Arab conflicts. The second condition was that all groups should prove their worth by fighting against Israel; the third was that a "clear evaluation of Palestinian action made with a scientific spirit" be carried out.[45]

With the PFLP decision on nominal representation and the *Fatah* demands as an immediate backdrop, the PNC deliberated from May 30 until June 4, and agreed to establish a central committee responsible for the overall management of all Palestinian activities, a unified military command to replace the PASC, and liaison committees in Jordan and Lebanon to foster better relations with the authorities in those two states.[46] The unified military command, comprising the eleven groups represented on the Central Committee of the Palestinian Resistance (CCPR), was intended to direct all guerrilla operations and training and to be divided into geographic regions, each with a commander. In mid-June, Arafat was appointed head of the military command. Though PNC sources were reported as saying that any organization would have the right to withdraw from the military command and carry out its own operations, the military command was supposed to have disciplinary powers enabling it to suspend membership or expel groups carrying out operations that endangered the "security of the Palestinian revolution."

At the top of the new organizational structure was the PNC, which would meet twice a year, and which delegated authority to the PLO-EC. Under the PLO-EC would be the CCPR and the unified military command.[47] The real agency of coordinating power in this scheme appeared to be the CCPR, for it was there, rather than in the PLO-EC, that all groups were represented.[48] In fact, within days a six-man secretariat (sometimes referred to as a politburo) made up of Arafat (*Fatah*), Habash (PFLP), Issam Sartawi (AOLP), Hawatmeh (PDF), Dhafi Jumayanni (*Sa'iqa*), and Kamal Nasser (PLO) was set up and given responsibility to oversee the implementation of CCPR decisions on political, military, and informational policy.[49]

During the PNC meetings on reorganization, sharp clashes between *Fatah* and the PFLP were reported over demands by Abu Mahir, the PFLP representative, that a political program defining the aims of the liberation struggle be adopted. Mahir insisted such a program identify reactionary Arab regimes as enemies of the Palestinian people; *Fatah* objected and reportedly threatened to withdraw from the PNC if the issue was put on the agenda.[50]

In addition to the ideological divergence inherent in the clash over Mahir's proposal, the tactical differences between the PFLP and *Fatah* were not bridged at the PNC meetings. This much was clear when, on June 5,

Ahmed Yamani of the PFLP said his organization would continue to pursue the enemy outside the occupied territory, and would consider itself entirely free to act as it wished in all areas not covered by agreements. Then, in comments indicative of persisting ideological differences, Yamani said the PFLP participation in the PNC was merely "symbolic" and the organization would continue to refuse association with most of the "bureaucratic and antirevolutionary" sections of the PLO. For this reason the PFLP had joined the CCPR, but not the PLO-EC. The main purpose, he went on, was to enable the PFLP to exert pressure toward the "aim of giving the Palestinian resistance a revolutionary character."[51]

It was not long before the new fedayeen organizational structure was tested. Soon after the close of the PNC session, serious fighting erupted in Jordan between the fedayeen and the army, with the PFLP and PDF as major instigators. The immediate effect on the guerrilla organizations was in the direction of consolidation. Following the appointment of Arafat as commander of all forces, the CCPR announced on June 15 that it was assuming all responsibility for the direction of Palestinian resistance groups, and was placing under its command all military and popular forces, including special forces of all organizations. The decisions of the CCPR, it was stated, would be binding on all resistance organizations militarily, politically, and in the public information sector. The following day the aforementioned secretariat was formed. Whether significant strides toward unity had really been taken, however, continued to be questioned by both guerrillas and outsiders.[52]

Another result of the Jordanian fighting was the apparent gain in prestige of the left-wing groups, especially the PFLP, which took a hard line against Hussein by demanding that the king disband his special forces and fire a number of top military commanders and political figures. When the "Voice of *Assifa*" also demanded that the Jordanian officers be removed, the development was taken by a number of observers to mean that *Fatah* was trying to avoid being outflanked on the left.[53] Still, the fact that not all differences among the fedayeen had been submerged was evident when Kamal Nasser, official spokesman of the CCPR, said that the Palestinians would listen to a four-man committee of Arab leaders set up to deal with the crisis, only to have the PDF criticize the same committee for interference in the internal affairs of the resistance.[54]

The latter contradiction was attributed by some as a key reason for a CCPR statement of June 24 to the effect that it would issue all communiqués.[55] Then, no doubt in reaction to statements of the left-wing groups which were complicating attempts to end the crisis, Arafat warned on June 26 that "our masses cannot any more tolerate an extremist demagogue who does nothing to change the status quo," a remark believed directed at Habash.[56]

Fatah was not the only party chagrined with the actions of the left-wing groups. Both Nasser and Libyan leader Mu'ammar al-Qadhdhafi were reported to have absolved *Fatah* and Hussein of guilt for the June fighting. More important, however, the Egyptian president, according to *Al-Ahram* (June 9, 1970), had a close understanding with Hussein and Arafat to curb the demands of the left-wing leaders, Habash and Hawatmeh. They were, in fact, curbed, since an accord reached in early July between Jordan and the CCPR did not meet the PFLP-PDF demands that the Jordan Special Forces be disbanded, officers responsible for the June fighting be punished, and troops in Amman be withdrawn.[57]

The Marxist groups were hardly pleased by this turn of events. Habash suggested that guerrillas should continue to struggle to achieve their demands, although the PFLP would abide by CCPR resolutions. A few days later he was quoted as saying the Jordanian compromise was a fedayeen retreat, "a real backing away." On July 22 Habash reiterated his demand that special groups in Jordan be dissolved so that the accord with Jordan could prevent further fighting.[58]

While the guerrillas and Jordanians were trying to reach a settlement, the strains within the resistance movement were further exacerbated when the PLA chief of staff, Colonel Othman Hadad, was relieved by Arafat. The Beirut publication *Al-Jarida* reported on July 5 that Hadad was an extremist who was removed in order to ease the situation in Jordan, and *Arab World* said on July 15 that his dismissal created tensions between *Fatah* and *Sa'iqa*, since Hadad was supported by the latter. As things turned out, Hadad defied Arafat's order, remained in office, and began to organize his forces against the PLA commander, Yahya.[59]

The fedayeen descent into disaster had only just begun with the fighting in June. Shortly after that crisis had passed, the fedayeen were stunned by Hussein's and Nasser's acceptance of the American cease-fire proposal to end the war of attrition on the Suez front. Led by *Fatah*, the PFLP, and the PDF, the CCPR rejected the Rogers plan and criticized Egypt's acceptance of it. In protest, armed men of the two left-wing organizations entered Amman to demonstrate, an action that was a violation of the already tenuous agreement with Jordan. *Fatah*, on the other hand, refrained from participation.[60]

Additional fissures made their appearance within the fedayeen movement when the two small pro-Nasser groups, the APO and the AOLP, defied the UCPR by calling Nasser's acceptance of the cease-fire a brilliant tactical move.[61] Although the AOLP indicated that the disagreement was a minor one, since the guerrillas could not be bound by any international agreement, it became involved in an outbreak of fighting with the PFLP in

Irbid, Jordan, on August 5. The next day clashes erupted in Amman when the PFLP raided an APO office. Even though conceding that they would violate the cease-fire, the AOLP and the APO warned that they would fight the PFLP if twenty-three prisoners taken by the PFLP were not returned. After guerrillas from the PFLP proceeded to raid an AOLP office in Lebanon, the other guerrilla organizations interceded to end the fighting and both the AOLP and APO decided to withdraw support for Nasser's acceptance of the American plan. Though the AOLP subsequently acknowledged that it had misinterpreted the situation and had been wrong, ill feeling remained toward the PFLP and was reflected in propaganda attacks against the latter.[62]

While these clashes were taking place, tension around the threat to the fedayeen resulting from the acceptance of the American plan continued to build. In response, the PNC met in emergency session in late August and passed resolutions formally rejecting the Rogers plan, and warning that anyone who worked outside the PNC would be considered a traitor. The latter point was clearly directed at Palestinian independents who might consider negotiating a peace with Israel.[63]

September 1970 proved to be a critical month for the fedayeen movement. Into an already tense atmosphere, created by periodic fighting between the Jordanians and the guerrillas since June, came the dramatic multiple skyjacking carried out by the PFLP. When the passengers and aircraft were held hostage in Jordan in defiance of the government and army, the regime perceived a challenge to Jordanian sovereignty. The military felt humiliation as it was forced to stand helplessly by. With the army's patience at the breaking point, the skyjackings proved to be the proverbial "straw that broke the camel's back." As a result, the Jordanian army moved against the fedayeen with savage fury until, on September 28, an agreement ended the fighting.

Although it was not clear at the time, the September civil war proved to be a major defeat for the fedayeen since, in addition to suffering substantial human and material losses (fedayeen numbers were reduced from 12,000 to an estimated 3,000 to 5,000, according to the *Journal of Palestine Studies*), they were pushed from the urban areas to northern Jordan. Most indicative of the state of affairs in the Palestinian resistance was the sharp decrease in fedayeen military activity against Israeli-held territories. Both casualties and incidents along the borders dropped to close to zero, as reflected in both the accounting of the IDF and decreased military reportage in fedayeen journals.[64] Despite claims by the fedayeen that they had won a victory, there was a sense of crisis within the movement that soon led to a great deal of soul-searching.[65]

As has been said, one cause of the September debacle was the PFLP skyjackings. These, in part, grew out of the disunity of the fedayeen and their lack of organizational discipline. Besides providing Hussein with a reason to strike hard at the fedayeen, the skyjackings also brought criticism from the Arab world, the Soviet Union, and the international community. In the final analysis, the human, material, moral, and political losses suffered by the fedayeen far outweighed the intended gain of securing the release of a few guerrilla prisoners. If the real objective was, as some suggested, to create a "revolutionary climate," the operation was undeniably counterproductive.

Although *Fatah* was angered over the PFLP's behavior, it had tried to stabilize the situation and prevent a split within guerrilla ranks by reaching an agreement with the International Red Cross on the release of the hostages. However, following a CCPR meeting on September 12, in which a decision was made to release the aircraft and the hostages, the PFLP, ignoring the majority vote, proceeded to destroy three jetliners. The CCPR response was to suspend the PFLP, condemn the skyjacking and the PFLP refusal to cooperate, and warn that a strong stand would be taken against any future PFLP act which harmed the revolution. The severity of the sanctions was mitigated somewhat by *Fatah*'s warning that it would not allow the PFLP to become isolated and vulnerable.[66] While expressing surprise, PFLP sources were quoted as saying in private that the suspension would increase the organization's freedom of movement and that at no time as a member of the CCPR had the PFLP abided by decisions which conflicted with its principles and policies.[67]

In addition to the problems created by the skyjackings, *Fatah* had another reason to be irate with the left-wing groups. When fighting between the Jordanians and the fedayeen was apparently to be ended by an agreed cease-fire on September 10, the PFLP and the PDF rejected the agreement. Thus, efforts by the moderate fedayeen to prevent the situation in Jordan from going from bad to worse were stymied.[68]

In the midst of these troubles in Jordan, the CCPR announced that it had decided to unite all Palestinian revolutionary forces—the PLA, fedayeen groups, and the militias—and to appoint Arafat as commander and General Yahya as chief of staff.[69] This proved to be the harbinger of a post-civil war attempt to once again reorganize the fedayeen movement in order to achieve a modicum of cohesion.

In early October, a joint military committee to coordinate actions of the leading fedayeen organizations was set up in Amman. In the interest of creating a permanent basis for military cooperation, the Military Leadership Committee (MLC) brought together representatives from *Fatah, Sa'iqa*, the PLA/PFL, the PFLP, and the PDF. According to a PFLP spokesman, the MLC was to have full authority for military decisions in

Amman. Since it was hoped that eventually the authority of the MLC would be extended to northern Jordan, a special committee was to study a broader and more permanent form of organization. The fact that impetus for establishing the MLC came from the PLO-CC rather than from the CCPR suggested that the PLO-CC, with the adherence of the PFLP, now had replaced the CCPR as the locus of coordinative power within the resistance movement. This impression was reinforced when Palestinian sources reported later in the month that the PLO-CC would establish offices in its name in Amman in order to serve all fedayeen groups. References to individual guerrilla organizations were to be abolished, as would references to the CCPR, and military communiqués were to be issued by spokesmen for the Palestinian revolution. Similar reforms were reported in Lebanon. In Lebanon, however, guerrilla-military coordination was still within the framework of the PASC.[70]

Although the PLO had apparently been restored as the agency of coordinative power in the resistance, it remained to be seen whether this organizational reshuffling would be any more effective than previous ones. Comments by the PFLP that the truce in Jordan was temporary, and that it would continue to oppose Hussein and imperialism, cast some clouds over the future, especially since the PLO was seeking to heal the wounds caused by the September fighting.[71]

In November, some answers began to emerge. The PLO-CC indicated that it wished to unify all guerrilla units in all countries in a popular liberation front along the lines of the National Liberation Front in Vietnam, starting from the smallest cells at the base of a pyramidal structure which would have the PLO-CC at the apex. Moreover, strong action was recommended against any deviation that involved adherence to particular persons, identities, or slogans associated with groups other than the Palestinian revolution. The past situation, in which groups acted on their own, was to be terminated and a single political and military strategy was to guide the resistance. As a first step in this new direction, the PLO-EC had earlier in the month demanded a purge of "incompetent elements" from the leadership.[72]

Near the end of November, Cairo's Middle East News Agency suggested that the military forces of *Fatah, Sa'iqa*, the PFLP, and PDF were to be absorbed into the PLA.[73] Immediately thereafter, there were contradictory reports. On the one hand, it was reported that the four main guerrilla organizations cited above had reached agreement on integrating their forces, had decided to isolate the Communist organization, *Al-Ansar*, and had agreed to let the six smaller groups retain a symbolic presence on the PLO-CC.[74] On the other hand, there were indications that plans for union had been thwarted by the PFLP, and Habash was quoted as saying that he was willing to join the move toward unity, but opposed the idea that actions planned by member organizations could be vetoed by a supreme military council "packed with *Fatah* men."[75]

When the PLO-CC met in Amman the following week, it appeared that the more pessimistic conclusion was accurate. After four days of talks, the PLO-CC announced that it would set up a permanent military command to coordinate the activities of the fedayeen groups.[76] For the time being, the more ambitious schemes for a military command structure with directive power were shelved, along with a plan for merging the guerrilla organizations under the PLA. Once more, attempts to establish a rational command structure, which would provide badly needed cohesion, were undercut by insurgent organizations jealous of their own autonomy and antagonistic toward their rivals in other groups. The appointment of a nine-man secretariat near the end of December scarcely concealed the fact that 1970 had been a disastrous year as far as attempts to unify the fedayeen movement were concerned.[77]

Unlearned Lessons: The Jordanian Expulsion, 1971

Despite the desperate need to reorganize and defend the revolution in the wake of the Jordanian civil war, disunity continued to plague the resistance movement, many of whose leaders seemed oblivious to the hard-learned lessons of the previous summer and fall. In what amounted to a veiled reference to *Fatah*, the PFLP and *Sa'iqa* issued a statement on January 4 condemning "unilateral acts and a trend towards autocracy by certain sections of the resistance movement."[78] However, it was renewed fighting with the Jordanians that led to the sharpest differences between *Fatah* and the PFLP. When a cease-fire negotiated with Jordan on January 14 agreed to the disarming of fedayeen militias in Amman, it drew a negative reaction from the PFLP, which reiterated its call for the overthrow of Hussein.[79] *Fatah*, which wanted to avoid friction with the Jordanian army and Hussein, vented its frustration by charging that the PFLP was in collusion with Jordan to wreck the resistance, and one of *Fatah*'s leaders, Kamal Adwan, warned that force would be used to prevent the revolution from being diverted from the task of fighting Israel. Habash was branded as "an adventurer who wants to make good his inferiority complex."[80] Underlying the verbal acrimony between the PFLP and *Fatah* was a sharp disagreement between the two over the PLO-CC's rejection of PFLP demands for an uprising against Hussein, which would have involved guerrilla raids against the Jordanian army, tactical attacks in Amman, and a boycott of the regime.[81]

The initial PFLP reaction to the Adwan warning was to reiterate its refusal to disarm its militia and deny that it provided Hussein with pretexts for attacking the fedayeen; shortly thereafter it pledged adherence to PLO-CC decisions.[82] The PDF, meanwhile, criticized both sides: the right wing, led by *Fatah*, for trying to isolate the resistance from the Jordanian masses, and the left wing for displaying "adventurist tendencies" which gave the Jordanian authorities "pretexts for liquidating the resistance and disarming the people."[83]

In the midst of this controversy, the commander of the PLA decided to make a bid for power. Citing the "lamentably deteriorating commando movement" and the need for unity to bring the PLO back from the brink of collapse, General Yahya urged all guerrilla organizations to merge into the PLO and the PNC to form a new collective leadership.[84] The move was generally interpreted as a challenge to Arafat.

In February, General Yahya pursued his opposition to the guerrilla leadership by publicizing a memorandum which demanded the dissolution of all Palestinian organizations and the merger of all fedayeen into a single unified command. Yahya also called for the formation of a special committee to investigate and establish responsibility for mistakes in running the resistance movement in the political, military, information, financial, and organizational fields.[85]

When the PLO-CC met in Damascus on February 20, Yahya, who was in attendance, renewed his demands and charged that Arafat was an "ignorant dictator." On the other hand, Yahya also tried to downplay his earlier statements by suggesting that what was going on was not a crisis but merely a presentation of views for debate! At the close of the PLO-CC meeting, Arafat and Yahya agreed that the eleven major guerrilla organizations should merge and that leftist guerrillas preaching the overthrow of Hussein should be curbed.[86] In response, the PDF issued a statement calling for the formation of a Palestinian-Jordanian "national front" to end the resistance's isolation from the Arab liberation movement and urging the conduct of a popular revolution against the Jordanian regime.[87] A week later the PFLP threatened to break from the commando movement if other guerrillas did not agree to attack the Jordanian regime and American interests in the Arab world. To underscore its warning, the PFLP decided that instead of Habash attending an upcoming PNC gathering it would send one "symbolic" delegate.[88]

As the eighth PNC convened on March 1, a major theme was once again the need for unity and a single unified command. In an interview, Arafat cited the need for military unity but stressed that this should be "unity in the real sense and not only some kind of coordinated work."[89] During the PNC, the "Arafat plan," which proposed unity in the political, military, and informational fields, was approved; unfortunately, there were no provisions for implementation. Instead, the PNC left plans for such unity for future determination by the PLO. Agreement was reached, however, on the prohibition of aircraft hijackings.[90]

Not everyone was pleased with the accomplishments of the eighth PNC. The PDF and the PFLP viewed the meeting as a complete failure because it did not commit the movement to the overthrow of Hussein. The PFLP argument, reflecting its ideological attitude toward "reactionary" regimes, particularly Jordan's, was that prior to the approval of Arafat's plan, a political-military program defining enemies, friends, and objectives had to be agreed upon.[91] The PLA, meanwhile, was disenchanted with the inability of the fedayeen to organize. The situation, in fact, led the commander of the PLA to comment that the conference, which had just observed a moment of silence for its war dead, "should have kept three additional minutes of silence for the loss of wisdom of the Palestine revolution."[92]

In contrast to the pessimism of the PLA and the left-wing groups was the relative optimism of the PLO and *Fatah*.[93] Several days after the PNC meetings, Kamal Nasser reported that the PNC had decided to streamline its organization by replacing the PLO-CC and the PLO-EC with one committee. Most significant, however, was the appointment of a committee to discuss the Arafat plan.[94] Late in the month, Arafat said in an interview that while force would not be used to obtain unity, *Fatah* would not tolerate disunity. To demonstrate his good faith, Arafat had appointed a *Sa'iqa* commander in Lebanon, despite the fact that the equality of *Fatah* and *Sa'iqa* forces would have allowed him to appoint one of his own men. That other organizations were not as committed to unity as *Fatah* became clear in April when, contrary to an agreement made after the Jordanian civil war making the PLO official spokesman of the resistance, the PFLP, PDF, and PFLP-GC issued independent communiqués on operations.[95]

In May, the PLA again complained about the inability of the resistance to achieve unity. With the term of the committee set up to devise a plan for unity about to expire, the PLA urged that a new PNC be established along with a single political-military command and that training, equipment, and operations be standardized. The unity committee, the PLA complained, had taken no steps in the direction of cohesion.[96] When a committee charged with forming a new PNC did meet the following month, the PLA withdrew in protest against its methods and the lack of movement toward unity.

While all this was transpiring there were grave problems on the operational level. In the wake of a vow by Hussein to launch a "final crackdown," the PLO had tried to defuse the situation by denying Jordanian charges that guerrillas had carried out acts of sabotage in Amman, Zerqa, and Russeifah. To the dismay of the PLO, the PFLP promptly stepped forward and claimed credit for the very attacks the PLO was denying.[97] Later in the month inter-fedayeen relations again worsened when the PASC arrested members of the PFLP-GC in Lebanon for a series of clashes and a shooting incident, a move that the latter claimed was part of a *Fatah* plan to destroy the smaller groups.[98]

A Syrian crackdown on left-wing guerrillas was also causing concern since weapons destined for the fedayeen were being confiscated. Underlying the move by Damascus was the fact that *Sa'iqa* was reported to have come under the control of the military wing of the Ba'th party. This meant that one of the larger guerrilla organizations would be at the bidding of a regime reportedly purging leftists and encouraging the PLA to cleanse its ranks.[99]

On July 7 the PNC met once again.[100] Since by this time Arafat was conceding that full unity was impossible due to ideological differences, it was not surprising that the fedayeen leaders were reported in favor of a national liberation front in lieu of one body.[101] Yet, in the face of another serious crisis in Jordan, fueled by the behavior of the left-wing groups, the PNC indicated that all guerrilla groups had agreed to join a single command under Arafat. In other developments, it was announced that the AOLP, APO, and PSF were to merge with *Fatah*. The issue of cohesion was also raised by the head of the PNF, who suggested that unity might help expedite a solution to a severe financial crisis facing the movement.[102]

At the conclusion of the PNC meetings, it was announced that a new PLO-EC had been formed, with members of all major fedayeen organizations represented. Notably absent from the new committee, but given the privilege of attending its sessions, was the PLA commander.[103] No doubt unsettling to the fedayeen at the time was a decision by three leaders, including the PNC president, to decline membership in the new PNC, because of the way it was formed and because of its past failures.[104]

As things developed, the PNC ended its session prematurely, when Hussein moved to eject the fedayeen once and for all from Jordan. The fact could not be ignored that the disunity of the fedayeen, which had been reflected in the sabotage and denunciation directed against the Hashemite regime, was largely responsible for this coup de grace. Indeed, it seemed that the fedayeen, refusing to heed the lessons of September 1970, were reliving history. As Salah Khalef of *Fatah* stated poignantly during a July 29, 1971 interview in *Fatah*, the PLO newspaper:

> These are the facts—the facts of the butchery of September. Now, what took place following the events of September? After September, an evaluation of all the confrontations and plots against the movement, universally faced by all revolutions, should have been undertaken, and reconstruction in light of

past experience should have taken place, so that the forces of revolution would take a unified course of action against the counterrevolutionary plots. The truth is that the resistance movement did not conduct any such an evaluation, and did not undertake any attempt to learn from the mistakes that preceded September. In all honesty, the Central Committee of the resistance movement continued, as it had done before September, to conduct laborious meetings, which were governed neither by systematic thought nor logic. They were not governed by what usually governs parallel historical sessions. Their task should have been directed towards defining a clear program around which all the various fedayeen organizations would unite to confront the massive assault on them by the Jordanian regime.[105]

Unhappily for the PLO, Khalef's words fell on deaf ears, because no sooner had Egypt and Saudi Arabia commenced on a mediation effort to repair the damage than the guerrilla organizations fell to squabbling among themselves.

Following two months of trips to Arab capitals by Saudi and Egyptian mediators, a meeting was finally scheduled for Jedda on September 8. However, when the PLO-EC split over whether or not the talks would be useful, Jordan withdrew. Besides reported disagreement within *Fatah* over the talks, the left-wing guerrilla organizations, as might have been anticipated, rejected the idea. In a statement issued on September 3 the PFLP criticized the meeting and other guerrilla groups for being indecisive. Then, in an interview appearing in the PFLP paper, *Al Hadaf*, Habash called for an "underground war of revolutionary violence" to overthrow Hussein's regime because there was no room for coexistence. The battle with Israel was explicitly relegated to second priority when Habash commented that the "resistance battle against the reactionary regime is the central battle facing the resistance movement now."[106] Shortly after Habash's remarks, the PDF indicated its support for his position and its newspaper, *Al Hurriya*, condemned the Egyptian, Lebanese, and Syrian regimes as a "grouping of neo-reactionary regimes designed to spearhead a fresh campaign to purge the leftists throughout the Arab world."[107]

On the other side, Arafat was once again prepared to negotiate with Jordan in the hope of salvaging something and testing Amman's will to abide by previous agreements.[108] At the time, however, there were fissiparous tendencies within *Fatah*, which was trying to elect a new executive committee following the deaths of two leaders in the Jordanian fighting. The problems experienced within the *Fatah* group were complicated by the fact that differences over the Jedda parley had become intertwined with a challenge to Arafat's leadership by younger officers. A group called "the free officers of *Assifa*" had issued a statement on

August 31 charging certain *Fatah* members with links to Jordanian intelligence and stating that Swiss bank accounts containing *Fatah* funds were in the names of five leaders rather than in that of the organization. Although *Fatah* denied the existence of the free officers and attributed the statement to foreign agents, there were reports that the group did exist, albeit comprising only three men. In any event, there were numerous reports of restiveness within *Fatah*, free officers' group or not.[109]

Within the political context just noted, the PLO-EC engaged in tense debates over the question of attending the Jedda meeting. When the PLO-EC finally voted seven to three to go to Jedda, the PFLP representatives walked out, and, at a subsequent news conference, branded the decision as "cowardly" and "shameful." The PFLP, however, stopped short of withdrawing from the PLO-EC, indicating instead that it would await the results of the Jedda talks before reassessing its position. If an agreement was reached at Jedda, the PFLP pledged to undermine it.[110]

Two days later the situation took a new turn when the fedayeen delegation to the Jedda talks failed to arrive. In reaction to these developments, Saudi Arabia and Egypt rescheduled the meeting and warned both sides that measures would be taken against them if they failed to appear. After stating that the Saudi border with Jordan would be closed and aid terminated if Hussein's representatives did not attend, the Saudi foreign minister said that his government recognized only *Fatah* and that it did not care about the "Reds" of the PFLP and PDF. If *Fatah* boycotted the gathering, the Saudi minister said, all aid to the organization would be stopped.

In the face of these pressures, both sides appeared at Jedda and engaged in three days of talks. The outcome was indecisive and the Amman delegation returned to Jordan for further instructions.[111] Matters were not helped by a PDF statement on September 16 calling for the overthrow of the Jordanian regime and contending that the Jedda talks were being carried out by right-wing fedayeen in violation of PLO directives.[112] By this time, however, the fedayeen became distracted by internecine violence within the PLA.

The problems within the PLA stemmed from a long-simmering rivalry between the commander in chief, Yahya, and the chief of staff, Othman Hadad. When an intelligence officer allied with Yahya, Rahman Baradi, was apprehended by Hadad's men and subsequently tortured to death (according to Lebanese police), Yahya called on Arafat to dismiss Hadad. Hadad then responded by demanding Yahya's dismissal. After at first biding its time, because of an apparent desire not to irritate Syria (which backed Hadad), the PLO-EC fired both men and appointed Misbah al-Budayri as commander in chief.[113]

In October, an attempt on Arafat's life once again illustrated the dissension and indiscipline within fedayeen ranks. While *Fatah* sources described the assassination attempt variously as the work of infiltrators into the movement or as that of a *Fatah* splinter group, *Al-Ahram* reported a more complex story on October 9. The guilty party, it said, was a long-time but reckless member of *Fatah*, Hussein Heibeh. The attempt on Arafat's life resulted from a series of events which began when a shipment of arms from Kuwait was intercepted by Heibeh's men and diverted to his bases. When Arafat came to look into the situation, his convoy was ambushed.[114] Even though Arafat escaped with his life, the fact that members of his own organization had tried to kill him further reflected both his and the organization's decline.

Despair, Diviseness, and Transnational Terrorism: 1972-1973

By the end of 1971, the Palestinian resistance movement had reached its nadir. Having lost many of its best fighting men, expelled from its principal staging areas in Jordan, and embittered by the perceived treachery of the Jordanian government, the PLO relocated in Lebanon and, to a lesser extent, Syria. In an attempt to pick up the pieces, the tenth PNC met in April 1972 and approved a merger plan put forward by Arafat and a new PLO-EC; the practical effect, however, was insignificant inasmuch as the various organizations retained their own camps, bases, forces and organizational affiliates abroad.[115] Indeed, any possibility that the traumatic events of the previous fourteen months and the debilitated state of the resistance would compel the leaders to bury their differences once and for all was soon laid to rest as new groups surfaced. *Fatah* was convulsed by disputes and the PLO leadership was shaken by the Israeli Beirut raid, which resulted in the deaths of three key leaders.

The emergence of new groups centered around the PFLP and *Fatah*. In early 1972, Abu Shihab defected from the PFLP with a group of followers and formed the Popular Revolutionary Front for the Liberation of Palestine (PRFLP). A more important product of the PFLP's endemic discontent, however, was revealed in July 1973 when the hijacking and destruction of a Japanese 747 aircraft was attributed to the "Sons of the Occupied Territory," a group believed to be under the control of Habash's chief lieutenant, Wadi Hadad, who was reported by the "Voice of Palestine" to be operating independently. Since the PLO had by that time reversed course and condemned hijacking, it argued that the act harmed the prestige and reputation of the revolution and ordered an investigation. The PFLP, which had temporarily suspended hijacking, did likewise.[116]

Fatah, too, was torn by dissidence during 1972-1973. Rejecting an agreement with the Lebanese government in the fall of 1972 to reduce forces

in and attacks from southern Lebanon, a group led by Abu Yusef al-Kayed
withdrew to a mountain stronghold where it engaged in hostilities with
Fatah loyalists that ended only after the intercession of the Algerian
ambassador to Lebanon. Besides the Lebanese issue, other factors gave rise
to the reported murder of *Fatah* agents in Rome and to leadership debates
that spilled over into the PLO. These factors included maneuvering
against Arafat, debates over the role of external terror, and the question of
whether or not to tack with political winds in the Arab world and seek a
political settlement with Israel.[117]

The most salient outcome of the turbulence within *Fatah*, as far as
general impact was concerned, was the formation of the Black September
Organization *(Ailul al-Aswad)*. Though previously opposed to terrorism,
especially transnational operations, the *Fatah* leadership had come under
increasing pressure from some members, who were traumatized by the civil
war in Jordan, to extract revenge and punish enemies (particularly Israelis
and Jordanians), regardless of their locations. In response, *Fatah* gave its
security and intelligence apparatus, *Jihaz al-Rasd*, the responsibility for
conducting terrorist incidents inside and outside the Middle East. A façade
of detachment was maintained by attributing attacks to the BSO.[118]

There was no single answer to why *Fatah* countenanced this course of
action. Rather, this compromise between avoidance of terrorist operations
and open support of them seemed to stem from several motives, namely (1)
preventing alienated radicals from leaving *Fatah*; (2) exercising control
over incidents which were bound to occur anyway; (3) demonstrating the
continued viability of the armed struggle at a time when alternative courses
of violent action (attacks within the target area and across the border)
showed little or no promise; (4) avoiding criticism in the Arab world and
outside it for terrorist incidents through the use of a cover group; and (5)
denying Israel an obvious target for reprisals.[119] As things turned out,
Fatah's attempt to have it both ways was exposed, with the result that the
PLO was subjected to Israeli reprisals which intensified tensions with
Lebanon because of the collateral costs inflicted on the latter. More
important, since the operations of the BSO not only had a negative
impact on the Arab image internationally but also affronted specific Arab
states, such as the Sudan and Saudi Arabia (e.g., the assassination of
American diplomats in the Saudi embassy in Khartoum in March 1973), the
PLO and *Fatah* witl.drew support for hijacking and BSO operations
declined precipitously.

The *volte face* on the part of *Fatah* did not bring an end to either
terrorism or factionalism, for in September 1973 an organization called
"Punishment Group" occupied the Saudi embassy in Paris and seized
hostages. Although sharp PLO criticism of this act stood in marked

contrast to the adulation of the BSO one year before, it also underscored another division in *Fatah* ranks, namely, the emergence of an independent group led by Sabri al-Banna (also called Abu Nidal), the former *Fatah* representative in Baghdad, which claimed to be part of *Fatah*, but in actuality defied the latter and castigated Arafat. Following the October War, the Nidal faction, which was based in Iraq, would resume operations and, along with other maverick groups, generate problems for the PLO in the Arab world and abroad.

The difficulties generated by the BSO were not the only ones experienced by the PLO during 1972-1973. In Lebanon, which had become the main staging area for guerrilla raids, a pattern of events analogous to the one in Jordan unfolded as Israeli reprisals and the Palestinian challenge to Lebanese sovereignty led to clashes with the army. These, in turn, resulted in compromise agreements negotiated by the pragmatists in the PLO. Here again, the situation in Jordan was replicated as left-wing groups refused to abide by the accords. In May 1973, this situation brought a major confrontation between the army and the fedayeen, principally the PDF. While the outcome was not as deleterious as in Jordan because, among other things, the PLO had strong support from the Muslim community, the fighting did take its toll in lives and resources and brought further curbs on guerrilla activity.[120]

As the fateful days of October 1973 approached, the fedayeen found themselves in a state of relative impotence, with guerrilla activities reduced to insignificance and terrorist operations abroad curtailed and disavowed by the PLO. Though Israeli countermeasures had a good deal to do with this situation, there was no gainsaying that the disunity of the resistance also played a major part. The words spoken by Salah Khalef in the spring of 1971 seemed more applicable than ever. Going directly to the heart of fedayeen problems Khalef had lamented, "We had twelve organizations which meant twelve leaderships, twelve different strategies and twelve different guns pointing in twelve different directions. From all that our ills grew."[121]

Unification Strategies

Looking back over several years of fedayeen activities, one could discern elements of three organizational schemes—division of labor, joint operations, and a unified command—which, as noted in Chapter 2, are designed to unify insurgent movements. Unofficially, there was some division of labor, with groups like the PFLP, BSO, and PSF specializing in operations outside the Middle East, the AOLP limiting itself largely to sniper actions, and the larger groups like *Sa'iqa* and *Fatah* emphasizing guerrilla raids. However, since there was an overlap and since some types of operations were not agreed upon by all groups, it would have been a mistake to depict this as effective coordination.

Joint operations involving various combinations of guerrilla organizations did take place on a number of occasions, usually under PASC auspices.[122] Since they were often cited in exaggerated communiqués, it was hard to establish their real significance. The fact that the fedayeen tried to establish a unified command on a number of occasions suggested that joint operations or a division of labor were considered unsatisfactory approaches.

Realizing that disunity was a basic factor contributing to many other problems, all the fedayeen organizations stressed the need for a centralized command. Nevertheless, since both the left-wing and right-wing organizations wanted the central structure to reflect their own ideologies and tactics, the various schemes put forth proved either stillborn (UCPR), short-lived and ineffective (CCPR), or persistent but unable to control all organizations (the PASC, PLO-EC, etc.). At no time did all the fedayeen organizations subordinate themselves to a central authority, at the expense of their own ideologies and tactics. Even emergency coordination during the crises in Jordan proved to be ephemeral, with left-wing groups soon returning to their denunciation of the king and moderate groups trying to reach a viable accord with him.[123]

In view of the inability to incorporate the rival organizations into a single, legitimate decision-making structure, there is little to be gained from analyzing the potential organizational formats which such a structure might have had. Not only would such formats have failed, but they most likely would have become a source of further internal conflict. Indeed, it was precisely fear of such conflict that led Arafat and his cohorts to sidestep Egyptian suggestions that they form a government-in-exile, reasoning that the various groups would engage in a struggle over the filling of positions such as president and foreign minister. Thus, the PLO forced a typical catch-22 situation. While it desperately needed a single institution to provide cohesion, the viability of such an institution was dependent upon a meaningful political consensus which did not exist. One answer to this dilemma was, of course, the use of force; but, for reasons discussed earlier, that, too, was eschewed.

Complexity and Functions

As noted in the previous chapters, the differentiation and extension of an insurgent organization have a major determinative effect on its ability to increase both popular and external support.[124] With regard to complexity, the PLO spawned a rather elaborate structure at the central level. Located at the apex was the PNC, the supreme authority for formulating policies and programs. During regular sessions, the PNC reviewed reports by the Palestine National Fund and the Executive Committee. The latter, a small committee selected from within the PNC, chose its own chairman. The Executive Committee's role was to supervise various bodies of the PLO, execute policy, prepare a budget, and make decisions and devise programs in accordance with the National Charter and PNC resolutions. In 1973 a central council was created to implement PNC resolutions and to coordinate activities of the PNC and the PLO-EC. Not surprisingly, the membership in these structures overlapped and generally mirrored the existing power structure of the PNC.

In addition to the formal political institutions of the PLO, there was a broad range of functional and service organizations handling workers, medical needs, education, welfare, and informational activities. The purpose of the auxiliary organizations was to mobilize the Palestinian masses through propaganda and the provision of services. Though such differentiation was necessary for the creation of a broad base of popular support, it was not sufficient, for success also depended upon extension of the organization to the various Palestinian communities.

As already noted in preceding chapters, one of the major PLO problems was the failure to extend its organization into the occupied areas in such a way as to create base areas governed by parallel hierarchies. Indeed, institutional control was exercised by Israel in 1970, with the result that it was the Israeli-guided local administration which performed instrumental functions by providing essential services. Although Israel could not provide channels for the expression of protest, neither could the fedayeen fully do so, once their rudimentary structures in the occupied areas were uncovered and destroyed.[125]

Several fedayeen organizations, particularly the PFLP and *Fatah*, had tried to organize in the occupied areas after the June War. Yet, despite *Fatah*'s claim in early 1968 that it had hidden bases in Israel and the occupied areas from which its guerrillas operated daily,[126] the organizational structures which did exist were never more than sabotage cells or networks. One observer has aptly summed up the organizational situation in the occupied areas in 1970, and put it into a meaningful perspective, by comparing it to other insurgencies:

> Although the commandos [claim] to have clandestine networks within Israel and its occupied territories—they seem to be quasi-intelligence rather than tactical combat networks—they have failed to establish either in Israel or the territories any apparatus comparable with those formed by the Viet Cong in Vietnam, the Pathet Lao in Laos, by Castro in Batista Cuba, the

Hukbalahaps in the Philippines or by some of the revolutionary groups in Central and South America and Africa.[127]

This state of affairs was acknowledged during the eleventh PNC meeting in January 1973, when *Fatah* indicated an interest in using Communist party cells in the occupied areas because of the loss of PLO networks. In addition to being an inadequate corrective measure, even this step entailed problems, since the inactive Communist organization, *Al-Ansar,* supported a political settlement and the remaining second echelon cadres on the West Bank opposed cooperation with the Communists for fear of an Israeli crackdown.[128]

All told, it appeared that in the case of the Palestinians, the revolutionary side could be subjected to a criticism usually reserved for the incumbent regime—namely, the failure to appreciate the primacy of the political dimension because of an overemphasis on military operations. This criticism, however, was not valid for the situation in the contiguous states.

It was not mere coincidence that it was in the refugee camps—where the fedayeen were able to organize the people and to perform, at least to some degree, instrumental and expressive functions—that the resistance enjoyed the highest degree of popular support.[129] In the summer of 1968 Israel learned from captured commandos that *Fatah* and other organizations had gained almost extraterritorial status on the East Bank, with *Fatah* virtually administering the Salt area.[130] Indeed, it was no secret at the time that the fedayeen had a number of supply and training bases in Jordan supplemented by "popular bases" in the refugee camps, where the insurgent organizations, especially *Fatah,* had begun to provide educational, medical, and welfare benefits (instrumental functions).[131] Of particular importance in this scheme was the Palestinian Red Crescent Society, which had been officially recognized on January 25, 1969, by the PLO as the official organization for first aid, medical services, and humanitarian needs. Its nationalist role was inherent in its stated primary goal, "to embody the Palestinian entity and confirm the existence of the Palestinian personality in connection with health, social and cultural affairs of the Palestinians, on both the local and international levels."[132]

Jordan was not the only country in which the fedayeen had established a parallel hierarchy, since there was confirmation from the head of the United Nations Relief Works Agency, Laurence Michelmore, in November 1969 that the fedayeen had taken control of the refugee camps in Lebanon.[133] A few months later the HPCPA in Lebanon acknowledged the fedayeen role in the camps, when it issued a directive which, among other things, said the security and safety of the revolution would be the task of the fedayeen, although Lebanese security forces would be allowed positions outside the camps. Similar remarks had been made by the interior minister of Lebanon.[134]

The fact that most recruits and support came from the refugee camps in Jordan and Lebanon was closely related to the ability of the fedayeen to maintain the balance of coercive and institutional control in their favor. Not only did the fedayeen organizational structure provide a number of services, but it also extended its scope by allowing women and children to play active roles in the movement. Women carried out operations (Leila Khaled of the PFLP, for example) and were heralded by the fedayeen for so doing, while the training camps for youngsters—the tiger cubs—were widely publicized.[135]

The fedayeen ability to establish parallel hierarchies in the refugee camps in Jordan and Lebanon enabled them to mobilize enough support to cause Israel substantial concern in 1968-1969. A fatal flaw in all of this, however, was the simple fact that the new political structures were parallel to the host states rather than to Israel. Since this meant that they were an affront to the sovereignty of the former, they eventually contributed to the hostilities with both Jordan and Lebanon.

As far as complexity on the military level was concerned, there was evidence that the guerrillas had a division of functions, at least formally. In addition to the regular PLA, which did little fighting, there were the terrorists and guerrilla raiders of the fedayeen groups and the part-time militias attached to several organizations, especially the PDF and the PFLP. However, unlike local guerrilla forces in other insurgencies (e.g., the Viet Cong in Vietnam), the Palestinian militias did not operate against the target regime. Since, instead, they were relegated largely to providing security against the military and police forces of the sanctuary states, especially Jordan, they could not be considered the functional equivalents of the local guerrilla forces in past insurgencies. Moreover, even if the militias could somehow have been deployed against Israel, they would still have had to overcome the same differences which plagued the parent organizations.[136]

While a rough division of functions did exist on the military level, the fact that the various elements could not be coordinated by any authoritative central command deprived them of any potential value they might have had. Indeed, the relationships among the PLA, guerrilla organizations, and militias were as badly coordinated as those among the parent insurgent organizations.

Summary and Conclusions

With the empirical analysis of the fedayeen organization completed, three tasks remain: (1) a summation of the underlying reasons for fedayeen disunity; (2) an analysis of the relationships among the organizational variables; and (3) an analysis of the relationships among organizational variables and the other major factors under consideration in the study.

Causes of Disunity

Three specific causes of fedayeen disunity are readily apparent. First, there were bona fide differences over ideology and tactics among several organizations. Second, there were personal rivalries and struggles for power among the fedayeen leaders themselves. Third, and superimposed on these cleavages, was the infusion of interstate differences into the guerrilla movement by organizations sponsored by Arab regimes. Thus, with the active participation of the Syrian-backed *Sa'iqa*, the Iraqi-supported ALF and the pro-Egyptian AOLP and APO, the fedayeen movement came to reflect many of the conflicts among Arab nations.

In addition to the three specific sources of disunity, there are two of a more general nature. The first is the high value placed on individualism in Arab society, which a number of observers have argued is responsible for the adulation of heroes and the resistance to discipline.[137] By this argument, Palestinian tendencies toward indiscipline and personalism are outgrowths of their political culture.

A second general cause of fedayeen disunity seems to be the modernization of the Palestinian community, as Professor Michael Hudson has discussed.[138] Since the literacy and educational levels of the Palestinians were relatively high for the Arab world, and many members of the diaspora found their way to metropolitan centers like Beirut, they were exposed to various modern ideologies. These ideologies, as pointed out earlier in the chapter, influenced a number of Palestinian intellectuals and found their way into the resistance. Just as the various ideologies led to profound differences among the Arab states, so, too, they led to grave differences among the fedayeen. Both specific and general causes, then, combined to produce the deep cleavages which defied attempt after attempt by the Palestinians to unify their movement.

Relationships Among Organizational Variables

In terms of scope, the fedayeen numbered approximately 25,000, excluding the 12,000-man PLA. Most of the cadres, guerrilla fighters, and their supporters came from refugee camps located in Jordan, Lebanon, and Syria. It was not by chance that the movement, for the most part, focused on camps where the fedayeen had established a shadow government which performed instrumental and expressive functions. Nor was it mere happenstance that the majority of Arabs in Israel and the occupied areas were outside the scope of the movement by the time Israel had neutralized the guerrilla organizational structures (1970). All of this confirmed the close link between popular support and organization. That is to say, participation in the movement within given areas varied quite strongly with the presence or absence of complex organizational structures (parallel hierarchies).

One reason the fedayeen were unable to extend their parallel hierarchy to the occupied areas was the weakness of the movement at the central level resulting from the chronic disunity. Indeed, without a well-planned and disciplined effort, it was almost impossible to implant even a low-level shadow government within the target area. As a result of the divisiveness within the resistance, organizational efforts within the target area amounted to little more than ad hoc activities by individual groups. Worse yet, the divisiveness often led to clashes among insurgents which in turn made it easier for the Israelis to detect and expunge fedayeen cells.

On the military level, there was a loose division of functions among regular forces, full-time guerrillas, and militias. However, the lack of cohesion within the resistance movement prevented these forces from being utilized in the systematic and well-organized manner which had characterized military operations in successful protracted insurgencies of the past (the Viet Minh against France, Mao against Chiang, etc.). Factionalism and lack of coordination remained the dominant reality. In general terms, it might therefore be proposed that severe disunity will prevent insurgent revolutionary military forces from operating effectively, even if they manifest a degree of functional differentiation.

Organization and the Other Major Variables

There was an interdependent relationship between organization and government response. To begin with, the overall effectiveness of the Israeli counterinsurgency program and the particular efficiency of the security and intelligence apparatus, especially between 1969 and 1971, not only frustrated fedayeen efforts to extend their organizational structures to the occupied areas, but also led to the detection and destruction of most of the cells implanted in 1968 and 1969. The result was consistent with the hypothesis that the scope and extension of an organization varies strongly and inversely with regime effectiveness. That is, where the government devises and implements a policy based on sound counterinsurgency principles (see Chapters 2 and 4), the membership in and extension of an insurgent organization is reduced to minimal levels.

As far as the government's impact on insurgent cohesion is concerned, the conclusions are more speculative. Although Israeli penetration of the fedayeen organizations was common knowledge, the covert nature of such action makes it difficult to ascertain the precise impact of agent provocateurs on internecine conflicts among the fedayeen. Those conflicts were rooted in other, more profound factors internal to the PLO, and the role of Israeli agents was probably limited to exacerbating cleavages rather than causing them.

On a more general level, the overall strength of Israel seemed to be a contributing factor to the ideological and tactical differences that plagued the Palestinians. In the first place, the formidable capability of Israel reinforced the proclivity of the left-wing organizations to stress revolution in the Arab world as a precondition for creating the assets necessary to overcome and defeat their Zionist adversary. Secondly, as the Israelis demonstrated their ability to effectively manage the threat internally and along the borders, a number of fedayeen groups turned to external terrorist operations, which had the eventual effect of accentuating tactical differences among the insurgents.

Turning the relationship around and treating organization as the independent variable, it is plausible to surmise that the Palestinians' inability to extend their organization to the target area reduced the burden on Israel and allowed the latter's attention to be focused elsewhere. The disunity of guerrilla organizations also benefited Israel since it impeded the extension of a complex organization into the target area, a development which would have increased the problems of the military government. Also, it caused attention and resources to be diverted away from the armed struggle and towards clashes involving rival groups and host governments. In both instances Israel was the main beneficiary since demands on its security forces were decreased. Thus, one could hypothesize that the effectiveness of a regime would vary moderately and inversely with the ability of the revolutionaries to extend their organization and create a cohesive movement.

The relationship between organization and popular support has already been discussed in several contexts. It is sufficient to repeat that the degree of popular support enjoyed by fedayeen organizations varied strongly with their ability to organize in a given area.

Although the question of external support remains to be discussed, several linkages with organization are already discernible. The most salient lesson drawn from the Palestinian case is that the inability of the resistance to discipline the various groups which were antagonistic to the regimes of external support states jeopardized the provision of political, moral, material, and sanctuary support by these states. Nowhere was this more clearly illustrated than in Jordan, where the rivalry of guerrilla organizations prevented their developing into a cohesive overall organization that could have achieved a modus vivendi with the regime. Instead, ideological hostility led some groups into an almost inevitable conflict with the regime. A modest theoretical implication can be drawn from this: that a lack of cohesion in an insurgent movement which contains organizations ideologically antipathetic toward external support states is likely to undercut external provision of tangible and intangible support over the long term.

Disunity aside, the fedayeen attempt to obtain external support, particularly sanctuary and freedom of movement, was also hindered by the need to organize the populations of refugee camps as the popular base of support. Since the establishment of parallel hierarchies undermined sovereignty of the host countries, it damaged relations with them. The explicit threats to the Jordanian government posed by left-wing groups, for instance, when combined with the organizational challenge to Jordanian authority in the camps, produced an untenable situation for Hussein. He responded by denying the commandos the last vestiges of support within his kingdom. The fact that the Israelis were effective in preventing the guerrillas from organizing in the occupied areas could not be overlooked in this context, since it made it imperative that the fedayeen organize in and operate from the sanctuary countries. Thus, rather than serving in an auxiliary capacity (as a safe haven and supply area), the sanctuaries in Jordan became the focal point of fedayeen strength. This, in turn, meant Jordan suffered more Israeli reprisals than might have been the case if the main base of insurgent strength had been in the occupied areas and Israel. It also meant that a larger number of commando forces were located in Jordan, a fact which combined with the ideological hostility of left-wing groups to increase the uneasiness of the regime.

Several general propositions are suggested by this summary. First, if a regime effectively prevents an insurgent movement from organizing within the target area, external support, in terms of sanctuary and freedom of movement, becomes critical. Second, if a sanctuary country is clearly in a position of military inferiority vis-à-vis the target state and lacks allies who will come to its defense, the costs inflicted by counterinsurgency reprisals are likely to increase. Third, a sanctuary state, defenseless against reprisals but perceiving itself to be militarily equal to or stronger than the insurgents, will curb the latter's operations as the costs of retaliation escalate. A fourth and closely related hypothesis is that external support will vary moderately with the cohesiveness of the guerrilla organization since the more cohesive the insurgent movement, the more capable it is to discipline and control elements hostile to the external support states.[139] The fifth hypothesis is that if an insurgent organization finds it necessary to establish a parallel hierarchy in an external support state, which governs part of the state's territory and population, violent conflict with the host state is almost inevitable.

The hypotheses and propositions just enumerated are designed not only to be tested in other cases, but also to underline the far-reaching and debilitating effects that insufficient or misdirected organizational efforts and disunity can have both in terms of organization and cohesion, and with regard to regime effectiveness, popular support, and external support. Also, of course, the hypotheses reflect the organizational deficiencies and consequences of the case from which they were drawn. Accordingly, in the Palestinian situation, one is left to ponder who the worst enemies of the fedayeen were: the Israelis or themselves?

7
External Support

The importance to insurgent movements of external support in the form of political and moral backing, the provision of sanctuaries, and material aid was discussed in Chapter 2. In cases where the regime being threatened demonstrates its effectiveness in dealing with insurgent activity within its boundaries, external support—especially material aid and the provision of sanctuaries—usually becomes a critical need. In particular, the tactic of relying on weapons seized from the enemy is not a practical means of equipping military units under such circumstances. Such was precisely the situation facing the fedayeen, who were unable to inflict serious military defeats on the Israelis, and hence could not depend on the capture of enemy weapons to sustain their operations. This meant that from the earliest stages of the revolution the fedayeen had to depend on outside sources for material support.

External support in the specific form of sanctuaries from which to operate freely also becomes crucial in cases where counterinsurgency forces deny the insurgents the ability to operate with impunity in the target country, or area, since the sanctuary then constitutes the main guerrilla base of operations. As Chapters 4 through 6 have indicated, a combination of Israeli countermeasures and fedayeen organizational shortcomings created a situation in which sanctuaries did, in fact, become the last fall-back positions for the guerrillas, particularly by the end of 1969, when insurgent organizational structures in the occupied areas were largely neutralized. Consequently, the fedayeen placed great emphasis on the importance of states adjacent to Israel as operational bases for conducting their people's war.

The response to the Palestinian quest for external support from potentially sympathetic states in the Arab world and the Communist bloc was far from uniform. At just about every point in time between 1967 and

1973, the response included an admixture of contradictions—enthusiasm and indifference, friendship and hostility, largesse and selfishness—which reflected the variability of both the attitudes of specific donors and the types of support rendered. In order to understand the rather convoluted situation involving fedayeen relations with important donor states, two considerations are important: (1) a brief summary of relations in each case, and (2) the identification and analysis of underlying explanatory factors, with particular reference to the four categories of external support. Our discussion begins with an examination of the state considered most important in the fedayeen scheme, the Hashemite Kingdom of Jordan.

Jordan

Historical Overview

There was little in fedayeen-Jordanian relations prior to the June 1967 War that augured a hopeful future for the fedayeen, inasmuch as the Hashemite regime had forcibly impeded Palestinian operations against Israel and arrested a number of insurgents.[1] Basically, three factors accounted for this state of affairs: fear of Israeli reprisals, concern that armed guerrilla units sponsored by unfriendly states (the PLO by Egypt and *Fatah* by Syria) might attempt to subvert the monarchy, and cognizance that the liberation of Palestine, however remote, would mean the loss of the West Bank.[2]

In spite of whatever trepidations they might have had, the fedayeen found they had little choice but to operate from Jordan after the war, if they were to carry out guerrilla attacks against Israel in the absence of an effective organization in the occupied areas. Besides, the defeat of the Jordanian army had removed an immediate threat, and the rising sympathy for the fedayeen among the Arab masses had generated pressures on Arab leaders to support the guerrillas.[3]

In view of constraints imposed by these conditions, it was not surprising that Jordanian behavior was inconsistent. On the one hand, the army periodically supported guerrilla incursions with covering artillery fire, while on the other hand, the king warned against the cost of operations across the border, indicated a willingness to accept Israel's existence, endorsed SC-242, and held secret meetings with Israeli representatives. This course of events was profoundly unsettling to the Palestinians since it clashed directly with the ultimate aim of the movement.[4]

Although the government made occasional efforts to control the fedayeen by detaining guerrillas and confiscating arms, activities along the border increased, Israeli reprisals followed, and the army continued to provide sporadic assistance to the guerrillas. After the Karamah battle in

March 1968, in which the army fought alongside the guerrillas, Hussein declared that "we are all fedayeen" and indicated that he would cooperate with "the best elements" among the commandos.[5] Though the Israeli propaganda apparatus quickly seized upon this as proof that "the rulers of Jordan [had] adopted an 'open door' policy towards the terrorist groups," the situation was far more complex.[6]

Caught between the hammer of Israeli reprisals and the anvil of rising sympathy for the Palestinians, Hussein vacillated in his attitudes toward the guerrillas from 1968 to 1970. Though pledging moral support for the insurgents, he continued to lament the economic dislocation caused by Israeli attacks, to search for a political solution that the Palestinians could only regard as anathema, to obstruct guerrilla operations and to guard against threats to the regime.

The incongruity of Jordanian and Palestinian interests led not only to sporadic minor clashes, but also to major confrontations involving the army and the guerrillas in November 1968, February 1970, June 1970, and September 1970. During the major conflicts, a more or less cyclical pattern of events emerged that was characterized by government efforts to control the guerrillas; fighting instigated by guerrilla groups ideologically hostile to the regime (*Sa'iqa*, the PFLP, and the PDF); involvement of the *Fatah*-PLO wing on behalf of their beleaguered comrades; creation of emergency organizational structures by the fedayeen to face the common threat; temporary accords between the government and the PLO negotiated by representatives from the Arab states; denunciation of the accords and the regime by left-wing groups; continued guerrilla attacks and Israeli reprisals; and renewed attempts by the government to control the guerrillas.[7] During such episodes Israel warned both sides of the consequences of renewed guerrilla activity; in September 1970, it actually mobilized forces, notably the air force, for possible action against the fedayeen should the Jordanian army find itself on the brink of defeat.[8]

As was noted in previous chapters, the September 1970 civil war in Jordan was a turning point in the relationship between the Palestinians and Jordan, because the severe defeats suffered by the guerrillas left the army in a preponderant position militarily. Despite an agreement negotiated in Cairo and some rather half-hearted attempts at accommodation between the government and *Fatah*, deep-seated hostility on the part of both sides persisted. Following renewed fighting in October, which forced the fedayeen to withdraw to bases near Jerash and Ajloun in the north, the situation remained unsettled for several months, with each side charging the other had either violated or failed to implement the Cairo accord. Additionally, there were armed clashes, promises by Prime Minister Tal to establish law and order, acts of sabotage and pledges to overthrow Hussein on the part of the PFLP and PDF, and attempts by *Fatah* to reconcile differences with the government. One episode of fighting in January 1971 moved the Damascus daily *Al-Thawra* to comment sardonically that a new accord to end the fighting was "an agreement for the implementation of the agreements in order to agree on reaching agreements."[9]

The sarcasm was soon justified as the two sides castigated and threatened each other, the left-wing guerrillas defied attempts by moderates to mitigate criticisms of the government, and new fighting broke out. Finally, on July 13, 1971, the military moved with air power, armor, and artillery to expel from the country an estimated 3,000 to 5,000 fedayeen located in the Jerash-Ajloun area.[10] Although the guerrillas appealed to the Arab states to intervene to save the revolution and Syria tried to achieve a truce through mediation, the attacks continued and Tal reported on July 19 that no guerrilla bases were left in Jordan and that 2,300 of 2,500 fedayeen had been taken prisoner. A day later, Tal said that 2,000 had been released, 700 leaving the country and the remainder laying down their arms. But, undoubtedly the best testimony to both the near absolute deterioration of the fedayeen position in Jordan and the hatred between the army and the guerrillas was the fact that some 100 guerrillas fled into Israeli hands in order to avoid being slaughtered by their Arab brothers. Closure of the Syrian and Iraqi borders with Jordan and sharp protests from the Arab states came too late to spare the fedayeen from the fate of being completely deprived of any operational presence in their "pillar base."[11]

Subsequent attempts by the Arab states to reconcile the PLO and Jordan broke down. Having finally expunged the fedayeen, King Hussein adamantly opposed any return other than token representation under strict army control, a condition unacceptable to the PLO. Besides losing their most important sanctuary, the fedayeen had suffered severe human and material losses. Frustrated and angry, they lashed out at Jordan through the operations of the BSO, assassinating Prime Minister Tal, wounding the Jordanian ambassador to Britain, and plotting against the monarchy.

The political violence directed againt the regime merely stiffened the government's resolve to deny fedayeen reentry into Jordan. Moreover, Hussein proceeded to announce a plan for a United Arab Kingdom during March 1972 which, although it would grant the West Bank local autonomy, nevertheless would leave it under Hashemite control.[12] This scheme, which Israel immediately rejected, led the PNC to commit itself to the overthrow of Hussein in January 1973 and Egypt to break relations with Jordan.[13]

Several attempts to reconcile the fedayeen and Jordan over the next seventeen months came to naught. In the meantime Hussein openly criticized the terrorism of the BSO and resisted its demands (e.g., the

Khartoum incident) to release from jail Palestinian leaders, including Abu Dawud. One month prior to the October War, however, Hussein reversed course and declared an amnesty for Dawud and others in the wake of a renewal of relations with Egypt and Syria which were secretly solidifying Arab ranks for the coming battle with Israel. An underlying motive was believed to be the Jordanian desire to have restored an annual $40 million subsidy, which had been suspended by Kuwait since 1970.

In any case, Jordan made it clear that the guerrillas could not return and that those who were released would be prohibited from engaging in political activity.

In looking back over several years of conflict in relations between the fedayeen and Jordan, the period between September 1970 and July 1971 stands out, for it was during this time that the guerrillas' flight from Jordan terminated the last advantage they had enjoyed—sanctuary. Moreover, besides being denied material support and losing the freedom of movement and sanctuary so vital for any semblance of guerrilla activity against Israel, the fedayeen suffered serious material and human losses. Since the commando losses in Jordan ended up being greater than their gains, their enterprise there had actually been counterproductive. Taking stock of the events during that period, Salah Khalef admitted that the movement had suffered a "political defeat" and "time was not in our favor."[14]

Types of External Support

As the foregoing account of fedayeen-Jordanian relations from 1967 to 1973 suggests, the Jordanians did extend *moral* support to the fedayeen by acknowledging the "just and lawful" cause for which the Palestinians were fighting. However, when it came to *political* support—agreement with and active support for the specific PLO objective—there was a clear divergence. Although agreeing with the insurgents that an independent Palestinian state should not be established alongside Israel (the scheme being discussed by independent Palestinians and some Israelis), Jordan did not endorse the goal of liberating Israel.[15] To the contrary, the king indicated several times that he was prepared to accept the reality of Israeli existence as part of a political settlement. This stand, of course, was totally rejected by the fedayeen and contributed on several occasions to fighting with Jordanian forces. It was also clear that Jordan was opposed to the idea of the PLO liberating the West Bank since that area was considered part of the Hashemite kingdom.[16] That Jordan was highly sensitive to the possibility that the West Bank might be permanently detached from Jordan was illustrated by its repeated rejection of the idea of a Palestinian state. The most Hussein would concede on this matter was a willingness to allow the West Bank population to control local affairs as part of a United Arab

Kingdom in which his government would continue to exercise ultimate power. What was obvious was that Hussein wished to be in a position to control the destiny of Palestinians within his kingdom rather than allowing the fedayeen to exercise such control.

In short, political support for the fedayeen was, in reality, non-existent, since Hussein was prepared to acknowledge Israel's existence and was not prepared to allow the guerrillas the primary role in determining the future of the West Bank Palestinians. This inherent contradiction between the PLO and Jordanian political objectives was a profound underlying cause of the numerous clashes between the two sides.

Despite growing strains between the fedayeen and Jordan, the latter did render some *material assistance* to the guerrillas until 1970. Most important was the periodic provision of intelligence about Israeli forces and occasional cover-fire for cross-border operations. However, there was no evidence that Jordan supplied the fedayeen with substantial financial aid or large amounts of weapons, ammunition, and medical supplies during the period of this study.

In 1970-1971 the worsening relations between Jordan and the fedayeen, the civil war, and subsequent clashes led to a termination of intelligence and artillery support for the insurgents and to the confiscation of fedayeen arms and ammunition. Thus, as suggested earlier, the situation became counterproductive for the guerrillas, with the army actually reducing the material supplies of the resistance rather than adding to them.

The most important contribution Jordan could have made to the fedayeen movement, as far as the guerrillas were concerned, would have been the granting of *sanctuary* and freedom of movement. As insurgent operations within the target area became increasingly ineffective, the guerrillas came to view Jordan as their indispensable primary base of operations for continuing the armed struggle. Three factors, however, prevented Jordan from extending these privileges to the fedayeen. First of all, the Israelis were not content to sit back and allow the guerrillas to infiltrate from, or fire across, the border. As pointed out in Chapter 5, the IDF employed a multifaceted strategy to deal with this problem, part of which involved search and destroy operations, commando raids, and air strikes against the Jordanian sanctuary. Since these resulted in a refugee flow toward the interior of Jordan and economic dislocations (e.g., the periodic attacks on the East Ghor Canal), the costs to Jordan became increasingly unacceptable. Indeed, since the army could not stop Israeli attacks, it became evident that the only solution was the cessation of guerrilla attacks which Israel was demanding. Although fedayeen operations had been tolerated at various times, because of the weakness of the army after June 1967, and because it seemed they might serve Jordanian strategy by increasing pressure on Israel to make concessions, by 1970-1971 there were repeated instances of the Jordanian army intercepting guerrilla units en route to the border. What had happened was that gains for Jordanian political-military strategy had proven to be negligible, given Israel's firm stand, whereas the costs of allowing the fedayeen to operate had risen. The question of gains and losses and Israeli reprisals, however, was not the only factor behind the transformation in Jordanian policy toward the fedayeen.

The fact that the guerrillas had established parallel hierarchies in the refugee camps was clearly a challenge to Jordanian sovereignty. Many times during the civil war and its aftermath, the right to impose law and order was cited by the regime as a reason for fighting with the fedayeen. In the end, Amman found it impossible to abide by temporary solutions which left Jordanian sovereignty in doubt.

Closely related to the challenge posed by the guerrilla organization within Jordan was the explicit threat to Hussein's regime from the left-wing organizations. The facts that the PFLP and PDF were self-declared enemies of Hussein and that *Sa'iqa* and the ALF were sponsored by regimes hostile to Jordan made the king uneasy about allowing them to organize armed forces within his borders.

In summary, several factors converged to produce the crackdown on the fedayeen. First of all, there was the Jordanian willingness to accept Israel and the contradictions between ultimate PLO and Hashemite aspirations regarding the West Bank. Second, there was the challenge to Jordanian sovereignty posed by the insurgent parallel hierarchy controlling the refugee camps. Third, there were explicit threats against the regime by the left-wing groups and efforts by them, and, eventually, the PLO, to assassinate Hussein and topple the regime. Fourth, there were continued costs to the economy from Israeli reprisals. And, fifth, in 1970 there were intensified frictions between the guerrillas and the army, which had not only gradually rebuilt its strength, but also consolidated control in the hands of Bedouin officers loyal to the king.[17]

While factors such as these were sufficient to produce violent interaction between the army and the fedayeen, once proximate causes such as the September 1970 multiple skyjacking were provided, they did not totally explain the government's eventual success. To understand the latter, one would have to acknowledge, inter alia, the role Israel and the United States played in deterring Syria from using its air force in the crucial days of 1970 and, no doubt, in the months thereafter.

Lebanon

Historical Overview

Prior to the June 1967 War, Lebanon opposed guerrilla operations against Israel from its territory. On numerous occasions Lebanese security forces intercepted fedayeen en route to Israel and publications of *Fatah* bitterly attacked Beirut authorities for putting obstacles in the path of the revolution. When the raiders did make it to Israel, the IDF often responded with limited reprisals. All in all, however, fedayeen operations from Lebanon were not crucial in events leading up to the June War.[18]

For more than a year following the war, the fedayeen maintained a relatively low profile in Lebanon, where they had been allowed to organize, recruit, and conduct fund drives. During this period the Palestinians, though unhappy, did not expend much energy castigating the Lebanese acceptance of SC-242. Nevertheless, by November 1968 the situation in Lebanon became somewhat restive as both pro and anti-guerrilla demonstrators took to the streets in the wake of the Jordanian fighting and the premier responded by warning that he would deal harshly with any seditious elements.[19]

If the Lebanese maintained a discreet silence about the organizational and recruitment activities within their borders, Israel did not. In fact, with one bold act—the December 1968 heliborne operation against the Beirut airport—Israel pushed Lebanon onto center stage. Besides being a reprisal for an El Al airliner incident in Athens, the operation was also intended to compel Lebanon to prevent future guerrilla operations from its territory.

The immediate results of Israel's attack and warnings were mixed. On the one hand, the fedayeen, in early 1969, stepped up their attacks against Israeli settlements from positions along the border, while on the other hand, Lebanese officials met with the Israelis in an effort to lower tension. Moreover, Lebanon took steps to disassociate itself from transnational terrorist operations by criticizing attacks on civilian aircraft.[20] Unfortunately for the government, however, at the very time it was denying responsibility for fedayeen violence, some 500 insurgents were taking up positions in the rocky, mountainous region of Mount Hermon in the southeastern part of the country. In time, the guerrillas would consolidate their control in this area, which the Israelis referred to as *"Fatah* land," and would carry out attacks against Israel which led inexorably to Israeli retaliation and subsequent attempts by the government to control the guerrillas. In fact, such a pattern characterized a series of armed clashes between the army and the guerrillas, the most notable occurring in April and May 1969, October 1969, December 1972, and May 1973. Two and one-half years after the October War, conflicts between the fedayeen and their opponents within Lebanon would culminate in a savage civil war.

In many ways, the periodic army-fedayeen conflicts in Lebanon resembled the situation in Jordan. In the first place, ending the human and economic toll exacted by Israeli military operations was a major consideration in Beirut, both among the wealthier Christians, who were well represented in the political power structure, and, at times, among the peasants in the south, who, as the most directly affected party, stood to lose their crops, homes, and perhaps lives. In the summer of 1970, such losses moved district and municipal leaders from villages in the south to pressure the government to reestablish its authority in the region, and led demonstrators in Beirut, who came from the southern villages, to demand protection against Israel. By the fall of 1970, the peasants were insisting that guerrilla activity against Israel be proscribed.[21]

Demands by local officials for imposition of government authority raised the larger question of the affront to Lebanese sovereignty posed by the implantation of fedayeen organizational control in refugee camps and in areas of southern Lebanon. Like its counterpart in Amman, the regime in Beirut constantly attempted to reassert its authority. However, it was rebuffed by the fedayeen and their left-wing supporters within the Lebanese body politic.[22]

The conflicts in Lebanon were also analogous to the Jordanian case in that they were terminated by accords negotiated by outsiders, particularly the Egyptians, that were then rejected and denounced by left-wing groups. (The PFLP reportedly controlled half of the refugee camps.) Not surprisingly, the left-wing reaction also included condemnation of the government itself.[23] However, while the PFLP and the PDF believed the government should eventually be toppled, unlike the situation in Jordan, they did not press the point, lest they antagonize Syria and leftist allies in Lebanon, who opposed such a course of action.

Juxtaposed with similarities between Jordan and Lebanon were some important differences. To begin with, the Lebanese political system was quite unlike the monarchy in Jordan. Essentially, it was a consociational democracy (also referred to as a confessional system) with democratic structures at the central level—president, prime minister, cabinet, and parliament—which were manned directly or indirectly through periodic elections. Underlying this was a feudal-like societal structure characterized primarily by competing religious groups led by strong local leaders. In order to satisfy the demands of the religious groups for equitable representation, a National Covenant, dating back to the 1940s, specifically allocated offices to designated groups following elections. Thus, the president was always a Maronite Christian, the prime minister a Sunni Moslem, the speaker of the Chamber of Deputies a Shi'a Moslem, and so on.[24]

The nature of the political system and the delicate balance of power it reflected had significant implications for the Palestinian presence in Lebanon since it provided both allies and enemies. To understand why this was so, it is necessary to point out that since the 1950s, the Moslems had become increasingly unhappy because they felt the Christians had acquired a disproportionate share of the political and economic pie, a situation made all the more intolerable by the generally held belief that the Moslem population had not only grown faster than the Christian, but probably exceeded it. Under such circumstances, the Moslem and Christian communities demonstrated a clear, although not complete, tendency to polarize at the left and right ends of the political spectrum respectively. Important Moslem leaders like Kemal Jumblatt found the Palestinians not just ideologically attractive; they also saw them as possible allies against their Christian opponents. Conversely, the Christians despised the socialist currents in the PLO and viewed the latter as a real threat to the maintenance of Christian political and economic hegemony.

This situation had several consequences for the fedayeen. First of all, trepidations about the Palestinian presence led Christian political leaders like Suleiman Franjieh and Pierre Jumayal constantly to pressure the government to control the guerrillas. Worse yet, they led to armed confrontations between private Christian militias and Palestinian organizations, skirmishes which had the immediate effect of diverting Palestinian political and material resources to imbroglios in Lebanon rather than against Israel, and the long-term effect of preventing the fedayeen from consolidating their power and control.

On the other side of the coin, the ideological-religious cleavages in Lebanon provided the PLO with both political and armed support from the left during major crises with the government and the army. The support from the left, when combined with Syrian military support in the form of augmented *Sa'iqa* forces or the intervention of PLA units from southern Syria, prevented the army from inflicting a decisive defeat on the fedayeen.

Although the Palestinian situation in Lebanon was relatively better than in Jordan, it was by no means an encouraging one. The fedayeen were able to carry out periodic guerrilla attacks across the border and to prepare, organize, and train in Beirut and the refugee camps for transnational terrorist operations; however, they were subjected to strong Israeli reprisals (during which the army usually stood by silently), resulting in interruptions of guerrilla activity and the previously mentioned clashes with the army. In April and May 1973, a series of events—Israeli attacks on refugee camps and the raid against the PLO headquarters in Beirut, a sabotage attempt by the BSO in the Beirut airport, and the kidnapping of two army corporals by the PDF—produced a major armed conflict during which Syrian-backed invasion forces saved the fedayeen from possible disaster. Though the PLO was able to maintain its presence, its military wings had been temporarily clipped and, as a consequence, the border with Israel remained relatively quiet through October 1973.

Types of External Support

During the period covered by this study, Lebanon consistently gave the fedayeen *moral* support. For the most part, this consisted of statements to the effect that the Palestinian resistance was justified and legal and was merely seeking to redress the grievances of the Palestinian community.

When it came to *political* support for the fedayeen goal of liberating Palestine, the Lebanese government was not enthusiastic. Although no doubt favoring the objective in the abstract, since it might relieve Lebanon of a large refugee burden, the Lebanese knew that its achievement was not likely in the immediate or intermediate future. The fact that the PLO was not about to achieve a quick victory meant that Lebanese interests could be jeopardized by the guerrillas' struggle to achieve their aims. Although there was no inherent territorial conflict between Lebanon and the fedayeen, as in the Jordanian situation (the commandos did not view sections of Lebanon as part of Palestine), there were other issues which divided the two sides.

As noted earlier, the Lebanese had both political and economic apprehensions about fedayeen activity, fearing that the confessional system might be upset and Israeli reprisals might result in severe damage to, and dislocation of, the economy. A more general concern was the possibility that Israel might use fedayeen activities from Lebanon as a pretext for annexing an area south of the Litani River. In light of these and other considerations, Lebanon decided to endorse SC-242 and the related quest for a political settlement, a move that placed it in direct conflict with the PLO.

While Lebanon did extend *material* support to the guerrillas by permitting them to recruit, train, and collect funds, and by contributing to the PLO, it was not one of the major benefactors of the insurgents. For arms and finances, the fedayeen turned elsewhere.

Lebanon was considered a front-line area for raids against Israel, next in importance to Jordan. While the government did permit a *sanctuary* and limited freedom of movement—probably out of concern for Arab and left-wing domestic pressure rather than affinity for the guerrillas—these concessions were always fragile, given the political and economic complications they caused. This situation led not only to severe violent episodes, but also to attempts to restrict both the fedayeen base area and operations along the Israeli border, especially after the guerrillas emerged in a weakened state from the Jordanian war.

Four reasons seemed to account for the PLO troubles in Lebanon. First, there was the general question of Lebanon's sovereignty, raised at several points by the establishment of de facto parallel hierarchies in fourteen of fifteen refugee camps and over a part of southern Lebanon. A second consideration was economic. Since Lebanon was the major commercial crossroads in the area and thrived on tourist trade, there was considerable apprehension that insurgent violence would damage the economy by discouraging visitors and bringing Israeli military operations against agricultural areas in the south. A third consideration, related to the economic element, was the human factor. Basically, this involved the exodus of refugees from the southern area because of Israeli reprisals. Aside from humanitarian concerns, Lebanon had to expend resources to alleviate the plight of the refugees. This situation also took on an explicitly political character, antithetical to fedayeen interests, when villagers from the south demanded in 1971 that guerrilla activities be terminated. The final factor underlying Lebanon's lack of commitment to the PLO was political. First and foremost was the concern that an independently organized and armed force like the guerrillas might upset the confessional system, by aligning with the Moslem section of the population. Linked with this consideration was the possibility that such interference might take the form of a lower-class movement led by the left-wing organizations, which were on record as believing the "reactionary" regime would have to be overthrown before Palestine could be liberated. In addition to the left-wing groups, Lebanon could not ignore the involvement of *Sa'iqa*, since the latter was controlled by Syrian Ba'thists who disliked the "bourgeois" politicians in Beirut and were suspected of having the longer-term aim of reincorporating Lebanon into a "Greater Syria."

Thus, in the final analysis, it was a combination of factors that caused Lebanon to oppose the fedayeen on the issues of political support and the rights of sanctuary and freedom of movement. When the fedayeen losses in terms of these two types of support were weighed against their exiguous gains in moral and material support, their 1973 status in Lebanon appeared unhealthy. Instead of being fully supported in their "just" cause, the guerrillas found they were, at best, unwelcome guests.

Syria

Historical Overview

The Syrian position on the fedayeen before the June War stood in marked contrast to that of Jordan and Lebanon. Besides supporting the concept of a people's war against Israel, arming guerrillas, and allowing them to organize and train on its own territory, Syria cooperated closely with *Fatah*. One thing the Syrians were reluctant to do, however, was allow commando raids from their territory, no doubt out of fear of Israeli reprisals. Thus, on several occasions Lebanese and Jordanian security forces intercepted guerrilla units coming from Syria to carry out operations across their borders. With the coming to power of a new, more hard-line Ba'thist group in Syria in February 1966, however, there was an increase in attacks across the Syrian border. Yet, despite the fact that Syria was the main sanctuary of the fedayeen, Israel chose to single out Jordan for some of its largest retaliatory strikes. Both this situation and the Ba'thist contention that Palestine could be liberated only after reactionary regimes were overthrown, severely strained relations with Amman. In fact, Hussein's post-June suspicions about *Sa'iqa* aims, noted in a previous section, were undoubtedly a carry-over from the prewar era.[25]

The Six-Day War served to reinforce Syria's militant stand toward Israel. In addition to boycotting the Khartoum conference and rejecting SC-242, Damascus reiterated its support for the concept of armed struggle as the best strategy for liberating Palestine, resumed training of fedayeen, and encouraged commandos to enter Jordan for eventual raids against Israelis.

Though Damascus supported guerrilla operations against Israel, it never looked with equal favor on all organizations. Indicative of this fact was the arrest of PFLP members—including George Habash—and confiscation of weapons during March and April 1968, the main concern being the perceived internal threat posed by the Ba'thists' old rival, the ANM, which, as noted in Chapter 7, was the main component of the PFLP. The possibility that Israeli reprisals also concerned the Syrian leadership in 1968 was suggested by a reported ban on guerrilla infiltration through the Golan Heights, the closure of a *Fatah* training base due to a refusal to submit to Syrian controls, and a decision to no longer recognize passports of fedayeen groups.[26]

Perhaps the most important development with respect to Syrian-fedayeen relations in the summer of 1968 was the first operation of *Sa'iqa* ("the Thunderbolt"), a fedayeen organization sponsored by the civilian wing of the Ba'thist party. The creation of *Sa'iqa* served several purposes. First, it enhanced Syrian prestige in radical Arab circles. Second, it helped deflect criticism of Syrian interference with the guerrillas. Third, it enabled Damascus to justify its policy of minimizing the presence of armed, independent guerrilla groups which, given Syria's fractious and unstable political system, could have aided enemies of the regime during internal crises. Fourth, *Sa'iqa* gave Syria a voice within Palestinian councils, and conferred some credibility on its rhetorical pledges of support for the PLO. Finally, it provided the civilian Ba'thists, led by Salah Jedid, an armed force to counterbalance their military rivals. Although infiltration of Lebanon was not a salient motive in 1968, *Sa'iqa* would later serve, along with the

PLA Yarmuk brigade which Damascus also controlled, as a valuable instrument for pursuing Syrian aims in Lebanon without risking the political and military costs that involvement of the regular army might engender.

As things turned out, Syrian-fedayeen relations from 1969 until the October War were marked by a good deal of vacillation. Activity along the border was intermittent. Increased Palestinian raids in February 1969, January through June 1970, January through March 1972, and September 1972 through January 1973 were countered by Israeli military retaliation. Israeli activity was particularly sharp during 1972-1973, when the IDF was pursuing its policy of active self-defense in a domestic atmosphere charged with emotion by Palestinian transnational terrorism. Deep penetration air strikes against fedayeen bases were accompanied by artillery barrages, sometimes directed on Syrian villages.[27] These attacks, designed, among other things, to disrupt and inflict losses on the fedayeen and to compel Syria to curb the raids, were eventually followed by long, relatively quiet periods along the border, particularly from January through October 1973.

Though Israeli military activity was, no doubt, a major reason for the lulls in guerrilla activity, there were other causes as well, not the least of which was the simple fact that Lebanon and Jordan were far more promising areas for guerrilla warfare, particularly between 1968 and 1970. It is also important to recall that a diminution of guerrilla activity everywhere occurred during the guerrilla-army clashes in Jordan and Lebanon, which occupied the attention of Syria and the other Arab states for months at a time.[28] Though perhaps less important, other impediments were generated by intrigues within the Ba'th party that created disruptions within *Sa'iqa*'s leadership (especially after Assad came to power and placed the organization under military control), and by the acrimonious relationship with Iraq, which resulted in arrests of ALF personnel in Syria and the confiscation of arms en route to them.[29]

Last, of course, special note should be made of the preparations for war which were under way in the spring of 1973 and no doubt accounted for a series of anti-Palestinian actions, including orders to the guerrillas to stay out of the Golan Heights, seizure of the Palestinian radio station, the arrest of sixteen *Fatah* members, and closure of guerrilla trails and camps.[30] Whatever specific reasons may have accounted for Syrian encapsulation of the fedayeen at various points in time, the cumulative effect was unfavorable for efficacious and systematic guerrilla warfare.

Types of External Support

When it came to *moral* support, Syria was more generous and committed than any front-line Arab state. Not only were the fedayeen concepts of armed struggle, people's war, and guerrilla methodology endorsed by Damascus, but they were greeted with great enthusiasm. This was consistent with both the prewar attitudes of Syria and the revolutionary outlook of its Ba'thist leaders.

The situation with respect to *political* support was more complicated. On the positive side, Syria rejected SC-242 and publicly endorsed the aim of liberating Palestine. By the time of the Assad coup in 1970, however, it appeared that Damascus was having second thoughts about its emphatic support for fedayeen aims. Although Syria continued to endorse the objective and methods of resistance—the Ba'thists could hardly do otherwise in light of their past rhetoric—it seemed to place less emphasis on the fedayeen cause and there were persistent reports that Damascus was privately prepared to accept a political settlement. The decision to join a loose confederation with Egypt and Libya in 1971 appeared to lend substance to this conclusion, given Egypt's desire to achieve a political solution. Moreover, the weakened state of the PLO could scarcely have raised Syrian hopes about the possibilities of a guerrilla success after the September civil war. In fact, Assad made it clear during an April 1972 visit to Kuwait that the Palestinian resistance would not be decisive in the battle of liberation.[31]

Before leaving the discussion of political support, it is important to note a long-term consideration that conditioned Syria's policy, namely, its historical frame of reference, which holds that Palestine was and is the southern part of a Greater Syria. This not only suggested a further reason for efforts to control and influence the fedayeen, but also raised a question as to whether Damascus would ever approve of the independent Palestine envisaged by the fedayeen.

The exact amount of *material* support given the insurgents by Syria was not ascertainable, although, compared to other front-line states, it seemed impressive. Aside from training and equipping the militarily respectable *Sa'iqa* organization and aiding the PLA contingent within its borders, Syria also sanctioned the invasion during the Jordanian civil war. Following the Assad coup, however, the Syrian government actually interfered with arms shipments to the fedayeen by confiscating supplies and, despite warnings to Hussein, avoided another military adventure on behalf of the guerrillas in Jordan during the July 1971 coup de grace.

If Syria had one thing in common with Jordanian and Lebanese policies toward the fedayeen, it was reluctance to allow the commandos freedom of movement against Israel. Although Syria did allow the guerrillas base areas and, when suiting its own purposes, the right to conduct operations across its borders, it clearly preferred that the guerrillas carry out their raids from Lebanon and Jordan, to spare Syria from Israeli reprisals and reduce the size of guerrilla contingents in Syria. Since the Ba'thists' hold on power was known to be precarious, and since some guerrilla organizations such as the PFLP were believed to be conspiring against the regime, the presence of Palestinian armed units was viewed as destabilizing. As pointed out earlier, this was no doubt one reason Syria sponsored its own fedayeen group.

While the creation of *Sa'iqa* did enhance—at least for a while—the quantitative and qualitative dimensions of fedayeen military operations, as well as meet a number of aims enumerated earlier, it also created some problems. For one thing, *Sa'iqa* exacerbated Palestinian relations with Jordan and Lebanon, both of which saw it as an instrument to be used against them by their ideological foes in Damascus. Because of *Sa'iqa*'s important position within the resistance, this meant the fedayeen were that much more suspect in Jordanian and Lebanese eyes. Yet another complication arising from *Sa'iqa*'s creation was its association with the civilian wing of the Ba'thist party. Since it was an armed force that could be used against the Assad faction, Assad sought to, and eventually did, bring it under control.

To sum up, by the spring of 1973, the general situation in terms of sanctuary and freedom of movement was not good. Though the guerrillas were still present in Syria, they were closely monitored and restricted by the government. Moreover, operations across the Syrian border and infiltration into Lebanon and Syria were reduced to insignificance.

Egypt

Historical Overview

Along with the three states already discussed, Egypt was important to the fedayeen, albeit not as a sanctuary. Instead, it was Egypt, the leading and most prestigious state in the Arab world, that the guerrillas looked to for moral, political, and material support.

Prior to the June War, Egypt had prompted the Arab League to establish the PLO and the PLA as the "vanguard" for the liberation of Palestine. As for the fledgling *Fatah* organization in Syria, Egypt kept aloof until the end of 1966, at which time the PLO began to coordinate with its rival, and Cairo correspondingly started to give substantial publicity to *Fatah* raids. Although offering the guerrillas moral, political, and limited material support, Nasser did not allow them to set up bases in his country, because he felt that such a move might provoke Israeli reprisals at times and places not of his choosing.[32] It should be remembered, however, that in the larger political-strategic context, fedayeen activity was not an overriding matter to Cairo, in part because of the relative impotence of the guerrilla organizations and Egypt's strategy of emphasizing the role of regular Arab armies in the conflict with Israel.

Shortly after the June War, Nasser seemed to move in the fedayeen direction when he endorsed the hard line against Israel at the Khartoum conference, called for the establishment of a people's resistance organization, and stated that the conflict with Israel was similar to the one in Vietnam.[33] As time went by, however, it became very clear that any inference that Nasser supported the fedayeen aims and strategy was erroneous. To start with, in November 1967, Egypt accepted SC-242, and an Egyptian spokesman told a press conference that his country agreed with Hussein's acknowledgement of Israel's right to exist, although it stopped short of diplomatic recognition.[34] While Cairo demanded that the rights of the Palestinians be restored and the occupied territories returned as part of a political settlement, the territorial issue always had the highest priority. In fact, at one point when peace talks appeared promising, January 1968, Egypt reportedly reached agreement with Jordan and the PLO (which was still under Egyptian influence) that guerrilla activity should be ended as a step toward a settlement. Though a more militant stance by Nasser followed, in the wake of an impasse in negotiations, there were other indicators of fundamental differences between Egypt and the Palestinians. When it came to defining precisely what was meant by the "restoration of Palestinian rights," for example, Egyptian officials (including the foreign minister) and the controlled press often mentioned repatriation or compensation, a formula most alarming to the PLO, inasmuch as it implied far less than the total liberation of Palestine.[35] Although the Israelis were skeptical of Egyptian aims and called attention to statements in which Egyptian spokesmen publicly backed the fedayeen aim of liberating Palestine, a closer look at the situation suggested that Nasser had in mind the possible creation of a Palestinian mini-state made up of the West Bank and the Gaza Strip.[36] Yet, because of the objections it raised among the Arabs, the mini-state notion was treated rather gingerly; it was only after the October War that it would become a central issue in the Arab world. The death of Nasser in September 1970 and Anwar as-Sadat's accession to power did little to close the basic gap between Egyptian and Palestinian aims. In fact, reliable sources close to the government went so far as to suggest that Sadat was willing to sign a peace treaty with Israel.[37]

Egypt also disagreed with the fedayeen when it came to the strategy of protracted armed struggle. Mohammed Heikal, Nasser's close confidant, put it this way in a January 1968 commentary in *Al-Ahram*:

> The people's war reflected today in the activity of the Palestinian resistance forces in Palestine cannot achieve—and nobody can ask it to achieve—a decisive result in the struggle. Anyone who thinks, for instance, that the

Palestinian revolutionary resistance will be able to accomplish the same results as the revolutionary resistance did in Algeria is doing an injustice to the Palestinian situation.[38]

On August 7, 1970, Heikal stated flatly in his weekly column that it was folly to believe the guerrillas could wage a successful war of liberation against Israel, since such a feat was beyond their capability.

When it came to tactical issues, the Egyptian view of fedayeen activity was mixed. On the one hand, officials and the media (*Al-Ahram, Al-Akhbar, Akhbar al-Yom,* for example) condemned hijacking because of its adverse effects on the Arab cause within the international community, whereas on the other hand, Cairo did provide moral and material support for the guerrilla and terrorist campaign in Israel and in the occupied areas.[39]

Affirmation of the just or moral nature of the Palestinian efforts was consistent. In 1969, for instance, Nasser commented on the fedayeen by saying:

> I admire them. As a man, I admire them because they are fighting for their rights. They waited for twenty years looking to the world to regain for them their deprived rights. Now they are fighting for their rights. I think everyone must agree with them because they have to fight.[40]

With regard to material support, Egypt contributed to the guerrilla campaign through provision of arms, amunition, radio time, medical services, health insurance, and intelligence information.[41]

Although, at first glance, the moral and material support rendered to the fedayeen appeared inconsistent with Egypt's disdain for the strategy of protracted people's war, it was never based on the assumption that such a strategy would succeed. Rather, it was intended to inflict costs on Israel that, when combined with those caused by Egyptian military actions, might serve the primary Egyptian aim of extracting Israeli concessions. It seemed more than mere coincidence that Cairo's support for the guerrillas was greatest during the longest period of diplomatic immobility (April 1968-July 1970).[42]

One thing Egypt steadfastly refused to do was allow the fedayeen an operational sanctuary for attacks against the Israelis in the Sinai. While this was no doubt due to the general Egyptian belief that a people's war would not be effective and that the topographical and demographic environment of the Sinai (open and sparsely populated) was unfavorable, there were other considerations as well.[43] For one thing, after the 1967 war, Nasser was struggling to regain his prestige within the Arab world, and reliance on the Palestinians would have been an admission of Egypt's military inability to handle the situation on its own front. Moreover, given the rising popularity of the fedayeen within the Arab world during 1968-1969, Nasser also may have been wary of the accolades accruing to the nascent hero figure, Yasir Arafat. A number of observers, in fact, pointed out that the *Fatah* leader was becoming something of a rival to Nasser. These considerations, as well as the internal security problem that would be posed by an independent guerrilla force operating in an unsettled Egyptian political milieu, seemed to be underlying motives for discouraging the fedayeen from establishing operational bases in and conducting attacks from Egypt.[44] By 1970, increasingly sharp differences with the PFLP and PDF reinforced the prohibition.

The problems with the leftists centered around tactics and ideology. Though Cairo's previously mentioned condemnation of transnational terrorism brought it into direct conflict with the PFLP, the ideological pretensions of the left seemed to be most bothersome. Nasser had already demonstrated his acute sensitivity to the Marxist threat within Egypt by incarcerating a number of domestic Communists and he, therefore, was no doubt very much aware that a similar challenge was implicit in the PFLP and PDF's longer-term commitment to revolution in the Arab world. Over the shorter term, however, the Egyptian regime bristled at what it called the "provincialism" of the fedayeen—its focus on Palestine in lieu of pan-Arabism—which some Palestinian revolutionaries had proposed as an alternative to Nasserism.[45]

The concrete effects of the differences with the left could be seen in Heikal's blaming the PFLP for the June 1970 fighting in Jordan, the clash between pro-Nasser guerrilla groups (the AOLP and APO) and the PFLP after Nasser's acceptance of the Rogers plan, and the deportation of PDF militants from Egypt.[46]

The general unevenness of Egyptian-Palestinian relations during the Nasser years carried over into the Sadat era. Though Sadat was critical of Jordanian expulsion of the fedayeen in 1971, he was reported to have rejected a Libyan plan to use force against Jordan, because it would have weakened the Arabs' overall military capability. Instead, he agreed to warn Jordan that "individual and collective" sanctions would be taken if Hussein did not revise his stand.[47] Nevertheless, when subsequent efforts to reconcile the fedayeen and Jordan collapsed in the fall of 1971, Sadat avoided breaking relations.

Two factors seemed to account for the absence of a stronger response. One was recognition that the PFLP and PDF had actively undermined the mediation efforts; the other was the affront to Egypt when the Jordanian minister was assassinated by Black September agents on Egyptian soil in November.[48]

The general strain in Egyptian-Jordanian relations continued, however, and set the stage for a rupture of diplomatic relations with Amman in 1972, the immediate precipitant being the king's United Arab Kingdom plan. Again, the principal concern seemed to be the possibility that Jordan might use the scheme as a framework for reaching a separate settlement with Israel, thereby damaging the Arabs militarily by neutralizing the eastern front. Though the PLO welcomed Sadat's moves, it was also quite aware they were done for Egyptian reasons, not Palestinian ones.

Fedayeen suspicions of Egypt's motives were multiplied a few months later when Sadat offered to recognize a Palestinian government-in-exile, a move he surely knew would sow further dissension in Palestinian ranks.[49] As if this were not enough, there was an Egyptian-Jordanian rapprochement in January 1973, and in the early summer Egypt's ambassador to the UN called for the creation of a sovereign Palestinian state as part of a peace settlement, a step *Falastin al-Thawra* soundly criticized because it would have meant recognition of "the legitimacy of the Zionist presence on Palestinian soil."[50] These events, followed by a restoration of relations with Jordan in September, aggravated the Egyptian-Palestinian situation even further.

Types of External Support

Since Egypt was the most important country in the Arab world, its support for the fedayeen was considered particularly significant. It was no doubt encouraging that in terms of *moral* support, Cairo was second to none. Like the other Arab nations, it repeatedly let it be known that the fedayeen cause was "lawful and just."

More important—especially in light of Egypt's role as *primus inter pares* in the Arab world—was the question of *political* support, since a total Egyptian commitment on this issue probably would have swung most Arab countries behind the Palestinian position. Unhappily for the guerrillas, however, Egyptian political support never measured up to their expectations. In the first place the commandos' demand for liberation of all of Palestine was incompatible with Egypt's limited aim of achieving return of the occupied areas. Whereas the Palestinian objective involved the destruction of Israel, the Egyptian goal and a host of official and unofficial statements allowed for the existence of Israel, albeit without diplomatic recognition. In spite of periodic suggestions that Cairo endorsed the fedayeen aim, statements which had the effect of increasing Israel's skepticism about Cairo's sincerity, it seemed that Egypt was clearly disposed to arrive at a political settlement guaranteeing Israel's right to exist. Although Egypt said many times that Palestinian rights would have to be considered in any political solution, it was suggested on several occasions that this demand could be satisfied by compensation, repatriation, referendum, and/or the creation of a Palestinian state. Since several students of the refugee question believed that if repatriation were offered, only ten percent would exercise the option to return, an agreement along these lines was not completely infeasible.[51]

Besides the contradiction between fedayeen and Egyptian political aims, Cairo made it clear more than once that guerrilla warfare could never be decisive in the struggle against Israel. This stand, of course, conflicted with the fedayeen proposition that a protracted armed struggle would succeed. On the question of external terror, Egypt's position was that such actions were the work of extremists and counterproductive to the Arab cause.

When it came to the problems in Jordan, Cairo was generally critical of the Jordanian side, even though Hussein was Nasser's ally in the search for a peace settlement. Yet, since Cairo confined itself to verbal condemnation of Jordan and attempted to mediate during the 1970-1971 period, despite the fedayeen requests for intervention, Egypt proved ineffective in stopping Hussein from applying his sanctions against the fedayeen.

As far as *material* support was concerned, Egypt did provide several types of assistance. In addition to limited provision of arms, ammunition, finances, medical help, military training, and intelligence information, Egypt granted the moderate fedayeen groups broadcast time over Radio Cairo. Radio time, however, was suspended at the insurgents' most critical hour, in 1970. It could be argued that the most important material aid Egypt rendered was indirect and not explicitly related to the guerrillas. This involved the Egyptian "war of attrition" on the Sinai front which, by causing Israel human and material losses, fit in with the fedayeen strategy of gradually depleting Israeli strength and weakening Israel's will to resist. However, as events in the summer of 1970 showed, these gains turned out to be short-lived once Nasser accepted the Rogers plan.

Egypt's ambivalent policy toward the fedayeen seemed the product of several factors, some of which impelled Egypt simultaneously to support the guerrillas and to restrict that support. Egypt's aid to the fedayeen was motivated by its leadership in the Arab world, a position which made it almost impossible to disavow the "sacred" Palestinian cause.[52] Closely related was Nasser's concern for his own prestige, under challenge within Egypt following the June War. Since Arafat gradually emerged as a hero among the Arab masses, Nasser could hardly allow him to achieve sole credit for championing the Palestinian cause. By extolling the fedayeen, the Egyptian president no doubt thought he could maintain his following among the masses in Egypt and the Arab world in general. In addition, the possibility should not be discounted that Nasser felt some genuine sympathy for the Palestinian fighters. Finally, Nasser's own political calculations may have induced him to support the guerrillas since the latter could be used as an instrument to pressure Israel into a diplomatic compromise.

The Egyptian disagreement with fedayeen political aims and Cairo's limitations on support for the guerrillas also resulted from a conglomeration of factors. While domestic turmoil in Egypt led Nasser to strike a forceful stance at several points, it also militated against granting the fedayeen a base of operations within the country because of the potential internal security threat involved. Likewise, the rivalry with Arafat motivated Nasser to support the fedayeen, and also led him to restrict support for the guerrillas lest they take center stage. In fact, as pointed out before, the pan-Arab aspect of Nasserism was perceived as being directly challenged by the "provincialism" of the resistance. Intermeshed with these considerations were the ideological and tactical differences with the PFLP and PDF because of their stated belief that the "petit bourgeois" regime in Cairo would eventually have to be toppled.

The shortcomings of the fedayeen (unfavorable environment, chronic disunity, and lack of accomplishment) appeared to be another major reason for Egypt's unwillingness to give the guerrillas full support. The reality of fedayeen impotence seemed to reinforce the Egyptian view that the only feasible military way to achieve Arab objectives was by conventional warfare conducted by the Arab armies.

A final consideration was the position of the Soviet Union. As the section on Russia will show, the Soviets were wary of the fedayeen because of their uncontrollable nature, and because the Palestinian aim clashed with the Russian desire for a political settlement in the Middle East. Since Moscow's influence in Cairo was substantial, due to Egypt's dependency on the Soviet Union for military hardware, Egypt could not easily ignore Soviet support for a political settlement and the existence of Israel.

The Peripheral Arab States

If external support from the front-line states was unsatisfactory, the situation in regard to the Arab nations geographically separated from the target area was not much better. Yet, since these peripheral states did provide assistance as well as cause problems, they merit our brief attention, beginning with the significant Persian Gulf states.

Iraq

Iraq extended complete moral and political support to the fedayeen during the 1967-1973 period. Following the June War, the Iraqis supported the fedayeen and were reported to be facilitating the movement of guerrillas toward Israel and the occupied areas. (The Iraqi army was said by a guerrilla captured at Karamah to be giving the resistance substantial assistance.) Though Iraqi army units in Jordan did not join Hussein's forces in directly aiding the Palestinians during the Karamah battle, the Baghdad government jumped on the commando bandwagon in the months thereafter by supporting pro-fedayeen demonstrations, raising funds for the PFLP, *Fatah,* and the PLF, and enthusiastically backing the idea of a war of national liberation.[53]

A coup in July 1968, which brought Sadaam Hussein, Ahmed Hassan Bakr, and the Ba'thists to power, did not appreciably affect the positive relations with the guerrillas. Continued moral and political support were evidenced by Iraq's refusal to attend the 1969 Islamic Summit Conference because the PLO had not been guaranteed the right to speak; by public affirmation of the Palestinian cause at the UN; by militant demands at the 1969 Arab Summit Conference that the destruction of Israel should be the Arab objective; and by denunciation of the Rogers plan in 1970. Likewise, material assistance to the fedayeen continued in the form of laws requiring Palestinians to pay taxes to the PLO, the provision of radio time, and the creation and equipping of the ALF. In addition, Baghdad not only provided weapons for the insurgents but it permitted Chinese weapons delivered at northern ports to be transported to them across its territory.[54] Several factors combined to produce such support, namely, Iraq's long-standing antipathy toward Israel; the revolutionary ideology of the Ba'th party, which led it to seek a leadership role in the Arab world; the need to undermine a similar claim by the Syrian Ba'thists; and the utility of focusing on an external foe as a means to create a modicum of cohesion in an otherwise divisive Iraqi policy.

While the kinds of support noted above were welcomed by the PLO, there were also a number of strains in the Iraqi-fedayeen relations. For one thing, Baghdad constantly restricted the Palestinian presence in Iraq, and at one point sought to manipulate it through the ALF. The government not only complained about infractions of agreements by the guerrillas, but it also banned public rallies and the collection of funds in 1969. The effort by the authorities to control the fedayeen was not astonishing, in light of the historical instability of the Iraqi political system. Like other Arab leaders, Iraq's rulers were wary of an armed, independent fedayeen force that might throw its weight behind dissidents plotting against the regime.[55]

The real test of the depth of the Iraqi commitment to the PLO came during the September 1970 civil war in Jordan. Although Iraq had criticized both Hussein and the PFLP and PDF during the June 1970 conflict in Jordan, the Egyptian acceptance of the Rogers plan shortly thereafter led Iraq to pledge that its 12,000-man force in Jordan would be at the disposal of the resistance and to charge Cairo with giving up the aim of liberating Palestine.[56]

In early September 1970, Iraq formally and informally warned Amman that its forces would protect the fedayeen if the fighting in Jordan continued. The admonition was underlined by the dispatch of the vice president and chief of staff to visit guerrilla forces in Jordan and the approval of radio broadcasts which castigated Hussein. However, when the Palestinians broadcast an appeal for help during the civil war, the Baghdad government not only stood silently by, but its forces in Jordan reportedly allowed Jordanian troops to pass through their positions. This led a PLO spokesman to accuse Iraq of backing down on its commitments, and Iraq to retort that its pledges did not necessarily involve direct military intervention. The military course, it was argued, was dangerous because it risked foreign intervention. That one of the fedayeen's most militant supporters had failed them in their most desperate hour was clearly evident.[57] As an editorial in *Free Palestine* succinctly put it:

> Some Arab governments are further to blame [for the Jordan massacres] because they were unable, or unwilling to match their verbal rejections of the Rogers proposals and support for the Palestinian Revolution with concrete acts when the moment of truth arrived. Invoking the pretext of "avoiding an American intervention" is a shameful cowering to imperialist threats and exposes the limitations of some anti-imperialist regimes.[58]

Though Iraq was able to improve its relations with the PFLP and the PDF over the next few years, [59] relations with *Fatah* remained cool, a factor that no doubt accounted for the active presence in Baghdad of Abu Nidal, a former *Fatah* member who was a severe critic of Arafat.

Saudi Arabia

After the June War, Saudi Arabia supported the guerrillas morally, politically, and materially. The Saudi view was that SC-242 was unacceptable; armed struggle was the only way to recover the Palestinian homeland; and the Palestinians themselves were responsible for its liberation, although Moslems everywhere should aid them.[60]

While Saudi Arabia reinforced its moral and political commitment with private and public financial aid to *Fatah* and the PLO, it was never happy with the Marxist guerrilla organizations, which were natural ideological enemies. The PFLP's destruction of part of the Tapline, running from the Saudi oil fields to Lebanon, during May 1969 intensified Saudi hostility, since it cost the Saudis substantial loss in revenue. Thus, left-wing groups became the target of strong denunciations and the Saudis demanded that they be purged. Since *Fatah* was on King Feisal's good side, it strove to remain so by apologizing for the Tapline episode.[61]

What financial aid Saudi Arabia gave to the fedayeen—reports claimed about $100,000 per month—was important enough to impel Arafat to pay periodic visits to Jedda, particularly when payments were delinquent.[62] Regardless of Saudi aid and the reasonably good relations it enjoyed with Riyadh, the PLO could not help but be chagrined when Saudi Arabia welcomed the 1970 cease-fire and voiced its hope for "an era of stability and tranquility in the region," even though King Feisal had previously lobbied for a militant solution to the Middle East conflict in talks with Nasser and twice called for a holy war against Israel.[63]

In 1971 Saudi Arabian policy was no less confusing. Although he publicly supported the Palestinian struggle to liberate the homeland in a joint communiqué with Lebanon in October 1971, Feisal had informed the American secretary of state in May that a political settlement was possible if Israel withdrew from the occupied areas.[64] Perhaps most discouraging to the fedayeen was the Saudi support for Hussein in July 1971, despite a long-standing rivalry with the Hashemites.[65]

The support for Jordan was no doubt generated by Feisal's concern that the overthrow of Hussein might bring to power a new regime under the influence of the PFLP and PDF, organizations committed to the destruction of the Saudi political system as well. Underlying and intensifying this concern was the king's obsessive fear of Communist expansionism in general.[66]

Saudi trepidation about Marxism did not, however, preclude a vigorous attempt to reconcile the fedayeen and Jordan in the late summer and fall of 1971. Since there was reason to believe that Feisal wanted some sort of compromise, in order to pursue his policy of bettering relations with Syria, Sudan, Egypt, and Libya, complete identification with Jordan might have undercut this wider policy if Amman remained intransigent.[67]

Although *Fatah* and the PLO chose to downplay their differences with the Saudis, because they did not wish to jeopardize financial assistance, the Marxist groups were vituperative in their condemnation of Feisal's regime.[68] There were occasions when moderate fedayeen spokesmen also displayed some impatience with Riyadh. In *Free Palestine*, which generally reflected the position of the PLO-*Fatah* wing of the resistance movement, Feisal's policy of considering the Palestine question as an Islamic one was depicted as an attempt to both circumvent involvement on the battlefield and force the "progressive" states to accept his philosophical viewpoint. Following the July 1971 expulsion of the fedayeen from Jordan, the same publication argued that the Jedda conference's aim of seeking conciliation under the Cairo agreement was tantamount to an abandonment of the armed struggle. Feisal's regime was then described as one of "the main pillars of U.S. imperialism in the area" which derived its power from being an "imperialist stooge."[69]

Although Saudi relations with the moderates eventually returned to normal, and in 1973 Riyadh was reportedly dispensing $1.2 million to *Fatah*, there was widespread conjecture among experienced observers that Feisal was really paying "protection money" to insure that his kingdom would be spared problems with the left, as well as terrorist attacks. Indeed, the persuasiveness of this argument is enhanced when one juxtaposes the well-known Saudi paranoia about communism with *Fatah*'s continuous effort to court the USSR; these overtures were certain to raise suspicions in the royal family about the longer-term political complexion and orientation of even the pragmatists in the PLO.

The fragile foundation upon which Saudi-PLO relations rested was further weakened by the BSO's assassination of diplomats at the Saudi Embassy in Khartoum during March 1973, especially since that event focused attention on the direct linkage between the BSO and the *Fatah* high command. In reaction, Riyadh's *Al-Hayat* indicated that the status of all Palestinians in the kingdom would be reconsidered, and indignantly pointed out that the "Voice of Palestine" in Baghdad had said the road to Tel Aviv passed through Amman and Riyadh.[70] Since the Saudis undoubtedly knew the renegade Nidal faction was behind the radio broadcast, rather than Arafat, they were presumably using the incident to express their underlying distrust of the movement as a whole. Given this outlook, the Saudi inclination toward a settlement involving acceptance of Israel following the October War was not particularly surprising.

Kuwait

As might have been expected, Kuwait's major connection with the Palestinian resistance movement was in the financial realm. Although Kuwait did extend moral and hedged political support to the fedayeen through its policy of not approving a political settlement unless it was accepted by "the Palestinian people," its involvement was a great deal more low-key than was that of many Arab states. The same was true of Kuwait's opposition to external terror tactics and activities of some PDF members within its own territory.[71]

The most important Kuwaiti support was material, notably financing from both public and private sources. In May 1968, with the government already deducting a three and one-half percent tax from the salaries of the Palestinians, the Council of Ministers decided on a general two percent on petrol sales and movie tickets to support the fedayeen. While the guerrillas were publicly grateful for this assistance, there were demands from Arafat in March 1969 that Kuwait release some four million dinars earmarked for the PLO, which had been blocked, and that Kuwait increase the tax on Palestinians to fifteen percent. In the same month, however, the rejection by the Economic and Financial Committee of the Kuwait National Assembly of a plan to pay Kuwaiti civil servants of Palestinian origin who served with the fedayeen suggested that Kuwaiti largesse was not unlimited.

In addition to private donations such as the contribution of 100,000 dinars by Sheik Sabah al-Salem al-Sabah to the families of the fedayeen killed in action, funds were periodically collected at Palestinian rallies and the Kuwaiti budget was allocating five million dinars for the guerrillas by 1970-1971.[72]

Besides direct subsidies, financial assistance was also used in an indirect and vacillating manner to assist the guerrillas. The subsidy to Jordan was suspended during the civil war, resumed in December 1970, resuspended in January 1971, and eventually renewed in 1973.[73]

Explanations for the limited assistance rendered by Kuwait were not hard to find. Besides the general need to fulfill its responsibilities in the Arab world, and thereby avoid threats from radicals, there was a sizable and active Palestinian population estimated at 140,000 inside Kuwait which needed to be placated lest it foment trouble for the regime.

Algeria

Algeria was perhaps the fedayeen's best friend among the North African Arab states, since its response was positive in terms of all the types of support it could offer—moral, political and material. Unfortunately for the guerrillas, such backing did little to help the movement in a substantial sense, because Algeria was a poor country and wielded marginal influence in the international community. The one type of aid that could have been important, given Algeria's standing, was sanctuary. However, the geographic separation of Algeria from the conflict area (1,350 miles from Israel) precluded this. In fact, even if Algeria had been in a position to be a sanctuary, it is altogether possible that its domestic politics and national interests would have led it to behave in much the same way as the front-line states.

As it was, Algeria exerted a reasonable effort on behalf of the Palestinians. The policy of the revolutionary government of Houari Boumedienne both before and after the June War was to extol the just nature of the Palestinian cause (moral support) and agree with and actively back the aim of liberating all of Palestine by means of a revolutionary war (political support). This support included strong denunciation of various peace proposals, condemnation of the idea of a Palestinian state alongside Israel, rejection of the notion of a peace settlement, and opposition to interference in the internal affairs of the fedayeen movement by other Arab states. Such interference was defined as including both the antifedayeen actions of Jordan and Lebanon and creation of small guerrilla organizations by several Arab countries.[74]

The Algerians were disposed to accept tactics of the more radical fedayeen organizations. In fact, not only was Algeria the sole Arab country to refrain from criticizing the Tapline attack, but its official daily, *El-Moudjahid*, approved the action on June 5, 1969.[75] Although Algeria did irritate the PFLP by releasing twelve Israeli passengers and an aircraft hijacked to its territory in the fall of 1968, it took a position in support of other hijackings, including those of September 1970. It even protested to the United Nations over Switzerland's handling of the trial of those responsible for the Zurich incident in 1968.[76] While Algeria adhered to an evenhanded approach to the June 1970 fighting in Jordan, it was severely critical of Hussein during the civil war.[77]

With respect to material support, Algeria proved to be generous, especially in light of its own underdeveloped economy. Shortly after the June War, the PLO revealed that Algeria was training guerrillas for operations against Israel, and by 1970 fedayeen were said to be attending officer training and commando courses with the same status as Algerian cadets. During the period after the June War, Algeria also provided the guerrillas with military materials and financial support, the latter coming from both private and government sources.

The Algerians made special efforts to alleviate the fedayeen plight during the time of troubles in 1970-1971. In addition to extending broadcast rights to the "Voice of *Assifa*" after Nasser's suspension of them in 1970, the Algerian government promised to replace all weapons lost in the fighting in Jordan during the summer of 1971. Unhappily for the Palestinians, the contribution of weapons was intercepted by Syria and came at a time when the resistance was in little position to put them to effective use.[78] While the exact figure on financial and military aid from Algeria is unknown, it can be assumed that such assistance was not decisive, given the fedayeen financial crisis of 1971.

Another Algerian contribution which cannot be overlooked is the confidence inspired by the Algerian revolutionary experience. The fedayeen often cited Algerian success against France as proof that they would succeed, and *Fatah* was quite clearly influenced by the writings of Frantz Fanon. What the guerrillas did not seem very attentive to were the differences between their situation and that of the Algerians.[79]

While Algerian support for the fedayeen was no doubt related to a degree of sympathy for the Palestinians, other factors seem to have been involved. One of these was the successful Algerian experience, which convinced the leadership that the idea of armed guerrilla struggle could succeed, and the satisfaction and prestige derived from seeing their model replicated. Three further explanations of the Algerian militancy on the Palestinian issue may have been an Algerian wish to divert attention from internal economic development problems, the need to keep Algerian revolutionaries active so that they would cause no trouble on the home front, and the desire to emerge ultimately as the principal progressive and revolutionary Arab state.[80] A final consideration may have been that such a policy involved few costs and risks since Algeria was relatively safe from Israeli attacks.

Libya

Like Algeria, Libya became a militant backer of the fedayeen, especially after the Qadhdhafi coup in September 1969, extending moral, political, and material support to the resistance movement.[81] Nevertheless, even though the new military junta in Tripoli was one of the most militant Arab regimes on the question of Israel and the aim of liberating the Palestinian "homeland," it did not take the position that guerrilla warfare was the only path to success. Indeed, Qadhdhafi's support of the role of Arab states, and his conceptualization of the liberation struggle in pan-Arab terms, implied that the fedayeen were only to be an auxiliary force in the conflict with Israel.[82]

The attempt to back both the Arab states and the fedayeen did not mean that Tripoli followed a neutral course in all disputes arising between the two parties. In the crises in Jordan and Lebanon, in fact, Libya supported the guerrillas, with the notable exception of the June 1970 fighting in Jordan. During the October 1969 crisis in Lebanon, for instance, Libya criticized Beirut and withdrew its ambassador in protest over restrictions on fedayeen activity; following the Jordanian civil war it maintained a steady barrage of criticism of Jordan, demanded Hussein's ouster, and terminated relations with, and aid to, Amman. In July 1971, Tripoli lobbied unsuccessfully for Arab military intervention to save the guerrillas. At times such as the last one, Qadhdhafi's demands were usually tempered by Cairo.[83] In fact, the enthusiasm of Qadhdhafi's own people seemed no greater than that of Egypt, given the poor response in the summer of 1971 to an appeal for volunteers to fight with the fedayeen.[84]

Although the Tripoli regime gave qualified moral and political backing to the resistance, its relationship with the fedayeen from 1967 to 1973 was complicated by its antipathy toward the left-wing organizations—

particularly the PFLP—and its affinity for Egypt. With respect to the PFLP, Libya's concern was both ideological and tactical. On ideological questions, both the monarch and the military regime were at odds with the PFLP, the monarch because he viewed it as a threat to the throne, and the military because it despised Marxism-Leninism as a foreign ideology antithetical to Islam. Thus, on at least three occasions, February 1968, March 1971, and June 1973, left-wing fedayeen or their supporters were arrested and/or deported from Libya. In January 1971, Qadhdhafi criticized both the PFLP and the PDF as "deviationist, secessionist organizations" preoccupied with Marxism-Leninism, which were guilty of embroiling *Fatah* in unnecessary crises; in August he referred to both groups as "unprincipled agents" more concerned with Marxism-Leninism than Palestine. After the PDF retorted by charging that Qadhdhafi was siding with "United States imperialism," the Libyan leader demanded that the left-wing organizations be purged by the PLO.[85]

Libya also differed with the fedayeen when it came to tactics, since Qadhdhafi believed operations within Israel and the occupied areas would be more effective than border raids and external terrorism.[86] Though the Libyan media had condemned terrorist acts outside the Middle East in 1968 and 1969, Tripoli had changed its tune by 1972. Following the Lufthansa hijacking in the fall of 1972, the director general of the Ministry of Information indicated that although the government opposed hijacking in principle, in some cases, such as the Palestinian one, it was "righteous."[87] The *volte face* on the part of Libya was probably due to Libya's realization that external terrorism was the only violent option left, since both the fedayeen organizations in the occupied areas and their border campaigns were in a shambles.

Qadhdhafi's vitriolic attacks on the left-wing groups reflected not only ideological and tactical disagreements with them, but also his belief that they were responsible for the chronic disunity of the resistance. As a zealous advocate of unity, within both the Arab world and the guerrilla movement, the Libyan leader often gave public vent to his frustration with the effects of factionalism in both realms. In a public address in April 1973, for example, he charged that the guerrilla movements existed only in radio broadcasts, after which Khalef and Hawatmeh quickly challenged him to prove his fealty to the cause by nationalizing American oil interests in Libya.[88] Aside from irritation with Qadhdhafi's criticism of the resistance, the fedayeen were also irked by his support of Nasser, and became even more so when Libya backed Egypt's acceptance of the Rogers plan in the summer of 1970. It also did not help matters when Qadhdhafi accompanied his support for the Egyptian president with a condemnation of the Palestinians for their parochial view of the struggle against Israel, arguing that Palestine was not for the Palestinians the way Vietnam was for the Vietnamese because the Palestine question was a matter for all Arabs.[89]

Despite the differences between the PLO and Libya, the latter did grant material assistance to the resistance in the form of training bases, a large PLO headquarters, asylum for hijackers and other terrorists, and an annual financial contribution estimated at $20 million, $11.5 million of which was derived from a six percent tax on Palestinian salaries and a three percent *jihad* tax on all Libyans.[90] From time to time, however, bases were closed and finances interrupted, depending on the vicissitudes of overall relations between the two parties.

Sudan

Until the time of the Khartoum incident, the Sudanese connection was relatively insignificant to the PLO. Although the Sudan gave the fedayeen moral support, qualified political support, and limited material assistance (radio time and PLO offices), it generally followed Egypt's lead in matters involving the conflict with Israel.[91] Unhappily for the PLO, Sudan's major impact was largely negative, and for this the fedayeen had only themselves to blame. By seizing the Saudi embassy and assassinating hostage diplomats in March 1973, the BSO affronted the Sudan's sovereignty and embarrassed it internationally. Enraged at both the act itself and perceived Libyan connivance, President Ja'far al-Numayri not only incarcerated the terrorists and other fedayeen believed to be in contact with Sudanese subversives, but, more importantly, also publicly revealed the direct relationship between the BSO and the highest levels of *Fatah*.[92] Thus, the myth of the BSO's autonomy was belied and *Fatah* became more accountable than ever for the acts of its stepchild. These developments, in turn, played a role in the PLO's subsequent reassessment and opposition to transnational terror.

Morocco

Morocco's involvement with the Palestinian guerrillas was generally negligible, although on several occasions it gave its blessing to the "sacred cause." Such periodic praise did not extend to the left-wing groups which King Hassan said were "wild and harebrained."[93] The most significant actions by Morocco were Hassan's January 22, 1970 pledge of more than one million pounds to the resistance and his promise of moral and diplomatic support to Arafat in November 1970. However, since Hassan did not bother to join in the severe castigation of Hussein for the July 1971 coup de grace in Jordan—Hassan had just escaped a coup attempt and was himself being criticized—it seemed clear Morocco's concern about the Palestinian question was, at best, marginal.[94]

Tunisia

Tunisia did little, if anything, for the fedayeen, perhaps because of its view, even before the June War, that Israel's existence was a fact of life. Both this policy and President Habib Bourguiba's stated willingness to mediate in the Arab-Israeli dispute were antithetical to insurgent aims.[95] While Tunisia did support the notion of guerrilla warfare in lieu of conventional combat, it seemed to view such action as a means to pressure Israel to accept withdrawal from the occupied areas as part of a political settlement.[96] The most Tunisia did for the fedayeen was to criticize Hussein and allow its premier to head the Arab mediation committee in Jordan after the civil war. Even this role, however, had little practical effect since Hussein proceeded to eliminate the commandos and the premier had to resign in frustration.

The Communist States

If unfulfilled expectations and disappointments marked the convoluted ties between the fedayeen and their Arab brothers, relations with the USSR were not much better, for, here again, the Palestinians found that while their interests and those of their beneficiary were sometimes parallel, they were never synonymous. Though the situation with regard to China was far better, the Chinese suffered from their limited ability to project influence into the Middle East. Moscow, by contrast, had an impressive potential capability for moral, political, and material support that the Palestinians believed could be mobilized on their behalf if Soviet leaders were favorably disposed. How successful the PLO was in obtaining such support is summarized below.

The USSR

The general thrust of Soviet foreign policy in the Middle East on the eve of the June 1967 War was to neutralize both American and Chinese influence in the area, and to enhance the prestige and security of the USSR. In serving those aims, Moscow aligned itself with the Arab states in their conflict with Israel, providing them with generous military and economic assistance. This action enabled the Russians to increase their own influence through the presence of military advisors and economic aid groups, and to obtain military bases and installations that strengthened and facilitated Soviet naval deployments on NATO's southern flank. Since overall strategic interests were clearly predominant in Soviet policy calculations, relations with the Arab states,which could provide concrete assets, took precedence over support for Communist parties. Indeed, for the most part, Moscow tolerated, though did not approve of, the arrest and detention of its Arab comrades by the Arab regimes. In this context, where state interests were more important than the pursuit of revolutionary aspirations, the small fedayeen organizations were generally treated with indifference.[97]

Following the June War, the Soviet Union's indifferent attitude was transformed into active interest, manifest in both moral and limited material support. Between 1968 and 1970, there was consistent Soviet media coverage of fedayeen activities as well as excoriation of both Israel's "repressive" security measures and its unwillingness to comply with the "just" demands of the Arabs.[98] Moral support was expressed in the media and statements by leading officials. *Pravda*, for instance, contended that the movement as a whole had a "liberating, just character," while Alexander Shelepin, a high-ranking Politburo member, characterized the resistance as a legitimate nationalist and anti-imperialist struggle during a November 1969 speech. Along these same lines, Ambassador Yacov A. Malik informed the UN that the fedayeen were "patriotic partisans."[99]

In addition to moral support, the USSR also extended limited material assistance to the fedayeen, principally in the period after the Jordanian civil war. In the wake of a February 1970 visit by Arafat to the Soviet Union, the generally well-informed *Africasia* indicated that the Russians had promised the PLO weapons, a claim echoed in a PLO report characterizing the visit as "one of our most important achievements on the international level."[100] *The New York Times*, meanwhile, reported that Soviet sources were acknowledging that the Arab states were supplying the guerrillas with Soviet weapons. A report in April 1970 by the Bulgarian ambassador to Baghdad that his country was giving arms to the fedayeen seemed to confirm the widespread assumption that the East European states were acting as third party suppliers.[101]

Although the Soviet Union paid relatively little attention to the fedayeen throughout 1971, during a visit to Moscow at the end of the year, Arafat was said to have secured a Soviet commitment to train guerrillas, supply weapons, and provide hospitalization for wounded guerrillas. On another journey to Moscow in July 1972, Arafat was reported (by both the Israelis and sources close to the PLO) to have obtained a pledge for the first direct weapons shipments to the insurgents, a pledge that was fulfilled by a shipment of small arms several weeks later.[102] By the time of the first visit the PLO's weakened capability had rendered it more "controllable" and hence less risky to deal with; by the time of the second visit, the Soviets probably saw moderate military assistance to the PLO as a way to regain some of the influence they had lost in the Middle East because of their difficulties with Egypt.

As heartening and useful as the moral and material support undoubtedly were to the Palestinians, they tended to obscure a more important and profound disagreement between the two parties over the ultimate goal and strategy of the resistance. As early as the Glassboro meeting between U.S. President Lyndon B. Johnson and Soviet Premier Aleksei Kosygin in July 1967, the Soviets made it clear that the Arabs must recognize Israel's right to exist, a position Moscow confirmed by acceptance of SC-242 the following November.[103] A year later, Soviet Foreign Minister Andrei Gromyko publicly underscored his government's policy before the UN General Assembly when he stated that:

> Now there are possibilities to achieve a turn towards peace in the Middle East, towards an end to the state of war between Israel and the Arab states and the ensuring of the sovereignty, territorial integrity and political independence of each state of this region and their right to live in conditions of security.[104]

In a Budapest press conference on November 11, 1968, Gromyko was even more explicit when he noted "the Soviet Union, while deploring Israel's views on the Middle East crisis, acknowledges Israel's rights as an independent state."[105] Soviet commitment to Israel's existence was also reflected in a February 1971 meeting between Arafat and the Russian ambassador to Jordan, during which the latter reportedly broached the idea of a Palestinian state made up of the West Bank and the Gaza Strip.[106]

The USSR was also unenthusiastic about fedayeen reliance on a strategy of armed struggle, independent of the general Arab liberation movement, since such a course of action had little chance of success as far as the Soviets were concerned. Unmistakable reservations along these lines were evident in a September 1968 article in the Soviet-supported *World Marxist Review*, which cited one of two dangerous trends in the Arab world as being the "romantic and reckless" course advocated by the progressive national patriotic element, which put forth slogans negating organizing mass struggle in favor of the sole method of separating the Palestine problem from the Arab national liberation movement. This policy, it was argued, was based on the slogan that the Palestinian movement was autonomous and ignored the true situation and relative strengths of the disputants.[107] The last point was clarified in the next issue of the *World Marxist Review* when the Jordanian Communist Fahmi Salfiti outlined the position of the Jordanian party (presumed to be the same as that of the Communist party of the Soviet Union) as follows:

> 1. Neither in Jordan nor in any other Arab country are conditions ripe for guerrilla activity in or outside the occupied territories.
> 2. The guerrilla organizations are based outside the occupied areas and

their activity, therefore, is usually the same as that of the regular Arab army commandos.

3. *Fida'iyin* activity differs from the armed struggle waged by the people in the occupied areas. Supporting *fida'iyin* organizations means supporting unrealistic political aims, aims that we reject. Their method of struggle is at variance with the objective conditions and strongly coloured by extremism. They tend to dissociate the resistance movement from the facts of life in Jordan and the rest of the Arab world, and from the world anti-imperialist movement. What is more, they ignore mass and political activity, and object to the existence of political parties in the present period.

4. The progressive Arab countries, such as Egypt and Syria, appreciate the correlation of strength in the region and the dangerous consequences of provoking the enemy. Therefore, they object to actions in the immediate proximity of the cease-fire line. Their support of the guerrilla organizations is given on tactical grounds for they desire to win sympathy among the masses, and possibly conceal weaknesses they are reluctant to discard. . . .[108]

Expressing similar skepticism about the potential of guerrilla warfare, G. Mirsky wrote in *New Times*:

Needless to say, guerrilla warfare cannot regain the seized territories. Political factors must be brought into play: Arab unity, stability of the progressive regimes in the Arab world, and primarily in the UAR, which unquestionably is the main force opposing the Israeli expansionists.[109]

Not only did the Soviets find the general strategy of armed struggle unappealing, but they also dissociated themselves from acts of terrorism, although not before some vacillation on the matter. Attacks on Israeli civilian airliners in 1969 were hailed by the media, and the Zurich raid in February was, according to *Pravda*, carried out by patriots defending their "legitimate rights to return to their homeland."[110] By 1970, however, Soviet concern over terrorism outside the Middle East was evident. For example, *Komsomolskaya Pravda* reprinted an article from the East German publication *Unsere Zeit* which condemned the PFLP as an extremist organization, led by a reactionary, which was responsible for hijackings and terror against airline offices.[111] The September 1970 multiple hijacking was an especially reprehensible act as far as Moscow was concerned, because, according to the Soviets, it damaged the Arab image and gave the United States and Israel a pretext to suspend peace talks, increase tension, intervene in Arab affairs, and generate anti-Soviet campaigns in the press.[112] Although chagrined and embarrassed by Palestinian transnational terrorism, Moscow's preferred reaction was to denounce terrorism in general terms and attribute its Palestinian incarnation either to extremists, especially in the PFLP, or to local Arabs acting independently. The

Fatah-BSO connection was conveniently overlooked by the Soviets, perhaps because they felt quiet diplomacy might be more effective in persuading Arafat to give up transnational terrorism.

The complications and costs associated with Palestinian external terrorism were among the reasons Moscow took a dim view of the PFLP and, until 1973, the PDF also, in spite of their affirmations of Marxism. Other factors behind the antipathy were leftist threats to regimes in Arab states friendly to Moscow (e.g., Egypt and Syria), the active role of the PFLP and PDF in upsetting peace negotiations, and the inclination of Habash and Hawatmeh toward Moscow's bitter rival, China.[113] Since the Soviet attitude toward the PFLP and PDF precluded reliance upon them as channels for ideological and political influence within the PLO, it supported the creation of *Al-Ansar* ("the Partisan Forces"), a resistance group composed of Communists from several states in the area. However, since *Al-Ansar* endorsed the Russian position on SC-242, the PLO rejected the group.[114]

The Kremlin was obviously uncomfortable with granting moral and material assistance to a movement whose aims and overall strategy it had disavowed. Consequently, in order to reconcile and rationalize this seeming contradiction, Soviet commentators frequently and disingenuously portrayed the fedayeen objective as the return of the occupied territories; the aim of liberating Palestine was carefully ignored.[115]

In the final analysis, Palestinian hopes of substantial support from the Soviet Union were undermined by Moscow's consistent, longer-term policy of cultivating the Arab regimes as the best means to increase its power and influence in the Middle East, while simultaneously reducing that of the West. What limited assistance the Soviets did render the Palestinians at various times seems to have had more tactical than strategic significance. By providing moderate aid, the Soviets increased the Palestinians' capability to attack Israel, thereby adding to the overall pressure on the Israelis to return the occupied areas. If the Israelis did so, it was the Soviets who would be in a position to claim a good deal of the credit. In the meantime, modulated assistance also functioned as a way to regenerate Soviet influence in the face of setbacks in Egypt and Sudan, and as a means to shore up Moscow's somewhat tenuous revolutionary credentials at a time when they were constantly under fire from Peking.[116] When all was said and done, however, the Kremlin's contributions paled into near insignificance when compared to the largesse it had bestowed on other revolutionary movements. The capability of the Soviets to sustain an insurgent movement with abundant military assistance was clearly demonstrable in Vietnam. Their choice not to do so in Palestine was equally clear. Indeed, when it came to praise for those extending aid to the fedayeen, the Chinese received the lion's share of the credit, not the Russians.

The People's Republic of China

The laudatory remarks the PLO made about the PRC were well deserved inasmuch as Peking gave moral, political, and material support to the fedayeen. In fact, shortly after the formation of the PLO in May 1964, China became the first non-Arab state to grant it diplomatic recognition, a development that may have contributed, in part, to a public indication by Ahmad ash-Shuqayri that the Palestinians would follow the Maoist model. Within a year, Peking dispatched military experts to Syria to train guerrillas, brought Palestinians to China for insurgency training, and began to send weapons to the PLO.[117] All things considered, however, the Chinese impact on the Middle East was modest on the eve of the June War.

Chinese policy after the Six-Day War emphatically rejected a peaceful solution to the Arab-Israeli conflict. Accordingly, Peking lashed out at the Western powers, Israel, and Moscow for what was considered collaboration with Washington. Security Council Resolution 242 was said to be part of a conspiracy to pressure the Arabs to capitulate, which had been adopted because of the betrayal of the "Soviet revisionist clique." Nevertheless, the Chinese argued that as long as a hundred million Arabs remained united and persevered, they would win final victory.[118] An article by Chou Tien-chih in *Peking Review* contended that the theory, strategy, and tactics of people's war would provide the keys to success. Thus, he advocated that the Arabs rely on the military theory and "the whole set of strategy and tactics of Chairman Mao" if they were to "win victory in a revolutionary war and defeat imperialism and its lackeys in that war." Since the Arab countries were perceived to be in the national-democratic stage of development, they were advised to rely on a union of the workers, peasants, revolutionary intellectuals, petit bourgeois, and national bourgeois to oppose imperialism.[119] In short, unlike the Soviet Union, the PRC gave enthusiastic backing to both the political goal and the strategy of the fedayeen. This happy convergence, of course, suited the Chinese quite well, as it not only gave them a means of countering the Soviets in the Middle East, but it also enhanced the legitimacy of Peking's claim that it was the leader of revolutionary forces in the Third World.

In order to establish the validity of the claim that the Maoist model should be emulated in the Palestinian cause, the Chinese media sought to create the impression that the revolution was gaining momentum and strength.[120] The reader of Chinese commentaries was constantly reminded that the fedayeen had the support of the Palestinians and the Arab masses, both of which constituted the water that sustained the fish. To prove the existence of such mass support, Chinese writers cited the growing resistance—strikes and demonstrations—in the occupied areas. Popular backing, according to *Peking Review,* provided guerrillas with information, food, shelter, concealment, and care for the wounded. With such support, the Palestinian movement was depicted as more powerful than American and Israeli "paper tigers."[121]

When dealing with the need for a vast countryside and base areas in order to conduct guerrilla warfare, Chinese analysts engaged in the Procrustean exercise of representing the geography of the conflict areas in such a way that it would appear similar to that of China. Thus, readers were told by *People's Daily* that guerrilla operations were being conducted "in the vast countryside and mountain areas dominated by Israel."[122] In addition to the operations in such favorable terrain, it was suggested that the fedayeen had actually set up bases in the occupied areas, thereby building a solid foundation for protracted war in the future.[123] In an apparent reconciliation with reality and the difficulties encountered by the insurgents when trying to establish bases, the Chinese subsequently referred to the occupied area bases as "mobile," whereas permanent bases and training camps were said to be located in Arab countries around Israel.[124]

Periodically, Chinese writers seemed to acknowledge, albeit implicitly, that the terrain in Palestine was really less than ideal. One *Peking Review* writer asserted that the guerrillas were "active in the broad rural and mountainous ranges" while in another passage he quoted a Palestinian leader as saying, ". . . although we have no jungles, the masses of people serve as our jungle."[125] The tacit admission of environmental deficiencies was unmistakable.

Nevertheless, there was little doubt the Chinese sought to create the impression that Palestinians, like the Chinese of twenty years previously, had gained the military initiative with continuous victories and expanding operations, enjoyed mass support, and operated from permanent and mobile bases in "endless" mountain chains. When portraying the events and environment in the Middle East this way, the Chinese avoided explicit comparisons with the Maoist model. Yet, for the reader acquainted with the Chinese guerrilla experience and Mao's writings, the hidden analogies were obvious.

If the relevance of specific assets of the Chinese model was dealt with implicitly, the general application of Mao's teaching and Chinese experience was not. Indeed, the Chinese were quite explicit that the Chinese path was the correct one and was a constant source of inspiration to the Palestinians.

At various times the Chinese injected a note of flexibility into their call for a guerrilla war based on the Maoist model by saying that the fedayeen would apply Mao's teachings to their own struggle.[126] Just how much the application could or would deviate from the Chinese experience was not spelled out. Two considerations seemed to suggest that the Chinese believed or hoped the divergences from the Maoist model would not be of great significance.

In the first place, the Chinese characterization of the Middle Eastern milieu along lines of the Chinese experience (popuar support, vast and rugged mountain chains, base areas, and so forth) left little room for basic dissimilarities with the Maoist model. A second indicator was a *Peking Review* reprint from *L'Humanité Nouvelle* that denounced Regis Debray's Cuban revolutionary model, because it denied the universality of Mao's thoughts.[127] Although some guerrilla leaders and independent analysts professed to see more similarity between the Cuban and Palestinian situations than between the Chinese and Palestinian situations, China apparently chose to overlook this comparison. This tendency was only natural, for to acknowledge similarities with the Cuban situation would be tantamount to recognition of a revolutionary path other than Mao's, a mortal sin during the cultural revolution.

Even though the Chinese went to great lengths to justify the relevance of the Chinese model to the Palestinian situation, they, at least by implication, conceded that two conditions of the Maoist formula remained unfulfilled: unity of the resistance forces and certitude about perseverance. Time and again, the Chinese analyses of the Palestinian situation would terminate with the statement that the Chinese were convinced the Palestinians and the Arabs would succeed as long as they unified their forces and persevered in the struggle.[128]

Although the existence of such failings provided a fallback position to explain possible guerrilla failure in such a way that credibility of the Maoist model would be maintained—defeat could always be attributed to lack of unity or perseverance—the Chinese reacted to Palestinian setbacks, particularly in September 1970, by blaming imperialism, social imperialism (the USSR), and reactionary elements in the Middle East and Israel.

The castigation of Israel, which was even more one-sided than similar Soviet condemnation, was aimed at gaining favor among the Arabs at the expense of the United States and the Soviet Union, the latter being charged with helping Zionism achieve its aims. China's unequivocal opposition to Zionism was intended to show the Arabs who their real friend was. A large number of articles included denunciations of Israeli "aggression, imperialism, and repression." At times Israel was referred to as "imperialism's running dog" and a "paper tiger" that was "panic stricken." Israel's "rabid repression" was functional, however, because it enabled the guerrillas to gain popular support, at least according to

Peking's spokesmen. In time, they said, the Palestinian efforts, backed by mass support, would combine with Israel's overextension and economic woes to bring about the downfall of Zionism.[129]

The Chinese moral and political support for the PLO led Salah Khalef to characterize China as "the only big power which adopts the guerrilla point of view," and Arafat to remark to *Al-Ahram* that "Chou [Chinese Prime Minister Chou En-lai] supports the guerrillas without limits to the very end."[130] Although political and moral support might have been helpful and encouraging, they were not orchestrated with a significant degree of support from other states. Moreover, the relative Chinese withdrawal from international intercourse during the cultural revolution severely undercut Peking's ability to translate its support of the fedayeen into effective action on the world platform. In short, China's limited capability and isolationist foreign policy seemed to prevent its political and moral support of the Palestinian guerrillas from having an effective international impact.

Although China may not have been able to muster an international effort to support the guerrillas, it did make important material contributions to the Palestinian effort. As noted earlier in this chapter, the Chinese were giving arms to the guerrillas, along with training, before the June 1967 War. As the fedayeen movement began to gather a degree of momentum after the war, China continued to provide material aid, although such activity was shrouded in secrecy and not acknowledged by Peking. Specific, accurate, and credible figures on Chinese arms deliveries to the various guerrilla organizations are unavailable, but a general picture of Chinese arms assistance can be painted on the basis of numerous reports on the matter.

The fact that the Chinese continued to give the fedayeen military assistance after the June War was confirmed by guerrilla spokesmen. In November 1967 Shuqayri claimed the Chinese were providing Palestinians with both arms and training, and in the spring of 1970 Arafat said it was no secret *Fatah* received Chinese aid.[131] A year or so later, Hani Abu Hasan, one of *Fatah*'s leaders, left no doubts on the matter when he stated that the Palestinian revolution "had recently received modern and effective weapons from China."[132]

Independent commentators also took note of the Chinese arms deliveries. In March 1970, for instance, *The Guardian* said the Chinese had "virtually armed the Arab guerrilla movement," and during August *The Times* of London quoted Asian diplomatic sources as reporting that Chinese arms, delivered at Aden in South Yemen, Basra in Iraq, and Latakia in Syria, were generally limited to rifles, grenades, mortars, antitank weapons, explosives, automatic weapons, and machine guns.[133]

The main route for delivery of the arms was said to extend from Iraq's ports on the northern tip of the Persian Gulf to Jordan. However, when Hussein closed the eastern frontier during September 1970, arms were diverted to Syria, where the subsequent coup by the more moderate General Assad appeared to make the logistical situation even more precarious.[134]

Along with arms assistance, the guerrillas continued to receive training. In March 1968, a captured Syrian guerrilla stated that China was training fedayeen, an admission which was confirmed the following year by a guerrilla leader in Lebanon, who, during a series of university lectures, noted that the guerrillas had received training in China and North Vietnam since early 1968.[135]

Israeli interrogations of captured fedayeen indicated that such training included courses in sabotage, guerrilla warfare, ideology, establishing harmonious relations with the people, and setting up spy and sabotage networks among the local people. By August 1970, it was reported that Chinese instructors had arrived in Amman to train members of the PDF, although some guerrilla estimates put the number of Chinese working with the fedayeen at no more than six.[136]

The total Chinese arms contribution to the revolution was unknown. But, even if one assumes that the Chinese assistance was substantial, the events of September 1970 showed it could not be very helpful to the fedayeen if local antagonisms led to the confiscation of weapons and blockage of supply routes. Such actions were, as noted in previous sections, taken by the Jordanians during and after the civil war. Moreover, even the "progressive" Arab states occasionally displayed a reluctance to play the role of funnel for Chinese arms, perhaps out of fear of irritating their main benefactor, the Soviet Union. Thus, in May 1969, the Kuwaiti newspaper *Al-Risala* reported that a ship carrying Chinese weapons for the fedayeen had been at sea for several weeks waiting to unload because no Arab state wished to receive the arms for fear of annoying the Soviet Union.[137] It was also instructive to note that the Chinese, unlike Soviets or Americans, lacked the overall capability (in particular, aircraft) to maintain a rapid flow of arms during a crisis. This fact simply accentuated the precariousness of supply lines extended to points as far away as China.

Thus far the assumption has been that Chinese aid has been substantial; however, there is reason to doubt this hypothesis. For instance, Israeli sources have been cited as estimating that the total value of Chinese material aid between 1965 and 1969 did not exceed $5 million. Moreover, most weapons captured by Israel are said to be outmoded Soviet weapons no longer used by the Chinese. In addition, *Le Monde*, in the fall of 1970, suggested that Chinese assistance was primarily moral and political, and military aid was limited. *The New York Times* several months later quoted informed sources in Lebanon as saying that Chinese assistance actually delivered was far less than a quarter of the aid promised during visits by guerrilla leaders to Peking in the previous two years.[138] The last report was not unusual, since several developing nations had complained in the past about receiving large promises and small deliveries from Peking.

Another indicator that Chinese aid was not as great as their propaganda suggested was the admission by Arafat that the guerrillas were paying for Chinese weapons. In an interview with the Lebanese magazine *Al-Sayyad*, he acknowledged that the fedayeen were "using Saudi money to buy weapons from China."[139]

Another important qualification related to Chinese military assistance is the reported tendency to favor the PFLP and the PDF.[140] Though the Marxism espoused by these two groups would make this tendency quite understandable, it is interesting to note that most of the moral and political support was given to the PLO-*Fatah* wing of the resistance, whereas the PFLP and PDF were, at best, given scant attention. Undoubtedly, the emphasis was related to *Fatah*'s emergence as the most powerful organization and leader of the fedayeen movement.[141]

Perhaps to legitimatize the more favored public treatment of the PLO-*Fatah* wing, Peking often quoted its leaders and guerrilla fighters as extolling the thought of Chairman Mao.[142] That *Fatah* gave far less attention to ideology than its PDF-PFLP rivals was not mentioned.

The political and moral support for the *Fatah* wing, coupled with limited material aid, enabled Peking to retain strong ties with the leading sector of the Palestinian movement, while material aid and quiet assistance for the PFLP and PDF organizations allowed the Chinese to solidify their links with a grouping with which they had a stronger ideological affinity. Moreover, it is possible that Peking's ultimate hope was for the left-wing groups, especially the PDF, to gradually assume control of the Palestinian movement and thus bring China's influence to even greater heights.

Whatever longer-term aspirations the Chinese had, by 1973 they appeared to be interacting with the PLO in a rather perfunctory way, a development that no doubt reflected the PLO's weakness, as well as China's preoccupation with domestic matters and significant changes taking place in relations with Washington and Moscow. Thus, another sad episode was added to the already pessimistic story of the fedayeen quest for external support.

8
The Uncertain Future

There is a general consensus among students of international politics and the Middle East that the October War had profound international and regional repercussions. Adequate testimony to this fact has been provided by the deluge of books and articles devoted to the analysis of petropolitics, superpower relations with the Middle East, military strategy, and efforts to reach a peace settlement. The second section of this chapter will focus on the specific, but more conjectural, question of the war's effect on the status of the PLO. However, since the strategic analysis of the PLO prior to the outbreak of hostilities is related integrally to what occurred after the fighting, the first task is to recapitulate the developments between 1967 and 1973.

Strategic Evaluation: Summary and Conclusions

The strategic condition of the Palestinian resistance on the eve of the October War was not impressive. Although the fedayeen had pursued their aim of liberating Palestine from Zionist control for more than six years, they had accomplished little more than compelling the world to acknowledge and take into account the importance of the Palestinian issue in any final settlement of the Arab-Israeli conflict. While there was no denying this was an important achievement per se, it by no means indicated that the strategy of protracted armed struggle had become an effective alternative to military action by the armed forces of the Arab states Neither protracted armed struggle nor the limited conventional engagements during the war of attrition softened the Israeli stand on the question of the occupied areas. In fact, such violence may have been partially responsible for the hardening of Israeli policy in the late summer of 1973. In any case, it was to regular military forces that the Arabs once again turned in order to achieve their political objectives.

Major Strategic Factors

As pointed out in Chapter 2, the strategy of protracted armed struggle involved the complex interplay of several major factors—the government response, the environment, popular support, organization, cohesion, and external assistance. Reduced to its essentials, the strategy called for the gradual erosion of the adversary's strength and will, through a combination of political activity and continually escalating violence in the form of terrorist actions and, especially, guerrilla warfare. Theoretically, success in such an undertaking was dependent upon both the establishment of bases and the acquisition of active popular support in the occupied territories. Moreover, since the Israelis were regarded as a formidable foe, external support was deemed necessary from the very beginning of the struggle. Critical to and underpinning all of this was the need for a solid organization.

The demands placed upon the Palestinians by the imperatives of their strategy were intensified by the Israeli counterinsurgency effort and environmental realities. While the military government's record was hardly unblemished, its response to organizational, terrorist, and guerrilla threats was generally effective. Through a skillful blend of economic development programs, liberal administrative policies, and highly efficient police work, the Israelis were able to stabilize the situation on the West Bank and in the Gaza Strip. Along the borders, guerrilla infiltration eventually was contained by means of military actions against sanctuary states, local defense measures, and, most importantly, by a nomadic territorial offensive which emphasized extensive border patrolling. Finally, transnational terrorism was countered by attacks on sanctuaries, augmented security for Israelis abroad, and clandestine operations against Palestinian terrorist agents.

Besides the problems created by the Israeli counterinsurgency efforts, the Palestinians also had to cope with a physical environment that was unfavorable for protracted armed struggle. Indeed, the mostly barren landscape and excellent road and communications systems were distinct assets for the Israelis.

Israel's counterinsurgency successes and the environmental deficiencies not only increased the pressure on the fedayeen to compensate by obtaining popular and external support and fashioning a complex and cohesive organizational apparatus, but they also made those tasks more difficult to accomplish. This difficulty was particularly acute when it came to popular support.

Although the fedayeen made a considerable effort to gain active popular support in the occupied areas, the results generally were discouraging. By late 1969 organizational cells on the West Bank were being uncovered at a rapid rate and the region was acknowledged to be increasingly hazardous for insurgent activities, a situation partially attributable to the indifference of most of the local Arab population and the willingness of some individuals within that community to betray the terrorists and guerrillas. It did not seem to be mere coincidence that by 1970 the fedayeen had come to de-emphasize the idea of popular bases in the target area in favor of accentuating the significance of their "pillar" base across the Jordan River.

A number of factors accounted for the failure to create popular bases within the West Bank and Israel. In addition to the effective Israeli counterinsurgency program, chronic disunity prevented the fedayeen from devising a coherent organizational scheme and strategy. At no time was there anything resembling the parallel hierarchies which had proven to be so important in mobilizing the people during successful protracted revolutionary wars in the past. If anything, the balance of both institutional and coercive control within the target area was in Israel's favor. This, plus the tendency of the fedayeen to fight among themselves and the decreasing incidence and effectiveness of insurgent operations, detracted from Palestinian attempts to seize the initiative and demonstrate the potency of the movement.

There was a significant degree of civilian resistance to Israel in the occupied areas in 1967-1968; in 1968-1969 the fedayeen were able to mount a number of terrorist and guerrilla operations. However, by 1970 their inability to gain active popular support was evidenced in several ways: by failure to obtain adequate concealment and sustenance on the West Bank, by the increased reliance on assassination to prevent betrayal, by the criticism of their activities from Arab notables, by the participation of a significant proportion of the Arab populations in Israeli-sponsored elections in Israel and the West Bank, and by the increasing calls of both traditional and modern leaders within the West Bank community for a nonviolent solution to the Palestinian question. In the Gaza Strip, the fedayeen were able to sustain a significant level of terrorist operations through mid-1971. Once again, however, the Israeli ability to isolate this region and to improve security by the second half of 1971 largely neutralized the impact of the fedayeen.

Where the fedayeen did achieve substantial success in mobilizing active support was in the refugee camps in Jordan and Lebanon and, to a lesser extent, Syria. Two key reasons for this success were the absence of Israeli security forces and the toleration of Palestinian organizational efforts in the camps by the governments of the aforementioned states. Nevertheless, in the long run, the insurgent organization in the refugee camps came to be viewed as a challenge to the sovereignty of the states concerned; in addition, the losses inflicted on the sanctuary states by Israel and the hostility directed at the regimes by the left-wing fedayeen groups brought confrontations with the Jordanian and Lebanese authorities. Such conflicts resulted in the expulsion of the fedayeen from Jordan in 1971 and a sharp reduction of their presence and operations in Lebanon by mid-1973. Though the insurgents were able to maintain control of the camps in Lebanon, this fact did not conceal their overall failure to harness the active popular support which was vital if they were to conduct a successful protracted insurgency.

One of the principal reasons why the fedayeen were unable to mobilize the people was their organizational failure. In the first place, the resistance was never able to surmount divisions rooted in personal, ideological, tactical, and inter-Arab state differences (the latter being manifest in the existence of groups like the ALF and *Sa'iqa*). Given the strengths of their adversary, such disunity was a luxury the Palestinians could ill afford; it diverted both resources and attention from the primary target, detracted from their image, precluded the creation and implementation of a coherent strategy, led to undisciplined behavior (which often worked at cross-purposes with the interests of the resistance as a whole), and undermined relations with the external support states that were so important in light of the guerrilla inability to set up popular bases in the target area.

The last-mentioned consequence of disunity was particularly significant in the fedayeen case because when the resistance lost financial backing, freedom of movement, and sanctuaries, it found itself in a state of profound stagnation. That these external support losses were, in large part, due to the explicit ideological challenge directed at Arab regimes by the left-wing organizations, to undisciplined and cavalier actions by individual fedayeen in sanctuary states, and to the dislike of the tactics of some fedayeen groups, was quite evident.

In terms of scope, the fedayeen organizations eventually embraced about 25,000 actual members. As indicated previously, these were largely recruited in and supported by the refugee camps in the border states. The existence of armed guerrillas within the sanctuary states, however, proved to be another factor which over the long term exacerbated relations with the host governments.

While the resistance did achieve a degree of organizational differentiation (complexity) in that it created auxiliaries such as youth groups, women's organizations, and welfare institutions, the impact of these structures was limited, for the most part, to the refugee camps. Since the organizational structures were parallel to the government structures in host states (rather than to those of Israel), Jordan, Lebanon, and Syria came to view the fedayeen apparatus as a threat to national sovereignty and to their right to maintain law and order within their boundaries. In the end, all three structural aspects of organization—scope, complexity, and cohesion—caused friction with the sanctuary states.

In the military realm, there was a rudimentary division of functions into those carried out by the regular forces of the PLA, the terrorist and guerrilla elements of the fedayeen organizations, and the part-time militias. Despite this seemingly efficient differentiation, no effective use was made of the various components because of the general lack of unity. PLA activity was rare and was hardly ever coordinated with the commando organizations, which themselves were divided. As for the militias (local guerrillas), they too, were uncoordinated because of the divisions among the parent fedayeen organizations. Moreover, since the militias were primarily located in Jordan, they could not be considered the functional equivalents of local guerrillas in other insurgent organizations such as the Viet Cong or Viet Minh. In the latter and in other cases, the role of local guerrillas was to harass the regime with acts of sabotage or terror, to assist main force units in their military operations, and to provide local security. In the fedayeen case, the militias' role was to provide defense against the military and security forces of the Arab governments, especially Jordan. Hence, the militias played no part in the direct conflict with Israel.

When it came to the organizational functions, the fedayeen were able to provide a number of educational, medical, and welfare services (instrumental functions) within the refugee camps and a channel for the expression of protest. But, since Israel was able to maintain an effective balance of coercive and institutional control in the target area, the fedayeen impact in terms of the performance of instrumental and expressive functions was neither adequate nor significant. The fedayeen inability to reach a level of activity that properly could be termed internal war was closely related to such organizational failings.

The rather gloomy strategic situation confronting the insurgents did not change much when it came to external support. Although in terms of moral support the fedayeen enjoyed the unanimous backing of the Arab world and China, plus the qualified support of the Soviet Union, the international community at large was not very responsive; and where the line between moral and political support was crossed, the situation became less favorable. For a number of reasons discussed in Chapter 7, several Arab states and the USSR refused to actively support the fedayeen aim of liberating all Palestine. While Syria did endorse the political goal of the PLO during the period of the Atassi regime, there were indications after the Assad coup that it might accept a political settlement with Israel.

Since the PLO did not have the capability to generate adequate material supplies—particularly weapons and ammunition—from within and could not rely on capturing appreciable amounts from the Israeli military forces, it was forced to turn to outside donors. In this search there was some initial success, with assistance in the form of finances, arms, and munitions coming directly from several Arab states, indirectly from the USSR, and directly but clandestinely from China. Yet, in spite of these external contributions, Arafat complained in 1970 that his movement lacked adequate weapons stocks and in 1971 the supplies that the fedayeen did have were depleted by confiscations in Jordan. At the same time, the financial contributions to the PLO began to lag. With conflicts between several donor states and the fedayeen as a backdrop, the impotence and confusion which marked the movement after September 1971 may have led some donors to decide that investment in a lost cause would not yield many political dividends. In any event, the material support which had been fairly solid in 1968-1969 had weakened seriously by 1971.

In light of the inability of the insurgents to establish a popular base in the target area, the need for sanctuary and freedom of movement in the states contiguous to the target area became essential. Unfortunately for the Palestinians, a concatenation of factors prompted these states to restrict or, as in the case of Jordan, to terminate fedayeen activity within their boundaries. With the PLO in an obviously weakened state after the civil war of 1970, such restrictive actions became even bolder, no doubt due in part to the PLO's loss of appeal among the Arab masses. Consequently, by the fall of 1971 the Palestinian commandos had little support in terms of sanctuary and freedom of movement.

Strategic Dissonance

All told, the strategic accomplishments of the resistance left very much to be desired. Though the analysis of the strategy of protracted armed struggle in previous chapters has attempted to describe and explain this failure, one area merits further comment here: the ambiguity and contradictions surrounding Palestinian strategic calculations, especially with respect to revolutionary models and stages of revolutionary warfare.

For *Fatah*, the Cuban model proved inspirational because it successfully overcame disadvantages similar to those facing the fedayeen—to wit, small area of conflict and small numbers of insurgents. One major difference, understressed or ignored by *Fatah*, however, was the fact that Castro started his revolutionary war against an adversary with weak political and military underpinnings. Since the Israeli regime, unlike Batista's, had firm foundations, an excellent military with high morale, and popular backing from the Jewish population, the fedayeen could not hope to succeed with an abbreviated campaign of guerrilla operations and psychological pressures. Hence, if there was to be any hope of success, the Palestinians would have to plan for a revolutionary war of long duration and in that situation the Cuban model was not as relevant as the Maoist, Viet Minh, Viet Cong, and Algerian experiences. To conduct an armed struggle along the lines of the last-mentioned models meant that substantial attention had to be paid to a number of complicated and interrelated factors, not the least of which were the progression of revolutionary warfare and a coherent long-term strategy.

Although many of the revolutionary leaders whom the fedayeen hoped to emulate had carefully analyzed the development of and problems associated with the various stages of protracted insurgency, the fedayeen did not appear to give the matter profound consideration. However, this is not to suggest that no thought was devoted to the issue.

In 1968, *Fatah* indicated that the revolution was in a stage involving hit-and-run tactics designed to avoid large losses while potential supporters were indoctrinated. In September 1969, it was suggested that this stage, the "strategic defensive," was about to be superseded by another phase due to the temporary occupation of the village of Al-Hamma by some fedayeen units. During the same month a fedayeen spokesman went further and contended that the Palestinians had, in fact, entered into a new stage, a claim echoed in *Free Palestine*, which reported that the fedayeen were in a stage of "mobile warfare" that was characterized by capturing areas for several hours and then withdrawing. The PFLP, however, was not as sanguine about these developments, a fact made explicit by Ghassan Kanafani, who referred to the state of the revolution at the time as "stagnant."[1] To the outside observer, the PFLP assessment seemed the more realistic.

When fedayeen activity in 1968-1969 was analyzed in terms of the Maoist model, it appeared that the Palestinian commandos had decided to engage in both terrorism and guerrilla warfare without the benefit of systematic political, psychological, and organizational preparation. This decision, which was more reflective of the Cuban military-foco short-duration model than it was of the Maoist-Vietnamese type of protracted warfare, led to a host of problems. For one thing, the fragile fedayeen organization which had been created was neutralized with relative ease by the Israeli security forces. Closely related to the organizational failing was the inadequate political preparation of the people in the target area, which precluded them from functioning as the water within which the fish (guerrillas and terrorists) could swim. Thus, although the fedayeen acknowledged the need for patience and commitment to a long struggle, they proceeded to act precipitously and unsystematically. By 1970 the claim of having entered a phase of mobile warfare had been proven hollow. If anything, Israel's destruction of the terrorist networks and its increasingly effective counterguerrilla operations, which forced the fedayeen into the interior of Jordan, suggested that Israel had seized the initiative.

Beyond the fact that the fedayeen had not assessed the progression of protracted warfare thoroughly and clearly, they did not agree on a basic organizational approach. For *Fatah* and some of the lesser groups, the military focus of the Cuban model was attractive because it was thought to avoid the unnecessary conflicts arising from maneuverings of political parties and groups. For the PFLP and the PDF, on the other hand, the idea of not having a tightly disciplined party in control of the revolution was considered a heretical and critical shortcoming. This basic disagreement, combined with other factors, precluded the emergence of a unified revolutionary movement and strategy. The result was that the two wings of the resistance proceeded to act upon different principles and assumptions and the movement as a whole took on an ad hoc, fragmented character, which, in the final analysis, proved to be its Achilles' heel.

It should not be inferred from the above that the PFLP/PDF and *Fatah* approaches were devoid of any merit. Certainly, the *Fatah* concern about the impact of party politics on the effectiveness of the resistance was well founded, given the obvious problems that the Marxist orientation of the PFLP and PDF caused the resistance in terms of winning both popular and external support. It was obvious that hostility of the left-wing groups toward most Arab regimes was a factor undermining external support. Yet, it was probable that even without the ideological conflicts, the Arab states would have been reluctant to support the guerrillas fully, given a number of other considerations noted previously. Where the absence of Marxism-Leninism might have paid more dividends was in mobilizing popular support, since communism not only had a limited appeal in the Arab world, but was considered hostile and foreign by most Muslims. This is not to suggest that the PFLP/PDF goal of a tightly knit revolutionary leadership was unwise. To the contrary, a small, cohesive leadership might have alleviated the fedayeen plight substantially, but only so long as the basis of cohesion was not Marxism-Leninism or one of its variants.

After all the data on the variables and subvariables have been analyzed, the inescapable conclusion is that the strategy of protracted armed struggle has been a near total failure, since fedayeen activity rates poorly in terms of all major strategic factors. While the problems associated with organization and cohesion and, to a lesser extent, popular and external support might have been attenuated by a well thought out and harmonious approach by the fedayeen groups, and while this might have increased Israel's human and material losses, successful revolutionary warfare would still remain a remote possibility because of the impressive strength of Israel after the June War and the telling implications of the environmental disadvantages. In other words, when the revolutionary warfare waged by the fedayeen is assessed in a systematic and comprehensive manner, the only conclusion is that it has failed. In view of the Israeli regime's effectiveness and the disadvantageous environment, it must be concluded that the Palestinian attempt to follow in the footsteps of the Chinese, Algerians, and Vietnamese by waging a protracted armed struggle was an ill-fated enterprise.

The Recrudescence of PLO Influence

Despite its weakness and strategic failures, the PLO experienced a dramatic political resurgence following the October 1973 war, highlighted by Arafat's triumphant appearance before the UN General Assembly on November 14, 1974. Though at first glance this development seems paradoxical, a closer examination of developments prior and subsequent to that historic event suggests that the PLO's political success was dependent, more than ever, on the support of the Arab states rather than on its own intrinsic strengths. Essentially, the PLO's political clout in both the Arab world and the larger international arena was increasingly the product of decisions made in the Arab capitals, especially Cairo. Though the PLO periodically called for an intensification of armed struggle, neither the sporadic acts of transnational terrorism nor the raids against Israeli towns and settlements, particularly in 1974, compared favorably to even the limited accomplishments of 1968-1969.

Transnational terrorism nevertheless exacted its costs and publicized the Palestinian cause. The more notable episodes included a Rome-Athens airline attack in December 1973 that resulted in the death of more than thirty civilians, a skyjacking to Dubai in November 1974, the firing of a bazooka at France's Orly Airport in January 1975, and the well-known Entebbe incident in June-July 1976. What was most striking about these and several lesser operations was their lack of overall strategic purpose. In fact, the PLO condemned the operations because they contradicted its new aversion to transnational terrorism, damaged the image of the Palestinians, and antagonized states from which the PLO was seeking political support (e.g., France). Furthermore, in the case of Entebbe, Israel was the main beneficiary since the daring rescue operation by the IDF won international acclaim and boosted morale inside Israel.[2]

In contrast to the transnational attacks, the terrorist raids inside Israel were sanctioned by the PLO. However, though such operations could be viewed as a renewed campaign to weaken Israeli resolve, they were better interpreted as a reaction to the Arab states' engagement in peace

negotiations and concomitant pressures exerted on the PLO to accommodate this trend. To understand this development, a brief look at the Arab
states' policies toward the Palestinian issue, as well as their effects on the
PLO, is necessary.

The Politics of Dependency: The Arab States and the PLO

The foreign policies of the Arab states were affected profoundly by the
October War and its diplomatic aftermath. Whether accurately or not, the
Arabs perceived that they had won the war and redeemed their honor and
dignity, which had been so badly tarnished in 1967. For the first time, the
Arab states had unified their ranks and successfully wielded both the
military and economic instruments of statecraft. Aided in large part by the
element of surprise, the Arab armies were able to inflict serious personnel
and material losses on the Israelis, while in the international arena the oil
embargo and production cutbacks had stimulated U.S. diplomacy and
resulted in the endorsement of Arab aims by Japan and the European
Economic Community (Holland excepted). The disengagement agreements negotiated by American Secretary of State Henry Kissinger on both
the Egyptian and Syrian fronts were viewed as useful preliminary steps
toward an eventual Israeli withdrawal from the occupied areas.

The October War had portentous political repercussions in Egypt.
President Sadat, overriding objections from some advisors, including
Heikal, embraced U.S. diplomatic initiatives and proceeded to excoriate
the Soviet Union for its prewar refusal to supply certain categories of
offensive equipment requested by Cairo. Though multilateral negotiations involving Israel were undertaken in Geneva, the Egyptians (until
1976) considered Kissinger's shuttle diplomacy the most promising
diplomatic approach. Internally, meanwhile, Sadat exploited his upsurge
in popularity by expounding his "October Plan," a wide-ranging program
calling for political liberalization and economic development, including a
new influx of both domestic and foreign capital.[3]

Closely related to these Egyptian moves was an apparent genuine desire
to arrive at a final peace settlement with Israel that would be based on the
1967 *status quo ante bellum*. While Sadat indicated that twenty-six years of
hostility and distrust would preclude the complete normalization of
relations which Israel desired, he nevertheless tacitly acknowledged the
continued existence of the Jewish state by pointing out to Arab audiences
that Egypt accepted the fact that America would continue to back Israel.[4]

Unfortunately, the Syrians were not as forthcoming on this matter as the
Egyptians, in part because Assad's political position was not as strong as
Sadat's. Yet, while Assad attempted to assuage the hawks among his
generals and political supporters by adamantly demanding the eventual

return of the Golan Heights, there were signs (e.g., the indirect acceptance of SC-242) that Damascus was coming to terms with the reality of the "Zionist entity." As in Egypt, although to a lesser extent, there was increased attention to rehabilitating the economy and permitting a limited revitalization of private enterprise through 1978.

Most of the other Arab states supported the efforts of Damascus and Cairo, with the Saudis echoing Sadat's acceptance of American backing of Israel's existence. Libya and Iraq, on the other hand, sharply dissented from this trend because of fears that it was leading towards the ultimate endorsement of Israel's legitimacy. Thus they supported factions within the resistance movement opposing any partial solutions to the conflict, the political catalyst being the emerging notion that the PLO should agree to the establishment of a mini-Palestinian state, composed of the West Bank, the Gaza Strip, and possibly (though implausibly) the Al-Hamma area at the entrance to the Golan Heights.

Prior to the October War, it should be recalled, all factions of the PLO had rejected negotiations with Israel on the basis of SC-242 because the resolution's acknowledgement of the right of all states in the area to peace and security was considered antithetical to the achievement of a "secular, democratic, nonsectarian state" in all of Palestine. Indeed, just four days after the outbreak of hostilities, one fedayeen spokesman warned that Arab military victories could lead to direct peace talks which would result in the recognition of Israel.[5] Such trepidations were soon reinforced by numerous reports that important elements within the PLO, led by the PDF, were giving serious consideration to the idea of a mini-Palestinian state. By January the issue had produced a bifurcation of the PLO as *Fatah* and *Sa'iqa* backed the PDF position of an "interim" state, whereas the PFLP, ALF, and PF-GC argued that such a state would play into the hands of imperialist and reactionary forces seeking to liquidate the revolution, because it would sap revolutionary strength and turn attention away from Israel and towards the inevitable problems of governing. Other factors, however, also accounted for the opposition of these groups, collectively known as the "rejectionist front."[6]

The PFLP, which had waged a constant struggle for influence within the PLO, was no doubt aware that its power vis-à-vis the *Fatah-Sa'iqa* wing was not substantial and that if it came to handing out portfolios in any government, it would not fare well. Ideologically, the PFLP considered the mini-state concept anathema, because the general ameliorating effects it might have would militate against revolutionary action within the Arab world (especially Jordan)—action that it considered a precondition for success against Israel.

The ALF's opposition was a reflection of the hard-line position of its parent, the Ba'th party in Iraq. Aside from their profound antipathy toward Israel, manifest from time to time in pogroms against their own Jewish population, the Iraqi authorities found that focusing on the external enemy was an effective means of deflecting attention away from their own lack of popular legitimacy. On the inter-Arab level, Iraq's position was linked to its historical quest for hegemony in the sense that the Palestinian question provided a ready-made issue around which Iraq hoped to mobilize support at the expense of its Arab rivals.

As for the PF-GC, its policy seemed to be derived from its lack of influence within Palestinian councils, its fanatical hatred of Israel, its exclusive stress on violent techniques, and its belief that interim political ploys were ineffective diversions from the task of totally liberating Palestine.

The fedayeen organizations which favored the notion of a Palestinian mini-state responded to different pressures and concerns. First of all, many of the PLO's supporters in the Arab world and the international arena, upon which the PLO had become increasingly dependent, endorsed the idea of a settlement with Israel and actively participated in the initial diplomatic stages, the Kissinger disengagement negotiations. Furthermore, three key benefactors, Egypt, Saudi Arabia, and the Soviet Union, were letting it be known that they favored creation of a Palestinian state. A second but related factor was the distinct possibility that PLO intransigence, coupled with its strategic weakness, might enable King Hussein to manipulate the continuing frustration in such a way as to reestablish Amman's preeminent position in any future bargaining with the Israelis over the West Bank. Third, the PLO pragmatists were no doubt aware that their claim to represent the Palestinian people was a mere assertion. Nowhere was this more true than in the politically hetereogeneous West Bank. Although the PLO had sympathizers on the West Bank, most of the population, along with the local political leaders, appeared to be keeping its options open. In the absence of widespread legitimacy, the idea of obtaining control of the area as the result of negotiations presented a significant political opportunity that the PLO pragmatists felt should be exploited. Finally, to some in the PLO, the Palestinian state idea made eminent strategic sense because it could provide a popular base and sanctuary from which the attempt to liberate Israel proper could be pursued.[7] From this perspective, fedayeen deficiencies in terms of popular and external support could be offset by a bold political move.

On the last point in particular, the rejectionist front was dubious. In its eyes, any mini-state that might emerge as part of a peace settlement would be so encapsulated by a web of restrictions and sanctions that it would be unable to carry on the revolution. Within the Palestinian resistance movement, the issue came to a head in the late winter and early spring of 1974. Both sides prepared working papers and engaged in heated arguments over the general question of PLO participation in peace talks at Geneva and the specific matter of the Palestinian state. In moves closely associated with the political in-fighting, the PF-GC and the PDF carried out the bloody terrorist attacks in the Israeli border villages of Qiryat Shemona and Ma'alot during April and May.

At Qiryat Shemona, the perpetrator, the PF-GC, killed or wounded some thirty-four people, the explicit and acknowledged objective being the prevention of a peace settlement. One month later, terrorists of the PDF seized a school and, in an ensuing exchange of fire with Israeli forces, extensive casualties were inflicted on hostage children. Unlike the Qiryat Shemona episode, the political purpose at Ma'alot appeared twofold. First, the PDF wanted to increase pressure for the inclusion of the PLO in peace negotiations at Geneva, and second, it wished to strengthen its own position and influence in any bargaining which might take place. At the same time, the PDF also wished to free a number of fedayeen incarcerated in Israel. In spite of the bloodletting, a close reading of the events which transpired at Ma'alot suggests that the PDF terrorists really did intend to exchange their hostages for prisoners. The carnage which followed was due largely to faulty communications between the terrorists and the Israelis and between the Israeli commanders on the scene and cabinet officials.[8]

When placed in the context of the severe political dissension within the PLO, the actions of Qiryat Shemona and Ma'alot and subsequent Israeli retaliatory attacks on Palestinian refugee camps in Lebanon constituted a dialogue of violence conducted at the expense of innocent civilians on both sides of the Lebanese border. While similar, albeit less spectacular, incidents were taking place in June at Kibbutz Shamir (PF-GC) and Nahariyya (*Fatah*), the pragmatists within the PLO gained the upper hand. At a closed session of the PNC a resolution was passed empowering the executive committee to search for a formula under which the Palestinian problem could be discussed. Most important, a ten-point program included euphemistic references to a "national authority" to be established on all Palestinian territories evacuated by Israel.[9] Although Arafat was forced to accept a provision to reconvene the PNC if a "fateful decision" arose affecting the Palestinian people, he was reportedly satisfied that his hands had not been tied. As might be expected, the "rejectionist front" was furious.

In an obvious attempt to forestall criticism from the radical wing of the movement, *Fatah* spokesmen, most notably Salah Khalef, were dispatched to argue the point that accepting a national authority would in no way diminish the commitment to the strategic goal of the movement. According to Khalef, the establishment of a national authority would enable the guerrillas to establish a "revolutionary base" for future actions against Israel.[10] Despite such efforts, tensions increased and led to an outbreak of fighting in Beirut between the PDF and PF-GC, resulting in over thirty casualties.

Behind the scenes the Egyptians, Saudis, and Soviets were playing key roles in support of PLO pragmatists. Sadat, in particular, was convinced that before further progress could be made in peace negotiations, the Arabs had to adopt a unified strategy which, in turn, made it imperative to avoid further delay as far as the Palestinian issue was concerned. While prodding the Palestinian pragmatists to accept the mini-state idea was viewed as a necessary step in this direction, it also was obvious that such a notion would remain stillborn if the controversy between Jordan and the PLO were not resolved. Although there were many factors underlying the Jordanian-PLO enmity, the essential difference between the two was the PLO's demand for control of the West Bank as against King Hussein's desire to conduct a referendum on the West Bank's future after it had been returned to Hashemite control. In PLO eyes a referendum under such circumstances would be nothing more than a sham designed to legitimize Amman's retention of the West Bank.

In July 1974 Sadat undertook a new initiative to reconcile the two sides when he affixed his signature to a joint Egyptian-Jordanian communiqué stating that the PLO was the legitimate representative of all Palestinians except those living in the Jordanian Hashemite kingdom.[11] However, it was never made clear whether the West Bank was considered part of the Hashemite kingdom. The PLO was naturally alarmed, since Hussein and Sadat had also endorsed a disengagement with Israel on the Jordanian front, a move which, if successful, would have resulted in portions of the West Bank reverting to Amman's control. Thus, it was not surprising that WAFA, the Palestinian news agency, reiterated that the PLO considered itself to be the representative of the Palestinian people "wherever they may be" and castigated Cairo and Amman for seeking to divide the Palestinian people and deprive them of their rights. The fact that Hussein had departed from previous policy by recognizing the PLO as the representative of Palestinians outside Jordan and had agreed that they should have separate delegations at the Geneva peace conference did little to allay the fears of the PLO.

In the weeks that followed, the PLO restated its opposition to the Egyptian-Jordanian communiqué and sought to demonstrate its strength by instigating terrorist attacks on the West Bank and obtaining Soviet backing for a Palestinian state. In the latter endeavor there was notable success; Soviet Foreign Minister Andrei Gromyko indicated that no one had the lawful right to deny the Palestinians statehood.

In the midst of these pressures, Egyptian Foreign Minister Ismail Fahmy was quoted by *Al-Ahram* on August 5, 1974 as saying that his government was committed to the principle that the West Bank should not be returned to Jordan since it was the land of the Palestinian people. In September the Egyptian *volte face* was amplified in a tripartite communiqué issued by the PLO, Egypt, and Syria which made it clear that all land liberated between the Jordan River and Israel should be turned over to a Palestinian national authority and that the PLO was the sole representative of the Palestinian people. Besides expected opposition from Jordan and Israel, there were angry denunciations by members of the rejectionist front.[12]

Objections within the PLO and the Arab world notwithstanding, Arafat pressed ahead with efforts to consolidate support for an impending showdown with King Hussein at the seventh Arab Summit Conference scheduled to be held in Rabat at the end of October. In a move designed to reinforce Cairo's backing, sources close to Arafat let it be known that the PLO was considering the formation of a provisional Palestinian government-in-exile, a move that had long been advocated by Sadat.

Alarmed by the new turn of events, the PFLP accused the PLO leadership of "deviation" and of accepting "surrender solutions." To underscore its chagrin, the PFLP withdrew from the PLO executive committee and indicated that its ALF and PF-GC allies would soon do likewise.[13] Though alleged secret contacts with the United States were cited as the proximate cause of the new rupture in fedayeen ranks, the need to extirpate, or, at a minimum, to mitigate the gathering momentum in favor of a Palestinian state, was the major concern of the rejectionists.

Despite this unwelcome development, which once again raised doubts about the claim of the PLO to represent all Palestinians, the Arafat wing continued its preparations for Rabat, and strengthened its hand by obtaining an overwhelming invitation from the UN General Assembly (which was dominated by Third World countries supporting the PLO) to participate in a discussion of the Palestinian question in November. The movement in support of exclusive PLO control over a future state in the Gaza Strip and West Bank proved too strong for Hussein to overcome. Following a sharp debate at Rabat, the king finally capitulated and the PLO was recognized as "the sole legitimate representative of the Palestinian people in any Palestinian territory that is liberated," thus setting the stage for Arafat's appearance at the UN.[14]

The PLO's political success at the UN paved the way for the adoption of several pro-PLO resolutions by the General Assembly. On November 22, 1974, Resolution 3236 recognized the right of the Palestinian people to self-determination, national independence, and sovereignty, while Resolution 3237 invited the PLO to participate as an observer in the General Assembly and in all international conferences held under UN auspices. A year later three more General Assembly resolutions supporting the PLO were passed. The first, 3375, requested that resolutions and measures be adopted to enable the Palestinian people to exercise their "unalienable national rights" in accordance with Resolution 3236 and again called for the participation of the PLO in all UN-sponsored deliberations and conferences on the Middle East. Resolution 3376 followed, establishing the Committee on the Exercise of the Inalienable Rights of the Palestinian People which was to recommend a program to implement those rights. Finally, the controversial Resolution 3379 equated Zionism with racism.[15]

Although such resolutions increased Israel's isolation in the international community, they did little to change conditions in the Middle East, since they did not reflect the asymmetrical structure of power in the region, which favored Israel. As a result both of military sales and assistance from the United States and of international strategic and tactical reforms in the IDF, Israel increased its military superiority vis-à-vis its adversaries. Moreover, the United States, which had become the major international actor in the region (in part because of the diminution of Soviet influence) did not support the General Assembly resolutions. Under such circumstances, there was little the Arabs could do about Israel's adamant refusal to accept the resolutions. Whatever residual capability the fedayeen had for independent action was eroded severely by the sanguinary Lebanese civil war in 1975-1976 which resulted in heavy Palestinian losses and the imposition of de facto Syrian control over fedayeen behavior and deployments. Thus, by 1977 the fate of the Palestinians was firmly in the hands of the Arab states and the international community.[16]

In spite of such developments, Israel was hardly able to rest assured, for in the midst of the conflict in Lebanon (spring 1976), a wave of strikes and demonstrations—some supportive of the PLO—swept the West Bank and northern Israel. To make matters worse, Israel was shocked by dramatic PLO gains in the West Bank municipal elections during April 1976.[17] Even though the emergence of pro-PLO sentiments was not associated with any appreciable resurgence of armed struggle, it nevertheless revealed the major flaw in Israel's counterinsurgency policy, namely, the absence of a viable political program for the area. By its inability or refusal since 1967 to accommodate independent Palestinian leaders or King Hussein, Israel had left the frustrated denizens of the West Bank little alternative to the PLO. An examination of Israel's attitude towards the Palestinian issue since 1967 suggests how this predicament arose.

Israel and the Palestinians

Although the Israeli government adopted a generally conservative policy towards the question of the Palestinians between 1967 and 1973, there were varying degrees of flexibility within its broad framework. The most rigid outlook was that of Prime Minister Meir, who argued that there was "no such thing as Palestinians" because when the Jews came to Israel "they did not exist." This attitude, which was characteristic of the older generation of Israeli political elites, was rejected by a number of prominent leaders, including Dayan, Allon, Hillel, Eban, and Arie Eliav.[18] While the latter group agreed that the emerging Palestinian national consciousness would have to be addressed in the negotiating process, they objected to the idea of a new state independent of Jordan in the area of Palestine. Instead, they entertained several alternatives.

Eban, for example, proposed that the Palestinians fulfill their national aspirations within the context of Jordan.[19] Another possibility was broached at the time of the Jordanian civil war by Allon, who asserted that if the Palestinians established a government in any part of the Arab world (Jordan), they could regard themselves as candidates for negotiations.[20] A third proposal by Shimon Peres suggested a unitary Arab-Israeli state based on ethnic federalism.[21] Underlying all three schemes was a consensus that negotiations with the fedayeen organizations should be avoided.

Once political stability returned to Jordan following the civil war, Israel settled on the position that the only negotiations over the West Bank would be with the Amman government. In the meantime, the policy of close economic and cultural, but not political, relations with the inhabitants of the West Bank had continued. Despite repeated political stirrings among West Bank intellectuals and political leaders, the Israeli government faced a dilemma. If Israel supported the increased political activity of the West Bank intellectuals and leaders, the latter would be branded as agents of Zionism; on the other hand, backing the West Bank elites was attractive because their position was more moderate than that of the fedayeen. In the final analysis, Israel clung to its position of preventing any political activity that might embarrass Hussein, apparently believing that it would be easier to reach agreement with Jordan than with any Palestinian grouping.[22]

As for the democratic-secular state proposed by the PLO, it goes without saying that Israel rejected this notion, because it undermined the raison d'etre of the state, and because of the basic distrust of groups that expressed unmitigated hatred for all Zionists. To Israelis, the distinction between the destruction of Israel and the destruction of Zionist institutions and structures was a fatuous one, given their inextricable linkage. Additionally, Israeli students of Arab affairs were quick to point out that the fedayeen organizations were themselves divided over the meaning of a democratic, nonsectarian, secular state. That some groups saw the idea as a tactical device to assuage world opinion did little to increase Israel's confidence in the ultimate goodwill of the Palestinian guerrillas.

In spite of Israel's misgivings about the PLO goal, the possibility of talks with the fedayeen was considered briefly in the summer of 1974. Following comments by the minister of tourism, Moshe Kol, that Israel should engage in talks with the Palestinians and Jordan, Aharon Yariv, minister of information, suggested publicly that Israel might negotiate with the PLO if the latter acknowledged Israel's existence and terminated hostilities against it (the so-called Yariv-Shemtov formula). Within a matter of days Israel's new prime minister, Yitzhak Rabin, contradicted Yariv by making it clear that there would be no talks with the fedayeen and no separate Palestinian state outside the Jordanian context.[23]

The reasons for Israel's retraction must remain a matter of speculation. Nevertheless, it did appear that the untimeliness of the Yariv statement had much to do with Rabin's haste in "clarifying" the issue. Aside from the fact that the new government was still trying to establish itself and hence did not wish to incur unnecessary wrath from either the Likud or the National Religious party, it no doubt occurred to many that the Yariv overture could well undermine the above-mentioned apparent success of King Hussein in his talks with Egypt.

Since the time of the Yariv controversy, Israel has maintained continuously and forcefully that it would neither directly negotiate with the PLO nor accept a mini-Palestinian state, a position reinforced by the public indignation at terrorist attacks inside Israel, by PLO successes at the UN between 1974 and 1976, and by the surprising Likud electoral victory in May 1977. The Likud success was particularly significant in that it brought to power a new coalition government, zealously nationalist and heavily influenced by religious considerations. Like their predecessors, the new Israeli leaders saw a mini-Palestinian state as a threat to Israel's security and thus refused to relinquish political control over the West Bank. In addition, however, the new government contended that since the West Bank was part of biblical Israel, it was really a "liberated territory" from which a complete withdrawal was unthinkable. To demonstrate its commitment, the government proceeded in the summer of 1977 to support the establishment of new Jewish settlements and the extension of financial, health, and social services equal to those in Israel to the West Bank and Gaza.

The belief that the West Bank was part of the historic land of Israel raised a new obstacle to negotiations with the PLO, since it accentuated the quintessential legitimacy conflict that divided the two sides. Simply stated, both Israel and the PLO claimed the moral right to control the same territory. Accordingly, the West Bank has assumed transcendent importance in the eyes of the Israelis, for they fear that conceding PLO control therein might lend legitimacy to that organization's larger purpose. It was this concern, more than any other, which motivated Israel in the fall of 1977 to reject not only an independent PLO role in the Geneva negotiations but low-level, official PLO representatives in a unified Arab delegation as well.[24] It also accounted for warnings that Israel would walk out of a peace conference if the issue of a mini-Palestine state were raised.

Conflict Resolution: An Impossible Dream?

Only an inveterate optimist could argue that political conditions in late 1977 were conducive to a resolution of Israeli-PLO differences. In fact, the distance between the two sides seemed greater than ever, with each side refusing to recognize the other, the Israelis opposing any PLO role in peace talks, and the Arab states, especially Syria, insisting on PLO participation as a condition for attendance at a Geneva conference. With such unpromising circumstances in mind, it is quite easy to visualize a scenario in which the Arab-Israeli conflict once more reaches an impasse, moderate Arab leaders are deposed or become militant, tensions escalate, and hostilities again erupt. While reconciliation is difficult to envisage, it is not impossible. Though the indicators of a possible compromise are admittedly fragile, they dare not be dismissed altogether, since the consequences of failure are too ominous. Accordingly, the grounds for a peaceful solution will be explored below.

The most important consideration affecting the realization of an Israeli-PLO settlement is the attitude of the PLO towards the existence of a Jewish state in the Middle East. The PLO will have to accept Israel's existence if there is to be a solution. Although the PLO continues to adhere to its claim of creating a secular, democratic, nonsectarian state in Palestine, there have been occasional hints that coexistence with Israel may be possible over the long term. During an interview following Arafat's 1974 UN speech, the head of the PLO Political Department (Farouk Qaddumi) suggested that his organization envisaged a three-step approach in pursuit of its goal. The first stage was to be the establishment of a "national authority" over the West Bank and the Gaza Strip; the second, the return of refugees to their homes; and the third, the creation of the democratic, secular state. During the first stage, which he said would last a long time, Jews and Arabs would have to learn to "coexist in peace."[25]

In certain respects, such remarks suggest an analogy with the evolution of the Soviet view concerning the future of communism. As is well-known to students of Soviet foreign policy, the ultimate objective of the Kremlin, a Communist world order, has taken second place to state interests as a determinant of day-to-day Soviet behavior, while continuing to justify both internal and external policies. The parallel to be drawn with the

Palestinians, of course, is that the "secular, democratic state" may, with the passage of time, be reduced to an ideological dream that rationalizes and justifies the existence and leading role of the PLO and provides the organization with a modicum of cohesiveness.

A more specific, albeit limited and cautious, indication that the pragmatists in the PLO could accept Israel's existence came from Zuhayr Muhsin, leader of the *Sa'iqa*, during December 1974. In an interview in the West German magazine *Quick*, Muhsin said that Israel would be recognized by a new Palestinian state if it accepted and implemented the UN 1947 partition resolution.[26] What is important here is that for the first time a major fedayeen leader suggested certain conditions under which the Israeli state might be accepted. While the conditions laid down by Muhsin were entirely unacceptable to Israel, they could be interpreted as a negotiating stance which in time might be amenable to compromise. Though a public declaration indicating unconditional acceptance of Israel would obviously be more reassuring, two political considerations seem to rule out such a move under current conditions: the fear that it would lead to serious violence with the rejectionists, and the PLO belief that recognition of Israel is its most important bargaining card for negotiations.

The last point is especially significant since it constitutes a tacit admission that armed struggle has not provided any appreciable leverage against Israel. The facts of the matter are that the PLO is impotent militarily and very much dependent on the Arab states. Under such conditions, the Arab states seeking a peace settlement have it within their power to compel the PLO to come to terms with and accept Israel. Indeed, as noted above, they already have been instrumental in the PLO's policy demarche on the question of a mini-state.

The willingness of the Arab states to use their considerable influence on the PLO is not a simple, straightforward matter, for residual commitments and general sympathy for the Palestinian cause in the Arab world make it politically hazardous to apply direct, heavy-handed pressure on the PLO. Nonetheless, this does not mean that face-saving formulas which have the effect of neutralizing the PLO threat to Israel cannot be adopted and implemented. It is an open question whether, in spite of its public stance, Israel will decide to explore seriously the possibilities along such lines through quiet diplomacy.

Though both the public and the Likud government show no disposition to move in such a direction, a number of Israelis, whose loyalty is above reproach, have made the case for negotiating with the PLO on the basis of the Yariv-Shemtov formula (e.g., the Israel Committee for Israeli-Palestinian Peace).[27] As of late 1977, however, their efforts, including contacts with PLO personalities, had not produced a decisive change in the situation.

Yet, since their proposal is serious, it is important to consider several critical matters which would require close examination if the proposal were adopted: namely, the channels for negotiations, Israeli assumptions about the PLO, the proper atmosphere for productive talks, and the specific political issues related to an Israeli-Palestinian accommodation.

The channels for negotiation would seem to be the least troublesome problem. Until such time as political conditions in Israel become more propitious, the government could adhere to its official policy of avoiding direct talks with the PLO as a separate entity while still pursuing contacts through third parties. Furthermore, the Israelis could have discussions with de facto PLO representatives at Geneva who are part of a combined Arab delegation. Finally, of course, there are ample opportunities for secret talks with the PLO similar to those held with King Hussein after the 1967 war. In short, channels for negotiations do not constitute an insoluble problem.

As for the assumptions about the PLO, Israel would have to consider some changes. In the first place, Israel would have to acknowledge the possibility that the pragmatists might agree to coexist with Israel as well as the fact that the PLO and the Arab states do not constitute a monolithic grouping with homogeneous strategic, tactical, and political views. In particular, Israel could distinguish among the actions of various fedayeen organizations and refrain from the tendency to treat all acts of terrorism as if they were sanctioned by the PLO. Should the PLO heed advice proffered by Moscow and limit its operations to military targets while the rejectionists try to undercut negotiations by striking at civilians, Israel could make a clear distinction between the two types of activity, especially when retaliatory steps are contemplated.

It is quite obvious that making distinctions among fedayeen attacks will not be an easy undertaking psychologically. Yet, over the longer term, a policy of differential response might have the effect of ending such operations if it leads to an agreement and a crackdown on the rejectionists by the PLO leadership and the major Arab states. As part of such a policy, Israel would have to overcome the temptation to attack refugee camps in response to the actions of the rejectionists since such ripostes would probably harden the position of the PLO pragmatists who might otherwise be seeking a compromise. Driving the pragmatists into the hands of the rejectionists by attacks on refugee camps would, of course, play into the hands of the latter. More discriminating military actions, such as patrols or limited search and cordon operations across the Lebanese border, are not only less dramatic but also less likely to escalate to the point where they increase tensions and undermine the peace process.

In addition to a more discriminating political-military strategy, there are other measures Israel might contemplate in order to foster a more favorable climate for discussions. A temporary Israeli postponement in the establishment of new settlements and towns on the West Bank and Gaza Strip would clearly be helpful.[28] Moreover, the Israelis could expand the opportunity for the lawful expression of support for the PLO in the occupied areas and could avoid countermeasures such as exiling those who organize and lead peaceful demonstrations. Since both steps would be temporary and subject to change, depending on PLO behavior, they would not seem to pose intolerable costs and risks. Indeed, by allowing PLO sympathizers to surface, there might even be a hidden benefit for the Israeli security-intelligence apparatus if the PLO pragmatists proved intransigent and reverted to terrorism.

In the event that a policy of military restraint and modulated goodwill gestures improved the atmosphere for negotiations, attention could then focus on the other substantive points of dispute. Of overriding importance would be arrangements designed to secure Israel against further threats to its existence. Here a number of questions arise: whether and where the Palestinians would be allowed to give concrete expression to their national consciousness; the political role of the PLO under new structural arrangements; sanctions and restrictions on violent behavior; revision of the Palestinian National Covenant; the future role of the Hashemite regime in Jordan; the rights and role of traditional and centrist politicians in the West Bank and Gaza Strip; future socioeconomic relations between Israel and the Palestinians; and resolution of the refugee dilemma.

Whether and how the Palestinians actualize their national awareness are perhaps the most vexing problems. That such an awareness exists and must be taken into account has been made amply clear by the Palestinians themselves. To dismiss it out of hand would probably be tantamount to an early termination of peace negotiations. If the Palestinian desire for national actualization is accepted, it is quite evident that it will have to be fulfilled in the geographic areas where Palestinian Arabs predominate, namely, the West Bank, the Gaza Strip, and perhaps Jordan.

The minimum requisite for Palestinian national actualization would seem to be a political entity of some sort. Here there are several alternatives available, each of which affects the basic nature of such an entity differently.

Two options, a Palestinian region with formal links to either Israel or Jordan, would grant the Palestinians control over local political matters but subordinate them to a non-Palestinian central governing authority. Though this could conceivably satisfy some Palestinians, the PLO would object to both possibilities inasmuch as they would leave Palestinian affairs in the hands of two distrusted and despised adversaries. Perhaps more important, the Arab states would probably find it difficult to endorse such schemes because of the Rabat commitment to the PLO. Though Rabat did not end the disputes and suspicions separating the Arab states and the PLO, it did put the Arab states on record as supporting the PLO's control over any areas of Palestine relinquished by Israel.[29]

The pledge made to the PLO also militates against a third alternative, the creation of a Palestinian state controlled by independent Palestinians. While such an arrangement might have been negotiated or initiated from 1971 to 1973, when internal conditions in Israel were not as astringent as after the October War, they received a serious setback at Rabat. This is not to say, of course, that independent Palestinians would have no role to play in a future independent Palestine; indeed, the active role of independent Palestinians might be a sine qua non for such a state.

The basic problem with the first three alternatives is that by denying the PLO political control over a new Palestinian state, they clash directly with the political pledges of the Arab states. One way to resolve this problem would be to give forthright consideration to the requirements of a Palestinian state controlled by the PLO which would pose no threat to the security or existence of Israel. Obviously, this would require a number of far-reaching restrictions on the PLO, beginning with the composition of a PLO governing apparatus.

Though the PLO can be expected to object to any interference in its internal affairs, it can be made clear that the inclusion of extremists, who are committed to continued armed struggle against Israel, is unacceptable, and that what is necessary is a PLO government made up of moderate PLO personalities and non-PLO Palestinians who are willing to grant Israel formal recognition. Since this initial step is necessary, but not sufficient, to guarantee Israel's security, there would have to be some ironclad guarantees made to Israel by outside powers, perhaps including the United States. Moreover, in order to reinforce its position, Israel would also have to demand that any agreements be ratified by all parties at Geneva and that Moscow reestablish diplomatic relations with Israel.

Given its historical distrust of exogenous guarantees, Israel undoubtedly would demand prevention of hostile acts against its territory, demilitarization, and an acknowledgement of the right to respond in self-defense should violations occur. An inability or unwillingness to meet these requirements would doom any possibility of a PLO-controlled state.

Closely related to the question of Israel's right of response is the matter of official PLO policy as far as the existence of Israel is concerned. In particular, the Palestinian National Covenant, which calls for the destruction of Zionism, must be revised. This could be done in one of two ways. The first, redrafting or amending the covenant, would be most difficult from a political standpoint, since it would be viewed by many in the PLO as a direct threat to the organization's legitimacy. Less controversial would be the careful drafting of a constitution or charter by a new PLO government-in-exile that does not threaten Israel's continued existence and that, in effect, supersedes the covenant.

The fate of King Hussein also will be of considerable interest to Israel. Since the king is not only a moderate who is willing to accept Israel's existence, but is also an erstwhile adversary of the PLO, it might be in Israel's interest to see to it that the Hashemite regime obtains guarantees against PLO threats as part of any accord.

Although not of equal importance, Israel could also seek assurances that non-PLO political personalities in the occupied areas be protected against purges and the like if a Palestinian government assumes power. This confidence-building step could be further augmented by agreements allowing for the maintenance of the new pattern of economic relationships that has emerged between Israel and the occupied areas since June 1967. Such agreements would benefit a new Palestinian government by alleviating its economic burden and would be of value to Israel because they would continue to provide incentives for stability and would contribute to improved understanding betweeen individuals.

Lastly, the status of the Palestinian refugees (approximately fifty percent of the total Palestinian population in 1976) will have to be improved, because as long as the refugees remain deprived both politically and economically (the phenomenon of relative aspirational deprivation), they will provide a basis of support for rejectionists seeking to continue the armed struggle. Dealing with this problem will not be easy, however, inasmuch as many inhabitants of the camps have been socialized to expect a return to the areas in Israel from which they fled in 1948 and thereafter. Since Israel would object to the right of mass repatriation, a combination of corrective measures will probably be necessary. In addition to compensation for property losses, the possibilities here include limited repatriation of refugees to Israel, resettlement of some in a new state, and a full political and economic integration for most in the Arab countries. To the extent that there is success in this endeavor, the security of Israel would be further enhanced. Over the short term, a successful resolution would have the effect of accentuating the differences between segments of the Palestinian community since it would compel the settled Palestinians (in the occupied areas and the Arab states) to consider whether or not it would serve their interests to support the refugees' aim of returning to Israel or alternatively, to stabilize their own situation by accepting a peace accord which recognizes Israel. In the longer term, the resolution of the refugee issue would, of course, remove a major factor underlying the violent behavior of the fedayeen.

Basically, the steps suggested above are designed to render the PLO impotent as a threat to Israel while at the same time accommodating the important but limited political support for the PLO in the Arab world. Israel's understandable reservations notwithstanding, the time for dealing with the PLO has never been better, for, as indicated by the political-military analysis in preceding chapters, the PLO's capability has eroded severely, and it is heavily dependent on Arab governments with which it has clashed as often as not. Indeed, because of the incompatibility between PLO aims and the international and domestic interests of most major Arab states, a settlement that enables the PLO to assume control of a Palestinian state, while significantly containing its power and influence, may be most welcome in Cairo, Damascus, Riyadh, and other Arab capitals.

It may well be the case, as Israel's distinguished Arabist Moshe Ma'oz argued in *Ha'arez* on February 22, 1974, that the fedayeen organizations have not changed their basic attitude towards Israel and are merely arguing about the proper means for destroying Israel. However, the only way the validity of such an interpretation can be tested is in the diplomatic arena, for it is there that both the Arab states and the PLO will be forced to come to grips with the criteria for an Israeli-PLO settlement. Should the Arabs in general prove unwilling to make the necessary concessions, Israel will be vindicated; should the PLO in particular remain intransigent and boycott negotiations, it may find itself completely left out of any solution. If, on the other hand, Israel refuses to put the Arabs and the PLO to the test, it may well bear the burden of blame for another, more costly and perilous war.

Appendix A
UN Security Council Resolution No. 242

UN SECURITY COUNCIL RESOLUTION NO. 242 (1967) OF 22 NOVEMBER,
1967 — SPECIAL REPRESENTATIVE TO THE MIDDLE EAST

The Security Council

Expressing its continuing concern with the grave situation in the Middle East,

Emphasizing the inadmissibility of the acquisition of territory by war and the need to work for a just and lasting peace in which every state in the area can live in security,

Emphasizing further that all member states in their acceptance of the Charter of the United Nations have undertaken a commitment to act in accordance with Article 2 of the Charter,

1. **Affirms** that the fulfillment of Charter principles requires the establishment of a just and lasting peace in the Middle East which should include the application of both the following principles:

(i) Withdrawal of Israeli armed forces from territories of recent conflict;

(ii) Termination of all claims of belligerency and respect for and acknowledgment of the sovereignty, territorial integrity and political independence of every state in the area and their right to live in peace within secure and recognized boundaries free from threats or acts of force;

2. **Affirms Further** the necessity

(a) for guaranteeing freedom of navigation through international waterways in the area;

(b) for achieving a just settlement of the refugee problem;

(c) for guaranteeing the territorial inviolability and political independence of every state in the area, through measures including the establishment of demilitarized zones;

3. **Requests** the Secretary General to designate a special representative to proceed to the Middle East to establish and maintain contacts with the states concerned in order to promote agreement and assist efforts to achieve a peaceful and accepted settlement in accordance with the provisions and principles in this resolution,

4. **Requests** the Secretary General to report to the Security Council on the progress of the efforts of the special representative as soon as possible.

Appendix B
Incidents and Casualties

The statistics in Appendix B, supplied by the Israeli Defense Forces, were cross-checked with several sources, especially *Arab Report and Record*. Since they appear to be accurate, they have been adopted as a convenient summary. Moreover, they provide the basis of Table 1 in Chapter 4.

TABLE B-1

FEDAYEEN INCIDENTS: 1967

	Jordanian Border			Lebanese Border			Syrian Border			Gaza		
	Number of Incidents	Israeli Casualties	Guerrilla Casualties	Number of Incidents	Israeli Casualties	Guerrilla Casualties	Number of Incidents	Israeli Casualties	Guerrilla Casualties	Number of Incidents	Israeli Casualties	Guerrilla Casualties
January	—	—	—	—	—	—	—	—	—	—	—	—
February	—	—	—	—	—	—	—	—	—	—	—	—
March	—	—	—	—	—	—	—	—	—	—	—	—
April	—	—	—	—	—	—	—	—	—	—	—	—
May	—	—	—	—	—	—	—	—	—	—	—	—
June	4	5[2]	1	1	—	—	5	—	—	6	8[3]	—
July	3	—	—	—	—	—	9	—	—	10	—	—
August	13	5	—	—	—	—	3	3	—	5	5[1]	—
September	9	3	—	—	—	—	—	1	—	5	—	—
October	20	11[3]	4	—	—	—	1	—	—	5	—	—
November	25	10	1	—	—	—	1	1	—	9	8[1]	—
December	23	4[2]	3	1	—	3	5	1	5	4	4[1]	2
Totals	97	38[7]	9	2	—	3	24	6	5	44	25[6]	2

NOTE: Figures in brackets represent those killed in action.

TABLE B-2

FEDAYEEN INCIDENTS: 1968

	Jordanian Border			Lebanese Border			Syrian Border			Gaza		
	Number of Incidents	Israeli Casualties	Guerrilla Casualties	Number of Incidents	Israeli Casualties	Guerrilla Casualties	Number of Incidents	Israeli Casualties	Guerrilla Casualties	Number of Incidents	Israeli Casualties	Guerrilla Casualties
January	36	14[3]	4	4	—	—	2	—	—	14	3	—
February	24	11[5]	47	1	—	—	4	1	—	6	—	—
March	48	61[11]	224	1	—	—	1	3[1]	—	17	2[2]	—
April	59	11[6]	23	—	—	—	1	—	1	12	—	—
May	80	24[6]	37	3	—	—	3	—	—	15	7[2]	2
June	94	20[2]	47	5	—	—	4	3[1]	3	22	1	2
July	83	31[3]	41	—	—	—	6	7	—	4	—	—
August	92	13[3]	57	1	—	—	3	—	—	14	6	—
September	93	38[7]	9	1	1	—	8	4[3]	4	12	9[3]	3
October	116	17[1]	28	7	11[4]	6	7	6[2]	6	14	5	5
November	116	23[3]	9	3	—	—	7	—	—	15	2	1
December	95	10[3]	24	3	4[3]	—	—	—	—	22	7[1]	—
Totals	916	273[53]	550	29	16[7]	6	46	24[7]	14	167	42[8]	13

NOTE: Figures in brackets represent those killed in action.

TABLE B-3

FEDAYEEN INCIDENTS: 1969

	Jordanian Border			Lebanese Border			Syrian Border			Gaza		
	Number of Incidents	Israeli Casualties	Guerrilla Casualties	Number of Incidents	Israeli Casualties	Guerrilla Casualties	Number of Incidents	Israeli Casualties	Guerrilla Casualties	Number of Incidents	Israeli Casualties	Guerrilla Casualties
January	61	5[1]	8	10	—	1	4	—	1	17	3[1]	—
February	98	14[2]	6	3	—	—	13	8[2]	12	24	5	—
March	67	13[4]	6	2	—	—	5	—	2	24	1[1]	3
April	177	44[6]	31	10	1	—	13	2	7	38	3[3]	—
May	199	25[6]	45	11	3[1]	—	21	2	10	34	—	—
June	172	33[9]	33	5	2	—	16	10[1]	8	42	11[4]	1
July	215	13[2]	44	22	4	10	36	13[2]	9	56	36[2]	7
August	263	34[7]	33	32	15[2]	—	43	4	9	52	11	9
September	293	18[8]	25	11	13[3]	5	30	11[4]	17	44	7[1]	8
October	237	10[1]	35	10	2[1]	6	28	8	8	45	15[1]	—
November	319	19[5]	10	13	—	—	26	4	1	54	18	4
December	331	15[2]	17	21	9[3]	16	41	6[1]	7	35	3	—
Totals	2,432	243[47]	293	150	49[10]	38	276	68[10]	81	465	113[13]	32

NOTE: Figures in brackets represent those killed in action.

TABLE B-4
FEDAYEEN INCIDENTS: 1970

	Jordanian Border			Lebanese Border			Syrian Border			Gaza		
	Number of Incidents	Israeli Casualties	Guerrilla Casualties	Number of Incidents	Israeli Casualties	Guerrilla Casualties	Number of Incidents	Israeli Casualties	Guerrilla Casualties	Number of Incidents	Israeli Casualties	Guerrilla Casualties
January	251	9[1]	44[33]	8	—	7[1]	61	1	10[5]	27	23[4]	5[5]
February	180	5[1]	17[10]	18	1[1]	12	53	—	8[6]	33	10	—
March	310	13[1]	43[17]	33	4[1]	26[13]	60	10[2]	20[4]	60	15[1]	10[10]
April	218	9[2]	41[23]	46	6[1]	25[9]	68	—	6[2]	46	4	12[10]
May	259	9[5]	68[53]	48	69[16]	64[42]	40	9[4]	4[1]	43	—	2[2]
June	175	43[6]	16[13]	38	9[1]	3[3]	46	4	7[7]	41	3	1[1]
July	236	9[5]	30[29]	37	16	18[17]	48	3[1]	—	40	9[1]	—
August	216	14[1]	42[26]	91	45[7]	19[10]	43	5[5]	13[6]	39	10	2[2]
September	25	—	6[4]	28	8[2]	27[14]	22	—	—	41	10[3]	4[3]
October	3	—	1[1]	13	5	5[4]	3	—	—	15	9[1]	1[1]
November	7	—	—	13	1	13[3]	3	—	—	35	9	4[4]
December	7	—	—	17	10[2]	25[21]	7	—	—	35	11[2]	1[1]
Totals	1,887	111[22]	308[209]	390	174[31]	224[137]	454	32[12]	68[31]	455	113[12]	42[39]

NOTE: Figures in brackets represent those killed in action.

TABLE B-5

FEDAYEEN INCIDENTS: 1971

	Jordanian Border			Lebanese Border			Syrian Border			Gaza		
	Number of Incidents	Israeli Casualties	Guerrilla Casualties	Number of Incidents	Israeli Casualties	Guerrilla Casualties	Number of Incidents	Israeli Casualties	Guerrilla Casualties	Number of Incidents	Israeli Casualties	Guerrilla Casualties
January	6	—	—	19	7[1]	10[10]	15	3	2[2]	35	12[3]	9[7]
February	5	—	3[2]	10	6[1]	8[7]	18	4	15[13]	33	9[1]	2[2]
March	5	—	6[5]	18	6[1]	11[8]	27	2	10[6]	28	7	10[9]
April	—	—	—	8	—	8[8]	6	—	2[1]	34	9	6[5]
May	4	—	—	8	—	3[2]	21	1	5[3]	38	13	2[2]
June	13	—	—	7	4	8[5]	8	—	8[8]	37	23[1]	—
July	12	—	15[15]	2	—	—	4	1	1[1]	28	4[1]	13[13]
August	—	—	—	—	—	—	—	—	—	—	—	—
September	—	—	—	—	—	—	—	—	—	—	—	—
October	—	—	—	—	—	—	—	—	—	—	—	—
November	—	—	—	—	—	—	—	—	—	—	—	—
December	—	—	—	—	—	—	—	—	—	—	—	—
Totals	45	—	24[22]	72	23[3]	48[40]	93	11	43[34]	233	77[6]	42[38]

NOTE: Figures in brackets represent those killed in action.

TABLE B-6

INCIDENT AND CASUALTY SUMMARY BY BORDER AREA

Border Area		Incidents	Israeli Casualties	Israeli Casualties per Month	Israeli Casualties per Incident
Jordan	1967[a]	97	38	5.4	.39
	1968	916	273	22.7	.29
	1969	2,432	243	20.2	.099
	1970	1,887[b]	111	13.8[c]	.063
	1971	45	——	———	———
Lebanon	1967	2	———	———	——
	1968	29	16	1.3	.55
	1969	150	49	4.0	.32
	1970	390	174	14.5	.45
	1971[d]	72	23	3.2	.32
Syria	1967	24	6	.8	.25
	1968	46	24	1.8	.48
	1969	276	68	5.6	.24
	1970	454	32	4.0	.07
	1971	93	11	1.5	.11
Gaza	1967	44	25	3.5	.56
	1968	167	42	3.5	.25
	1969	465	113	9.4	.24
	1970	455	113	9.4	.24
	1971	233	77	11.0	.33

[a]1967: June-December

[b]1,845 from January to August 1970

[c]1970: January-August only (no casualties after the civil war)

[d]1971 figures are for January-July only

TABLE B-7

YEARLY INCIDENT AND CASUALTY TOTALS

	Incidents	Israeli Casualties	Israeli Casualties per Month
1967[a]	167	69	9.8
1968	1,158	355	29.4
1969	3,323	473	39.8
1970	3,186	430	35.8
1971[b]	443	111	15.8

[a]June-December only   [b]January-July only

Appendix C

Refugees: Location by Country

TABLE C-1

REFUGEES: LOCATION BY COUNTRY

		Living in Camps	Living Elsewhere
In May 1967			
JORDAN: East Bank	392,586		
West Bank	330,101		
Total	722,687	32.2%	67.8%
GAZA Strip	316,776	63.7%	36.3%
LEBANON	160,723	46.9%	53.1%
SYRIA	144,390	16.0%	84.0%
Total	1,344,576	39.6%	60.4%
In May 1971			
JORDAN: East Bank only	766,615		
GAZA Strip	306,938		
LEBANON	171,673		
SYRIA	155,607		
Total	1,400,833		

In both tables the number of Palestine Arabs—original inhabitants—of the West Bank are not included: they are considered Jordanian citizens and not refugees. Their number is estimated at 600,000.

There are also about 200,000 Palestine Arabs in countries not mentioned in the above tables.

There are also approximately 300,000 Palestine Arabs living within the pre-1967 borders of Israel.

Source: Arab Report and Record, Special Supplement, June 1971, p. 315.

Appendix D
Terrorists Killed According to Organizational Affiliation

TABLE D-1

TERRORISTS KILLED ACCORDING TO ORGANIZATIONAL AFFILIATION

12 June 1967-20 May 1970

Period	El-Fatah	Popular Liberation Forces	Popular Front for the Liberation of Palestine	Sa'eka	Other Organizations	Unidentified	Total
1967 (12 June - 31 December)	66	5	1	—	4	11	87
1968	450	54	39	9	1	128	681
1969	219	53	75	71	58	110	536
1970 (1 January - 20 May)	105	16	24	31	35	56	267
TOTAL	840	128	139	111	98	305	1,621

Source: Israeli Defense Forces, June 1, 1970.

Appendix E
Estimated Fedayeen Order of Battle

TABLE E-1

ESTIMATED FEDAYEEN ORDER OF BATTLE

(Major Organizations Only)

Fatah	10,000
Saiqa	7,000
PFLP	3,000
PDF	1,000
ALF	3,000
PFLP-GC	500
PAO	350
AOLP	700
PSF	200
	25,750

PLA — 10,000-20,000

Source: The New York Times, September 19, 1970. The 25,000 total was a figure cited by a number of other sources. Not all of the 25,750 were actually commandos. Some were support and political elements. According to The New York Times, February 11, 1970, Israel estimated that the fedayeen could muster only 5,000-6,000 fighters. In any event, the precise total of fedayeen was unknown and the list above must be regarded as no more than an estimate.

Notes

Abbreviations Used in Notes

AP	Associated Press
ARR.	*Arab Report and Record*
CSM	*The Christian Science Monitor*
DSB	*The Daily Star* (Beirut)
FBIS/ME	*Foreign Broadcast Information Service, Middle East and North Africa* (previously Africa), *Daily Report*
JPS	*Journal of Palestine Studies*
NYT	*New York Times*
UPI	United Press International

Notes

Chapter 1

1. For an excellent summary of the history of Palestine see John K. Cooley, *Green March, Black September* (London: Frank Cass, 1973), pp. 1-41.

2. The reader interested in the debate surrounding the nature and dimensions of Palestinian nationalism should consult and juxtapose the following: Shlomo Avineri, ed., *Israel and the Palestinians: Reflections on the Clash of Two National Movements* (New York: St. Martin's Press, 1971), and the lengthy review of the Avineri volume by Ahmad R. Haffar in *Journal of Palestine Studies* (hereafter *JPS*), Autumn 1972, pp. 120-127.

3. A detailed history of Palestine, particularly the evolution of Zionism and its role in the area, is beyond the scope of this paper. The interested reader will find a burgeoning literature on various facets of the topic. The following are especially informative: Walid Khalidi, ed., *From Haven to Conquest, Readings in Zionism and the Palestine Problem Until 1948* (Beirut: The Institute for Palestine Studies, 1971), particularly the introductory section; J. C. Hurewitz, *The Struggle for Palestine* (New York: Norton, 1950); Christopher Sykes, *Crossroads to Israel* (New York: World Publishers, 1965).

4. The reader interested in the Palestinian viewpoint on this should consult Fayez A. Sayegh, *The Palestine Refugees* (Washington, D.C.: AMARA Press, 1952).

5. Rashid Hamid, "What is the PLO? " *JPS*, Summer 1975, pp. 90-91.

6. For one account of the psychological predicament of the Palestinians in exile see Fawaz Turki, "The Palestinian Estranged," *JPS*, Autumn 1975/ Winter 1976, pp. 82-96. On their nationalist prose and poetry see Cooley, *Green March*, pp. 45-67.

7. William B. Quandt et al., *The Politics of Palestinian Nationalism* (Berkeley and Los Angeles: University of California Press, 1973), p. 50.

8. Hamid, "What is the PLO? " pp. 94-95.

9. Walter Laqueur, *The Road to War* (Baltimore: Penguin Books, 1968), pp. 67-74. The PLO's close ties with Egypt and its problems with other Arab states, especially Jordan, are revealed in the following polemical tracts by Ahmad as Shuqayri: *Forty Years of Political Life on the Arab and International Scene* (Beirut: Dar al-Nahar, 1972); *On the Road to Defeat with the Arab Kings and*

Presidents (Beirut: Dar al-Audah, 1972).

10. Michael Hudson, "The Palestinian Resistance Movement: Its Significance in the Middle East Crisis," *Middle East Journal*, Summer 1969, p. 299, and Laqueur, *Road to War*, p. 68, place the origin of *Fatah* in 1956 while Abdullah Schleiffer, "The Emergence of Fatah," *Arab World*, May 1969, p. 16, traces *Fatah* to a 1957 summer meeting of a dozen or so Palestinians on a beach near Kuwait City.

11. Leila S. Kadi, comp. and trans., *Basic Political Documents of the Armed Palestinian Resistance Movement* (Beirut: Palestinian Liberation Organization Research Center, 1968), p. 18.

12. Fred J. Khouri, *The Arab-Israeli Dilemma*, 2nd ed. (Syracuse, N.Y.: Syracuse University Press, 1976), pp. 234-241. Several smaller Palestinian groups also operated at the time, including Heroes of the Return (military wing of the Palestinian branch of the Arab Nationalist Movement), Youth of Revenge Organization (another ANM group), and the Palestine Liberation Front led by Ahmad Jibril.

13. See the Palestinian National Charter, especially Articles 1, 8, 14, 15, 19, 20, 21, 22 and 23, in Kadi, *Basic Political Documents*, pp. 137-142.

14. *The Liberation of the Occupied Lands and the Struggle Against Direct Imperialism*, pp. 16-17. Also quoted in Hudson, "Palestinian Resistance Movement," p. 299. Fedayeen statements and literature have been replete and consistent with reference to the aim of destroying Zionism. See, for instance, *Free Palestine*, September 1970, p. 15; editorial in *Fatah* (Beirut), November 18, 1971; interview of Abu Ammar with Yasir Arafat in *Free Palestine*, February 1971, p. 1; *Arab Report and Record*, January 1-15, 1969, p. 19 and January 16-31, 1971, p. 78; *Daily Star* (Beirut), May 17, 1971.

15. Disagreement on the meaning of a "secular, democratic, nonsectarian state" has been clearly evident within fedayeen ranks, with some groups striving to give the concept a meaningful content and others choosing to use it merely as a slogan for assuaging world opinion. See, for example, the accounts of a symposium of six fedayeen organizations on the question of the democratic Palestine state entitled *The Democratic Palestinian State* (n.p., March 1970). The same account can be found in *Al-Anwar* (Beirut), March 8 and 15, 1970. See also *Free Palestine*, March 1969, pp. 6-8; *New York Times*, September 16, 1969; *New Middle East*, April 1970, p. 6. For three articles critical of the concept of the democratic state as articulated by the fedayeen, see Y. Harkabi, *Three Articles on the Arab Slogan of a Democratic State*, trans. Y. Karmi (n.p., n.d.). This booklet can be obtained from the embassy of Israel. The articles reproduced therein can also be found in *Ma'ariv* (Tel Aviv), April 3 and 17, 1970; July 10, 1970.

There has been inconsistency on the question of which Jews could remain in the new Palestinian state. While the most recent position of the fedayeen has been that any Jew renouncing Zionism could stay, there have been suggestions that only those who were there prior to 1917 or, alternatively, 1947, could do so. The 1917 date seemed to be implicit in Article 6 of the Palestinian National Charter since that section clearly states that only those who resided in Palestine prior to the "Zionist invasion" were acceptable. Since the "Zionist invasion" is generally understood to date to 1917, the conclusion is obvious. See Kadi, *Basic Political Documents*, p. 137.

For references to the 1947 date, see the comments of a fedayeen leader cited in *The New York Times*, June 17, 1968; *Arab Report and Record*, March 1-15, 1970, p. 164. On the indications that all Jews rejecting Zionism could stay, see ibid., *Free Palestine*, June 1970, p. 1; interview of Abu Omar cited in *Arab Report and Record*, July 1-15, 1970, p. 402; Arafat's comments to C. L. Sulzberger in *New York Times*, October 30, 1970; *Free Palestine*, April 1970, pp. 1 and 6; interview of Abu Omar in *Free Palestine*, September 1970, p. 6. Perhaps the best source is the fedayeen statement entitled "Towards a Democratic Palestine," *Fatah* (Beirut), 1970, reprinted in *Arab Views*, February 1970, pp. 4-6. The sincerity of the willingness to accept all Jews renouncing Zionism appeared to be compromised, however, by the acknowledgement on page 6 that *Fatah* engaged in active negotiations with several Arab states to allow Jewish emigrants to return to their countries of origin.

16. While some individuals and groups within the fedayeen movement seemed more inclined toward certain revolutionary models than others, there has been an attempt to study and borrow from all of them. That the Chinese, Cuban, Algerian, and Vietnamese experiences have influenced fedayeen thinking in a substantial way is evident from their publications, interviews, and statements. Of particular importance in this regard was a two-part series of pamphlets entitled Revolutionary Studies and Experiences (Beirut and Amman: *Fatah*, 1967-1970). The following pamphlets are part of the series: *The Chinese Experience, The Vietnamese Experience*, and *The Cuban Experience* in part one, and *The Vietnamese Revolution* in part two. More accessible commentaries on the influence of these models may be found in Y. Harkabi, *Fedayeen Action and Arab Strategy*, Adelphi Papers no. 53 (London: The International Institute for Strategic Studies, 1968), pp. 7-8 and 13-17; Tom Little, *The New Arab Extremists*, Conflict Studies no. 4 (London: Current Affairs Research Services Center, 1970), pp. 11-12; the interview of George Habash cited in *Arab Report and Record*, March 1-15, 1969, p. 112; the interviews of K. Kudsi (*Fatah*) in *Free Palestine*, August 1969, p. 6; and September 1969, p. 6.

17. Kadi, *Basic Political Documents*, p. 138.

18. Ibid., p. 139 (Article 15); *Free Palestine*, June 1969, p. 1.

19. Lawrence C. Mayer, *Comparative Political Inquiry* (Homewood, Illinois: Dorsey Press, 1972), pp. 62-64; Eugene J. Meehan, *The Theory and Method of Political Analysis* (Homewood, Illinois: Daisy Press, pp. 132-134.

Chapter 2

1. On the questions of legitimacy and parts of the political system see Charles F. Andrain, *Political Life and Social Change* (Belmont, California: Duxbury Press, 1971), pp. 137-144; David Easton, *A Systems Analysis of Political Life* (New York: John Wiley and Sons, 1965), pp. 171-219.

2. Military coups fall within the broad scope of our definition. Even though those who engineer coups occupy supportive roles in the political system, they are not, strictly speaking, part of the "ruling authorities." Indeed, one of the reasons for coups is to seize control of the highest offices or to create new ones.

3. While the Kurds at one time had a secessionist goal, their demands during the

recent and ill-fated round of fighting were essentially reformist (to wit, increased revenues from oil, more social services, and a substantial degree of political autonomy within the framework of Iraq).

4. On this distinction see Ted Robert Gurr, *Why Men Rebel* (Princeton: Princeton University Press, 1970), pp. 10-11.

5. On terrorist aims see Brian Jenkins, "International Terrorism: A Balance Sheet," *Survival*, July/August 1975, pp. 158-160. Although much attention has been paid to terrorism since the upsurge of its international and transnational variants in the late 1960s and early 1970s, the construction of a reasonably precise, general definition agreeable to most or all scholars has remained elusive. For a representative sampling of more recent attempts to grapple with the definitional problem see David Fromkin, "The Strategy of Terrorism," *Foreign Affairs*, July 1975, pp. 692-693; H. Edward Price, Jr., "The Strategy and Tactics of Revolutionary Terrorism," *Comparative Studies in Society and History*, January 1977, pp. 52-53; Jay Mallin, "Terrorism As a Military Weapon," *Air University Review*, January-February 1977, p. 60; U.S. Central Intelligence Agency Research Study, *International and Transnational Terrorism: Diagnosis and Prognosis* (Washington, D.C., Library of Congress Photoduplication Sevice, April 1976), pp. 8-9; and Martha Grenshaw Hutchinson, "The Concept of Revolutionary Terrorism," *The Journal of Conflict Resolution*, September 1972, pp. 383-385. The last mentioned is a particularly admirable effort to define terrorism carefully, albeit only in its revolutionary variation.

6. Julian Paget, *Counter-Insurgency Campaigning* (New York: Walker and Company, 1967), p. 15.

7. Samuel P. Huntington, "Guerrilla Warfare in Theory and Policy," in *Modern Guerrilla Warfare*, ed. Franklin Mark Osanka (New York: Free Press of Glencoe, 1962), p. xvi; Arthur Campbell, *Guerrillas* (New York: John Day Company, 1968), p. 3.

8. Otto Heilbrunn, *Partisan Warfare* (New York: Frederick A. Praeger, 1962), pp. 39 and 160.

9. The cohesion and organization factors are sometimes treated as one variable. Since both are very important in regard to the Palestinian case, they will be treated separately. For a similar listing of strategic factors see Virgil Ney, "Guerrilla Warfare and Modern Strategy," in *Modern Guerrilla Warfare*, pp. 25-38.

10. Mao Tse-Tung, *Selected Military Writings of Mao Tse-Tung* (Peking: Foreign Language Press, 1963), p. 260.

11. Comparative studies that have examined popular support suggest that it may be useful to break it down into five categories: passive and active support for the insurgents; passive and active support for the government, and neutrality. See Bard E. O'Neill and Stephen J. Rossetti, "Conclusion," in *Political Violence and Insurgency*, eds. Bard E. O'Neill, D. J. Alberts, and Stephen J. Rossetti (Arvada, Colorado: Phoenix Press, 1974), pp. 461-464.

12. For an analysis of the role and traits of the intelligentsia in the Third World see Harry J. Benda, "Non-Western Intelligentsias as Political Elites," in *Political Change in Underdeveloped Countries*, ed. John H. Kautsky (New York: John Wiley and Sons, 1967), pp. 235-251. On their role in insurgencies see David A.

Wilson, *Nation Building and Revolutionary War* (Santa Monica, California: The Rand Corporation, 1962), p. 7; Gil Carl AlRoy, *The Involvement of Peasants in International Wars*, Center for International Studies Research Monograph no. 24 (Princeton: Princeton University Press, 1966), pp. 16-19.

13. Gurr, *Why Men Rebel*, p. 337.

14. Ney, "Guerrilla Warfare," p. 34.

15. Gabriel A. Almond, *The Appeals of Communism* (Princeton: Princeton University Press, 1954), p. 62. On the basic distinction between esoteric and exoteric appeals see ibid., pp. 65-66, and Morris Watnick, "The Appeal of Communism to the Underdeveloped Peoples," in *Political Change in Underdeveloped Countries*. The same dichotomy is implicit in Peter Van Ness, *Revolution and Chinese Foreign Policy* (Berkeley and Los Angeles: University of California Press, 1970), pp. 118-119; Gurr, *Why Men Rebel*, p. 195.

16. V. I. Lenin, *Imperialism—The Highest Stage of Capitalism* (New York: International Publishers, 1969), pp. 1-128. Other aspects of Leninist thought, such as the leading role of the intellectuals within the revolutionary party, enhance its attractiveness for many intellectuals. See John H. Kautsky, *Communism and the Politics of Development* (New York: John Wiley and Sons, 1968), p. 77.

17. Almond, *Appeals of Communism*, p. 65.

18. Gurr, *Why Men Rebel*, p. 205; quotes from pp. 199 and 198 respectively.

19. A striking passage on the manipulation of mass grievances can be found in Mao Tse-tung, "On Methods of Leadership," *Selected Works*, vol. 4 (New York: International Publishers, 1958), p. 113.

20. The impact of terrorism has led some scholars and practitioners to contend that terror is the most powerful weapon for establishing community support. Roger Trinquier, for example, calls it the principal weapon of modern (revolutionary) warfare and suggests that by making the people feel insecure it causes them to lose confidence in the government and to be drawn to the guerrillas for protection. See Roger Trinquier, *Modern Warfare* (New York: Frederick A. Praeger, 1964), pp. 16-17. It has been argued that the Chinese communist ability to get popular support without large-scale terror is atypical, because most insurgencies start without the degree of popular backing that Mao had and therefore must resort to terror. See, for example, Brian Crozier, *The Study of Conflict* (London: Institute for the Study of Conflict, 1970), p. 7.

21. Jerry M. Silverman and Peter M. Jackson, "Terror in Insurgency Warfare," *Military Review*, October 1970, pp. 62-64; Paget, *Counter-Insurgency Campaigning*, p. 65.

22. Ibid., pp. 64-67. Richard L. Clutterbuck in *The Long, Long War* (New York: Frederick A. Praeger, 1966), p. 63, cites an example of the ineffectiveness of terror in the Malayan situation. In the fall of 1951 the Malayan Communist party realized that intimidation was not gaining popular support and, therefore, issued a directive proscribing attacks on innocent people.

23. J. K. Zawodny, "Unconventional Warfare," in *Problems of National Strategy*, ed. Henry A. Kissinger (New York: Frederick A. Praeger, 1965), pp. 340-341. Peter Braestrup, "Partisan Tactics—Algerian Style," in *Modern Guerrilla*

Warfare, p. 393, argues that such was the case with the French in Algeria; see also Bernard B. Fall, *The Two Viet-Nams*, 2nd ed. rev. (New York: Frederick A. Praeger, 1967), pp. 348-352.

24. Clutterbuck, *The Long War*, pp. 178-179.

25. Silverman and Jackson, "Terror in Insurgency Warfare," p. 67.

26. On the political aspects, see the depiction of the agent's role in Andrew R. Molnar, James M. Tinker, and John D. LeNoir, *Human Factors Considerations of Underground in Insurgencies* (Washington, D.C.: American University Center for Research in Social Systems, 1966), p. 109; Vo Nguyen Giap, *People's War People's Army* (New York: Bantam Books, 1968), p. 50.

27. George B. Jordan, "Objectives and Methods of Communist Guerrilla Warfare," in *Modern Guerrilla Warfare*, pp. 404 and 409; Paget, *Counter-Insurgency Campaigning*, p. 22.

28. Edward L. Katzenbach, Jr., and Gene Z. Hanrahan, "The Revolutionary Strategy of Mao Tse-tung," *Modern Guerrilla Warfare*, pp. 144-145.

29. Mao Tse-tung, "On Protracted War," *Selected Works*, vol. 2 (London: n.p., 1954), p. 211ff., quoted in Heilbrunn, *Partisan Warfare*, p. 56.

30. Douglas Hyde, *The Roots of Guerrilla Warfare* (Chester Springs, Pennsylvania: Du Four Editions, 1968), pp. 86-88. He also cites his conversations with Huk leaders in the Philippines, who said that the government ability to sever the leaders from the rest of the movement was a key reason for their downfall.

31. Ibid., pp. 36-37 and 43.

32. See Gurr, *Why Men Rebel*, pp. 274-316, for an expanded discussion of the structural and functional aspects of organizations.

33. The commentary on auxiliary organizations, like that on parallel hierarchies, is extensive. See, for example, Fall, *The Two Viet-Nams*, p. 134; Hyde, *The Roots of Guerrilla Warfare*, p. 34. An especially good source for the treatment of the role of auxiliary organizations is Douglas Pike, *Viet Cong* (Cambridge: M.I.T. Presss, 1966), chapters 6 and 10.

34. Tomas C. Tirona, "The Philippine Anti-Communist Campaign," in *Modern Guerrilla Warfare*, p. 204.

35. On the question of military differentiation, see Ney, "Guerrilla Warfare," pp. 35-36; Heilbrunn, *Partisan Warfare*, p. 25; Pike, *Viet Cong*, chapter 13; Anthony Crockett, "Action in Malaya," *Modern Guerrilla Warfare*, p. 310; Brooks McClure, "Russia's Hidden Army," *Modern Guerrilla Warfare*, p. 89; James E. Dougherty, "The Guerrilla War in Malaya," *Modern Guerrilla Warfare*, p. 302.

36. Gurr, *Why Men Rebel*, pp. 297-301.

37. John J. McCuen, *The Art of Counter-Revolutionary War* (Harrisburg, Pennsylvania: Stackpole Books, n.d.), p. 69.

38. Cited in George B. Jordan, "Objectives and Methods of Communist Guerrilla Warfare," in *Modern Guerrilla Warfare*, p. 404. See also p. 407.

39. Many writers cite the significance of external material aid. See, for instance, Ney, "Guerrilla Warfare," pp. 31-32; Gurr, *Why Men Rebel*, pp. 269-270; Frank Trager, *Why Vietnam* (New York: Frederick A. Praeger, 1966), p. 77; and Bernard B. Fall, *Street Without Joy* (Harrisburg, Pennsylvania: Stackpole Books, 1963), p. 294.

40. Hyde, *The Roots of Guerrilla Warfare*, pp. 86-88.
41. On this point see Mao Tse-tung, "On Protracted War," *Selected Military Writings*, pp. 200-201; A. H. Shollom, "Nowhere Yet Everywhere," in *Modern Guerrilla Warfare*, p. 19; C. E. S. Dudley, "Subversive Warfare—Five Military Factors," *The Army Quarterly and Defence Journal*, July 1968 p. 209.
42. Heilbrunn, *Partisan Warfare*, pp. 44-45.
43. Gurr, *Why Men Rebel*, pp. 363-364.
44. The relationship between primordial cleavages and insurgent fortunes is extremely complicated. Where insurgent organizations draw their support from ethnic minorities, for example, they may establish a popular base sufficient for terrorism or guerrilla warfare. Whether this will enable them to achieve their aims depends in large part on the nature of the aims. If the insurgents have revolutionary aims which will require them to gain support from other communities, the initial reliance on minorities may not be equal to the task. Reformist insurgents, on the other hand, may find a minority base of support adequate for limited violence. Since the reformist goals do not challenge the regime or the authorities, the authorities may decide on a conciliatory approach rather than continued conflict. See O'Neill and Rossetti, "Conclusions," pp. 467-470, 474.
45. Walter C. Sonderland, "An Analysis of the Guerrilla Insurgency and Coup d'Etat as Techniques of Indirect Aggression," *International Studies Quarterly*, December 1970, p. 345.
46. Ibid.
47. McCuen, *Counter-Revolutionary War*, pp. 43-44.
48. Ibid., pp. 71 and 181-182.
49. Ibid., pp. 58-59 and 96.
50. Arthur Campbell, *Guerrillas*, pp. 73-89. See also *Modern Guerrilla Warfare*: Frederick Wilkins, "Guerrilla Warfare," pp. 10-11; Walter D. Jacobs, "Irregular Warfare and the Soviets," p. 61; McClure, "Russia's Hidden Army," pp. 96-97; Ernest von Dohnanyi, "Combatting Soviet Guerrillas," pp. 102-105.
51. See *Modern Guerrilla Warfare*: Kenneth M. Hammer, "Huks in the Philippines," p. 102; Boyd T. Bashore, "Dual Strategy for Limited War," pp. 193-196 and 199-201; Tomas C. Tirona, "The Philippine Anti-Communist Campaign," pp. 206-207.
52. The decision of the Sudanese government to meet demands for greater autonomy on the part of the rebels from the three southern provinces is an example of a regime terminating an insurrection by agreeing to reallocate political power. See *New York Times*, February 28, 1972.
53. In situations where the installation of the regular administrative apparatus is impossible in the short run because of a paucity of resources and trained personnel, the government should use civic action teams to help meet the needs of the population and to establish a government presence. On civic action, see Heilbrunn, *Partisan Warfare*, p. 157; Paget, *Counter-Insurgency Campaigning*, p. 178; Hyde, *The Roots of Guerrilla Warfare*, pp. 44-45. If it is possible, local administrators, as well as police and militia personnel, should be drawn from the local population. One advantage is that the additional frictions and suspicions that emerge when a group interacts with elements whom they consider foreign will be avoided.

Moreover, there is also a military advantage since use of local people will free regular and regional troops for operations against guerrilla units and bases.

54. In other words, each law must be enforceable, fairly applied, and avoid falling unfairly on particular groups in the population. For a discussion of regimes' coercive measures, see Gurr, *Why Men Rebel*, pp. 236-259; Sir Robert Thompson, *Defeating Communist Insurgency* (New York: Frederick A. Praeger, 1966), p. 53; Charles Wolf, Jr., *Insurgency and Counter-Insurgency: New Myths and Old Realities* (Santa Monica: The Rand Corporation, 1965), pp. 4 and 22. Thompson argues that harsh security measures can be followed only in areas within the scope of government control. If they were sporadically applied in areas under insurgent control, the people would have little choice but to support the insurgents. Arguing along similar lines, others have suggested that if collective sanctions are to be morally acceptable, they must be implemented in a context within which the government can provide security against insurgent reprisals. See Heilbrunn, *Partisan Warfare*, pp. 151-158; Paget, *Counter-Insurgency Campaigning*, p. 169; Campbell, *Guerrillas*, pp. 232-233; Trinquier, *Modern Warfare*, pp. 43-50.

55. On the question of resettlement and its successes and failures, see Clutterbuck, *The Long War*, pp. 56-63 and 66-72; Campbell, *Guerrillas*, pp. 36, 148 and 218; Paget, *Counter-Insurgency Campaigning*, p. 36; Heilbrunn, *Partisan Warfare*, pp. 36 and 153; McCuen, *Counter-Revolutionary War*, pp. 231-234.

56. Trinquier, *Modern Warfare*, pp. 23-27 and 35-38; Campbell, *Guerrillas*, pp. 300 and 323; Paget, *Counter-Insurgency Campaigning*, p. 164; Clutterbuck, *The Long War*, pp. 95-100.

57. McCuen, *Counter-Revolutionary War*, pp. 119-124 and 166-181. French mobile operations in the Atlas Mountains in Algeria are cited by McCuen as a model that might be emulated. Moreover, he suggests that counter-organizations using native tribes could prove useful in some underpopulated areas, the French experience with the Moi and Thai tribes in Indochina being examples.

58. Ibid., pp. 128-142.

59. Ibid., pp. 195-231; Hyde, *The Roots of Guerrilla Warfare*, pp. 94-95; Clutterbuck, *The Long War*, p. 161.

60. McCuen, *Counter-Revolutionary War*, pp. 235-245; 258-309.

61. Ibid., pp. 240-249; Trinquier, *Modern Warfare*, pp. 101-103. Trinquier favors using counterguerrillas drawn from the population of the sanctuary country. That he may have overestimated the possibilities here is suggested by Bernard Fall in the foreword to Trinquier's book.

62. Clutterbuck, *The Long War*, p. 161.

63. McCuen, *Counter-Revolutionary War*, p. 31.

64. John S. Pustay, *Counterinsurgency Warfare* (New York: The Free Press, 1965), pp. 54-59.

65. Ibid., pp. 59-71; McCuen, *Counter-Revolutionary War*, p. 33.

66. Pustay, *Counterinsurgency Warfare*, pp. 71-72; McCuen, *Counter-Revolutionary War*, pp. 34.

67. Gurr, *Why Men Rebel*, pp. 294-295; Pustay, *Counterinsurgency Warfare*, p. 36 and 72; McCuen, *Counter-Revolutionary War*, pp. 34-35.

68. Pustay, *Counterinsurgency Warfare*, pp. 72-74; McCuen, *Counter-Revolutionary War*, pp. 34 and 36.

69. Pustay, *Counterinsurgency Warfare*, pp. 75-76.

70. Ibid., pp. 76-78; McCuen, *Counter-Revolutionary War*, pp. 37-40.

71. Che Guevara, *Guerrilla Warfare* (New York: Vintage Books, 1961), p. 1.

72. Pustay, *Counterinsurgency Warfare*, pp. 46-47.

73. Guevara, *Guerrilla Warfare*, p. 112.

74. Crozier, *The Study of Conflict*, p. 7.

75. Regis Debray, *Revolution in the Revolution*, trans. Bobbe Ortiz (New York: Monthly Review Press, 1967), pp. 20-21, quote p. 85; Crozier, *The Study of Conflict*, p. 8.

76. Debray, *Revolution in the Revolution*, pp. 83-84.

77. Ibid., p. 105.

78. Ibid., p. 106. Italics are from Debray. Despite Debray's claims, the idea of military action preceding popular support was already present in the literature on insurgency. It was one of several possibilities raised by Ximenes on "La Guerre revolutionnaire et ses donnés fondamentales," *Revue Militaire d'Information*, February-March 1957, pp. 9-29.

79. For a succinct account of the differences between the Maoist and Debray schemes see Arthur Jay Klinghoffer, "Mao or Che? Some reflections on Communist Guerrilla Warfare," *Mizan*, March-April 1969, pp. 94-99.

80. Carlos Marighella, "On Principles and Strategic Questions," *Les Temps Modernes* (Paris), November 1969.

81. Robert Moss, *Urban Guerrilla Warfare*, Adelphi Paper no. 79 (London: International Institute for Strategic Studies, 1971), p. 3.

82. Carlos Marighella, "Minimanual of the Urban Guerrillas," in Moss, *Urban Guerrilla Warfare*, p. 26.

Chapter 3

1. Abraham S. Becker, *Israel and the Occupied Palestinian Territories: Military-Political Issues in the Debate* (Santa Monica, Calif.: The Rand Corporation, 1971), pp. 19-27; Gil Carl AlRoy, "The Prospects of War in the Middle East," *Commentary*, March 1969, p. 59.

2. Official Israeli statistics put the population figures in the occupied areas as follows: West Bank—600,000; East Jerusalem—66,000; Golan—6,400; Gaza—356,000. See *Arab Report and Record*, January 1-15, 1968, p. 13 (hereafter cited as *ARR*).

3. *New York Times*, June 29 and 30, 1967 (hereafter cited as *NYT*).

4. *NYT*, July 9, 1967.

5. *NYT*, July 29 and 31, 1967.

6. *NYT*, August 10, 11, and 16, 1967.

7. *NYT*, September 2, 4, and 11, 1967.

8. *NYT*, September 25, 27, and 28, and October 1, 1967. For a discussion of the origins, recruitment, structure, and purposes of the *Nahals*, see Irving Heymont, "The Israeli Nahal Program," *Middle East Journal*, Summer 1967, pp. 314-324.

9. Jerusalem Domestic Service in Hebrew, October 30, 1967, in *Foreign Broadcast Information Service Daily Report, Middle East, Africa, Europe*, October 31, 1967, pp. H1-H2 (hereafter cited as *FBIS/ME*); *NYT*, October 31, 1967.

10. *NYT*, November 6 and 7, 1967; *Africa Diary*, December 17-23, 1967, p. 3714. In private, Hussein was said to expect that Israel would not effect a total withdrawal.

11. *NYT*, February 13, 1968.

12. *ARR*, February 16-29, 1968, p. 56.

13. *NYT*, March 21 and 22, 1968; Y. Harkabi, *Fedayeen Action and Arab Strategy*, Adelphi Papers no. 53 (London: The International Institute for Strategic Studies, 1968), p. 29.

14. *ARR*, June 16-30, 1968, p. 179.

15. Eric Roleau, "Hawks and Doves in Israel's Foreign Policy," *The World Today*, November 1968, p. 499; *Time*, May 3, 1968, p. 33.

16. Becker, *Israel and Occupied Palestinian Territories*, pp. 57-67; James Feron, "Yigal Allon Has Supporters, Moshe Dayan Has Disciples," *New York Times Magazine*, April 27, 1969, pp. 92-97. In mid-July Dayan visited the West Bank and Gaza and told Arab leaders that since Israel assumed that the present situation would last for some time, it was prepared to begin large-scale, long-term planning and improvements in the occupied areas. See *NYT*, July 29, 1968. Sapir was also concerned that the retention of the occupied areas would, over the longer term, lead to a situation where Arabs outnumbered Jews. Support for this fear may be found in Dov Friedlander and Calvin Goldscheider, "Peace and the Demographic Future of Israel," *Journal of Conflict Resolution*, September 1974, pp. 497-498.

17. *ARR*, June 16-30, 1968, p. 178.

18. On the Allon plan, see Becker, *Israel and Occupied Palestinian Territories*, pp. 27-32; *Le Monde* (Paris), June 11, 1968; *NYT*, June 18 and 24, 1969. One writer argues that the Allon plan represented the most Israel could concede without the cabinet falling. See E. R. J. Owen, "Israel and the Arabs," *World Today*, December 1968. p. 491.

19. *ARR*, July 1-15, 1968, p. 199.

20. *NYT*, December 27 and 30, 1968. One observer cites an Israeli official as saying that the Beirut raid, in addition to being a reprisal for the Athens attack, was designed to display Israel's concern about the increased guerrilla activity in southern Lebanon. See D. K. Lewis, "Beirut Communique," *Interplay*, December 1969/January 1970, p. 52.

21. *NYT*, December 30, 1968.

22. A PFLP attack on an Israeli airliner in Zurich during February 1969, for instance, was not answered with any unusual display of force. *ARR*, February 15-28, 1969, p. 86; *NYT*, March 2, 1969. An increase in guerrilla raids, particularly along the Syrian border, led to the policy of "active self-defense," according to *NYT*, March 16, 1969.

23. *ARR*, January 1-15, 1969, p. 19.

24. *Middle East Journal*, Summer 1969, p. 371; *NYT*, March 18, 1969; *ARR*, March 16-31, 1969, p. 132.

25. *Middle East Journal*, Summer 1969, pp. 364-365; *NYT*, April 7, 1969; *ARR*, March 1-15, 1969, p. 109.

26. *NYT*, April 11, 1969.

27. On the Israeli elections, see the summary in *Mid East*, February 1970, pp. 25-26; *ARR*, October 16-31, 1969, p. 451.

28. *NYT*, November 6, 1969; *Times* (London), November 14, 1969; *Jerusalem Post*, November 13, 1969.

29. *NYT*, November 14, 1969; *ARR*, November 16-30, 1969, p. 504; *Jerusalem Post*, November 23, 1969.

30. *NYT*, December 17, 1969. The same report quotes Dayan as saying that 516 homes had been destroyed since 1967. *NYT*, December 21, 1969, section IV, carried a report which indicated that most Israelis supported the neighborhood punishment policy.

31. *NYT*, December 16, 1969.

32. On the incident, see *NYT*, February 22-25, 1970. On February 21, a spokesman for the Popular Front for the Liberation of Palestine—General Command (a PFLP splinter group), code named Abu Mariam, took responsibility for the attack on the Swiss aircraft, saying a high-ranking Israeli official was on board (*NYT*, February 22, 1970). As indignation mounted, the PFLP-GC reversed its position and denied any role in the incident and the Unified Command of the Palestinian Resistance, of which the PFLP-GC was a member, denied any responsibility and condemned the act as barbaric (*NYT*, February 24, 1970). Nevertheless, the attack seemed to be part of a pattern of attacks on airliners and El-Al offices. Beyond the circumstantial evidence, this analyst, during an interview on October 27, 1970, with an intimately informed and very reliable source, was told that there was no doubt the PFLP-GC carried out the attack. Unhappily, the name of the informant cannot be divulged. On February 26, 1971, the head of the Swiss Federal Ministry of Transport said a thorough investigation had confirmed a "probability bordering on certainty" that the disaster had been caused by Arab guerrilla sabotage. See *ARR*, February 15-28, 1971, p. 129. Following the Qiryat Shemona attack in April 1974, a PFLP-GC military statement took credit for the Swiss incident. See Voice of Palestine in Arabic, April 12, 1974, in *FBIS/ME*, April 16, 1974, p. A5.

33. *NYT*, February 17, 1970.

34. Israel planned to take over some 700-800 acres. Hebron was important to the Israelis because it was the burial place of the Jewish patriarchs. Shortly after the June War some one hundred religious Jews had moved into the Hebron area and, following a cabinet debate, were settled in an army compound. During December 1970 Dayan told a United Jewish Appeal banquet that Israel could never surrender Hebron because Abraham and Sarah were buried there. See *Africa Diary*, January 22-28, 1970, p. 5309; *NYT*, May 16, 1968.

35. According to *NYT*, July 24, 1971, Dayan believed it was possible that the Jews in Hebron could live under Arab rule if the area were returned as part of a settlement, a belief shared by some settlers.

36. On developments in the Hebron situation during March and April, see *NYT*, March 10 and 26, 1970; *ARR*, March 16-31, 1970, p. 197; April 1-15, 1970, p. 230; *ARR*, April 16-30, 1970, p. 259.

37. *ARR*, May 16-31, 1970, p. 314; *Mid East*, August 1970, p. 23.

38. *ARR*, April 16-30, 1970, p. 259.

39. On the Gahal crisis, see *NYT*, August 4, 1970; *Jerusalem Post*, August 2, 3, and 5, 1970. The last source contains the text of Premier Meir's statement to the Knesset on the acceptance of the Rogers plan.

40. On the question of fedayeen activities and the cease-fire, see *NYT*, August 15, 1970; Associated Press dispatch in *Denver Post*, August 11, 1970; *Washington Post* dispatch in *Denver Post*, August 8, 1970.

41. Following attacks on Israeli settlements of Yardena and Maoz Haiyim, an Israeli raid struck a Jordanian army base which, it was claimed, aided the guerrillas. See *NYT*, August 15, 1970; on Israeli strikes against Lebanon, see *NYT*, August 10 and 19, 1970.

42. *NYT*, August 29, 1970.

43. *NYT*, September 19, 1970.

44. *NYT*, September 7, 1970; *Daily Star* (Beirut), September 27 and 28, 1970 (hereafter cited as *DSB*).

45. For a summary of Israeli thinking about the Cairo pact, see *NYT*, September 29, 1970.

46. *NYT*, December 30, 1970.

47. See *NYT*, November 20, 1970, on Sadat's speech. On Israeli activity in the occupied areas, see *ARR*, October 1-15, 1970, p. 572; *ARR*, October 16-31, 1970, p. 600; *ARR*, December 16-31, 1970, p. 702.

48. On the Meir interviews dealing with the disposition of the occupied areas, see *NYT*, March 13, 1971; *Times* (London), March 13, 1971; *ARR*, March 1-15, 1971, p. 151 and *ARR*, February 15-28, 1971, p. 126.

49. *NYT*, March 10, 1971.

50. For a critical account of Israel's actions in Jerusalem, see Abdullah Schleifer, "Report from the Occupied Zone," *Arab World*, May/June 1968, pp. 6-7.

51. *DSB*, January 26, 1971.

52. For a description of the Sharm el-Sheik area and its significance, see *NYT*, April 2, 1971. On April 2, 1971, the Israeli Housing Ministry indicated it would develop Golan in order to increase the population by thirty percent, according to *ARR*, April 1-16, 1971, p. 206. Although a key Israeli planner, Dr. Elisha Ephrat, confirmed that Israel had a thirty-year development plan for the West Bank, he stressed that it had no political significance. See *DSB*, February 13, 1971. In April a Mapai convention passed a resolution indicating an intention to keep Sharm el-Sheik, Golan, Gaza, and East Jerusalem, according to *NYT*, April 8, 1971, and *DSB*, April 8, 1971.

53. For the full text of Dayan's speech, see "Speech of Defense Minister Dayan to the Labor Party Convention," *New Middle East*, May 1971, pp. 46-48.

54. *NYT*, April 6, 1971.

55. Jerusalem International Service in English, in *FBIS/ME*, April 15, p. H1.

56. Jerusalem Domestic Service in Hebrew, August 19, 1971, in *FBIS/ME*, August 20, 1971, p. H1; *NYT*, August 20, 1971. For an account of the United States' reaction and opposition in Israel, see *NYT*, August 21, 1971.

57. The findings of the survey are reported in *NYT*, April 19, 1973. On the Galili Document, see item from *Ha'arez*, August 30, 1973 in *FBIS/ME*, September 5, 1973, pp. H1-H2.

58. For accounts of the political and military developments prior to the war, see Chaim Herzog, *The War of Atonement* (Boston: Little, Brown and Co., 1975), pp. 1-39; Mohamed Heikal, *The Road to Ramadan* (New York: Quadrangle/New York Times Book Co., 1975), pp. 155-203; D. K. Palit, *Return to Sinai* (London: Compton Russell Ltd., 1974), pp. 1-73; Heikal's interview of the war minister and commander-in-chief of the Egyptian Armed Forces, General Ahmad Isma'il, Cairo MENA, in *FBIS/ME*, November 20, 1973, pp. G6-G15; see also the interview of the Egyptian chief of staff, Lieutenant General Sa'id ad-Din ash-Shadhili, in *FSIS/ME*, November 23, 1973, pp. G1-G6.

59. Quoted in Michael Hudson, "The Palestinian Resistance Movement: Its Significance in the Middle East Crisis," *Middle East Journal*, Summer 1969, pp. 299-300.

60. Interview of King Hussein by Leon Janos in *Time*, April 18, 1969, pp. 26-27.

61. Randa Khalidi El-Fattal, "Palestine Liberation Movement," *Arab World*, May 1969, p. 22.

Chapter 4

1. Benjamin Beit-Hallahmi, "Some Psychological and Cultural Factors in the Arab-Israeli Conflict: A Review of the Literature," *Journal of Conflict Resolution*, June 1972, p. 270.

2. *Administration of Justice in the Areas Administered by Israel* (Jerusalem: Ministry of Foreign Affairs, Division of Information, 1974), pp. 2-6.

3. In August 1967, two Arabs caught with submachine guns received eight- and fifteen-year sentences, setting a pattern which would continue for several years. Another terrorist from Jordan was given twenty years for laying mines. See *NYT*, July 28 and August 3 and 29, 1967.

4. An early example of the punishment for captured fedayeen was the case of M. A. Y. Hemayes, a Palestinian leader, sentenced to life by a Hebron military court in the fall of 1967 for carrying arms and forged papers and for belonging to a terrorist organization. Such trials and convictions were recounted regularly by *ARR* during the period 1968-1971. By the fall of 1971, however, Israeli courts were reported to be relatively inactive, a fact reflecting the improved internal security situation. On the latter, see *ARR*, October 1-15, 1971, p. 548.

5. *ARR*, September 1-15, 1968, p. 273; March 16-31, 1971, p. 183; *NYT*, September 4, 1968 and November 6, 1972.

6. The promise of lenient treatment, made by Dayan on August 1, 1971, did not include a general amnesty. See *ARR*, August 1-15, 1971, p. 426. On the release of the guerrillas from Jordan, see *ARR*, September 16-30, 1971, p. 522.

7. *Le Monde* (Paris), January 20, 1968; *NYT*, January 19 and 21, 1968; *Guardian*, January 26, 1968.

8. *NYT*, July 26 and 27, 1967.

9. *NYT*, August 9, 10, 20, and 22, 1967. For an Arab account of the civilian resistance in the fall of 1967 and Israeli counteractions, see *Arab World*, September/October 1967, pp. 3-5.

10. *ARR*, October 16-31, 1968, p. 339; *NYT*, October 29, 1968.

11. On the strikes, demonstrations, and boycotts, see *Middle East Journal*, Autumn 1968, p. 476; Winter 1969, pp. 64-66; Summer 1969, p. 364; *NYT*, November 5 and 11, 1968; *ARR*, November 1-15, 1968, p. 364.

12. *NYT*, August 1 and 2, 1967. At the end of September, Israel permitted the governor to return, according to *NYT*, September 29, 1967. On March 7, 1968, he was again deported, this time to Jordan, according to *ARR*, March 16-31, 1968, p. 83.

13. *ARR*, November 16-30, 1970, p. 655; *NYT*, November 19, 1970. According to both sources, the Israelis put the number deported in a three-year period as "somewhat less than 100." Arab sources claimed the figure was between 120 and 130.

14. Kollek's warning followed an explosion in a Jerusalem market that resulted in Israel's restoration of barriers between East and West Jerusalem and interruption of traffic between the East and West Bank. See *NYT*, November 24, 25, and 28, 1968.

15. *ARR*, October 1-15, 1968, p. 313.

16. By December restrictions on movement were substantial, with traffic between East and West Banks nearly eliminated. See *NYT*, December 1, 18, and 9, 1968.

17. *NYT*, August 6, and September 9 and 16, 1967. This should not be confused with demolition of sixty buildings in the Bal al-Magharaheh quarter of Jerusalem that left some 680 homeless. The latter was done for security reasons, according to the Israelis.

18. *Middle East Journal*, Summer 1968, p. 324.

19. *ARR*, August 1-15, 1968, back cover; *NYT*, August 19 and 20, 1968.

20. *Ha'arez* (Tel Aviv), September 5, 1968.

21. *NYT*, November 23, 1968.

22. *ARR*, November 1-15, 1968, p. 364; February 15-28, 1969, pp. 86-87.

23. *NYT*, November 24, 1969.

24. *Facts About the Administered Areas* (Jerusalem: Israel Information Center, n.d.), pp. 45-50; *NYT*, August 15, 1968.

25. *NYT*, October 31, 1970; Amnon Rubinstein, "No Man's Land Remains in Jerusalem," *New York Times Magazine*," May 11, 1969, p. 126. For a descriptive assessment of the Arab economic advantages resulting from this occupation, see Freda Utley, "Upside Down Victory in the Holy Land," *Arab World* January/February 1969, pp. 3-5. A more analytical piece is Abdul Ilah Abu-Ayyash "Israeli Regional Planning Policy in the Occupied Territories," *JPS*, Spring/Summer 1976, especially pp. 83-105. Abu-Ayyash argues that Israeli economic planning in the occupied areas is guided by a core-periphery model that is inherently colonialist and exploitative. Although such a conceptualization restricts interpretation because it overlooks the benefits to inhabitants in the periphery, it is useful because it reminds us that Israeli economic policy is partially motivated by material self-interest.

26. Peter Duval, "How Israel Feeds the Palestine Revolution," *New Middle East*, June 1971, p. 32. The economic boom was also cited by General Gazit as one factor contributing to the stability of the West Bank. See *Daily Star* (Beirut), June 6, 1971 (hereafter cited as *DSB*).

27. *Jerusalem Post* (weekly), October 6, 1969.

28. Odeh Remba, "Israel and the Occupied Areas: Common Market in the

Making?" *New Middle East,* November 1970, p. 37.

29. An earlier Israeli indication that a labor shortage in the West Bank would preclude issuance of work permits beyond the 20,000 was obviously not implemented. See Nora Levin, "Gaza and the West Bank," *Interplay,* July 1970, p. 37; Remba, "Israel and the Occupied Areas," pp. 36-37.

30. *NYT,* June 28, 1973.

31. Interview of Nabil Shaath entitled "Liberation: Creating Something New in the Middle East," *Free Palestine,* July 1971, p. 5.

32. On civic action programs, see *Middle East Journal,* Winter 1968, p. 59; *Facts About Israel: 1971* (Jerusalem: Ministry of Foreign Affairs, Information Division, 1971), pp. 171-174; *The Health Services of Judaea and Samaria* (Jerusalem: Military Headquarters, Judaea and Samaria, Department of Health, 1974), pp. 3-49; *Facts About the Administered Areas,* pp. 55-56 and 62-73.

33. *Facts About Israel,* p. 170.

34. *NYT,* January 15, 1968, reported Israel was allowing Arabs to run their administration with fewer than a dozen Israeli advisers; on the vacation program, see *NYT,* June 17, 1968.

35. *NYT,* September 1 and November 7, 1967.

36. *Facts About the Administered Areas,* pp. 22-23; *DSB,* July 3, 1971; *ARR,* July 1-15, 1971, p. 367.

37. Quoted in Duval, "How Israel Feeds the Palestine Revolution," p. 32.

38. Amos Elon, "The Israeli Occupation," *Commentary,* March 1968, p. 43, noted that Israeli citizens at times made the job of the Arab police difficult, because they ignored the latter.

39. Ibid., pp. 43-44; Remba, "Israel and the Occupied Areas," p. 35; Levin, "Gaza and the West Bank," p. 34.

40. Elon, "Israeli Occupation," p. 43; *ARR,* June 16-30, 1968, p. 179, reported that on June 21, 1968, thirty-two Arab policemen passed out of the first Israeli training course. Occasionally, Israel was forced to dismiss Arab policemen for lack of loyalty. See, for example, *ARR,* November 16-30, 1968, p. 384.

41. Allon, in a September 12 interview in *Ha'arez* (Tel Aviv), indicated that he was sorry Israel had not pushed on to Jebel Druze during the June War so an independent Druze state allied to Israel could have been created.

42. *Ma'ariv* (Tel Aviv), November 3, 1970; *DSB,* November 10, 1970; *Free Palestine,* February 1971, p. 71; *NYT,* May 4, 1973. In February 1973, four Druze espionage rings were uncovered in the Golan Heights. See *NYT,* February 12, 1973.

43. *ARR,* October 1-15, 1968, p. 314; *Free Palestine,* March 1970, p. 5.

44. Elon, "Israeli Occupation," pp. 45-46; *NYT,* July 8, 1967.

45. *ARR,* September 16-30, 1968, p. 292.

46. Maharaj K. Chopra, "Israel Beyond Cease-Fire," *Military Review,* April 1971, p. 15; comments of Professor Marver H. Bernstein in "What Future for the Palestine Arabs," *Interplay,* June/July 1970, p. 4; Shlomo Avineri, "The Palestinians and Israel," *Commentary,* June 1970, p. 39.

47. Since even a cursory reading of *The New York Times* or the Middle Eastern press from 1967-1971 revealed countless incidents of Israeli security forces breaking up guerrilla cells, there is no need to belabor the point here. The interested reader is directed to *Arab Report and Record* issues from January 1968 to December 1971 as a

convenient source for this, as well as for numerous references to cordon and search operations.

48. *Free Palestine*, October 1969, p. 3.

49. *NYT*, March 4, 1968; *ARR*, September 1-15, 1968, p. 271. The willingness of captured fedayeen to provide information was evidenced a number of times. See *ARR*, January 1-15, 1969, p. 17 on the capture of Abu Fahem in December 1968; *Jerusalem Post* (weekly), November 26, 1969, on disclosures of the head of a Galilee sabotage ring; Y. Harkabi, *Fedayeen Action and Arab Strategy*, Adelphi Papers, no. 53 (London: International Institute for Strategic Studies, 1968), pp. 26-27.

50. On the Jerusalem market and Hebrew University incidents, see *ARR*, March 1-15, 1969, p. 109; *NYT*, March 2, 7, and 8, 1969. Both the PFLP and the PDF claimed credit for the Hebrew University blast, thus casting some doubt on conclusions about an expanded PFLP apparatus.

51. *NYT*, March 2, 1973.

52. See Sulayman Abdullah Schleifer, "Report from the Occupied Zone," *Arab World*, May/June 1968, p. 5.

53. There were many clashes between Israeli patrols and fedayeen units. See *ARR* issues from 1968 to 1971. Comments on effectiveness of Israeli territorial defense measures (ambushes, patrols, and so on) can be found in Harkabi, *Fedayeen Action*, pp. 26-27. For a good descriptive account of Israeli patrolling, see Zeev Shiff and Raphael Rothstein, *Fedayeen: Guerrillas Against Israel* (New York: David McKay Co., 1972), pp. 93-99. By 1976 the Israeli defense against guerrilla infiltration was augmented further by civilian guard patrols around villages and towns. Until 1974 the potential of local defense had not been fully exploited.

54. *ARR*, September 1-15, 1968, p. 271; *NYT*, September 8, 1968. The barrier, according to *Time*, December 13, 1968, pp. 35-56, consisted of an outer line of eight-foot-high barbed wire and an inner five-foot-high line ten yards away. The space between contained mines. At irregular intervals along the fence were electronic sensing devices which raised an alarm in adjacent guard posts when the infiltrator tried to cross. The guards alerted nearby army units, equipped to react quickly with helicopters and powerful searchlights. Other comments about the effectiveness of the fence are to be found in *ARR*, June 16-30, 1971, p. 339.

55. *NYT*, November 6, 21, and 22 and January 12, 1968. One observer argued Israel had no viable alternative to cross-border raids in dealing with the fedayeen sanctuaries. He pointed out the political climate in the Arab countries was such that the popularity of the fedayeen precluded a total prohibition on guerrilla activity. Since the fedayeen were not a government, Israel found it could not approach them on the diplomatic level. Another possibility, an appeal to international organizations to help prevent fedayeen raids, also held little chance for success, given the weakness of the United Nations. He concluded that reprisal raids were the only rational response to fedayeen attacks. See David L. Jones, "Reprisal: Israeli Style," *Military Review*, August 1970, pp. 93-97.

56. On the clash and Hussein's reaction, see *NYT*, February 16 and 17, 1968. Hisham Sharabi, *Palestine Guerrillas: Their Credibility and Effectiveness* (Washington, D.C.: Georgetown University Center for Strategic and International Studies, 1970), p. 19, argued that reprisals failed as a deterrent. However, Sharabi

did not deal with the possible compelling effect resulting from the pressure directed at Arab governments.

57. Success might be conceded on the basis of casualty figures and destruction of the Karamah base. On the other hand, the fact that the guerrillas immediately reoccupied Karamah led many observers to conclude that the action could not be construed as an Israeli victory. See *ARR*, March 16-31, 1968, p. 72.

58. A review of statements by Israeli spokesmen indicates Israeli losses were twenty-three killed, seventy wounded, and three missing in action. See *NYT*, March 23, 1968. Israel claimed approximately 150 fedayeen were killed. For an Arab view of significance of the Karamah battle, see Sebastian Sting, "Karamah Means Dignity," *Arab World*, May 1968, pp. 47-50.

59. See, for example, *NYT*, March 23, 1968; David Waines, *The Unholy War* (Wilmette, Il.: Medina University Press International, 1971), pp. 188-189; David Meter, "Frustration Breeds Mid-East Tension," *Arab World*, May 1969, p. 39.

60. *ARR*, March 16-31, 1968, p. 73; *NYT*, March 22, 1968.

61. *NYT*, March 31, 1968. Previously, Prime Minister Eshkol had defended the raid as a success. See *NYT*, March 23, 1968.

62. *NYT*, April 1 and 27, 1968. As Appendix B, Table B-3 indicates, incidents and casualties along the Jordan border actually increased in the several months after Karamah, thus affirming Bar Lev's prognostication.

63. *NYT*, April 9, 1968. Israeli forces went eighteen miles inside Jordan, and claimed all guerrillas were killed, a fedayeen base destroyed, and attack plans for three Negev towns captured.

64. Occasionally, as in the case of the Ghor al-Safi operation of January 21, 1970, Israel reverted to larger-scale search and destroy operations like the Karamah raid. But with the international community seemingly accustomed to Israel's cross-border attacks, world reaction was not as severe as in the Karamah episode. On the Ghor al-Safi raid see *NYT*, January 22, 1970; *ARR*, January 16-31, 1970, p. 80.

65. *ARR*, May 1-15, 1968, p. 124. In May 1969 Israel disclosed its guerrillas had been crossing into Jordan for a year, laying mines, and ambushing guerrilla units. See *NYT*, May 10, 1968.

66. *NYT*, December 5 and 21, 1968; *ARR*, December 16-31, 1968, p. 428. Israel claimed, according to the latter source, that air strikes were followed by a decrease in number of incidents in the north of the Jordan Valley.

67. For a thought-provoking debate about the Beirut raid by two prominent international lawyers, see Richard A. Falk, "The Beirut Raid and the International Law of Retaliation," *American Journal of International Law*, July 1969, pp. 415-443; Yehuda Blum, "The Beirut Raid and the International Double Standard: A Reply to Professor Richard A. Falk," *American Journal of International Law*, January 1970, pp. 73-105.

68. *NYT*, January 4, 6, and 7, 1969.

69. *NYT*, January 9 and 17, 1969. Yet the Israeli ambassador to the United Nations complained of the upsurge in fedayeen activity, according to *ARR*, March 16-31, 1969, p. 131.

70. See Appendix B, Tables B-2, B-4, B-6, and B-7.

71. On the policy of active self-defense and the Syrian strikes, see *ARR*, February

15-28, 1969, p. 86; March 16-31, 1969, p. 133; *NYT*, February 24, 1969.

72. According to *NYT*, July 6, 1969, Israeli leaders were reported as conceding that air strikes could not end border incidents. Instead, their aims were to give Israel a respite, keep the enemy off balance, keep the initiative, boost morale, and achieve long-term aims.

73. *NYT*, March 9, 1969.

74. See the articles by James Feron and Dana Adams Schmidt in *NYT*, June 29, 1969, Section 4. Prime Minister Meir told the Knesset that Israel would not interfere with canal repairs as long as Jordan stopped the army and fedayeen from shelling across the border. See *NYT*, July 1, 1969.

75. *Christian Science Monitor*, August 22, 1969 (hereafter cited as *CSM*); *NYT*, September 23 and 24 and January 2, 1970. Since the canal was a $15 million showpiece of American aid, the United States let it be known that it would like to see it spared.

76. Examples of Israeli warnings can be found in *ARR*, June 1-15, 1970, p. 345.

77. *NYT*, September 27 and 29, 1970; *DSB*, September 27 and 29, 1970. Given the sharply diminished fedayeen activity along the Jordan border after September 1970, there was little need for Israeli military action. Thus, there were but few scattered incidents through December 1971. On those that did occur, see *NYT*, November 12, 1970. Israel, through Allon, again manifested its sensitivity to developments in Jordan during April 1971, when warnings were addressed to Syria and Iraq not to intervene on behalf of guerrillas fighting the Jordanian army. See *New Middle East*, May 1971, p. 50.

78. *NYT*, October 9, 1969, November 4 and 5, 1969 and March 7, 1970; *ARR*, March 1-15, 1970, p. 164. Israeli leaders issued periodic warnings to Lebanon throughout 1971.

79. *DSB*, May 28, 1970; *New Middle East*, July 1970, p. 50. A large search and destroy operation on May 12 was condemned by the United Nations Security Council. See *NYT*, May 29, 1970. Bar Lev indicated the raid was aimed at warning the Lebanese government and people of disadvantages associated with supporting the guerrillas and at destroying fedayeen bases. See *ARR*, May 1-15, 1970, pp. 283-284; *New Middle East*, June 1970, p. 50.

80. *ARR*, September 1-15, 1970, p. 510; September 16-30, 1970, p. 541; *NYT*, September 6 and 24, 1970.

81. See Appendix B, Table B-6.

82. *NYT*, October 29, 1970. Following the firing of rockets into Israel, villagers from the Marjyun border district demanded that Lebanese police and troops prevent guerrilla rocket firing from the area.

83. *DSB*, April 10, 1971. A postal employee in a Lebanese village reported that the Israelis arrived with a map marking guerrilla houses and destroyed only those. *NYT*, June 15, 1972.

84. *NYT*, March 10, 1972.

85. *NYT*, June 24 and 29, 1972.

86. *NYT*, September 17 and 18, 1972. During the raids, ten guerrillas were captured and several months later were brought to trial by Israel in accordance with a revision in the criminal code that extended the code to crimes committed abroad against Israel's security. Previously, such individuals had been detained without

trial under administrative orders. See *NYT*, July 24, 1973.

87. *NYT*, October 16, 1972.

88. Quoted in AP dispatch in *Denver Post*, November 22, 1972. Citing official figures, *Davar* (Tel Aviv), January 10, 1973, indicated that in 1972 there were 122 incidents and 5 casualties along the Syrian border and 30 incidents and 45 casualties along the Lebanese frontier.

89. *NYT*, May 6, 1973.

90. *NYT*, May 7 and 11, 1973.

91. *NYT*, January 24, 1973.

92. *NYT*, November 29, 1969. The same source indicated it was presumed these agents had warned Greece of an impending Athens attack.

93. *NYT*, September 8 and 11, 1970; *DSB*, September 15, 1970.

94. On the detention, see *NYT*, September 13, 15, and 19, 1970.

95. *JPS*, Winter 1972, pp. 158-160; *NYT*, September 9, 1972.

96. *NYT*, September 22, 1972.

97. *Newsweek*, September 25, 1972, p. 49.

98. Cited in *Newsweek*, October 2, 1972, p. 30.

99. Jerusalem Domestic Service in Hebrew, October 12, 1972, in *FBIS/ME*, October 13, 1972, p. H2. The issue of covert attacks against the terrorists outside the Middle East led to a debate over the prudence and effectiveness of such a course of action. See *JPS*, Winter 1973, pp. 142-149. In July 1973, Meir confirmed that Israel was fighting terrorists all over the world. See Jerusalem Domestic Service in Arabic, July 30, 1973, in *FBIS/ME*, July 30, 1973, p. H3.

100. Here there was some success. According to *NYT*, October 22, 1972, a number of Arab students were expelled from Europe and new security controls were directed at Arab travelers.

101. See *NYT*, April 12, 1973; *Newsweek*, April 23, 1973, p. 35.

102. See *Times* (London) dispatch in *NYT*, July 26, 1973; *NYT*, August 15, 1973.

103. *Time*, March 5, 1973, p. 21.

104. *JPS*, Summer 1973, pp. 129-131; 139-142.

105. *CSM*, September 12, 1973.

106. Zuhair Muhsin, leader of *Sa'iqa* admitted that his group was responsible, in an interview in *Al-Anwar* (Beirut), October 11, 1973. A detailed account of fedayeen external terrorism and the Israeli response between 1967 and 1973 may be found in Charles Dean Wise, "Political Terrorism: An Israeli Case Study" (M.A. thesis, University of Oklahoma Graduate College, 1976), pp. 56-73.

107. *International Herald Tribune*, cited by *ARR*, November 1-15, 1969, p. 477; Sharabi, *Palestine Guerrillas*, pp. 8-9. The data in Appendix B, Table B-7, indicates that in terms of Israeli casualties along the borders, 1969 was the high point of fedayeen activity.

108. *NYT*, November 16, 1969.

109. *ARR*, November 1-15, 1969, p. 478; *NYT*, November 13, 1969. According to *Arab World*, August 27, 1969, as quoted in a news item in *Mid East*, December 1969, p. 24, Dayan offered to provide collaborators with guns to protect themselves after the killing of five Arabs outside Hebron.

110. *Mid East*, December 1969, p. 23; February 1970, pp. 26-27. A particularly critical article on Israeli security measures was written by E. C. Hodgkin of *Times*

(London), on October 28, 1969. Hodgkin claimed about 7,000 homes had been destroyed; Dayan, according to *NYT*, December 17, 1969, put the figure at 516.

111. *Daily Telegraph* (London), November 26, 1969, as cited in *ARR*, November 16-30, 1969, p. 503; *NYT*, November 26, 1969.

112. See Appendix B, Tables B-3 and B-7.

113. *Facts About the Administered Areas*, p. 38.

114. Cairo Voice of Palestine in Arabic, January 3, 1973, in *FBIS/ME*, January 10, 1973, p. A1.

115. *NYT*, April 13, 1970; AP dispatch in *Denver Post*, March 11, 1970; *Mid East*, June 1970, p. 25; AP dispatch in *Denver Post*, January 14, 1970. The last source indicates that there were eighty murders in 1970, many due to guerrilla rivalries.

116. *NYT*, April 13, 1970; *ARR*, March 1-15, 1970, p. 166. In an interview with a staff member of *The Daily Star* (Beirut), an active participant in the Gaza resistance said most members of that resistance were "sick and tired" of parties and organizations and therefore fought under the PLA banner. See *DSB*, June 20, 1971.

117. *NYT*, January 1, 1971.

118. *NYT*, January 1, 1971, said that official statistics indicated nine times more incidents in Gaza than in the West Bank during 1970.

119. *NYT*, January 11, 1971.

120. *ARR*, January 16-31, 1971, p. 79; *DSB*, January 18, 1971; January 23 and 28, 1971; besides fueling the already existing anti-Israeli feelings in Gaza, actions of the border police proved to be a propaganda windfall for the Arabs and fedayeen. See, for example, *Free Palestine*, June 1971, p. 3; July 1971, p. 8.

121. *ARR*, February 1-14, 1971, p. 100; February 15-28, 1971, p. 131.

122. *ARR*, March 1-15, 1971, p. 157; March 16-31, 1971, p. 183.

123. *DSB*, June 20, 1971.

124. On the Gaza plan and resettlement, see *NYT*, July 22 and 29, 1971; August 20, 1971; *DSB*, July 24 and 30 and August 1, 15, 16, and 31, 1971. In a report to the General Assembly on September 19, the secretary general said 15,000 persons were displaced by the Gaza resettlement, of which 1,600 were moved to al-Arish and 150 to the West Bank. The rest were settled elsewhere in Gaza. See *ARR*, September 16-30, 1971, p. 504; Dayan's report on the resettlement scheme in *NYT*, November 3, 1971. Reports on the sharp improvement in the security situation in Gaza in the last half of 1971 can be found in *NYT*, December 18, 1971. On the 1972 developments see *Hatzofeh*, as quoted in *JPS*, Spring 1973, pp. 139-140.

125. *NYT*, May 9, 1972.

126. *NYT*, October 24, 1972.

127. *Sunday Times* (London), June 19, 1977; W. J. Mallison, Jr., "The Geneva Convention for the Protection of Civilian Persons: An Analysis of Its Application in the Arab Territories Under Israeli Occupation," *Arab World*, December 1969-January 1970, pp. 16-22; Sharabi, *Palestine Guerrillas*, pp. 14-16; *Israel and the Geneva Conventions* (Beirut: Institute for Palestine Studies, 1968), pp. 7-63; George Dib and Fuad Jabber, *Israel's Violation of Human Rights in the Occupied Territories*, 3d ed. rev. (Beirut: Institute for Palestine Studies, 1970); The Arab Women's Information Committee, *The Arabs Under Israeli Occupation: 1969* (Beirut: Institute for Palestine Studies, 1970).

128. On the July surrenders, see *ARR*, July 16-31, 1971, pp. 377 and 298;

September 16-30, 1971, p. 52; *DSB*, July 19 and 20, 1971; *New Middle East* September 1971, pp. 42-43. The released fedayeen were to be under surveillance and Israel had obtained guarantees of good conduct from relatives and prominent Arabs.

129. The casualty figures given by Israeli military sources can be found in *DSB*, October 10, 1971. On Israeli taxation and defense spending, see *NYT*, January 5, 1971.

130. *Free Palestine*, January 1971, p. 3. Others also argued this point. See, for instance, "A Conversation With Paul Jacobs: Divide Palestine, or Continue War," *Interplay*, November 1970, p. 15; Avineri, "Palestinians and Israel," p. 40.

131. The unfavorable nature of the terrain has been noted, inter alia, by the following: Harkabi, *Fedayeen Action*, pp. 18, 27, and 31; Waines, *The Unholy War*, p. 174; Barbara C. Aswad, "The Involvement of Peasants in Social Movements and Its Relation to the Palestine Revolution," in *The Palestinian Resistance to Israeli Occupation*, ed. Naseer Aruri (Wilmette, Ill.: Medina University Press International, 1970), p. 23; Ania Francos, "The Palestinian Revolution and the Third World," in ibid., p. 43; Constantine Zuraik, "Today and Yesterday—Two Prominent Aspects of the New Meaning of Disaster," *Middle East Forum*, 1967, p. 19.

132. See, for example, *Free Palestine*, September 1970, p. 1.

133. *Palestine Resistance Bulletin*, March 1971, p. 3; Harkabi, *Fedayeen Action*, p. 41; Edmund Ghareeb, "An Interview With Abu Amar," *Arab World*, May 1969, p. 28.

134. *Al-Ahram* (Cairo), August 18, 1968.

135. Naji Alush, *The Road to Palestine* (Beirut: Dar al-Tal'ia, 1964), as cited in Harkabi, *Fedayeen Action*, p. 18.

136. J. Gaspard, "The Critical Power Balance in the Lebanon," *New Middle East*, December 1969, pp. 8-9; *NYT*, January 30 and February 3, 1969.

Chapter 5

1. On the reference to popular support as a "revolutionary law," see the interview of Khalil Kudsi, a *Fatah* representative, in *Free Palestine*, August 1969, p. 6. The need for mass support was a consistent and frequent theme in all fedayeen literature, left-wing or moderate.

2. Michael Hudson, "The Palestinian Arab Resistance Movement: Its Significance in the Middle East Crisis," *Middle East Journal*, Summer 1969, pp. 4-5. *Fatah* and pro-*Fatah* sources are replete with references to Israeli imperialism. See, for example, *Free Palestine*, November 1970, pp. 2-3; June 1971, pp. 4-5; August 1969, p. 5.

3. On the role of Fanon in Palestinian thinking, see *Free Palestine*, March 1971, p. 6; *Dialogue with Abu Amar* (n.p.: Palestine National Liberation Movement, *Fatah*, n.d.); Y. Harkabi, *Fedayeen Action and Arab Strategy*, Adelphi Papers no. 53 (London: International Institute for Strategic Studies, 1968), p. 14; Ehud Yaari, "Al-Fath's Political Thinking," *New Outlook*, November/December 1968, pp. 30-31.

4. The nationalist aspect was particularly appealing to the young. See E. R. J.

Owens, "Israel and the Arabs," *World Today*, December 1968, p. 493. The attraction of guerrilla warfare for youth should also be noted. One writer has suggested that its appeal to youthful Palestinians stemmed from the fact that it was a romantic part of the culture of youth. See Randa Khadidi El-Fattal, "Palestine Liberation Movement," *Arab World*, May 1969, p. 21.

5. On the influence of Marxism-Leninism on left-wing fedayeen organizations, see Leila S. Kadi, comp. and trans., *Basic Political Documents of the Armed Palestinian Resistance Movement* (Beirut: Palestine Liberation Organization Research Center, 1968), pp. 143-247. For secondary sources see Gerard Chaliand, *The Palestinian Resistance* (Baltimore: Penguin Books, 1972), pp. 80-96; Robert Anton Mertz, "Why George Habash Turned Marxist," *Mid East*, August 1970, pp. 32-36. Mertz argues persuasively that the PDF, which at one time was part of the PFLP, is more serious about Marxism-Leninism. Yet he avoids writing off the PFLP interest in Marxism-Leninism, noting that some of its writings are serious about this aspect, while others tend to treat it as an expedient ideology for liberating Palestine.

6. Mertz, "Why George Habash Turned Marxist," p. 195, pointed out that most members of the left-wing groups were admittedly middle-class intellectuals.

7. *Le Monde* (Paris) [weekly], July 16, 1969. A good summary and analysis of education in the Palestinian exile community may be found in Ibrahim Abu Lughod, "Educating a Community in Exile: The Palestinian Experience," *JPS*, Spring 1973, pp. 94-111.

8. For Dayan's remarks, see *NYT*, March 9, 1969. The other observer was Edward Hughes, whose remarks can be found in *Time*, March 29, 1968, p. 30. Others also stressed the fact that the fedayeen were young and educated. See *NYT*, December 27, 1968; *Jerusalem Post* (weekly), March 23, 1969; Gil Carl AlRoy, "The Prospects of War in the Middle East," *Commentary*, March 1969, p. 56. Harkabi, *Fedayeen Action*, p. 29, argues that fedayeen phraseology was persuasive for those who were converted or wished to be converted. These findings are generally supported by a recent quantitative analysis of commando membership. See Yasumasa Kuroda, "Young Palestinian Commandos in Political Socialization Perspective," *Middle East Journal*, Summer 1972, p. 265.

9. *Guardian Weekly*, September 6, 1969.

10. Hudson, "Palestinian Resistance Movement," pp. 293-294, points out that the loss of their land was particularly distressing to the Palestinians since attachment to the land was an important aspect of their life-style and culture. A young fedayeen captive suggested during an interview that the appeal of the resistance was based on getting the land back and avenging Arab honor. See Amnon Rubinstein, "'Damn Everybody' Sums Up the Angry Mood of Israel," *New York Times Magazine*, February 9, 1969, p. 97.

11. On the popularity of Arafat and assassination attempts against him see *NYT*, December 3 and 27, 1968; *ARR*, August 1-15, 1969, p. 333. On Arafat's background and career see Thomas Kiernan, *Arafat: The Man and the Myth* (New York: W. W. Norton and Co., 1976). Though clearly unsympathetic to Arafat, Kiernan's work is nonetheless interesting, informative, and provocative.

12. *NYT*, November 16, 1969. In July 1968, traitors were warned to surrender to the fedayeen or lose their lives, according to *ARR*, July 16-31, 1968, p. 215.

Although the assassinations of collaborators became prominent in mid-1969, there were incidents in the previous period. See, for example, *ARR*, March 16-31, 1969, p. 129; May 16-31, 1969, p. 215; June 1-15, 1969, p. 250.

13. *NYT*, October 10, 1968, and November 25, 1968; *ARR*, October 1-15, 1968, p. 313.

14. The issues of *Arab Report and Record* from 1968 to 1971 contain numerous accounts of all types of terror.

15. *NYT*, May 29 and 30, 1969; *Jerusalem Post*, January 12, 1970.

16. Hisham Sharabi cited the fedayeen objective of provoking Israeli counter-terror. See Hisham Sharabi, *Palestine Guerrillas: Their Credibility and Effectiveness* (Washington, D.C.: Georgetown University Center for Strategic and International Studies, 1970), p. 38.

17. While Israel made attempts to minimize brutality, those incidents which did occur probably increased the alienation of the victims and created some new active supporters. See David Waines, *The Unholy War* (Wilmette, Ill.: Medina University Press International, 1971), pp. 175-177.

18. The linkage between military success and increased volunteers and support, demonstrated at Karamah in 1968, was obviously not lost on the fedayeen.

19. Kuroda, "Palestinian Commandos," pp. 257-260.

20. Harkabi, *Fedayeen Action*, p. 27, calls attention to the tendency of captured fedayeen to inform on comrades as a fact well known to the population. Saleh Khalef (Abu Iyad) explicitly links disunity of the fedayeen to lack of popular support in an interview in *Free Palestine*, November/December 1971, p. 8.

21. Harkabi, *Fedayeen Action*, p. 41. Harkabi noted a letter from a fedayeen officer published in *Al-Anwar* (Beirut), claiming that since 1965 the guerrillas had killed 7,000 Israelis, as a good example of exaggerated casualty reporting. Arab doubts about fedayeen claims are noted in *NYT*, August 11, 1969; *New Middle East* April 1970, p. 7; *Mid East*, August 1970, p. 19.

22. For Qaddumi's comments, see *DSB*, December 16, 1970. Conceit, exhibitionism, and opportunism were admitted as fedayeen sins in a later interview with Qaddumi (using the sobriquet Abu Lutf). See *Free Palestine*, April 1971, p. 5. Others made similar observations. See, for example, *Al-Thawra* (Syria), October 2, 1968; and *An-Nahar* (Beirut), weekly supplement, October 6, 1968, cited in Harkabi, *Fedayeen Action*, p. 42; David Meter, "Frustration Breeds Mid-East Tension," *Arab World*, May 1969, p. 41; Edward R. F. Sheehan, "In the Flaming Streets of Amman," *New York Times Magazine*, September 27, 1970, p. 26.

23. Leonard Fein, *Politics in Israel* (Boston: Little, Brown & Co., 1967), pp. 59-60.

24. Ibid., p. 61. Similar comments, two years after Fein's book, were made by Shmuel Toledano, the Israeli prime minister's advisor on Arab affairs. See *Davar* (Tel Aviv), January 21, 1973.

25. On the distrust separating the Israeli Arabs from those outside Israel, see Herbert Pundik, "Israel's Arabs Establish Their Identity," *New Middle East*, August 1969, p. 33; *NYT*, July 28, 1968, and January 29, 1971. The latter quoted a prominent Palestinian nationalist in East Jerusalem as saying the Israeli Arabs were of no concern to West Bank Palestinians because "they were lost two decades ago." Don Peretz reported a study by Israeli sociologists in 1968 indicating the Arab

defeat increased respect for the state among Arab school children, while at the same time intensifying feelings of hatred toward Israel. See Don Peretz, "Arab Palestine: Phoenix or Phantom," *Foreign Affairs,* January 1970, pp. 329-330.

26. Waines, *The Unholy War,* p. 187; *NYT,* July 28, 1968, and October 25, 1969.

27. *Time,* January 5, 1970, p. 27.

28. On the question of Palestinian hopes of winning Jewish support, see *Free Palestine,* July 1970, p. 6; *JPS,* Summer 1973, pp. 165-167. Interviews with prominent left-wing spokesmen such as Uri Avnery and Uri Davis revealed that even left-wing circles were skeptical about the possibility of a democratic-secular state as proposed by the fedayeen. See "A Conversation With Paul Jacobs," *Free Palestine,* September 1970, p. 4; "Interview With Uri Avnery," ibid., November 1970, p. 4; "Uri Davis Speaks to *Free Palestine,*" ibid., May 1971, pp. 6-7.

29. The *Fatah* claims were made over the radio. See *NYT,* February 7, 1968, and March 31, 1968, Section 4; *ARR,* February 1-15, 1968, p. 43. Though Arafat himself was involved in organizational efforts on the West Bank in 1967, he emphasized immediate military action in lieu of creating bases and obtaining recruits. See Zeev Shiff and Raphael Rothstein, *Fedayeen: Guerrillas Against Israel* (New York: David McKay Co., 1972), p. 75.

30. It is difficult to establish the extent to which given acts of civil disobedience were spontaneous as opposed to being instigated by the fedayeen. What is clear is that the fedayeen welcomed the civil resistance as part of the liberation struggle and sought to promote it. See, for example, *Free Palestine,* June 1969, p. 5.

31. The evidence of partial support has been cited in a number of accounts. See *Mid East,* February 1970, pp. 26-27, for instance.

32. The problem prompted the "Voice of *Assifa*" to warn traitors on July 22, 1968 to surrender and stand trial or be killed. On the broadcast and other indicators of nonsupport, see *ARR,* July 16-31, 1968, p. 215.

33. *Daily Telegraph* (London), November 26, 1969, cited in *ARR,* November 16-30, 1969, p. 503; *NYT,* November 26, 1969; Rubinstein, "Angry Mood of Israel," p. 93.

34. On the guerrilla threats, see *ARR,* October 16-31, 1969, p. 451.

35. *Free Palestine,* December 1969, p. 3. Interestingly, the article on the elections mentions but does not deny, the reported fedayeen threats. The same article points out that even Israelis had called attention to the fact that the Arabs' desire to have their identification cards stamped may have been a key factor in their voting. Also see *Mid East,* February 1970, p. 26.

36. *NYT,* May 3, 1972.

37. AP dispatches in *Denver Post,* February 3 and 4, 1970. In a move in the other direction, seven Arabs withdrew from newly elected posts in the Jerusalem government because of pressure from "extremist circles."

38. Cited in *New Middle East,* March 1971, p. 42. An article in *The International Herald Tribune,* July 15, 1971, claimed Arafat ceased to be the romantic charismatic figure and had become just another politician in the eyes of the Arab masses. See *ARR,* July 1-15, 1971, p. 366.

39. *NYT,* September 9, 1967.

40. *ARR,* January 1-15, 1968, p. 14; *NYT,* December 30, 1967.

41. *NYT,* February 18, 1970.

42. *New Middle East*, May 1970, pp. 5-7. For the summary of the *Fatah* broadcast, see ibid., pp. 46-47. For hostile fedayeen comments, see ibid., p. 7. For a good example of the new thoughts on the West Bank in regard to independence, see *Survival*, April 1970, pp. 132-135.

43. *DSB*, August 14 and 25, 1970. Abu Iyad charged the petitions were circulated by monopolists and farm owners. Perhaps the most accurate description of Palestinian opinion at the time was made by a Palestinian who wrote the following:

> Since the June 1967 war the PLO has become even more unrepresentative. The bulk of the Palestinians are in Israeli-occupied territory, and they have not recently been consulted about their views on the question of a settlement. In Jordan, also, there has never been any organized or realistic polling of opinion amongst the Palestinians about the basis for a settlement of the dispute. The same is true in regard to Palestinians in the wider diaspora of the Arab world. Nobody, therefore, can now say with any degree of accuracy or truthfulness what the Palestinian Arabs want.

See Sarih, "Frankly Speaking," *New Middle East*, July 1970, p. 40. Sarih's comments raise a question about the argument that fedayeen programs represented a broad consensus among Palestinians. For the latter, see Hisham Sharabi, *Palestine and Israel: The Lethal Dilemma* (New York: Pegasus, 1969), pp. 201-208.

44. *New Middle East*, September 1970, p. 18. The increased apathy toward the fedayeen was also illustrated by the fact that a PFLP call for a general strike to protest Israeli detention of Arabs during the September civil war in Jordan was largely ignored. See *DSB*, September 18, 1970.

45. *New Middle East*, September 1970, p. 18.

46. The Amman government, it should be recalled, was also opposed to the idea of an independent Palestinian state, a position underlined by its refusal to allow notables associated with the idea from visiting Jordan after the civil war. See *NYT*, December 11, 1970.

47. See *DSB*, October 10 and 19, 1970; *ARR*, October 16-31, 1970, p. 600; Dan Gillon, "Report on the Present State of Opinion on the West Bank," *New Middle East*, November 1970, pp. 6-7; *NYT*, December 8, 1970. Another meeting of traditional leaders was held on September 26 in East Jerusalem, during which a proposal to condemn Hussein's actions was watered down to a statement expressing "shock" at events in Jordan.

48. See, for example, *DSB*, November 23 and 25, 1970; *Free Palestine*, November 1970, p. 8.

49. Gillon, "Opinion on the West Bank," pp. 6-7. Gillon reported that the vacillation of the traditional and the new leaders precluded their being effective. The Palestinian press on the West Bank also condemned post-civil-war actions against the guerrillas. See *New Middle East*, February 1971, p. 13.

50. *Al-Basheer* (Bethlehem) and *Al-Quds* (Jerusalem) both took the West Bank politicians to task for their inability to give forceful articulation to their views on a settlement, according to *New Middle East*, March 1971, p. 41.

51. This conclusion was underscored by an *Al-Quds* (Jerusalem) article in March 1971 that criticized the hard-line guerrilla stand at the eighth PNC as putting Palestinians "back on the road of invective and libel." See *New Middle East*, April

1971, p. 12. On the continuous activity of the independent Palestinians through 1971, see *New Middle East*, May 1971, pp. 13 and 25; "The Palestinian Memorandum to Rogers," *New Middle East*, June 1971, pp. 30-31; *NYT*, May 5, 1971; *DSB*, February 17, 1971.

52. Such observations were actually appearing as early as 1968. See, for example, *NYT*, June 26, 1968; Harkabi; *Fedayeen Action*, pp. 26-27.

53. An attribution of blame for terrorist activities to the fedayeen appeared in *NYT*, April 13, 1970.

54. *NYT*, August 20, 1970. This point has been argued persuasively by P. J. Vatikiotis, "A Middle East Perspective—Fashion and Reality," *New Middle East*, April 1971, p. 36. One scholar has pointed out that even before June 1967 there was no social cohesion between Palestinians in West Bank towns and those in the refugee camps. See Shlomo Avineri, "The Palestinians and Israel," *Commentary*, June 1970, p. 36.

55. James P. Brown, "No Peace Without the Palestinians," *NYT*, January 25, 1971.

56. Interview with Nabil Shaath entitled "Liberation: Creating Something New in the Middle East," *Free Palestine*, July 1971, p. 5. Also see Rubinstein, "Angry Mood of Israel," p. 93.

57. Hisham Sharabi, "The Palestinian Revolutionary Struggle," *Arab World*, May 1960, p. 9, argues that the fact that the refugees in the occupied areas had little to lose would spur support for the resistance. However, Sharabi failed to appreciate the different status of the West Bank Arabs and its implications for protracted revolutionary warfare. This oversight was no doubt related to the general thrust of the article, which sought to convince the reader that revolutionary armed struggle would succeed. This led Sharabi to acknowledge criticism that conditions in the Palestinian struggle were different from other successful insurgencies, but to ignore implications of those differences and ways they might be overcome. The best Sharabi could do was assure his reader that the Palestinian struggle would succeed because of Zionist contradictions. Another curious argument indicates faith in success because the Palestinian revolution, like a number of successful revolutions seemed hopeless at the outset. He did not point out a number of revolutions that failed were also hopeless at the outset.

58. *Free Palestine*, November 1969, p. 2. There was a consensus among observers that most guerrillas were from the refugee camps. See, for instance, *CSM*, December 24, 1968; November 14 and 22, 1969; *NYT*, February 18, 1969; March 2 and 14, 1969. David P. Forsythe, "UNRWA, The Palestinian Refugees and World Politics: 1949-1969," *International Organization*, Winter 1971, p. 43.

59. "Human Rights and the Palestinian," *Mid East*, December 1967, p. 15. Similar comments are found in Peter C. Dodd, "Human Dignity in Exile: The Problem of the Arab Refugees of 1967," *Middle East Forum*, 45, (1968) pp. 91-95 and 99; Harkabi, *Fedayeen Action*, p. 14; Sharabi, *Palestine and Israel*, pp. 180-181.

60. For a good description of the refugees' conditions and desires, see James A. Michener, "What to Do About the Palestinian Refugees," *New York Times Magazine*, September 27, 1970. For a suggestive essay on the revolutionary potential of the refugees, see Barbara C. Aswad, "The Involvement of Peasants in Social

Movements and Its Relation to the Palestine Revolution," in Nasser Aruri, ed., *Palestine Resistance to Israeli Occupation* (Wilmette, Ill.: Medina University Press International, 1970), pp. 22-24.

61. *Free Palestine*, March 1969, p. 1.

62. *Free Palestine*, January 1970, pp. 6-8. A report in *DSB*, August 9, 1970, claimed that the Palestinian Red Crescent handled 50,000-60,000 people per month. Also see John M. Mecklin, "Fire and Steel for Palestine," *Fortune*, July 1970, p. 89; Aswad, "Peasants in Social Movements," p. 23. Neville Brown, "Palestinian Nationalism and the Jordanian State," *World Today*, September 1970, p. 375, argues that *Fatah* provided most services.

63. For an empirical, quantitative analysis of the political socialization of the Palestinians, see Kuroda, "Palestinian Commandos," pp. 253-270.

64. *Guardian*, December 29, 1970.

Chapter 6

1. See Appendix E, Table E-1. A year and a half after the Jordanian civil war the *NYT* reported that the number of active guerrillas was 7,000 and the PLA strength was 8,000. See *NYT*, April 14, 1972.

2. See Appendix C, Table C-1.

3. Editorial in *Free Palestine*, October 1969, p. 1. The need for unity was a theme stressed by all the fedayeen organizations. See, for example, *The Palestine Revolution* (n.p., n.d.), Message from the Palestine National Liberation Movement (*Fatah*) to the Seventeenth Annual Convention of Arab Students in the United States and Canada, Ann Arbor, Michigan, August 26-31, 1968, pp. 8-9 and 14; *Democratic Popular Front for the Liberation of Palestine* (Manchester, England: Committee for Solidarity with the Palestine Revolution, 1969), pp. 11 and 26-29. Even a cursory reading of almost any fedayeen or pro-fedayeen publication will reveal the persistent concern about the need for unity.

4. Observers rightfully pointed out that the adverse effect to the Arab cause resulting from Shuqayri's violent rhetoric prior to the June War was a consideration in his removal. See, for example, Shlomo Avineri, "The New Status Quo," *Commentary*, March 1968, p. 50.

5. *ARR*, January 1-15, 1968, inside cover; *Middle East Journal*, Spring 1968, p. 175; *NYT*, January 21, 1968.

6. *ARR*, February 1-15, 1968, p. 42; *Daily News* (Kuwait), January 1, 1970.

7. Y. Harkabi, *Fedayeen Action and Arab Strategy*, Adelphi Papers no. 53 (London: Institute for Strategic Studies, 1968), p. 38.

8. *Daily News* (Kuwait), January 1, 1970.

9. The allocation of fifty seats to the PLO was thought to be due to its extensive financial backing from the Arab League, according to *NYT*, July 14, 1968.

10. The smaller groups were the Palestine Liberation Front and the Return Hero's Organization, according to *ARR*, October 1-15, 1968, p. 316. The third group cited was Vengeance Youth, the nucleus of the ANM. The ANM was a semiclandestine political organization which had been actively but unsuccessfully involved in the Arab nationalist struggle since 1948. On its origins and

development prior to its transformation into the PFLP, see Robert Anton Mertz, "Why George Habash Turned Marxist," *Mid East*, August 1970, pp. 31-35.

11. Inter alia, the summary of events surrounding the PNC conclave in Cairo on July 1 and 17 is based on the following: *ARR*, May 1-15, 1968, p. 128; May 16-31, 1968, inside cover; July 1-15, 1968, p. 199; July 16-31, 1968, p. 214; *NYT*, July 14 and 16, 1968; *Le Monde* (Paris), August 10, 1968.

12. On the PLO-PLA crisis, see *ARR*, July 16-31, 1968, p. 216; August 1-15, 1968, p. 234; November 1-15, 1968, back cover; *NYT*, August 4 and 11, 1968; *Middle East Journal*, Autumn 1968, p. 478; *Le Monde* (Paris), August 10, 1968. Budayri was favored by the Syrian regime.

13. *An-Nahar Arab Report*, October 11, 1971, p. 2.

14. *ARR*, September 1-15, 1968, p. 272; September 16-30, 1968, p. 292; *DSB*, November 28, 1969.

15. *Guardian* (Manchester), September 3, 1968.

16. *ARR*, November 16-30, 1968, front cover and p. 383. Also see Abbas Kelidar, "Shifts and Changes in the Arab World," *World Today*, November 1968, p. 509.

17. *ARR*, October 1-15, 1968, p. 315; October 16-31, 1968, pp. 339-340 and back cover; November 1-15, 1968, p. 364. According to the November report, the planning council was set up to act as an independent advisory board which would submit projects to the PLO for approval.

18. *NYT*, November 6 and 11, 1968.

19. On the events in January and February 1968, see *ARR*, January 1-15, 1969, p. 19; January 16-31, 1969, p. 43 and front cover; May 1-15, 1969, p. 195; February 1-14, 1969, p. 65; February 15-28, 1969, pp. 73-74 and 89; *NYT*, February 2, 5, and 21, 1969; March 4, 1969; Mertz, "George Habash," p. 36; Michael Hudson, "The Palestinian Arab Resistance Movement: Its Significance in the Middle East Crisis," *Middle East Journal*, Summer 1969, p. 298; J. Gaspard, "Palestine, Who's Who Among the Guerrillas," *New Middle East*, March 1970, pp. 13-14. The PFLP-GC split because it wished to avoid preoccupation with ideology in favor of concentrating on the struggle against Israel.

20. Leila S. Kadi, comp. and trans., *Basic Documents of the Armed Palestinian Resistance Movement* (Beirut: Palestine Liberation Organization Research Center, 1968), p. 32; Mertz, "George Habash," p. 36. As Mertz points out, the PFLP moderates did not drop the Marxist-Leninist ideology. For them it was partly utilitarian and partly commitment. Similar comments are found in Gaspard, "Who's Who Among the Guerrillas," pp. 13-14; *ARR*, Special Supplement, June 1971, p. 314. The reader interested in a detailed comparison of the PDF and PFLP views should consult Kadi, *Basic Political Documents*, pp. 143-247.

21. See the PDF pamphlet *On Terrorism, Role of the Party, Leninism Versus Zionism* (Buffalo: Palestine Solidarity Committee, State University of New York at Buffalo, n.d.), pp. 2-5 (also found in the PDF paper *Al-Hurriya* (Beirut), September 12, 1969); interview with secretary-general of the Central Committee of the Popular Democratic Front for the Liberaiton of Palestine, Nayef Hawatmeh, in *An-Nahar* (Beirut), August 17, 1973 as excerpted in *JPS*, Autumn 1973, pp. 198-199.

22. See the remarks of George Habash in Oriana Fallaci, "A Leader of the *Fedayeen*: We Want a War Like the Vietnamese War," *Life*, June 12, 1970, p. 34.

Though the position on finances was an outgrowth of the PFLP's Marxist-Leninist ideology, which depicted reactionary states as organic parts of the world imperialist system, it no doubt also reflected PFLP chagrin with the fact that such money strengthened its rivals.

23. On the differences over tactics, see Hudson, "Palestinian Arab Resistance," p. 299; *NYT*, March 2, 1969; Gaspard, "Who's Who Among Guerrillas," p. 14. Habash was not reticent about defending attacks on civilians and operations outside the Middle East. Indeed, he indicated they would continue. See *ARR*, March 1-15, 1969, p. 112; *NYT*, March 4, 1969. PFLP statements corroborated Habash's public view. See *ARR*, March 16-31, 1969, p. 133. Although *Fatah* officially disapproved of attacks on civilians, it carried out a number of raids against civilian areas, justifying them as reprisals for Israeli attacks on Arab civilians. See *Free Palestine*, June 1969, p. 23; *Fatah* General Command Operations Order 546, August 27, 1969, reprinted in *New Middle East*, October 1969, p. 4.

24. J. Gaspard, "Palestine: The Struggle of a People to Become a Nation," *New Middle East*, September 1970, p. 31.

25. *ARR*, May 16-31, 1969, p. 214; June 1-15, 1969, pp. 241 and 250; June 16-30, 1969, p. 270; September 16-30, 1969, p. 404. The last contains the estimated losses by country resulting from the Tapline explosion.

26. *ARR*, June 16-30, 1969, p. 270. *Fatah* mentioned the fact that the PFLP refused to cooperate and coordinate with the PASC. In March, both the PFLP and the PDF had claimed credit for a Hebrew University blast and the PASC had indicated it was convinced the PDF did it. See *ARR*, March 1-15, 1969, p. 109.

27. Cited in *ARR*, June 1-15, 1969, p. 246.

28. *NYT*, June 15, 1969; *ARR*, June 1-15, 1969, p. 250; *International Herald Tribune* (Paris), June 16, 1969. The four groups were identified as: (1) a splinter from the PFLP led by Subhi Ghoshey; (2) The United Palestine Struggle (an extreme leftist group in Gaza); (3) the ALF; and (4) the PFLP-GC. In addition, *Fatah* was apprehensive about reported Jordanian plans to establish a guerrilla organization called *Fatah al-Islam*.

29. *Al-Jumhuriyah* is cited in *ARR*, July 1-15, 1969, p. 294. See also *ARR*, September 16-30, 1969, p. 404; *NYT*, July 5, 1969.

30. Interview with K. Kudsi (*Fatah*) in *Free Palestine*, August 1969. Kudsi said he hoped the PASC would play the leading role in the revolution. The implication was, of course, that it was not yet doing so.

31. On the PNC meeting, see *ARR*, September 1-15, 1969, pp. 376-377; *NYT*, September 2, 1969.

32. *ARR*, November 1-15, 1969, p. 474; *NYT*, November 6, 1969.

33. Citations and comments are found in *ARR*, November 1-15, 1969, p. 456; November 16-30, 1969, p. 503.

34. *ARR*, December 1-15, 1969, pp. 523-524; December 16-31, 1969, p. 552. Another PDF-*Fatah* disagreement over a raid would occur within a month when both claimed credit for an Elath explosion that caused a large number of casualties.

35. *ARR*, January 16-31, 1970, p. 81. Some observers concluded—somewhat precipitously it now appears—in 1969 and early 1970 that the resistance had taken meaningful steps toward unity. Hudson, "Palestinian Arab Resistance," p. 299, for

example, said that fusion rather than fission was the dominant theme in the fedayeen movement and in a later article he cited the PASC and the PLO as confirmation of the increased cohesion. See Michael Hudson, "Fedayeen are Forcing Lebanon's Hand," *Mid East*, February 1970, pp. 10-11. Time, however, would show that the PASC and the PLO were impressive in form but lacking in substance, since ideological, tactical and personal rivalries would continue to defy attempts to unify the movement. An even more optimistic appraisal claimed that there were still five or six guerrilla organizations after the mergers. See Abdullah Schleifer, "The Emergence of *Fatah*," *Arab World*, May 1969, p. 20.

36. The UCPR, which included seven members of the PASC, consisted of the following organizations: *Fatah, Sa'iqa*, the PFLP, PDF, ALF, PFLP-GC, APO, AOLP, Popular Arab Liberation Forces, and the Popular Organization for the Liberation of Palestine (POLP). See *ARR*, February 14-28, 1970, p. 136.

37. *ARR*, February 1-14, 1970, p. 110; *NYT*, February 12, 1970; *Free Palestine*, April 1970, p. 4.

38. *ARR*, February 15-28, 1970, p. 137.

39. *New Middle East*, May 1970, p. 9. The same source contains the Habash quote and accounts of the seminars (pp. 8-9).

40. Ibid., p. 9.

41. The statement is reprinted in *Mid East*, August 1970, p. 43. Groups identified in the new CCPR were *Fatah, Sa'iqa*, the PFLP, the PDF, the PFLP-GC, the ALF, the AOLP, the POLP, the PSF, the PLO (PLF), and the APO. A communist group, *Al-Ansar*, did not sign the May 6 statement. Although its application to the CCPR had been made in March, *Fatah* objected to *Al-Ansar*'s membership on the grounds that it had accepted SC-242. In August 1970, *The National Flag*, the paper of the AOLP, indicated that the PFLP and the PLF lobbied for *Al-Ansar*'s admission to the movement whereas *Fatah*, the AOLP, and the APO objected. See *DSB*, August 15, 1970. On the creation of *Al-Ansar*, see *ARR*, March 1-15, 1970, p. 163.

42. *NYT*, May 23, 1970; *DSB*, May 23, 1970; *Africa Diary*, June 25-July 1, 1970, p. 5016.

43. *ARR*, May 16-31, 1970, p. 312; *DSB*, May 29, 1970.

44. *ARR*, May 16-31, 1970, p. 312; *DSB*, May 29, 1970.

45. *ARR*, May 16-31, 1970, p. 312.

46. *Mid East*, August 1970, p. 19, reported that the PASC had merely carried out police operations and issued communiqués.

47. *ARR*, June 1-15, 1970, pp. 343-344; *DSB*, June 5 and 6, 1970; *Mid East*, August 1970, p. 19. Of the fedayeen organizations in the CCPR only *Fatah, Sa'iqa*, the PDF, and the PLF were represented on the PLO-EC, according to *NYT*, June 13, 1970.

48. This point was explicitly made by Ahmad Yamani of the PFLP. See *ARR*, June 1-15, 1970, p. 344.

49. *DSB*, June 17, 1970; Eric Pace, "The Violent Men of Amman," *New York Times Magazine*, July 19, 1970, p. 35. Pace noted that despite the CCPR most guerrilla organizations seemed to reserve day-to-day decision-making to themselves. Similar comments were made by John M. Mecklin, "Fire and Steel for Palestine," *Fortune*, July 1970, p. 135.

50. *ARR*, June 1-15, 1970, p. 344; *DSB*, June 4, 1970.

51. *ARR*, June 1-15, 1970, p. 344; *DSB*, June 6 and 12, 1970; *NYT*, June 5, 1970. *NYT* reported that attacks on civilian airliners were proscribed at the PNC meeting. This was contrary to Yamani's assertions. That *NYT* was in error was suggested by a report in *DSB* on June 5, 1970 to the effect that just what constituted a legitimate commando operation was not defined at the PNC.

52. On the Jordanian clashes and reports of PFLP instigation, see *Al-Ahram* (Cairo), June 9, 1970, and *Al-Thawra* (Baghdad), June 10, 1970, as cited in *New Middle East*, July 1970, p. 8. On the formation of the secretariat and the CCPR assumption of command, see *ARR*, June 16-30, 1970, p. 373. For skepticism that unity had been achieved with the new organizational moves, see *Sa'iqa*'s views in *ARR*, July 1-15, 1970, p. 402; also, the comments of *Le Nouvel Observateur* cited in *ARR*, July 16-31, 1970, p. 433.

53. *ARR*, June 16-30, 1970, p. 374; *DSB*, June 11, 12, and 17, 1970; Pace, "The Violent Men of Amman," p. 41.

54. *DSB*, June 24, 1970.

55. *ARR*, June 16-30, 1970, p. 373; *DSB*, June 25, 1970.

56. *DSB*, June 28, 1970. Similar indirect criticism of the left-wing groups was made by Arafat in an interview appearing in *Free Palestine*, August 1970, pp. 1 and 6.

57. *DSB*, July 11, 1970; *NYT*, July 11, 1970.

58. *DSB*, July 14, 18, and 24, 1970. *Sa'iqa* and the ALF also expressed reservations about the July 10 accord. See *ARR*, July 1-15, 1970, p. 402.

59. *DSB*, July 11, 1970; *NYT*, July 11, 1970.

60. *ARR*, July 16-31, 1970, p. 430; *DSB*, July 25-29, 1970.

61. *ARR*, July 16-31, 1970, p. 430; *DSB*, July 31 and August 7, 1970. The AOLP broke with *Fatah* in 1968. The APO was a splinter group from the PFLP which was led by Ahmad Zaarour. Both organizations were minor ones, whose actions were limited in scope.

62. On the internecine conflict, see *ARR*, August 1-15, 1970, p. 462; *DSB*, August 3, 6 through 8, 10 through 13, and 15, 1970; *NYT*, August 6 and 7, 1970.

63. *ARR*, August 16-31, 1970, p. 488; *NYT*, August 28 and 29, 1970. The importance of unity for facing up to Arab regimes that might accept settlement was stressed by the fedayeen as far back as May 1970, according to *Arab Report* as cited in *Mid East*, August 1970, p. 20.

64. See Appendix B, Tables B-6 and B-7. Prior to the civil war, the editions of *Free Palestine* carried a summary of the prior month's fedayeen military activity. After the civil war, there was no military summary. On the reduced fedayeen manpower, see "The Palestinian Resistance and Jordan," *JPS*, Autumn 1971, p. 164.

65. In May 1971, Nabil Shaath admitted that the guerrillas had lost the battle of Amman. See the interview with Shaath entitled "Liberation: Creating Something New in the Middle East," *Free Palestine*, July 1971, p. 4.

66. *DSB*, September 13 through 15, 1970; *NYT*, September 1 through 15, 1970, p. 508. One observer indicated that *Fatah* was also perturbed by the hijacking because some of its members were defecting to the more exciting PFLP. See Edward R. F. Sheehan, "In the Flaming Streets of Amman," *New York Times Magazine*,

September 27, 1970, p. 109.

67. *DSB*, September 15, 1970.

68. *DSB*, September 10 and 15, 1970.

69. *ARR*, September 16 through 30, 1970, p. 538.

70. *NYT*, October 10 and 12, 1970; *DSB*, October 18, 1970; *ARR*, October 16-31, 1970, p. 601; November 16-30, 1970, p. 655. An editorial in *Free Palestine*, December 1970, p. 2, argued that the need for unity was the most important lesson learned from the civil war.

71. On the PFLP remarks, see the PFLP statement in *New Middle East*, November 1970, p. 49; *DSB*, October 15, 1970; *ARR*, October 1-15, 1970, p. 551. The PLO desire to avoid friction with Jordan could be seen in the arrests of militiamen by the PLO for violations of the agreements. See, for example, *DSB*, November 10, 1970.

72. *DSB*, November 13, 16, and 26, 1970; *NYT*, November 4, 1970. The merger reflected the long-held *Fatah* view that parties should be avoided because they could only allow for a coalition which contained the seeds of a schism. This outlook was, of course, contrary to the left-wing view which held that party identity and ideology could not be cast aside. See Ehud Yaari, "*Al-Fath*'s Political Thinking," *New Outlook*, November/December 1968, p. 32.

73. Cited in *ARR*, November 16-30, 1970, p. 655.

74. *DSB*, November 27, 1970. Events surrounding the smaller groups at the time were somewhat confusing. The PSF was suspended from operating in Lebanon by the HPCPA and several of its members were arrested for an attack on PASC forces. The AOLP was absorbed by *Fatah* and the following month the PASC raided an AOLP office and arrested its leader, Issam Sartawi, who had reportedly come to Lebanon to broach the idea of a Palestinian state. To further complicate matters the Syrian coup by Assad put *Sa'iqa* in an uncertain position since Assad was a rival of *Sa'iqa*'s civilian chief, Salah Jedid. Accounts of these developments can be found in *ARR*, November 1-15, 1970, p. 616; November 16-30, 1970, pp. 638 and 655; *DSB*, November 21, 1970, and January 1, 1971.

75. Cited in *ARR*, November 16-30, 1970, p. 655.

76. *ARR*, December 1-15, 1970, p. 680.

77. The same day the secretariat was announced, it was reported that 1,000 defectors from the PLO had established a new organization called the Yarmuk Brigade in southern Syria. See *ARR*, December 16-31, 1970, p. 702.

78. *ARR*, January 1-15, 1971, p. 48.

79. *DSB*, January 17 and 19, 1971; *NYT*, January 18, 1971.

80. On the *Fatah* reaction to the PFLP stand, see *ARR*, January 16-31, 1971, p. 78; *DSB*, January 18,1971.

81. *DSB*, January 16 and 30, 1971.

82. *DSB*, January 19 and 22, 1971.

83. *DSB*, January 21, 1971; *ARR*, January 16-31, 1971, p. 78. The fedayeen fissions once again led Qadhdhafi to blast disunity, especially "deviationist, secessionist organizations" (the PDF and PFLP). See *ARR*, January 16-31, 1971, p. 62.

84. *DSB*, January 28, 1971. The problem of discipline became more serious, with

fedayeen organizations losing control of some members during clashes with the Jordanians the following month. See *DSB*, February 27, 1971.

85. *DSB*, February 18 and 20, 1971. The latter issue contains a detailed listing of Yahya's proposals.

86. On the PLO-CC meetings of February 20-22, see *DSB*, February 21, 1971; *Le Monde* (Paris), February 20, 1971; AP dispatch in *Denver Post*, February 21, 1971; AP dispatch in *Los Angeles Times*, February 25, 1971, pt. 1.

87. *ARR*, February 15-28, 1971, p. 129.

88. *DSB*, February 28, 1971.

89. *Free Palestine*, February 1971, p. 1. The PDF also stressed the need for unity, albeit in a united front in which the left should strive "to insure the hegemony of proletarian ideology." See *Palestine Resistance Bulletin*, March 1971, p. 1; also pp. 2-7, for repeated references about the need for unity and ways to achieve it.

90. *ARR*, March 1-15, 1971, p. 156; *New Middle East*, April 1971, p. 50; *Free Palestine*, May 1971, p. 2. *Al-Ansar* reportedly agreed to reject SC-242 in return for its recognition by the PNC. In September the PFLP indicated it still approved of hijackings. See *DSB*, September 9, 1971.

91. *ARR*, March 1-15, 1971, p. 156; *DSB*, March 1 and 13, 1971.

92. *Near East Report*, July 7, 1971, p. 107.

93. Examples of optimistic statements by *Fatah* can be found in *ARR*, March 16-31, 1971, p. 184; *DSB*, March 12, 1971.

94. *DSB*, March 12, 1971. The discussion of the unity plan was to be limited to three months. A military committee was also set up to reorganize the resistance forces. See *DSB*, March 7 and 16, 1971; *Free Palestine*, April 1971, p. 1.

95. *DSB*, March 23 and April 8, 1971.

96. *DSB*, May 29, 1971.

97. *DSB*, June 3, 1971. One knowledgeable observer stated flatly that there was "little doubt that much of the initial shooting was due to the simple fact that the fedayeen were totally disunited." See J. Gaspard, "Palestinian Waterloo at Ajloun—Military Myths and Political Realities," *New Middle East*, September 1971, p. 12.

98. *DSB*, June 15, 1971.

99. *ARR*, July 1-15, 1971, p. 35; *NYT*, July 5, 1971. There were reports that Syria favored turning over the Algerian arms to the PLA. Since Syria was friendly to the PLA, this was plausible. See *Daily Star Sunday Supplement* (Beirut), July 11, 1971, p. 12.

100. *Free Palestine*, August 1971, p. 8, indicated that the PNC was increased by four to 155 due to the extension of representation to four minor organizations—PSF, the POLP, APO, and AOLP.

101. *DSB*, July 12 and 13, 1971. For a discussion of the "objective and subjective" factors which, according to the PDF, made a merger impossible, see *Palestine Resistance Bulletin*, October 1971, pp. 2 and 11. Among the factors cited were the class divisions of the Palestinian people, their geographical dispersion, the interference of the Arab states, and the lack of democracy in "national relations."

102. *ARR*, July 1-15, 1971, p. 366; *DSB*, July 10, 1971; *Free Palestine*, August 1971, p. 8.

103. *DSB*, July 14, 1971; *ARR*, July 1-15, 1971, p. 366.

104. *DSB*, July 6, 1971.

105. Interview of Abu Iyad (also known as Salah Khalef) reprinted in *Free Palestine*, September/October 1971, p. 6.

106. Cited in *DSB*, September 4, 1971; see also *DSB*, September 5, 1971; *NYT*, September 6, 1971.

107. Cited in *DSB*, September 7, 1971.

108. *DSB*, September 5, 1971.

109. On *Fatah*'s problems, see *An-Nahar Arab Report*, September 13, 1971, p. 1; *DSB*, September 3 and 5, 1971.

110. *DSB*, September 8, 1971; *NYT*, September 9, 1971. The ALF joined the PFLP in rejecting the policy. Those in favor were the four *Fatah* representatives, two from *Sa'iqa* and one independent.

111. *JPS*, Autumn 1971, pp. 168-170; *An-Nahar Arab Report*, October 4, 1971, pp. 1-2. The major obstacle to reconciliation was Jordan's refusal to allow the fedayeen to return to bases inside the country, especially after the price paid by the army in forcing them out.

112. *DSB*, September 17, 1971. That the Jordanian government had not lost sight of the continued hostility of the left-wing groups was reflected in the remarks of its spokesmen. See *DSB*, October 5, 1971.

113. *ARR*, September 16-30, 1971, p. 521; October 1-15, 1971, p. 547; *DSB*, September 26 and October 8, 1971; *NYT*, September 29, 1971; *An-Nahar Arab Report*, October 4, 1971, p. 4. As with most such events, this conflict was complicated. Prior to Baradi's capture, followers of Haddad had been captured by Yahya's forces, thus setting off a chain of events leading to Baradi's death.

114. Cited in *DSB*, October 10, 1971; see also *DSB*, October 7 and 8, 1971.

115. The new PLO-EC was comprised of four representatives from *Fatah*, two from the PFLP, two from the PDF, two from *Sa'iqa*, one from the ALF and two independents. The PSF, APO, and PF-GC had virtually suspended operations. See *NYT*, April 14, 1972.

116. *JPS*, Summer 1972, p. 154; Riad El-Rayyes and Dunia Nahas, *Guerrillas for Palestine* (New York: St. Martins Press, 1976), pp. 39-41; *NYT*, July 25 and 27, 1973. The PRFLP split came after Habash refused to purge the PFLP leadership. The group dissolved in 1974.

117. *Ha'arez* (Tel Aviv), March 22, 1973, reported on the Rome incidents. The controversy within *Fatah* pitted Khalid al-Hassan (a rightist) against Salah Khalef (a leftist). Hassan argued against terrorism, criticized the Khartoum assassinations, favored closer relations with the Arab regimes, blamed the fighting in Jordan on the left-wing guerrillas, and emphasized the need to buttress the main forces. Khalef favored closer ties with the left-wing groups and considered attacks on any group as an attack on the overall movement. In this dispute al-Hassan lost and was removed from the PLO-EC. See *Middle East Intelligence Survey* (Tel Aviv: Middle East Information Media, 1973), pp. 2-3; El-Rayyes and Nahas, *Guerrillas for Palestine*, pp. 33-34.

118. The linkage between *Fatah* and the BSO was revealed by the Khartoum incident in March 1973 and by the interrogation of Abu Dawud in Jordan. See "Abu

Dawud Testimony Before Jordanian Military Tribunal," Amman Domestic Service in Arabic, March 24, 1973, in *FBIS/ME*, March 26, 1973, pp. D-1–D-12, especially D-10 and D-11; Christopher Dobson, *Black September: Its Short, Violent History* (New York: Macmillan Co., 1974), pp. 38-40 and 45-50. Previously, there were numerous reports attributed to Israeli and European intelligence services, Arab informants and Palestinians which explicitly identified the links between *Fatah* and the BSO as: (1) funding; (2) command direction; (3) *Fatah* membership. See, for example, *NYT*, September 8 and 18, 1972. A particularly good piece of investigative reporting on the subject is Eric Pace, "The Black September Guerrillas: An Elusive Trail in Six Countries," *NYT*, October 12, 1972. For an apologia for the BSO, see Mury Gilbert, *September Noir* (Paris: Sindbad, 1972).

119. On point (1) see Dobson, *Black September*, pp. 38-39; on point (2) see Dobson, p. 62. With regard to the latter, Dobson points out that, unlike the frequently indiscriminate operations of the PFLP, the BSO targets were people or establishments which could be classified as pro-Israel. On point (3) see Abu Iyad's comments cited in *Time*, February 12, 1973, p. 29.

120. *NYT*, May 3, 1973; *Time*, May 14, 1973, p. 41.

121. *ARR*, April 16-30, 1971, p. 231.

122. *ARR*, November 16-30, 1969, p. 504; *NYT*, April 17, 1969; *Mid East*, August 1970, p. 19; *Free Palestine*, March 1969, p. 4.

123. Even sympathizers of the fedayeen lamented the unity crisis. See the discussion of the unity problem in light of the Algerian and Vietnamese models in Ania Francos, "The Palestinian Revolution and the Third World," in Naseer Aruri, ed., *The Palestine Resistance to Israeli Occupation* (Wilmette, Ill.: Medina University Press International, 1970), pp. 45-47.

124. Few pro-fedayeen or fedayeen writers gave much thought to organizational problems. For one who did, see Tareq Y. Ismael, "Toward a Revolutionary Strategy," in Aruri, *Palestinian Resistance*, p. 83.

125. Actually, Israel did provide a limited degree of expressive protest by allowing Arab papers like *Al-Quds* (Jerusalem) to criticize the government openly.

126. On the PFLP cells, see *ARR*, November 16-30, 1969, p. 503; *NYT*, August 10, March 2 and 8, 1969. On the *Fatah* cells, see *ARR*, November 16-30, 1969, p. 503; *NYT*, November 4, 1967; February 7, 1968; Edward Ghareeb, "An Interview with Abu Ammar (Arafat)," *Arab World*, May 1969, p. 28. A number of non-Arab observers have cited the early PFLP and *Fatah* attempts to organize in the occupied areas. See, for example, Harkabi, *Fedayeen Action*, p. 26; John B. Wolf, "The Palestinian Resistance Movement," *Current History*, January 1971, p. 29.

127. Tom Lambert, "Will Israeli Reprisals Eliminate Palestinian Commando Resistance," *DSB*, May 31, 1970. Harkabi, *Fedayeen Action*, p. 26, points out that Israel's main problem was not destroying guerrilla networks, since they were not significant. Rather, it was preventing them from being set up in the first place.

128. *Middle East Intelligence Survey*, pp. 1-2.

129. It was interesting to note that in the one sector of the occupied areas where Arafat said the fedayeen spent thirty percent of their resources, Gaza, the fedayeen had a modicum of popular support. See *DSB*, July 8, 1971. One guerrilla supporter argued that while "something of a shadow government" had been created, there

was a need to assess the movement's organizational capability. In another context, he described the fedayeen organization as rudimentary. See Ismael, "Toward a Revolutionary Strategy," pp. 86-87. For a brief assessment of the relative organizational abilities of the Palestine groups, see Gerard Chaliand, *The Palestinian Resistance* (Baltimore: Penguin Books, 1972), pp. 67-129. Chaliand's obvious sympathy with the PDF is natural since he is a Marxist.

130. *NYT*, August 6, 1968. There was subsequent confirmation of the fedayeen status in the camps. See *ARR*, Special Supplement, June 1971; *NYT*, February 27, 1970; Neville Brown, "Palestinian Nationalism and the Jordanian State," *World Today*, September 1970, p. 370.

131. Hudson, "Palestinian Arab Resistance," p. 292; *Daily News* (Kuwait), January 1, 1970; Schleifer, "The Emergence of Fatah," p. 20; Neville Brown, "Jordan's Precarious Truce: How Long Will It Last?" *New Middle East*, June 1970, p. 10; *ARR*, Special Supplement, June 1971, p. 313. In early 1971, in the midst of declining fortunes, *Fatah* turned its offices in the refugee camps into social centers, according to *DSB*, January 5, 1971.

132. *Free Palestine*, March 1970, p. 6. For a good article on the Palestinian Red Crescent Society, see *DSB*, August 9, 1970.

133. *NYT*, November 14, 18, and 26, 1969.

134. *ARR*, February 1-14, 1970, p. 91; February 15-28, 1970, p. 119; *NYT*, February 27, 1970.

135. On the role of women, see *Free Palestine*, June 1969, p. 5; Ghareeb, "An Interview with Abu Ammar," p. 28; David Waines, *The Unholy War* (Wilmette, Ill.: Medina University Press International, 1971), p. 186.

136. On the militias and their role, see *DSB*, June 9, September 17, and December 17, 1970; Brown, "Palestinian Nationalism," p. 375. Joe Alex Morris reported in *DSB*, November 10, 1970, that the militias were disproportionately attached to the PFLP and PDF.

137. See Morroe Berger, *The Arab World Today* (Garden City, N.Y.: Anchor Books, 1964), pp. 136-155. Two commentators explicitly linked this to fedayeen disunity. See Mecklin, "Fire and Steeel," p. 87; Wolf, "The Palestinian Resistance Movement," p. 26.

138. Hudson, "Palestinian Arab Resistance," pp. 295-297.

139. The term "moderately" is used because it is possible that the rhetoric of the groups which were hostile to the regime would have been sufficient to bring an end to popular support even if the hostile organizations were disciplined. In addition, intervening variables such as regime reprisals can end external support.

Chapter 7

1. See Walter Laqueur, *The Road to War* (Baltimore: Penguin Books, 1968), pp. 69-73; Fred J. Khouri, *The Arab-Israeli Dilemma* (Syracuse, N.Y.: Syracuse University Press, 1968), pp. 231-232 and 280; Nadav Safran, *From War to War* (New York: Pegasus, 1969), p. 45; Malcolm Kerr, *The Arab Cold War: 1958-1967*, 2nd ed. (London: Oxford University Press, 1967), pp. 153-155.

2. Kerr, *Arab Cold War*, pp. 161-162.

3. One Jordanian official with whom I discussed this matter freely acknowledged that the fedayeen not only constituted a strong force in the Jordan River valley in 1968-1969, but they also gained considerable support from the local people and some elements of the army.

4. Hussein's willingness to accept Israel's existence was well known. See, for instance, the BBC interview cited in *ARR*, January 1-15, 1969, p. 21; interview of King Hussein by Leo Janos, *Time*, April 18, 1969, p. 29. On the contradictory aspects of Jordanian policy, see *NYT*, July 25, September 6, and October 5, 21, and 28, 1967. Similarly, the meetings between Jordanian officials and the Israelis were well known, although denied by Amman for various reasons. See *Middle East Journal*, Winter 1969, p. 66; *NYT*, October 18-19, 1969. John K. Cooley, *Green March, Black September* (London: Frank Cass, 1973), p. 5, estimates that Hussein held up to ten to twelve meetings with the Israelis from 1968 to 1972.

5. *NYT*, March 26, 1968.

6. See *War by Terror*, rev. ed. (Jerusalem: Ministry for Foreign Affairs, Information Division, 1970), p. 16. Even prior to the Jordanian civil war, a number of clashes between the fedayeen and Jordanian forces exposed the Israeli contention as simplistic propaganda.

7. Convenient and easily accessible sources that provide good information on the episodes of violence are as follows: For the November 1968 clash, *ARR*, October 1-15, 1968, front cover; October 16-31, 1968, p. 339; November 1-15, 1968, p. 350; *Middle East Journal*, Winter 1969, p. 71; *NYT*, October 15, 18, 20 and November 5, 6, 16, 24, and 25, 1968. On the February 1970 incidents, see *ARR*, February 1-14, 1970, p. 89; *Free Palestine*, April 1970, pp. 4 and 6; *NYT*, February 12, 14, 16, and 22, 1970. For June 1970, *ARR*, May 1-15, 1970, pp. 265-266; *New Middle East*, June 1970, p. 50; *NYT*, April 16, 17, and 18, and May 30, 1970; J. Gaspard, "Palestine— The Struggle of Arab People to Become a Nation," *New Middle East*, September 1970, pp. 31-32. Gaspard erroneously concludes that the fedayeen were so successful in June that they had achieved the power of ultimately deciding what would happen to the army and government (p. 32). Fedayeen strength was also prematurely judged by Shlomo Avineri, "The Palestinians and Israel," *Commentary*, June 1970, p. 38. On the September 1970 civil war, see *ARR*, September 1-15, 1970, pp. 493-495; September 16-30, 1970, pp. 517-521, 530 and 537; *DSB*, September 1-4, 10-11, 14-17, 21, 23, 25, and 27, 1970; *NYT*, September 1, 3, 5, 8, 9-14, 16-19, 21-26, and October 2 and 11, 1970.

8. Marvin Kalb and Bernard Kalb, *Kissinger* (Boston: Little, Brown and Co., 1974), pp. 201-206. The Kalbs assert that Jordan actively sought possible military support from Israel.

9. *ARR*, January 1-15, 1971, p. 31.

10. On the July coup de grace, see "The Palestinian Resistance and Jordan," *JPS*, Autumn 1971, pp. 162-166; *ARR*, July 1-15, 1971, pp. 349-350; July 16-31, 1971, pp. 376-377, 391, and 395; *DBS*, July 1 and 14-20, 1971; *NYT*, July 8, 14, and 21, 1970.

11. One of the principal reasons for Hussein's success was the near absolute loyalty of the army, which, if differing at all from the king, usually took a harder line against the fedayeen. The army's loyalty was due to the fact that its hard core was largely composed of loyal and apolitical Bedouins, whose tribal allegiance had

been transformed into support for Hussein. Also important was the religious dimension, which emphasized the king as a descendant of the Prophet, and the high pay and material privileges extended to the military. On these points, see *An-Nahar Arab Report*, September 13, 1971, p. 2; Neville Brown, "Jordan's Precarious Truce—How Long Can It Last?" *New Middle East*, June 1970, p. 11; Tom Little, *The New Arab Extremists* (London: Current Affairs Research Center, 1970), p. 17. Hussein's 56,000-man army was one-third Bedouin from Jordan, one-third Bedouin from adjacent Arab states, and one-third Palestinian. The crucial armored brigades were almost entirely Bedouin. See Edgar O'Ballance, *Arab Guerrilla Power* (London: Faber and Faber, 1974), pp. 144-145.

12. For the full text of Hussein's proposal, see Amman, Domestic Service in Arabic, March 15, 1972 in *FBIS/ME*, March 15, 1972, pp. D1-D6. On the Arab reaction, see *JPS*, Summer 1972, pp. 155-157.

13. Aims of the Political Programme of the Palestinian Revolution adopted by the Eleventh Palestine National Congress, Cairo, January 12, 1973 in *JPS*, Spring 1973, pp. 171-172.

14. Interview of Abu Iyad, *Free Palestine*, September/October 1971, p. 7.

15. A good example of the distinction between moral and political support can be found in the comments of the Jordanian ambassador to the United Nations in 1968. See Muhammad H. El-Farra, "The Case for the Palestinian Resistance," *Arab World*, May 1969, pp. 4-5. Although El-Farra gave moral sanction to the resistance by equating it to the anti-Nazi resistance, he carefully avoided contradicting Jordanian political aims in that he linked it to the Israeli occupation.

16. This was a point that Arab radicals always made when they argued that Hussein was ultimately unreliable. Politics aside, the West Bank was important to Jordan since it accounted for nine-tenths of the tourist industry.

17. One of the principal reasons Hussein moved in September was pressure from the army, which felt it had been humiliated. Reports that fedayeen had paraded soldiers around towns with their hands over their heads no doubt increased the hatred and helped explain the ferocious fighting of the Bedouins. Even guerrilla leaders later complained of the "domineering attitude" of certain commandos as a mistake. See the comments of Farouk Qaddumi in *DSB*, December 16, 1970. With this situation as a backdrop, the initial Jordanian inaction in the face of the multiple skyjacking in September led to army pressure on Hussein to act. The king reported that the army was particularly discontented and recounted that one of the squadron chiefs, when queried about why he was flying a brassiere from the antenna of his tank, replied it was because "We are women." See Edward R. F. Sheehan, "In the Flaming Streets of Amman," *New York Times Magazine*, September 27, 1970, p. 111.

18. On relations between Lebanon and the fedayeen prior to the June War, see Laqueur, *Road to War*, pp. 69 and 71-72; Khouri, *Arab-Israeli Dilemma*, pp. 242-243; Safran, *War to War*, p. 46; Y. Harkabi, *Fedayeen Action and Arab Strategy*, Adelphi Papers no. 53 (London: International Institute for Strategic Studies, 1968), p. 7. The last three authors give little attention to Lebanon, no doubt because in a relative sense it was not as important as other border states in the pre-June 1967 period.

19. *NYT*, November 13-16, 1968.

20. *Times* (London), January 23, 1969; *ARR*, January 1-15, 1969, p. 6; *NYT*, January 2-7 and February 20-23, 1969.

21. *DSB*, July 1-3 and 8, 1970; *Fatah* (Beirut), July 1 and 17, 1970; *ARR*, July 16-31, 1970, p. 414; August 1-15, 1970, p. 462; October 1-15, 1970, p. 555; October 1-16, 1970, pp. 582 and 589; *NYT*, July 8, 14, and 20, and August 10, 19, and 26, 1970; *DSB*, October 5, 13, and 26, 1970.

22. On the role that the issue of sovereignty played in the conflicts, see the *An-Nahar* report cited in *DSB*, April 21, 1970; *Times* (London), December 5, 1969; *ARR*, December 1-15, 1969, p. 510; January 16-31, 1970, p. 64; February 1-14, 1970, p. 91; February 15-28, 1970, p. 119; *ARR*, June 1-15, 1970, p. 325; *NYT*, December 3, 5, and 7, 1969, January 20, 1970, May 23, 1973; *DSB*, June 1, 6, 11, 18, and 30, 1970; and *L'Orient Le Jour* (Beirut), February 10, 1970.

23. See, for instance, *ARR*, November 16-30, 1969, p. 503; *NYT*, November 6, 1969, June 30, 1972. For Habash, the Lebanese government was "reactionary and rotten." See Oriana Fallaci, "A Leader of the Fedayeen: We Want a War Like the Vietnam War," *Life*, June 12, 1970, p. 34.

24. The elements of the consociational model and their relevance to Lebanon may be found in Arend Lijphart, "Typologies of Democratic Systems," *Comparative Politics*, April 1968, and "Consociational Democracy," *World Politics*, January 1969. For an excellent analysis of why it failed in Lebanon, see Michael C. Hudson, "The Lebanese Crisis: The Limits of Consociational Democracy," *JPS*, Spring/Summer 1976.

25. On Syrian-fedayeen relations prior to the June War, see Laqueur, *Road to War*, pp. 67-72; Khouri, *Arab-Israeli Dilemma*, pp. 242-244; Safran, *War to War*, pp. 26 and 130; Harkabi, *Fedayeen Action*, pp. 22-24.

26. *ARR*, April 16-30, 1968, p. 107; May 1-15, 1968, pp. 120 and 124; September 16-30, 1968, p. 287; *NYT*, April 12 and 16, August 11, and September 20, 1968. *NYT*, May 23, 1968, reported that the ANM, the Syrian Arab Socialist Union and the Arab Socialist Party had united in the hope of overthrowing the Ba'thist regime. On the arrest of Habash, also see Robert Anton Mertz, "Why George Habash Turned Marxist," *Mid East*, August 1970, pp. 35-36. As might have been anticipated, the propaganda apparatus in Israel chose to either downplay or ignore the Syrian actions against the PFLP, thus leaving the impression that Damascus supported the group. See, for example, *War by Terror*, p. 13. Besides the threat posed by the PFLP, the Syrians did not appreciate the good relations the PFLP maintained with Iraq. See Neville Brown, "Palestinian Nationalism and the Jordanian State," *World Today*, September 1970, p. 375.

27. In November 1972, an Israeli commander was quoted as admitting attacks against villages. See *NVT*, November 22, 1972; AP dispatch in *An-Nahar Arab Report*, November 22, 1972. For accounts of fedayeen activity and Israeli reprisals, the following are convenient sources: *ARR*, March 1-15, 1970, p. 163; March 16-31, 1970, p. 185; June 1-15, 1970, p. 322; *NYT*, February 24-25, 1969; January 25, September 9 and 10, October 31, November 10-11 and 22, and December 28, 1972; January 7, 9, and 24, 1973.

28. The Syrian involvements in the Jordanian civil war has been recounted in

previous contexts. Suffice it to recall that Syria used PLA armored units but refrained from employing its air force in the face of Israeli and American pressure. This ill-fated adventure was generally believed to be a major factor behind Assad's successful seizure of power after the civil war. When Hussein moved to expel the fedayeen in 1971, the Syrian response included warnings to Amman, mediation efforts, and closure of the border. Military intervention was eschewed. On Syrian behavior in July 1971, see *ARR*, July 16-31, 1971, p. 398. On the Syrian criticism of Jordan, see ibid., pp. 377 and 395; *NYT*, July 21 and 23, 1971; *DSB*, July 20 and 21, 1971. J. Gaspard, "Palestinian Waterloo at Ajloun—Military Myths and Political Realities," *New Middle East*, September 1971, p. 33, reported that Syria refused to let guerrillas cross the border to help their beleaguered brethren. He also pointed out (p. 34) that the protests from Damascus did not really pick up until Hussein had completed his task.

29. On the impact Syrian power struggles had on *Sa'iqa*, see *ARR*, August 1-15, 1970, p. 451; August 16-31, 1970, p. 478; October 16-31, 1970, pp. 581-589; November 1-15, 1970, p. 616; November 16-30, 1970, pp. 644-645; December 1-15, 1970, pp. 664-673; *DSB*, August 12 and 25, 1970; October 23 and 26, 1970; November 8, 16, and 26, 1970; *New Middle East*, December 1970, p. 11. The PDF was explicit about its view of the Assad faction, saying that it was a wing that was willing to accommodate imperialism. See the editorial in *Palestine Resistance Bulletin*, June 1971, p. 1. For a brief but insightful article on the Syrian coup and the development of the Assad-Jedid rivalry, see J. Gaspard, "Damascus After the Coup—Syria's New Master Breaks with the Past," *New Middle East*, January 1971.

30. On these measures, see *L'Orient-Le Jour* (Beirut), February 9, 1973; *NYT*, January 24; September 17, 20, and 23, 1973. By fostering relative calm on the Golan Heights and by carrying out the Vienna kidnapping mentioned in previous chapters, Syria undoubtedly hoped to distract Israeli attention while war preparations were taking place.

31. *JPS*, Summer 1972, p. 162.

32. Laqueur, *Road to War*, pp. 69-73.

33. *NYT*, July 24, 1967.

34. *Africa Diary*, December 17-23, 1967, p. 3714; *NYT*, November 23, 1967.

35. See, for instance, *ARR*, January 16-31, 1969, pp. 38, 43, and inside cover; the interview of Nasser by Eric Roleau in *Le Monde* (Paris), February 19, 1970. The January 1968 agreement with regard to ending guerrilla activity was reported by *DSB*, January 24, 1968.

36. Nasser's thinking on the mini-state was revealed by Simon Malley, the well-informed editor of *Africasia*. See *DSB*, August 29, 1970. For the Israeli view, see *War by Terror*, pp. 11-12 and 24-25.

37. On Sadat's policy, see *ARR*, January 16-31, 1971, p. 71; February 15-28, 1971, pp. 120-121; *DSB*, January 21-22 and 26, February 17, 20-21 and 26, 1971; *NYT*, November 20, 1970; December 9 and 28, 1970, February 19, 1971.

38. *Al-Ahram* (Cairo), as cited in *Africa Research Bulletin*, February 15, 1968, p. 961. As expected, the fedayeen were critical of Heikal, charging him with ignorance on the subject of guerrilla warfare and not understanding the mass support enjoyed by the resistance. See *Free Palestine*, September 1970, p. 1. Interestingly, Nasser was

reported to have reached agreement with the PLO and Jordan during talks in January 1968, that guerrilla activities should be ended as a step toward peace.

39. Egyptian criticism of hijacking can be found in *Al-Ahram* (Cairo), September 8, 1970, and a number of other Egyptian publications cited in the following: *NYT*, September 9 and 13, 1970; *ARR*, September 1-15, 1970, p. 504; *DSB*, September 10 and 15, 1970. The remarks attributable to an Egyptian spokesman were found in *DSB*, June 11, 1970. Other acts of external terrorism such as the Swissair disaster in 1970 and Athens attack in 1969 were also condemned by Egypt. See *NYT*, December 2, 1969, February 27, 1970.

40. Cited in "The Arab-Israeli Conflict and the United Nations," *International Review Service* vol. 14, 1969, p. 27.

41. *ARR*, January 16-31, 1969, pp. 38, 43, and inside cover; *NYT*, February 21, 1969.

42. On the increased support for the guerrillas beginning in 1968, see *ARR*, April 1-15, 1968, inside cover and p. 96; *Africa Report*, June 1968, p. 33; *NYT*, April 11-13 and 30, 1968. Another factor which may have prompted the militant posture was Nasser's desire to deflect attention from domestic discontent (riots by workers and students) at the time.

43. Mohamed Heikal, *The Cairo Documents* (Garden City, N.Y.: Doubleday and Co., 1973), pp. 315-316.

44. Nasser's uneasiness about allowing any armed force other than the Egyptian military the right to operate in Egypt was demonstrated by his hesitation in creating a Popular Defense Army made up of his own people. See *ARR*, November 1-15, 1968, p. 360; *NYT*, November 5, 1968. The Egyptian president's concern about his own prestige relative to that of the guerrillas was cited by a number of observers on several occasions. See, for example, *NYT*, October 19 and December 27, 1968; J. Gaspard, "Palestine: Who's Who Among the Guerrillas," *New Middle East*, March 1970, p. 15; Andre Fontaine, "Collision Course," *Survival*, April 1970, p. 129.

45. See *New Middle East*, April 1970, pp. 6-7; May 1970, pp. 4-6 and 47. The Marxist organizations, of course, advocated an eventual socialist revolution in Egypt, since the latter was considered a "petit bourgeois" country. See, for example, *Democratic Popular Front for the Liberation of Palestine* (Manchester, England: Committee for Solidarity with the Palestinian Resistance, 1969), p. 17.

46. *ARR*, July 16-31, 1970, p. 430; August 1-15, 1970, p. 462; August 16-31, 1970, p. 481; *DSB*, July 25, 29, and 31, and August 3, 1970; *New Middle East*, July 1970, p. 8; *NYT*, June 12, 1970.

47. On the Libyan plan, see *ARR*, July 16-31, 1971, p. 395.

48. The PFLP charged that Egyptian efforts to reconcile Hussein and the fedayeen were an attempt to finish off the resistance. By that time, however, the left-wing organizations and Cairo had reached the point of no return, with Egypt demanding the PLO-EC purge the extremists and the PFLP and PDF branding the Egyptian regime as "reactionary." See for example, *Palestine Resistance Bulletin*, June 1971, p. 1; *DSB*, September 7, 1971.

49. *NYT*, October 1, 1972.

50. *NYT*, June 21, 1973. Also see Voice of Palestine in Arabic, June 26, 1973 in

FBIS/ME, June 27, 1973, p. A2.

51. Khouri, *Arab-Israeli Dilemma*, pp. 165-166: James Michener, "What to Do About the Palestinian Refugees," *New York Times Magazine*, September 27, 1970, p. 119.

52. A good discussion of restrictions imposed on decision-making by the perceived "national role" can be found in K. J. Holsti, *International Politics: A Framework for Analysis* (Englewood Cliffs, N.J.: Prentice-Hall, 1967), pp. 172-173.

53. *Middle East Journal*, Summer 1968, p. 326; *ARR*, April 1-15, 1968, p. 88; June 1-15, 1968, p. 158; June 16-30, 1968, p. 164; *NYT*, March 22, April 2 and 14, and June 5, 1968. Iraq's support of the fedayeen and its generally militant stance on the Arab-Israeli issue, besides being derived from the revolutionary ideology of the Ba'thist party, seemed to be related to the need to focus on an external enemy in order to create some sense of political cohesion in its fragmented polity and society. It may also have been influenced by a desire to divert attention from economic problems. On Iraq's domestic problems, see Abbas Kelidar, "Shift and Changes in the Arab World," *World Today*, November 1968, p. 508.

54. *ARR*, October 1-15, 1969, p. 424; December 16-31, 1969, p. 532; July 16-31, 1970, p. 429; *DSB*, July 30, August 4, 20-21, and 29, and October 6, 1970; *Fatah*, August 19, 1970; *NYT*, September 1 and 23, and October 23, 1969; January 10 and 24, February 12, July 27, and August 31, 1970. The creation of the ALF, it should be noted, was also intended to give Baghdad a voice in PLO decision-making and counterbalance and offset the influence of *Sa'iqa*.

55. On the restrictions, see *Al-Nida* (Beirut), April 16, 1969, as cited in *ARR*, April 16-30, 1969, p. 160; *Mid East*, May/June 1969, p. 26; *NYT*, June 15, 1969; *Time*, May 16, 1969, p. 37.

56. On the Iraqi stance in June, see *Al-Thawra* (Baghdad), June 4, 1970, as cited in *ARR*, June 1-15, 1970, p. 321. Actually, there was some vacillation in the Iraqi commentary on events in Jordan. After first warning Hussein on June 7, *AlThawra*, on June 10, condemned PFLP and PDF for instigating the trouble and praised Hussein and *Fatah* for their efforts to end the fighting. See *New Middle East*, July 1970, p. 8. Since the PDF branded the Iraqi regime as "petit bourgeois" and implied it had to be overthrown because it was incapable of mobilizing peasants and the workers for the liberation effort, Iraq had reason to be wary of that organization. See *Democratic Popular Front for the Liberation of Palestine*, p. 17. For the Iraqi reaction to the Rogers plan, see *ARR*, July 16-31, 1970, p. 429; *DSB*, July 30, August 4, 20-21, and 29, 1970; *Fatah*, August 19, 1970; *NYT*, July 27 and August 31, 1970.

57. On the Iraqi political-military role during the Jordanian civil war, see *ARR*, September 1-15, 1970, pp. 492-493 and 516; September 16-30, 1970, p. 539; *NYT*, September 5 and 22, 1970; *DSB*, September 3, 17, 19, 22, and 28, 1970. A report in *AlAhram* (Cairo) on September 22 that Iraq had promised to support Hussein if Syria intervened was highly dubious and seemed to be a function of the acrimony between Cairo and Baghdad. In fact, according to the Beirut weekly *Al-Ahrar* on September 22, Iraq had proposed joint action with Syria, only to be turned down by Damascus. See *ARR*, September 16-30, 1970, p. 530, on this point. In October, Arafat denied Iraqi soldiers had allowed Jordanian troops to pass through their

positions during the civil war. Since Arafat was trying to obtain Iraqi support at the time, however, it is difficult to gauge the veracity of his comments. See *ARR*, October 1-15, 1970, p. 549.

58. Editorial in *Free Palestine*, December 1970, p. 2. For similar comments, see the January 1971 remarks by *Fatah* leader Abu al-Hassan, as reported in *DSB*, January 8, 1971; the editorial in the PDF monthly *Palestine Resistance Bulletin*, June 1971, p. 1.

59. *CSM*, September 19, 1973.

60. *ARR*, January 1-15, 1968, p. 13; August 1-15, 1968, p. 224; September 1-15, 1968, p. 273; Tom Dammann, "Saudi Arabia's Dilemma: An Interview with King Feisal," *Interplay*, September 1970, p. 17; *DSB*, April 24, 1970.

61. Since Feisal was a militant anti-Communist, his dislike of the PFLP was natural. On the Tapline incident and Saudi hostility toward the left-wing guerrillas, see *ARR*, June 1-15, 1969, pp. 233, 241 and 250; September 16-30, 1969, p. 404; Sarih, "Frankly Speaking," *New Middle East*, December 1969, p. 13. There were reports of large-scale arrests in Saudi Arabia of Yemen and Palestinian workers suspected of being associated with the PFLP after the Tapline incident. The Saudis denied the reports. See *Mid East*, July/August 1969, p. 23; *NYT*, June 18, 1969.

62. *ARR*, August 1-15, 1970, p. 462; December 16-31, 1970, p. 692; *NYT*, August 16, 1970; January 18, 1971; *DSB*, December 21, 1970; *Mid East*, June 1970, p. 26.

63. *Free Palestine*, October 1969, p. 4; *NYT*, December 19, 1969, August 16, 1970. Dammann, p. 16, notes the contradiction in the Saudi policy which favored both peace and a holy war.

64. *DSB*, October 3, 1971; *NYT*, May 3, 1971.

65. *NYT*, July 23, 1971. Saudi Arabia was also the only Arab state to continue its financial payments to Jordan, according to *NYT*, September 14, 1971.

66. Sarih, "Frankly Speaking," *New Middle East*, July 1970, p. 40. *Free Palestine*, September/October 1971, p. 3., argued that Feisal's support of Jordan was partially due to his need for a buffer against the revolutionary regimes. Feisal's desire to contain revolutionary change may well have been a consideration in his decision to aid *Fatah*. The assistance, it was probably reasoned, would give the king leverage over *Fatah* and help induce it to control the left-wing groups. See Neville Brown, "Jordan's Precarious Truce," p. 12.

67. *An-Nahar Arab Report*, October 4, 1971, p. 2.

68. See, for example, Fallaci, "A Leader in the Fedayeen," p. 34.

69. *Free Palestine*, September/October 1971, pp. 1 and 3.

70. UPI dispatch, *Colorado Springs Sun*, March 5, 1973.

71. *New Middle East*, June 1970, p. 35; September 1970, p. 9; *ARR*, February 1-14, 1969, p. 52; September 1-15, 1970, p. 507; October 16-31, 1970, p. 581; *DSB*, October 21 and December 31, 1970; February 11, 1971. On the PDF trouble, see *Mid East*, July/August 1969, p. 22. Sarih, "Frankly Speaking," *New Middle East*, December 1969, p. 14, reported that close to 500 Palestinians were forced to leave Kuwait in 1969 because they were demanding a more active involvement for Kuwait in the Palestinian struggle.

72. Information on Kuwait's financial support can be found in *ARR*, May 16-31,

1968, p. 132; March 1-15, 1969, p. 97; March 16-31, 1969, p. 119; February 1-14, 1970, p. 118; June 16-30, 1970, p. 374; *Mid East*, May/June 1969, p. 26; February 1970, p. 29; *NYT*, December 25, 1969; *Daily News* (Kuwait), January 11, 1970.

73. *ARR*, September 16-30, 1970, p. 520; December 1-15, 1970, p. 662; January 115, 1971, p. 31; *DSB*, December 22, 1970; *NYT*, March 5, 1971.

74. On Algeria's prewar stance, see *Africa Diary*, January 12-19, 1967, p. 3213. On Algeria's postwar moral and political backing of the fedayeen, see the following: *NYT*, July 30, 1967; December 23, 1969; *ARR*, March 16-31, 1968, p. 69; April 1-15, 1969, p. 138; May 16-31, 1969, p. 197; October 16-31, 1969, p. 434; November 16-30, 1969, p. 481; April 1-15, 1970, p. 201; July 16-31, 1970, p. 405; *DSB*, February 19 and December 31, 1971; *New Middle East*, March 1971, p. 4; *Free Palestine*, March 1971, p. 7; June 1971, pp. 6-7. Ben Bella, it should be noted, was not close to the resistance. Informed observers attributed this to Nasser's influence. See *NYT*, December 3, 1968.

75. *El-Moudjahid* (Algiers), June 5, 1969, as cited by *ARR*, June 1-15, 1969, pp. 233 and 250.

76. *ARR*, September 1-15, 1970, p. 489; *NYT*, September 1, 1968; December 23, 1969.

77. *ARR*, September 16-30, 1970, p. 513; *NYT*, June 17, 1970; Sarih, "Frankly Speaking," *New Middle East*, December 1969, p. 14. This did not prevent the PDF from branding Algeria as a "petit bourgeois" regime that was incapable of mobilizing the masses. On the latter, see *Democratic Popular Front for the Liberation of Palestine*, p. 17.

78. On material support, see *ARR*, November 16-30, 1968, p. 369; September 1-15, 1970, p. 489; July 16-31, 1971, pp. 373 and 398; *NYT*, November 16, 1967, December 3, 1968; February 6, 1969; July 7, 1971; *DSB*, April 26 and June 7 and 21, 1970; *Free Palestine*, July 1971, p. 7.

79. Ehud Yaari, "Al Fath's Political Thinking," *New Outlook*, November/December 1968, p. 28. As Yaari pointed out, *Fatah* overlooked the fact that the FLN was defeated militarily. The importance of Algeria as a model for the fedayeen has been cited by a plethora of observers. See, for example, Irene Gendzier, "Algeria and Palestine: Warning or Model," *New Middle East*, October 1970, p. 14.

80. For a discussion of some of these points, see J. Gaspard, "Algerian Mentor Gives a Helping Hand," *New Middle East*, June 1971, pp. 33-34.

81. The new regime's outlook was an admixture of revolutionary rhetoric and Moslem fundamentalism, with a militant posture on the Israel question. For an account of the coup, see Eric Rouleau, "Oil and Monarchies Don't Mix," *Africa Report*, November 1969, pp. 24-27.

82. Examples of Libya's public identification with the idea of armed struggle and the fedayeen objectives of a secular, democratic state can be found in *ARR*, October 16-31, 1970, p. 584; *DSB*, November 10, and December 31, 1970. For an account of the Qadhdhafi view of the structure of the armed struggle, see Gaspard, "Algerian Mentor," p. 492.

83. *ARR*, July 1-15, 1969, p. 283; September 16-30, 1970, pp. 519 and 521; March 16-31, 1971, p. 166; April 1-15, 1971, p. 193; *NYT*, October 14 and 23, 1969, August 2 and September 14, 1971; *DSB*, September 6, 1970.

84. *DSB*, August 9, 1971. In one month only thirty-five volunteers showed up in Benghazi, Libya's second largest city, and Qadhdhafi was said to have been upset by the poor response.

85. *ARR*, February 1-15, 1968, p. 35; January 16-31, 1971, p. 62; February 15-28, 1971, pp. 112-113; March 1-15, 1971, p. 142; August 1-15, 1971, p. 413; *Africa Report*, April 1968, p. 27; *NYT*, March 8, 1971; *DSB*, February 20, 1971; AP dispatch in *Denver Post*, September 8, 1971. A PFLP spokesman referred to Libya as a "petit bourgeois" state whose government would have to be changed in the long run by a socialist revolution. See John M. Mecklin, "Fire and Steel for Palestine," *Fortune*, July 1970, p. 135.

86. See Naseer Aruri, "Introduction," *The Palestine Resistance to Israeli Occupation*, ed., Naseer Aruri (Wilmette, Ill.: Medina University Press International, 1970), p. 5; *ARR*, December 16-31, 1968, p. 415; February 15-28, 1969, p. 76.

87. *NYT*, November 2, 1972.

88. See "Al-Qadhdhafi Speaks to Nation on Arab, Domestic Issues," Full Text, Tripoli Domestic Service in Arabic, April 15, 1973 in *FBIS/ME*, April 17, 1973, p. T4ff; *NYT*, May 1, 1973. In response to earlier criticisms, *Fatah* had characterized Qadhdhafi as a young and inexperienced dictator. See the partial text of Qadhdhafi's March 31, 1970 speech at Tripoli in *New Middle East*, May 1970, p. 47, and *Al-Assifa*'s reply on April 7.

89. *ARR*, August 1-15, 1970, p. 463; September 1-15, 1970, p. 492.

90. AP dispatch in *Denver Post*, July 4, 1973.

91. On the relations between the Sudan and the fedayeen, see *ARR*, September 1-15, 1968, p. 265; December 16-31, 1968, p. 428; April 1-16, 1971, p. 196; July 16-31, 1970, p. 421; August 16-31, 1970, p. 487; March 16-31, 1971, p. 166; *DSB*, July 30, 1970. The Sudanese ability to help the fedayeen was severely limited by its own developmental problems and by a rebellion by blacks in its southern region.

92. Numayri was the first Arab leader to acknowledge publicly the BSO-*Fatah* linkage. At first, only the local connection, involving Libya, was emphasized. A few days later, the command and control exercised by *Fatah* leaders in Beirut was revealed. See text of Numayri speech on fedayeen action to the nation, Omdurman Domestic Service in Arabic, March 6, 1973 in *FBIS/ME*, March 7, 1973, p. T7; *NYT*, March 8 and 11, 1973.

93. *DSB*, November 19, 1970; *NYT*, August 27 and September 28, 1969.

94. *ARR*, January 16-31, 1970, p. 81; July 1-15, 1971, p. 350; *DSB*, November 19, 1970.

95. *Intelligence Digest*, November 1967, pp. 10-11; *Der Stern* (West Germany), October 9, 1967, as cited in *Africa Report*, January 1968, p. 34.

96. *ARR*, March 1-15, 1969, p. 104; March 16-31, 1969, p. 125.

97. This is not to argue that the Soviets did not support and seek to control Communist parties, and thereby create periodic problems in the area; it is only meant to suggest that where such support might undermine larger national interests, the former had to be sacrificed. For an account of Soviet relations with local Communists, see A. Yodfat, "The USSR and the Arab Communist Parties—A Chilling Account of Great Power Penetration," *New Middle East*, May 1971, p. 33.

98. The interested reader will find ample evidence by reviewing the weekly

indices of *Pravda* and *Izvestia* in *Current Digest of the Soviet Press* issues between 1968 and 1971. See, for instance, September 25, 1968, p. 22; February 12, 1969, p. 19.

99. *Pravda,* as cited in *ARR,* December 16-31, 1968, p. 425. On Shelepin's comments, see *ARR,* November 1-15, 1969, p. 474; *Free Palestine,* March 1970, p. 2. It should be noted that Shelepin saw the Palestinian struggle as one aimed at liquidating the consequences of the June War, not one aimed at destroying Israel. On Malik's remarks, see *NYT,* January 23-24, 1970.

100. See Simon Malley, "Arafat au Kremlin," *Africasia,* March 15, 1970, pp. 5-6. The PNC report was published in *An-Nahar* (Beirut), and cited in *ARR,* June 1-15, 1970, p. 344.

101. See *NYT,* January 17 and February 7, 1970. UPI cited Palestinian sources as saying *Fatah* acquired Katyusha rockets via Czechoslovakia. See J.C.K., *Peking and the Palestinian Guerrilla Movement,* Radio Free Europe Research Report, Communist Area, September 1, 1970, p. 4. For information on the Bulgarian ambassador's remarks, see *DSB,* April 26, 1970. An AP report of March 22, 1971, according to *ARR,* March 16-31, 1971, p. 184, quoted Israeli sources as saying a number of Palestinian guerrillas were being trained in the Soviet Union in the use of sophisticated weapons. *NYT,* January 1, 1972 reported PLA officers were being trained in the USSR and *Fatah* personnel were to follow suit. No mention was made of the type of weapons involved.

102. *NYT,* December 30, 1971, January 1 and September 18 and 28, 1972. The Soviets had trained PLA officers for some time prior to 1971. On the direct arms shipment in the fall of 1972, see *NYT,* September 22, 1972.

103. *NYT,* July 8, 9, and 29, 1967.

104. "Andrei Gromyko, Union of Soviet Socialist Republics Statement of Policy," delivered before the UN General Assembly, October 3, 1968, reprinted in *International Policy Debate* (New York: International Review Service, Inc., 1968), p. 28.

105. *ARR,* November 16-30, 1968, p. 387.

106. United Press International, cited by *ARR,* February 15-28, 1971, p. 130; *DSB,* February 16 and 21, 1971. Jean Riollot, "The Soviet Attitude Towards the Palestinian Organizations," *Radio Liberty Dispatch,* February 13, 1970, p. 4, cited Radio Moscow in Yiddish to Israel on August 14, 1969, as making a rare reference to the idea of an Arab state in Palestine based on the November 29, 1947 UN General Assembly Resolution. The broadcast commented that "An Arab state in Palestine would be a real step toward a solution of the Middle East problem. Supporters of this movement point out that as a result of the Six-Day War, Palestine has been restored to its 1947 frontiers and, therefore, the creation of an Arab state in Palestine would not necessarily cause difficulties now. Such a solution could provide enough living space for the vast majority of the Arab refugees and would mean security for Israel."

107. George Batal, Amjad Rashad, and Mohammed Harmel, "Vital Tasks of the Arab National Movement," *World Marxist Review,* September 1968, p. 53.

108. Cited in Aryeh Yodfat, "The Soviet Union and the Palestinian Guerrillas," *Mizan,* January/February 1969, pp. 13-14.

109. G. Mirsky, "Israel: Illusions and Miscalculations," *New Times,* October 2, 1968, p. 7.

110. *Pravda*, February 27, 1968, as reported in *Current Digest of the Soviet Press*, May 19, 1969, p. 21; *NYT*, February 28, 1969.

111. *Mizan*, Supplement A, March/April 1970, p. 4.

112. See *Izvestia*, September 10, 1970, as reported in *New Middle East*, October 1970, p. 49; *Za Rubezhom*, September 24, 1970, as cited in *New Middle East*, November 1970, p. 44; *Pravda*, September 13, 1970, as cited in *Mizan*, Supplement A, September/October 1970, p. 4; *New Times*, September 23, 1970, p. 1.

113. Despite obvious Russian distaste for the PFLP, Habash still referred to Moscow as a friend, albeit a lesser one than China. See *ARR*, June 1-15, 1970, p. 345. Other examples of Soviet criticism of left-wing groups may be found in *Pravda*, September 17, 1970, as cited in *Current Digest of the Soviet Press*, October 10, 1970, p. 12; *New Middle East*, November 1970, p. 44; *Mizan*, Supplement A, September/October 1970, p. 4; *NYT*, January 18, 1971; George Toubi, "The Middle East: Prospects and Dangers," *World Marxist Review*, November 1970, p. 72.

114. Mention of *Al-Ansar* was made by Nicolas Chaoui in "Leninism and Problems of Revolutionary Movements in the Arab Countries," *World Marxist Review*, May 1970, p. 65. Chaoui pointed out that a popular guard formed to defend Lebanese frontiers would participate in the operations of *Al-Ansar*.

115. See, for example, *Current Digest of hte Soviet Press*, Febuary 12, 1969, p. 10, and March 5, 1969, p. 19; *ARR*, December 1-15, 1969, pp. 518-519. When the Soviets referred to the restoration of the legitimate rights of the Palestinians, they said it would have to be in accordance with SC-242.

116. The Soviets were critical of what they referred to as Maoist "rank demagogy and adventuristic exhortations," which, along with anti-Soviet fabrications,were said to serve the Chinese aim of driving a wedge between the USSR and the Arabs. See A. Repin, "The Soviet Union and the UAR," *New Times*, July 10, 1968, p. 5. Moscow also opposed the revolutionary warfare model promulgated in Peking, because it not only ran counter to the Soviet desire for a political solution, but also attracted support for the PRC in the area. On August 26, 1970, Radio Moscow commented that:

... Peking, above all else ... is now devoting itself to propaganda aiming to undermine the efforts to create conditions, which could lead to a political solution of the present Middle East crisis. To this end Mao's supporters rely on the doctrine they have thought up about revolution being the inevitable way of struggle and they reject any other means of ensuring the rights and interests of any people. It appears that Peking is opposed to the Arab peoples liberating the territories occupied by Israel and establishing their rights except by means of bloodshed, destruction, devastation and tragedy brought by war. *New Middle East*, October 1970, p. 49.

117. W. A. C. Adie, *China, Israel and the Arabs* (London: Institute for the Study of Conflict, 1971), pp. 3-7; R. Medzini, "China and the Palestinians—A Developing Relationship," *New Middle East*, May 1971, p. 35. Shortly after the June War Israel seized large amounts of Chinese arms in the Gaza Strip and Qantara area according to *NYT*, June 26, 1967; see also *NYT*, August 9, 1967.

118. *Peking Review*, November 3, 1967, pp. 24-25; December 1, 1967, pp. 32-33.

119. Chou Tien-chih, "Lessons of the Arab War Against Aggression," *Peking Review*, September 8, 1967, pp. 22-26.

120. The Chinese, like the Soviets, reported the exaggerated fedayeen claims without question. In July 1968, for example, they claimed the guerrillas had inflicted 4,000 casualties on the Israelis in one year. See *Survey of the Mainland China Press*, July 31, 1968, p. 22.

121. The theme of broad popular support for the fedayeen was consistent. See, for instance, *Peking Review*, March 15, 1968, p. 37; May 24, 1968, p. 35; *Survey of the Mainland China Press*, September 25, 1969, p. 28; *Peking Review*, September 25, 1970, p. 3. *Survey of the Mainland China Press*, January 19, 1971, p. 106.

122. *People's Daily* (Peking), June 5, 1968, reprinted in *Survey of the Mainland China Press*, June 11, 1968, p. 23. Through 1971 the vast countryside theme remained consistent. See *Peking Review*, June 14, 1968, p. 233; January 16, 1970, pp. 25-26; February 20, 1970, p. 24.

123. *Peking Review*, June 28, 1968, p. 22.

124. *Peking Review*, November 22, 1968, p. 20; May 23, 1969, p. 28.

125. *Peking Review*, June 28, 1968, p. 22.

126. *Survey of the Mainland China Press*, February 12, 1969, p. 16.

127. *Peking Review*, July 26, 1968, p. 11; *Survey of the Mainland China Press*, April 11, 1969, p. 26; June 23, 1970, p. 61.

128. Occasionally, self-reliance was included as a necessary condition for victory. See, for example, *Survey of the Mainland China Press*, January 8, 1970, p. 158.

129. *Survey of the Mainland China Press*, July 31, 1968, pp. 22-23; *Peking Review*, August 2, 1968, p. 26; November 22, 1968, p. 20.

130. *ARR*, January 1-15, 1971, p. 48; April 1-15, 1970, p. 229.

131. *NYT*, November 25, 1967; *Mizan*, Supplement A, March/April 1970, p. 25.

132. *ARR*, August 16-31, 1970, p. 487; *NYT*, January 7, 1971.

133. *Guardian*, March 23, 1970; *Times* (London), August 19 and 23, 1970; Sheehan, "Flaming Streets of Amman," p. 109; Medzini, "China and the Palestinians," p. 36.

134. *Al Hurriya* (Beirut), October 5, 1970, cited PDF sources as admitting that Iraq allowed Chinese arms to cross its territory, according to *DSB*, October 5, 1970. It was also reported that Iraq diverted some arms to its own fedayeen.

135. *ARR*, March 16-31, 1968, p. 73; *NYT*, December 3, 1969.

136. *Times* (London), September 19, 1970; *Sunday Telegraph* (London), August 30, 1970; *Le Monde* (Paris), October 12, 1970. There were claims in Medzini, "China and the Palestinians," p. 37, that Chinese Communists were fighting alongside the fedayeen during the civil war. In reaction to such reports, a PDF spokesman denied the presence of Chinese experts with guerrillas outside Jordan. On the latter, see J. C. K., *Peking and the Palestine Movement*, p. 1.

137. Sevinc Carlson, "The Chinese Intrusion," *New Middle East*, December 1970, p. 38.

138. *Le Monde* (Paris), September 27 and 28, 1970; *NYT*, February 10, 1971; *Times* (London), September 19, 1970. In the latter paper Beirut correspondent Paul Martin reported Chinese military assistance accounted for only a small percentage of the fedayeen arsenal. J. C. K., *Peking and the Palestine Movement*, pp. 4-6, concurs with the thesis that Chinese political and moral support were more important than its material aid; Medzini, "China and the Palestinians," p. 36, quoted the Israeli figures in the text.

139. *NYT*, February 10, 1970, citing *Al-Sayyad*.

140. *Times* (London), September 19, 1970; *Guardian*, March 23, 1970. During August 1970 Chinese officials reportedly came to Damascus to discuss arms deliveries. Some AK-47 automatic rifles were reported to have been delivered and, according to *The Daily Telegraph* (London), August 26, 1970, went to the PDF.

141. The conclusion is based on a thorough review of all articles and news items on the Palestinians in the *Survey of the Mainland China Press* and *Peking Review* from 1967 to 1971. Fatah and its military wing, *Assifa*, were praised for their operations and popular support. See, for example, *Peking Review*, August 2, 1968, p. 26; May 24, 1968, pp. 25-36; July 18, 1969, p. 22. The visits by *Fatah* representatives to Peking were always given good press coverage. Guerrilla operations were usually attributed to *Fatah* and "other organizations," as in the case of *Peking Review*.

142. See, for instance, *Survey of the Mainland China Press*, April 11, 1969, p. 26.

Chapter 8

1. *NYT*, November 1, 1968; interviews with K. Kudsi in *Free Palestine*, September 1969, pp. 1 and 6; and November 1969, p. 2; interview with Yasir Arafat in *Free Palestine*, August 1970, pp. 1 and 6; *ARR*, September 16-30, 1969, p. 402; January 16-31, 1970, p. 81.

2. The transnational operations were carried out by small maverick groups, the PFLP and Nidal's so-called "Black June" faction in Iraq. The Black June group was also responsible for attacks against the Semiramis Hotel in Syria (September 1976) and the Intercontinental Hotel in Jordan (November 1976), as well as an assassination attempt against the Syrian foreign minister. The main benefactors of the group were Libya and Iraq.

3. Sadat's program was outlined in his "October Paper" which was presented to a joint meeting of the Arab Socialist Union Central Committee and the People's Assembly on April 19, 1974. See Text of President As-Sadat's "October Paper," Supplement, Daily Report, *FBIS/ME*, May 13, 1974, pp. 1-34.

4. See, for example, Cairo Domestic Service in Arabic, Text of NBC Television Interview of Sadat, September 25, 1974, in *FBIS/ME*, September 26, 1974, p. D5.

5. *Washington Post*, October 12, 1973.

6. In the fall of 1974 the PSF joined the rejectionist front. Its policy was outlined in a joint statement by the Iraqi Ba'th party and the rejectionist front on October 12, 1974. See *FBIS/ME*, October 15, 1974, pp. A4-A6.

7. While defending the notion of a mini-state (national authority), Abu Iyad (Salah Khalef), *Fatah*'s second in command, noted in both speeches and interviews that it would not mean recognition of nor reconciliation with Israel. A typical case in point is the interview in *Ash-Sha'b* (Algeria), quoted by Algiers "Voice of Palestine" in Arabic, August 24, 1974, in *FBIS/ME*, August 27, 1974, pp. A1-A2.

8. Summary of findings of the Horev committee, Jerusalem Domestic Service, July 10, 1974, in *FBIS/ME*, July 11, 1974, pp. N3-N6; *Jerusalem Post*, Weekly Overseas Edition, July 16, 1974.

9. For the ten-point program see Cairo "Voice of Palestine" in Arabic, June 8, 1974, in *FBIS/ME*, June 10, 1974, pp. A6-A11. A point-by-point critique from the Israeli perspective may be found in *Near East Report*, July 10, 1974, pp. 158-159.

The latter argues, quite correctly, that the ten points do not alter the National Covenant's commitment to the destruction of Zionism.

10. Interview in *Ash-Sha'b*, quoted in *FBIS/ME*, August 27, 1974, pp. A1-A2.

11. Egyptian-Jordanian Joint Communique, Cairo "Voice of the Arabs" in Arabic, July 18, 1974, in *FBIS/ME*, July 19, 1974, pp. D1-D2.

12. For the tripartite statement see Cairo "Voice of the Arabs" in Arabic, September 21, 1974, in *FBIS/ME*, September 23, 1974, pp. D2-D3. The interplay of several considerations seemed to account for Egypt's turnabout. For one thing, it was an open secret that Sadat had long believed that the only way to solve the Palestinian dilemma was to create a state within which the Palestinian need for self-determination could find concrete expression. Secondly, the Egyptian president was of the opinion that a unified Arab diplomatic strategy was a requisite for successful negotiations. Third, Sadat was aware that his principal military ally, Syria, strongly supported the notion of a Palestinian state. In addition to the factors mentioned above, Sadat's opting for the PLO was no doubt influenced by two short-term political calculations: the costs and risks he would incur in the Arab world and the Israeli political stance. In terms of the former, Sadat probably concluded that alienating Hussein and the smaller guerrilla groups was less damaging than the anger and resentment he would face from the PLO, the majority of Arab states, and the radicals throughout the region and in Egypt, were he to side with Hussein. When it came to the Israeli part of the equation, Sadat found little reason to have second thoughts about the matter, since Israel and Jordan were hopelessly deadlocked on the West Bank issue. In casting his lot with Arafat, however, Sadat did not find the Israeli stance any more tractable since the Israelis had developed a strong aversion to the idea of a Palestinian state.

13. See "Statement Issued by the Popular Front for the Liberation of Palestine," *JPS*, Winter 1975, pp. 165-170, for the reasons behind the withdrawal from the PLO-EC.

14. See "The Palestine Resolution of the Seventh Arab Summit Conference," *JPS*, Winter 1975, p. 178.

15. For the full text of the resolutions, see *JPS*, Spring 1975, pp. 188-189; Autumn 1975/Winter 1976, pp. 298-300. For a Palestinian analysis of what Palestinian "rights" consist of, see Ghayth Armanazi, "The Rights of the Palestinians," *JPS*, Spring 1974, pp. 88-96.

16. In Lebanon, a long-simmering conflict between the Christians and left-wing Muslims suddenly burst into a civil war that was triggered by a Christian attack in April 1975 on a bus-load of Palestinians who were allied with the left-wing Muslims. Although for several months thereafter the PLO found itself allied with Syria, in a March 1976 *volte face*, Damascus began to assist the Christians. During the period in which the PLO was aligned with Syria in Lebanon, it had joined the chorus of criticism directed at the second Egyptian-Israeli disengagement accord (September 1975) emanating from Damascus. Essentially, both Syria and the PLO felt that Cairo's pledge not to use force against Israel had undermined what leverage the Arabs could use to extract concessions on the Golan Heights and Palestinian issues. Having alienated President Sadat, the PLO was then forced to seek his support against Syria when the latter intervened and changed sides in Lebanon. Thus, when Syria and Egypt mended their fences in the fall of 1976 and an accord was reached terminating the Lebanese civil war, the PLO found itself isolated. In

short, by managing to antagonize the two major confrontation states, the PLO engendered the distrust of both and largely forfeited its freedom of movement to the Arab states as far as its role in negotiations with Israel was concerned.

17. *CSM*, April 14, 1976; *NYT*, April 14, 1976. The rejectionist front criticized the elections, arguing that the outcome was deceptive because it would provide a basis for capitulationists within the resistance to disavow the goal of the movement and come to terms with Israel. The pragmatists, on the other hand, welcomed the outcome as a victory for the revolution. For these views, see *JPS*, Spring/Summer 1976, pp. 224-229.

18. Shlomo Avineri, "The Palestinians and Israel," *Commentary*, June 1970, pp. 42-44.

19. *Le Figaro* (Paris), June, 22, 1970. Eban's views were further developed and elegantly presented in "A New Look at Partition," *Jerusalem Post Magazine*, June 25, 1976.

20. *DSB*, September 26, 1970; Abraham S. Becker, *Israel and the Occupied Palestinian Territories: Military-Political Issues in the Debate* (Santa Monica, Calif.: The Rand Corporation, December 1971), p. 77.

21. *New Middle East*, April 1970, p. 4.

22. *NYT*, March 30, 1971; *Al-Quds* (Jerusalem), September 27, 1970, published what it said was a secret document which revealed that Jordan asked the United States to bring pressure to bear on Israel and make her desist from supporting a Palestinian state. Israeli historian Yaacov Talmon also indicated that Israel had an understanding with Jordan not to support a Palestinian state. Both of these items are cited in Aziz Shihad, "Must History Repeat Itself," *New Middle East*, January 1971, p. 36. In an interview the minister of police reiterated Israel's decision to deal with "the central authority which is in Amman," arguing that while the West Bank Palestinians might be alienated from the Hussein regime, they were not necessarily alienated from Jordan. See *New Middle East*, December 1970, p. 16.

23. There was a question as to whether Yariv was speaking for himself or deliberately tossing a political straw into the wind. In a conversation with the author, an Israeli close to Yariv endorsed the latter interpretation. The other cabinet member associated with the proposal was Victor Shemtov, minister of health.

24. Israel was willing to accept members of a unified Arab delegation who were de facto, as opposed to official, representatives of the PLO.

25. See account of Qaddumi's comments in *Wall Street Journal*, November 22, 1974.

26. *Quick* (Munich), November 28, 1974, pp. 24-25G; see also the interviews of Naftali Feder, national secretary of Israel's Mapam party, who discussed PLO aims with a fedayeen representative in Prague, in *Le Nouvel Observateur*, January 6-12, 1975; *L'Expresso* (Rome), January 12, 1975.

27. *JPS*, Spring/Summer 1976, pp. 200-201.

28. According to a poll taken by *Ma'ariv* (Tel Aviv), 46.7 percent of the Israelis interviewed agreed that further settlements would damage the prospects for peace. See the citation of the poll in *Washington Post*, November 2, 1977.

29. The Jordanian solution has much to commend it since over half of Jordan's population is Palestinian and the Palestinians play an important role in the economy, administration, parliament, and cabinet. The difficulty, of course, is that the regime's key authoritative decision-makers are non-Palestinians.

Index

Index